Fathers in a Motherland

Fathers in a Motherland

Imagining Fatherhood in Colonial India

SWAPNA M. BANERJEE

OXFORD
UNIVERSITY PRESS

Oxford University Press is a department of the University of Oxford.
It furthers the University's objective of excellence in research, scholarship,
and education by publishing worldwide. Oxford is a registered trade mark of
Oxford University Press in the UK and in certain other countries

Published in India by
Oxford University Press
22 Workspace, 2nd Floor, 1/22 Asaf Ali Road, New Delhi 110002, India

© Oxford University Press India 2022

The moral rights of the author have been asserted

First Edition published in 2022

All rights reserved. No part of this publication may be reproduced, stored in
a retrieval system, or transmitted, in any form or by any means, without the
prior permission in writing of Oxford University Press, or as expressly permitted
by law, by licence or under terms agreed with the appropriate reprographics
rights organization. Enquiries concerning reproduction outside the scope of the
above should be sent to the Rights Department, Oxford University Press, at the
address above

You must not circulate this work in any other form
and you must impose this same condition on any acquirer

ISBN-13 (print edition): 978-9-39-105024-5
ISBN-10 (print edition): 9-39-105024-5

ISBN-13 (eBook): 978-9-35-497255-3
ISBN-10 (eBook): 9-35-497255-1

ISBN-13 (OSO): 978-9-35-497285-0
ISBN-10(OSO): 9-35-497285-3

DOI: 10.1093/oso/9789391050245.001.0001

Typeset in Minion Pro 10.5/14
by Newgen Knowledge Works Pvt. Ltd.
Printed in India by Rakmo Press Pvt. Ltd.

To

The memory of my Mother,
The Source of My Strength and Inspiration

and
Katherine Ulrich, my chief interlocutor and copyeditor extraordinaire

Contents

Preface and Acknowledgements   ix

1. The Familial and the Familiar: In Search of Fathers and Children in Indian History   1

2. "Fathers" at the Crossroads: Literary Activism and Fatherhood in Nineteenth-Century Bengal   51

3. Fathers in a Motherland: Children as Social Imaginaries in the Scientific Literature of Nineteenth-Century Bengal   96

4. Imagining Fatherhood: Representations of Fathers in Autobiographical Literature of Colonial Bengal   134

5. Rabindranath Tagore: The Father and the Educator   194

6. Beyond Bengal—Gandhi and Nehru: Fathers at Home and Fathers of the Nation   234

Conclusion   275

Selected Bibliography   281
Index   303

Preface and Acknowledgements

This book had an accidental and a delayed birth. Its origins lay in my attempt at restoring children, the ubiquitous subaltern, into the pages of history, a task I embarked upon following my endeavour to recuperate histories of domestic workers. The trope of childhood that pervaded nineteenth-century Bengali literary sources inspired me to locate the "child" in Indian history. To that effort, I collected vernacular publications from colonial Bengal—didactic texts; scientific journals on health and hygiene; leading periodicals; textbooks; children's literature; biographies and autobiographies; fictions that contained information on children. As I started scrutinizing the sources, especially the scientific journals and the nineteenth-century periodicals, what stood out to me was the lack of "real" presence of "children" in this literature. The history of children, I knew, ought to be mediated as children left very few direct records. What struck me was the authorial voices of the male intelligentsia who were writing about an "imaginary" body of children in nineteenth-century Bengal. As I delved further into different genres of literature, I noticed that the Indian male social reformers, trained in Western-style education and conversant with liberal ideas of reform and enlightenment, were advocating an alternate pedagogy parallel to colonial education that was propagated in the school curriculum. I further noticed a striking overlap between the familial interests and the public commitments of these leaders. For instance, many of the educational experiments that these leaders pursued emanated from the urgency of educating their own children. Family, as extended, multigenerational units, operated both as constraints and facilitators and children, in particular, acted as enabling agents. Also apparent was the stark contradiction between the public rhetoric and the personal lives of these leaders, which was understandable if one was sensitive to their locations in the complex grid of power hierarchy within and outside of the family. Concurrently, it also became evident that through the promulgation of an alternate moral script and pedagogy the leaders and reformers developed their own conception of masculinity that was distinct from the dominant notion of manliness that the colonial critique generated, especially about Bengali men.

This new project thus shifted my focus from children to the larger familial world, especially the fathers who were "absent-present" in the historical literature I searched. The attention to fathers and their experiments with education also offered me the scope to engage with the current historiography on masculinity, pedagogy, and most importantly, gender and family history. That family, children (daughters and sons), fathers, mothers were integral to an understanding of the national and anticolonial history of India is central to the making of this book. Concerned with the everyday and the ordinary, I stayed away from the fraught accounts of paternity and property rights that are abundant in legal cases and juridical records. I also tried to keep the language of the book straightforward so that it might be accessible to a wider readership. I attempted to retain the story-elling aspect of history by maintaining the simplicity of the prose and adopting a biographical approach, unravelling the intimate lives of the historical actors and the gamut of their emotions that played out in the familial as well as the public domains.

A few words about certain technical aspects of the book are in order here. All translations in English from Bengali or Sanskrit, unless otherwise stated, are mine. Throughout this book, I have retained the spelling of the sources for both cities and the names of individuals. Thus, colonial-era British publications use Calcutta, Bombay, Behar, and so forth, while for Bengali-language publications, I transliterated the spelling of the original, providing in brackets the alternative spelling in cases—like Thakur [Tagore]—where the Anglicized spelling is likely to be more familiar. There are multiple spellings of the names of the personalities I discussed in the book. I retained the spellings that were used by the authors in the texts that they wrote and I used as my sources.

Over the years parts of this book appeared as chapters and journal articles. I thank the editors, the anonymous reviewers, and the publishers for giving me permission to use in this book sections of my previous publications: "Through the Ages of Life: Rabindranath Tagore—the Son, Father, and Educator (1861–1941)" in *Enfances Familles Générations*, December 2017. https://journals.openedition.org/efg/1508; "Everyday Emotional Practices of Fathers and Children in Late Colonial Bengal, India," in

Stephanie Olsen et al., eds., *Childhood, Youth and Emotions in Modern History* (London: Palgrave Macmillan, 2015), pp. 221–241. "Emergent Youth Culture in Nineteenth-Century India: A View from Colonial Bengal," in Christine Feldman edited *Lost Histories of Youth Culture* (New York: Peter Lang, 2015), pp. 239–255. "Children's Literature in Nineteenth-Century India: Some Reflections and Thoughts" in GRAAT (Groupe de Recherches Anglo-Américaines de Tours) from Université Francois Rabelais, Tours, France, 2007, pp. 337–351 (OpenEdition books: http://books.openedition.org/pufr/4974). The pictures in the book, especially those without source citations, come from Wikimedia Commons.

A book whose ideas evolved over more than a decade surely incurred debts to a multitude of individuals and institutions. My initial foray into the world of children to unravel the story of Indian families was made possible by the generous support of the NEH-funded senior research fellowship of the American Institute of Indian Studies; summer fellowships and Humanities Research grants from the University of Florida; the PSC-CUNY grants; and the CUNY-Central research grant of the City University of New York. The Wolfe Fellowship from Ethyle R. Wolfe Institute for the Humanities, the Whiting Fellowship for excellence in teaching, travel grants from the School of Humanities and Social Sciences and the History Department of Brooklyn College, the sabbatical fellowship, and the Endowed Chair position in Women's and Gender Studies gave me the much needed time and resources to research and write this book.

When I embarked on this project, the faculty members of the Center for Studies in Social Sciences Calcutta (CSSSC) played a crucial role. Professor Gautam Bhadra, in his characteristic generosity and support, directed me to archives and sources that were invaluable for gaining insights into the world of children's literature in colonial India. Professor Tapati Guha-Thakurta steered me to the burgeoning scholarship on children, while Professor Pradip Bose (who passed away recently) introduced me to the interdisciplinary world of psycho-analytical literature, and to the health sciences and periodicals of nineteenth-century Bengal. With Professor Partha Chatterjee, I had the opportunity to share my ideas at every stage as they morphed over the years. Both at the Centre, Kolkata, and at Columbia University, New York, Professor Chatterjee spent long hours sharing his valuable insights and guiding me to relevant primary and secondary sources. While my discussion with him filled important holes in my work, I have not been able to do justice to the new areas of exploration he suggested to unveil native fatherhood. I am forever grateful for his mentorship and time. In addition, the Centre's archive and the library proved to be great resources in locating historical records. The archivist Abhijit Bhattacharya, along with Kamalika Mukherjee and Ranjana Dasgupta were vital in helping me out with the visual archive and digital sources. Abhijit, in particular, has always been prompt until the very end in fielding any questions I had from afar. Manaswita Sanyal helped me navigate the collection of Hiteshranjan Sanyal Memorial Collection at the CSSSC archive.

From its inception to the completion of this research, Professor Geraldine Forbes, my friend, philosopher, and mentor, has always been with me. Mere words cannot express my gratitude to her. She shared texts, documents, books, comments, and finally pictures from her own rich collections of photographs, to make this project complete. Gerry's kindness and love expressed in all possible ways are hard to capture and repay. I am also indebted to Professor Sekhar Bandyopadhyay for sharing critical insights on the character of my father-activists. It was he who alerted me that these fathers were "reformers and not revolutionaries" and that I needed to tailor my expectations from these historical subjects. Professor Bandyopadhyay also shared important documents, especially from the Bengali Dalit community. Towards the end of this research, Professor Tanika Sarkar's inspiring words made a world of difference to me. Professor Peter Gran, helped give shape to my initial proposal and sharpen my argument. In our intermittent conversations, he never failed to challenge me on theoretical grounds which forced me to grapple with critical questions of hegemony and power. Professor David Ludden, with his broad vision, directed me to look into areas that I would have ignored otherwise. Professor Kathleen Uno remained a constant source of moral support who supplied me with healthy food, trained me in numerous yoga sessions, indulged me in massages, and always kept an eye on my health and emotional well-being.

The History Department of Brooklyn College, my home institution, has been my main source of support and intellectual sustenance. The vibrant environment of the department and the collegiality of my colleagues encouraged me to forge ahead with this project. Without the wisdom and care of our Chairs, David Troyansky, Christopher Ebert, Gunja Sen

Gupta, and Philip Napoli, this project would not have seen the light of the day. David Troyansky especially has been my partner-in-crime who read through several drafts of my proposals and chapters. Karen Stern, my office-mate, bore with my endless lamentations. Jocelyn Wills and Gunja Sen Gupta were the most ardent facilitators, as were Brigid O'Keeffe and Lauren Mancia. The retired colleague Margaret L. King, a specialist in children's history of medieval Italy, was always forthcoming with ready references. Prudence Cumberbatch, the then Coordinator of Women's and Gender Studies when I was the Endowed Chair, was truly a friend when I was in need! Her deft scheduling gave me work-life balance and allowed me to make progress on the book. Our secretaries, Anne Ciarlo and Lorraine Greenfield of the History Department, and Irva Adams of Women's and Gender Studies, complied with my numerous requests to photocopy documents that I gathered from different libraries. No less important are the staffs of Brooklyn College library, and especially, Sherry Warman of the Inter-library loan, who never failed to deliver my needs in a timely fashion.

The inspiration and challenges from my undergraduate and graduate students in and outside of the classroom acted as major incentives to take a closer look at my research. As we grappled with the history of women and men in colonial South Asia, the construction of gender, family and nation-state, the politics of colonial masculinity and femininity, my students posed searching questions that made me pause and rethink my position. My students also compelled me to convey complicated ideas and notions in the most direct manner. I benefited from their reflections and analysis as much as they learned from the literature I shared with them. My Research Assistant Cheyenne Stone, as a Mellon Transfer Student Research fellow, helped me compile a master bibliography on fatherhood and masculinity. As Kurz fellows, Nathaly Soto, facilitated putting together the bibliography and Jean-Michel Mutore, in particular, was crucial in locating pictures in the correct resolutions for the book. My students are my true "teachers" and I cannot thank them enough.

Several chapters of the book evolved originally as conference and seminar papers. Professor Samita Sen, the former Director of the School of Gender and Women's Studies, Jadavpur University, Kolkata, India, invited me to share my work on fathers and fatherhood in colonial Bengal. A session chaired by late Jasodhara Bagchi, a pioneer of Women's and

Gender Studies in India, that was attended by other stalwarts, invigorated me to carry forward the burgeoning project. At an international conference, "Childhood, Youth and Emotions in Modern History," organized by the Center for the History of Emotions at Max Planck Institute for Human Development, Berlin, Dr Stephanie Olsen, the organizer and a research fellow at the Institute, gave me the opportunity to share my research on the affective relationship between fathers and children in colonial India among a select group of scholars working on related topics. The invitation extended by Professor Raffaella Sarti to deliver a comparative paper on the "new" pedagogy of Tagore, Gandhi, and Nehru in the "Men at Home" conference at the University of Urbino, Italy, was crucial for crafting two chapters of the book. The connections I forged in these conferences turned out to be long-term friendships. I owe many thanks to these friends and the organizers.

Over the years, the biennial conferences of the Society for the History of Children and Youth in the US and abroad, the Berkshires Conference of Women's History, the Annual South Asia Conference at the University of Wisconsin, Madison, the Association of Asian Studies' Annual Meetings, the American Historical Association's Annual Meetings, and the Annual Conference of Social Science History Association, the European Social Science and History Conferences, and a special conference "Stories for Children, Histories of Childhood/Histoires d'enfant, histoires d'enfance" at the University of Tours, France were important venues where I presented my research. I am indebted to the organizers, co-panellists, Chairs, and discussants of those panels.

I owe an enormous debt to friends and professional colleagues who in so many ways heightened my understanding of the intersecting forces that complicated relationships between "family men," children, and the colonial state. Gautam Chando Roy, who is an avid researcher on children in colonial India, made me aware of important sources and possible areas of exploration. Ishita Pande alerted me to possible pitfalls in the questions I asked while her searching engagement with the colonial archive and "age" served as important reminders of how complex the narrative of gender, law, sex, age, and power was. Sudipa Topdar's works on colonial education were major sources of knowledge and scholarly conversation as we met in conferences and exchanged ideas. While Sarada Balagopalan's works on children deepened my understanding of childhood in the

PREFACE AND ACKNOWLEDGEMENTS xv

South Asian context, she created opportunities to present my fledgling ideas in conferences that engendered meaningful conversations with scholars working on similar areas. Indrani Chatterjee was instrumental in accentuating my argument that the new fatherhood was not so much a break but a continuation of the "guru" model that the colonial state displaced. Sumit Guha was equally forthcoming with relevant literature. Mrinalini Sinha's words of encouragement and useful advice always restored faith in what I was doing. While her notion of colonial masculinity has been the axis around which this book evolved, my work hoped to respond to her urgings of a more contextualized analysis of masculinity that straddled the so-called private and public domains. Equally supportive was Antoinette Burton whose own works gave me the assurance to explore home as the archive. Discussion with Sumathi Ramaswamy on Gandhi and children added further insights to my work. Emma Alexander, Kristin Alexander, Rachel Berger, Nupur Chaudhuri, Durba Ghosh, Dilip Menon, Arun Nag, Margrit Pernau, Barbara Ramusack, the late Satadru Sen, have all brought new awareness to the topic of my research. Sheryl Kroen has listened to many rounds of my arguments: as a Europeanist enmeshed in the Enlightenment discourse, her references to Locke and Rousseau in matters of pedagogy and education opened new lines of thought. Kathryn Burns offered her characteristic insights in finding the right words to describe the double standards I noticed among the nineteenth-century Indian elite males. Victoria Haskins and Claire Lowrie, as collaborators on a different project, but with intersecting interests in home, masculinity, and carework, have been major influences in developing this work. They are crucial in the process of writing this book.

To my long-time friends, many of whom are fellow historians and scholars, I am always indebted. Sanjukta Das Gupta-Prayer has been with the project through thick and thin. With Simonti Sen I tested my most nebulous thoughts and shared the roughest drafts of my chapters. Not only did she put up with the constant "torture" I put her through but this manuscript would not have been completed if she had not unearthed and scanned obscure Bengali sources for me at lightning speed! Paula Banerjee and Padma Anagol have also lived with this book for the past several years. As members of an editorial team engaged in a project honouring our mentors, we forged a sisterhood that allowed me to vent my frustrations, fears, angsts, and worries. I got from them much needed love and protection and benefited from their expertise and visions. I wish I could have incorporated all the valuable suggestions they made over the years. Sima Roy Chowdhury has been my support in more ways than one: in my times of nervousness and scrambling for time, her kind words and urging to follow a regular schedule of writing brought me closer to the path of progress. Debjani Banerjee is an empathetic scholar always willing to share her insights from the field of South Asian literature. She and Rajat Basu provided the most comforting meals and space for me to relax in. There are not enough words to express my gratitude for the inspiration and assistance I received on an everyday level from Jaha Hamida and Muttalib Khandker, Nandita Biswas and Kalyan Ghosh, Piyali and Rahul Chatterjee, Arindam Banerji, Malini Schueller, Rupa and Ashis Bose, Rakhi Basu, Nilanjan Mukherjee, Anandarup Chakraborty, Chitrali Chaudhuri, Pooja Ghosh, Teesta Bose, Kriti Chakrabarty, Raili Roy, Ramita Tadimalla, Samarth Nagarkar, Ruhaan, my friends in New Jersey and others whose names might be escaping me now.

I write this acknowledgement with a heavy heart. The bedrock of my strength and inspiration, my mother, who left this world in the midst of the pandemic, generated a colossal void that has been hard to reckon with. Even in her last days, she insisted that I prioritize my academic work and did not hesitate to admonish me, saying that my frequent conversations with my sisters (thanks to WhatsApp) slowed my writing process. It is my deepest regret that my mother could not see the book in print. My sisters, Suparna, Srirupa, and Sunetra are always my comrade-in-arms in foraging sources, and each lending a patient ear to my frustrations and triumphs. Sunetra, especially came to my aid as a first reader of the chapters and offered useful comments. Siddhartha and Bapi, Dadabhai, Boumoni are all integral to the writing of this book. No less important are our children Swagata, Pico, and Pablo, who posed challenges but were also sources of enormous joy. Pablo provided the necessary distraction while Swagata offered worthy suggestions to the early drafts. Pico faced a major competitor in this project as my attention and time were split between him and the writing of the book. In its final stages, he turned out to be a critical reader, my chief technical assistant, and even an editor. The pictures would not have made their way into the book without Pico's help. My mother-in-law has been always with me and showered her blessings in whatever I ventured in my personal and professional life. Words are not enough to express my thanks to Arijit, my biggest facilitator, who nurtured me in moments of crisis and despair and put up with my innumerable demands and tantrums. From being the first sounding-board and an astute reader of my writings, a diligent co-parent, and a partner who indulged me in my passion for food, wine, and travel, he always had more faith in me and in this project than I could ever muster.

No one has been more engaged with this project than my chief interlocutor, friend, and copyeditor, Katherine Ulrich. Her intervention made a significant difference to my thought process and the writing of this book. Finally, my thanks go to the production team at Oxford University Press and the reviewers of the manuscript who made the book infinitely better. I am thankful to Nandini Ganguli, who actively saw through the process and brought the book to successful completion.

The gestation period of this book has been unusually long. It was strapped in between my multiple professional responsibilities and commitments to several competing research agendas that interrupted the writing process. Even at the very last stage, although the manuscript was in press since early 2020, the COVID-19 pandemic and a personal loss further slowed the process. I hardly need to emphasize that any errors and shortcomings in this book are all mine.

1
The Familial and the Familiar
In Search of Fathers and Children in Indian History

Pita Dharma Pita Swarga Pitahi Paramantapa
Pitori Preetimapanne Priyontay Sarvadevata

Father is dharma, Father is heaven, Father is the supreme subject of meditation
If Father is contented, all other gods and goddesses will be satisfied.

Bhumergariyashi Mata Swargaduchhatara Pita
Matarang Pitarang Bidddhi Sakshat Pratakshyadevatam

Mother is superior to Earth, Father is higher than Heaven
Worship your parents that way; they are the real Gods.

Chanakya-Sloka[1]

---

[1] Jagadishchandra Ghosh, ed., *Chanakya-Sloka* (Kolkata: Presidency Library, 2009, 11th ed.). These slokas, in their different variants, also occur in the *Mahabharata* and are often attributed to Manu. Chanakya, also known as Kautilya or Vishnugupta, is an ancient Hindu polymath, a statesman and philosopher, who was believed to be the prime minister of the king Chandragupta Maurya (321–297 BCE) and the author of the treatise in statecraft *Arthasastra*. According to Daniel H.H. Ingalls, Chanakya-slokas (verse maxims) are the most popular secular works of Sanskrit literature. The slokas are like "proverbs" and constitute the "bed rock of common sense and prejudice." The verses aimed to teach *niti*, "the age-old art of getting along in the world," and are mostly indifferent to the "morality or immorality of the means." One of the purposes of *niti* is self-protection and out of these popular verses on self-defense and self-interest grew the royal art, *raja-niti*. Daniel H.H. Ingalls, "The Cāṇakya Collections and Nārāyaṇa's Hitopadeśa," *Journal of the American Oriental Society* 86, no. 1 (January–March 1966): 1. For a recent historical reassessment of Chanakya as a political man and his relevance for the current political culture in India see Prathama Banerjee, "Chanakya/Kautilya: History, Philosophy, Theater and the Twentieth-Century Political," *History of the Present* 2, no. 1 (Spring 2012): 24–51.

Fathers in a Motherland. Swapna M. Banerjee, Oxford University Press. © Oxford University Press India 2022.
DOI: 10.1093/oso/9789391050245.003.0001

In popular Indian sayings, often quoted to Indian children, both fathers and mothers are equally important. In the Indian epic the *Mahabharata*, Yudhisthira, the eldest Pandava brother, known for his righteousness, was confronted with a series of ethical questions by a nature spirit (*yaksha*). The spirit asked, "What is weightier than the earth? What is it that is higher than the sky?" Yudhisthira responded, "The mother is weightier than the earth; the father is higher than the sky."[2] The glory of mothers and fathers are extolled in several classical Indian texts: mother was held superior to heaven and earth; father, compared to heaven and *dharma*, was held as the highest object of meditation; a father's contentment would satisfy all other gods. The simultaneous exhortation of fathers and mothers in ancient Sanskrit *slokas* and the many legends associated with their glory establish the supreme importance of both parents in Indian culture.[3] The same texts that ascribe equal importance to both parents however assign different and unequal treatment of women compared to men.[4] This gendered power differential is inscribed in familial practices and in the arena of the household. The household is where production, distribution, and consumption are organized and socialization between individual and collective members, connected or not connected by blood-ties, are played out. Although the nature and practices of households changed over time, the power of the father remained crucial in Indian history and culture. However, despite the exaltation of parents and the thoroughly entrenched patriarchal culture, fathers and children in familial and extra-familial settings are waiting to receive scholarly attention.

---

[2] Manmatha Nath Dutt, ed. & publisher, *A Prose English Translation of the Mahabharata* (translated literally from the original Sanskrit text) (Calcutta: H.C. Dass, Elysium Press, 1895), 447. This episode of a riddle contest between Yudhisthira and a crane (*baka*), also known as "Dharma Baka Upakhyan" or the "Yaksha Prashna" is part of "Bana-Parva" or "Aranya-Parva" of the *Mahabharata*. https://books.google.com/books?id=Wy0MAAAAIAAJ&pg=PA449#v= onepage&q&f=false (accessed on June 18, 2016).

[3] *Manusmriti* or *The Laws of Manu* further adds to the list a teacher and older brother, in addition to father and mother, as persons commanding highest respect from an individual (male). *The Laws of Manu* is an encyclopedic compendium of 2,685 verses detailing the Hindu thought on every aspect of human life, of how it is and how it should be lived. Composed around the beginning of the Common Era or a little earlier, this text embodies the quintessential ideas of dominant Hinduism and reflects on Hindu family life, psychology, concepts of the body, sex, relationships between humans and animals, caste purification, pollution, material possession, politics, and any other conceivable aspect of human life. Wendy Doniger with Brian K. Smith (trans.), *The Laws of Manu* (Delhi: Penguin Books, 1991), 40–41.

[4] See for example other *slokas* by Chanakya that attributed limited power to women. Most of his family-oriented slokas, in fact, are about what constitutes an ideal son.

Appropriating the familial and the familiar, this book weaves stories of fathers and children into the histories of gender and family in colonial India. As the first academic history of fatherhood in this period, it argues that notions and practices of fatherhood acquired new meanings over time, particularly in the late years of British colonial rule; that fatherhood extended beyond breadwinning for children to include literary, pedagogical, and scientific/medical "imagined fathers"; that new norms were defined to extend the parameters of fatherhood; that fathers were taking a more active part in child-rearing and socialization; that there were differences in their attitude towards boy- and girl-children, so that fatherhood differs, depending on the gender of the child. Most importantly, this study examines how fatherhood was tied to the self-fashioning of educated Indian men and their conception of masculinity and manliness.

Set primarily in colonial Bengal with the imperial British capital in the city of Calcutta (now Kolkata)[5] until 1911, the work focuses predominantly on Hindu and reformed-Hindu communities, the Brahmos, the latter professing monotheism and opposing idolatry, who were in the forefront of progressive social reforms concerning women, children, and family in nineteenth- and twentieth-century India.[6] As products of colonial education and serving the administration on different levels, the fathers—literal and metaphorical—were exposed to the ideas of the West and as "modern" individuals were instrumental in translating concepts that traversed both the non-West and the West. Similar processes can be discerned among Muslim communities as well.[7] My focus on the Hindus

---

[5] The book uses "Calcutta" instead of "Kolkata" since it refers mostly to the colonial period. In referring to sources in the footnote, it uses "Kolkata" depending upon what the publishers indicated as their location.

[6] For more on Brahmos, see David Kopf, *The Brahmo Samaj and the Shaping of the Indian Mind* (Princeton, NJ: Princeton University Press, 1979). For women, Meredith Borthwick, *Changing Roles of Women in Bengal (1849–1905)* (Princeton, NJ: Princeton University Press, 1984).

[7] A sharp distinction between the educated Hindu and Muslim communities seems facetious as there is an "interdependent material field of *sociality* with equivalence, cross-connections, parallels" rather than the discrete fields that they have come to seem in 20th-century scholarship. Indrani Chatterjee, *Unfamilar Relations* (New Delhi: Permanent Black, 2004), 16. For the fallacy of drawing sharp communal lines between Hindus and Muslims, see Ayesha Jalal, "Exploding Communalism: The Politics of Muslim Identity in South Asia," in *Nationalism, Democracy, and Development: State and Politics in India*, eds. Sugata Bose and Ayesha Jalal (New Delhi: Oxford University Press, 1997), 76–103.

and the reformed Hindu community is not to privilege one over the other or to exclude other groups, but is determined by the sources I examined.[8]

My work studies fatherhood in its broadest possible sense mainly within the context of colonial Bengal, although it also draws on examples beyond Bengal. It discusses middle-class men, mostly from upper castes, as fathers to their own children and as metaphorical fathers of an "imagined community" of children of an incipient nation.[9] Undefined and unaddressed as a sociological category in historical scholarship, the "fathers" that I examine were members of the native intelligentsia, with roots in the villages. While there was continuity in rural elite structures in eighteenth- and nineteenth-century India, the establishment of British rule provided the context for a new urban-based elite group to develop in major port cities and presidency capitals. Known as the respectable middle class, and often referred to as westernized elites, these fathers were engaged in teaching, medicine, and law and filled up the lower rungs of the British civil service.[10] The middle class can be best described as the class that acted always in "response to, in reaction against, or together with, people who are Muslims, low castes, peasants and labourers and the colonial ruling classes."[11] The fathers, mostly Hindu upper castes, ranging in age from young to matured adults, represented that newly settled urban community, who often were the absentee landlords, and hence their lives straddled both the city and the village.

The book begins with the establishment of the Calcutta School Book Society in 1817 and concludes with the first prime minister-ship of Jawaharlal Nehru in the wake of India's liberation from British colonial rule in 1947. It explores specific moments in colonial Indian history when educated men as biological fathers as well as literary activists and

---

[8] Some recent works that document similar processes among Muslim communities are Ruby Lal, *Coming of Age in Nineteenth-Century India* (Cambridge: Cambridge University Press, 2015); Sonia Nishat Amin, *World of Muslim Women in Colonial Bengal, 1876–1939* (Leiden: Brill, 1996); Margrit Pernau, *Ashrafs Into Middle Classes: Muslims in Nineteenth-Century Delhi* (New Delhi: Oxford University Press, 2013); Gail Minault, *Secluded Scholars: Women's Education and Muslim Social Reform in Colonial India* (New Delhi: Oxford University Press, 1998).

[9] For caste politics in two comparable states, Bengal and Kerala, see, Sekhar Bandyopadhyay, *Caste, Culture and Hegemony: Social Dominance in Colonial Bengal* (New Delhi: Sage Publications, 2004). Dilip Menon, *Blindness of Insight: Essays on Caste in Modern India* (New Delhi: Navayana Publishers, 2006).

[10] Sanjay Joshi, ed., *The Middle Class in Colonial India* (New Delhi: Oxford University Press, 2010); *The Fractured Middle Class* (New Delhi: Oxford University Press, 2001).

[11] Tanika Sarkar, *Hindu Wife, Hindu Nation* (New Delhi: Permanent Black, 2001), 2.

educators assumed guardianship and became crucial agents of change. I seek to understand the significance of the ideas of "fatherhood" (*pitritvo*) and "childhood" (*shaishab*) mainly in the writings of this indigenous literati of Bengal in emerging nationalist culture. These male intellectuals, often subjects of derogatory criticism by the colonial government, were among the first to question traditional social customs and envision new models of womanhood, family, children, nation—and, I argue, new ideas of fatherhood as well. As the sources make clear, the *shikshito sampraday* (educated community) of colonial Bengal took the middle-class child to be the future citizen subject, if male, and to be the "good" mother and housewife, if female. A close reading of the sources reveals that these male writers were also asserting themselves as "fathers" (*pita*) both in their biological capacity and as moral guardians of an incipient nation. Ascribing fatherhood to this native group, my work demonstrates that both "children" and "fathers," as plural and unstable categories, are critical not just for childhood and masculinity studies but for understanding the evolving national identity of India as well. Emphasizing the connection between masculinity and fatherhood, I argue that the study of masculinity in late colonial India remains incomplete without an examination of fathers and fatherhood.

This book works in tandem with the arguments of scholars who have deliberated on notions of colonial masculinity, the constitution of patriarchy, and the heterogeneous and paradoxical nature of the Indian middle class. Mrinalini Sinha's pioneering work on colonial masculinity demonstrated the "multiple axes" around which power was exercised among or within the colonizers and between colonizers and the colonized.[12] Sinha treated both the British officials and the Indian elites as imperial social formations whose history could be recuperated only through a densely contextualized study of the experiences in the colonies. By attending to major public events, Sinha demonstrated the way the British men and women deployed tactics of colonial masculinity to justify their claims and the way the Bengali elites both accepted and resisted the politics of colonial masculinity. The British designated the middle-class Bengali Hindus, the most typical representative of this group, as "effeminate *babus*."[13] In

---

[12] Mrinalini Sinha, *Colonial Masculinity: The "Manly Englishman" and the "Effeminate Bengali" in the Late Nineteenth Century* (Manchester, UK: Manchester University Press, 1995), 1.
[13] Sinha, *Colonial Masculinity*, 2.

the words of Thomas Babington Macaulay, who was instrumental for introducing English as the official language in India (1835), the Bengalis were "feeble even to effeminacy" and were "weak, even to helplessness." The Bengali men were routinely identified with the "frailty of women" and the "powerlessness of the submissive slave."[14] The stereotypes were further bolstered in the aftermath of the Rebellion of 1857–1858 and the transfer of power to the British Crown when the recruitment in the Indian army was reorganized based on a classification of "martial" and "non-martial" communities. Marathas, Rajputs, and Sikhs, considered "manly," thus came to replace the "effete, unmilitary and cowardly Bengalis" in the British Indian army.[15] The response this critique generated among educated Hindu middle-class men was two-pronged: on the one hand, they had internalized this criticism; but, on the other, they used this critique as a springboard to launch their challenge against the colonial regime. Tanika Sarkar argued that the Hindu patriarchy's initial capitulation to the colonial critique of Indian men's effeminacy and enfeebled bodies actually signalled a hegemonic aspiration: the weak body of the Hindu male indicated the negative impact of colonial rule on the indigenous society.[16] Simultaneously, the internalization of the critique spurred on responses and reactions, however contradictory and limited, to challenge colonial domination.[17]

My work seizes this moment of counteraction by the colonial elites: it steers our gaze from the public debates and controversies to the more personal realms of family life. By positioning the reformers and leaders as fathers, I contend that fatherhood, just like newly conceived models of motherhood and mother-craft, assumed new significance in the changing society and culture of colonial India. I locate these fathers as modern

---

[14] Thomas Babington Macaulay, "Critical, Historical, and Miscellaneous Essays," *The Works of Lord Macaulay* (Boston, 1860), 5: 19–20. Cited in Indira Chowdhury, *The Frail Hero and Virile History: Gender and the Politics of Culture in Colonial Bengal* (New Delhi: Oxford University Press, 2001), 4.

[15] Thomas Metcalf, *Aftermath of Revolt: India 1857–1970* (Princeton, NJ: Princeton University Press, 2015 [1964]); Indira Chowdhury, *The Frail Hero and Virile History: Gender and the Politics of Culture in Colonial Bengal* (New Delhi: Oxford University Press, 2001).

[16] Sarkar, *Hindu Wife, Hindu Nation*. Essays in Bharati Ray, ed., *From the Seams of History: Essays on Indian Women* (New Delhi: Oxford University Press, 1995).

[17] In the late 1920s, a similar process of women questioning the beneficence of colonial rule has been richly illustrated by Mrinalini Sinha, "Refashioning Mother India: The Sarda Act and Women's Collective Agency," in *Specters of Mother India: The Global Structuring of an Empire* (Durham: Duke University Press, 2007), 152–196.

subjects, as family men,[18] whose masculinity was constituted by their intellectual and affective relationships with their children (biological and metaphorical or imaginary) rather than only via heteronormative relationships based on muscular strength and as breadwinners. Their power as social reformers emanated from their being leaders of a vulnerable community which they attempted to salvage by educating future citizens with new sense and sensibilities. Subjugated Indian men, especially the educated intelligentsia, turned the colonial critique of Indian masculinity on its head by shifting the focus from the denigration of Indians to a sharp critique of the colonial system of education. It was not through outright rejection but through negotiation, selective acceptance and partial disavowal of colonial education that Indian men sought to reclaim themselves and their future generation. As part of the growing literature on family history in South Asia, my work thus connects domestic practices with pedagogical innovations and nationalist politics, thereby bridging the gap between private and public and nationalist and imperialist concerns.

Patriarchal power and authority being so ubiquitous, fathers and fatherhood have been naturalized in Indian history. While historical literature examined the role of mothers and wives as the cornerstone of an ideal Indian family in colonial India, it has not questioned the male authorship that was instrumental in laying out the attributes of wife- and motherhood on Indian women. Scholars explored how Indian patriarchy trained women in values of global domesticity of the Victorian era and the hierarchical relationship between husband and wife.[19] But, the relationship between fathers and children (both biological and putative) as a foundational unit of Indian patriarchal structure demands serious attention. Attempting to redress the imbalance, my work locates and identifies specific scenarios when fatherhood was asserted at home and the outside world through new behavioural and pedagogical practices. Straddling

---

[18] For a parallel work on post-War England see Laura King, *Family Men: Fatherhood and Masculinity in Britain, 1914–1960* (Oxford: Oxford University Press, 2015).

[19] Judith Walsh, *Domesticity in Colonial India: What Women Learned When Men Gave Them Advice* (Lanham, MD: Rowman & Littlefield, 2004); Tanika Sarkar, *Hindu Wife, Hindu Nation*; Rochona Majumdar, *Marriage and Modernity* (Durham: Duke University Press, 2009); Mytheli Sreenivas, *Wives, Widows, and Concubines* (Bloomington: Indiana University Press, 2008); Samita Sen, "Motherhood and Mothercraft: Gender and Nationalism in Bengal," *Gender and History* 5, no. 2 (1993): 231–243.

the domains of the home and the world, the book seeks to understand the different ways the authority and power of the father were invoked and constituted metaphorically and in everyday experiences. It is a book that does not ignore women's history—rather it seeks to find the many ways girls and women of a specific caste, class, and ethnic status were defined and subjugated through patriarchal norms and authority that were likewise being defined, constituted, and subjugated, this time in conversation with colonial ideals. It is an attempt to problematize modern Indian patriarchy that subjected women to new cultural domination in the course of the nineteenth century.[20] Fatherhood as a cornerstone of patriarchy worked through assumption, appropriation, enunciation, and performance of paternal responsibilities. The ideas and practices of fatherhood took a new turn and became a mode of self-fashioning in the course of the nineteenth and twentieth century.

Fathers, a Polysemic Trope: Received Wisdom from the Hindu Worldview

The father (*pita*) is someone who gives birth; who initiates children (boys) to spirituality/lord through the sacred thread ceremony; one who gives knowledge; who gives food; and one who protects from fear. To improve the character of a son, a father will fondle him for five years; for ten years, he would beat the son; then from the sixteenth year, the father would be a friend to the son.[21] This is a summary of the Chanakya *slokas* that provide the scriptural basis of the role of a father. The father-son (not daughter) dynamic was a staple of ancient Indian texts, particularly the *Upanisads* and the *Puranas*, including the two epics. According to *Brihadaranyaka Upanisad*, the father "passes on to the son his very vital force (*prana*)"; the son "by receiving his father's bequest, redeems him from his sin": "When [a father] ... departs this world, he enters into his son with [all] these faculties (*prana*). Whatever wrong he might have done his son frees him from it all."[22] This mutually enforcing relationship between fathers and

---

[20] Partha Chatterjee, "The Nation and Its Women."
[21] Ingalls, "The Cāṇakya Collections," 2.
[22] *Brihadaranyaka Upanisad* 1.5.17, in R.C. Zaehner, trans., *Hindu Scriptures* (New York: Everyman's Library, 1966), cited in Brian Hatcher, "Father, Son, and Holy

sons, bolstered by philosophical justification, attests to the privileged position of fathers in the annals of Indian history.

Filial obligations and fatherly responsibilities (*pitritva*) varied between a son and a daughter. Proverbs, maxims, as well as Puranic legends, construct or signal the low status of women as girls and wives. Some of the clearest expressions of these viewpoints can be found in the Hindu legal codes (*dharmashastra*).[23] While *The Laws of Manu* warned that "no learned father should take a bride-price for his daughter, no matter how small,"[24] it perpetually relegated women to a secondary status by proclaiming that "[A] girl, a young woman, or even an old woman should not do anything independently, even in (her own) house. In childhood a woman should be under her father's control, in youth under her husband's, and when her husband is dead, under her sons'. She should not have independence."[25] The responsibilities of the father, husband, and son were further underscored: [A] father who does not give her [the daughter] away at the proper time should be blamed, and a husband who does not have sex with her at the proper time should be blamed; and the son who does not guard his mother when her husband is dead should be blamed."[26] When it came to matters of property, Manu prescribed that a "Man with no son may make his female child an appointed daughter" by following a certain formula.[27]

The extent to which such rulebooks were followed in the centuries following is unclear, but the British made these texts, particularly the *Manavadharmashastra* or *Laws of Manu*, a source for colonial jurisprudence and legislation on a variety of topics, especially laws and cases relating to marriage, divorce, legitimacy, adoption, guardianship, inheritance, religious endowments, and other related matters.[28] For the British,

---

Text: Rabindranath Tagore and the Upanishads," *Journal of Hindu Studies*, no. 4 (2011): 119–143 (here 123–124).

[23] For Hindu ideology and practice relating to women's roles see Susan Wadley, "Women and the Hindu Tradition," *Signs* 3, no. 1, Women and National Development: The Complexities of Change (Autumn 1977), 113–125.
[24] Doniger, *Laws of Manu*, 48.
[25] Doniger, *Laws of Manu*, 115.
[26] Doniger, *Laws of Manu*, 196.
[27] Doniger, *Laws of Manu*, 213.
[28] Sir William Jones, one of the founders of modern Indology, first translated the text in English in 1794. The historical and religious significance of the text was further attested by the fact that Max Müller included it in his monumental work, *Sacred Books of the East* series. British scholars regarded the text as "'one of the world's premier compositions in ancient law, more valuable in every sense than Hammurabi and able to hold its own in comparison to the covenant

the text provided the basis for constructing a complex system of jurisprudence that supplemented "general laws" with "personal laws" determined by one's religious affiliation. And, "Hindu laws" or *dharmashastras* were applied to 80% of the population in colonial India. Even in contemporary India, Manu is the authority for the formulation of the Hindu marriage code that distinguishes itself from Muslim and governmental or secular marriage laws.[29]

Paternal authority, like most kin-based relations in India, assumes multiple meanings and is a diffused concept, not restricted to biological linkage alone.[30] As the foundation of a heteronormative, agnatic culture, fatherhood was tied to intersecting social-economic and cultural processes, deeply rooted in property rights. Indrani Chatterjee discusses the heterosexualization of South Asian households in the colonial era: while precolonial economic units were organized in a variety of patterns, including the celibate monastic lineages, colonial authorities and print cultures valorized "the formation of conjugal heterosexual households on the basis of 'love marriages' (Walsh 2004) and biological adulthood (from twelve years in 1891 to fourteen in 1929 and eighteen in 2012)."[31] Paternal authority was exercised by senior males in positions of spiritual, economic, or political power, and biological fatherhood was not a prerequisite. In a multigenerational, patrilineal, patrilocal household it was

---

and the Priestly codes of Moses.'" Wendy Doniger with Brian K. Smith, "Introduction," in *The Laws of Manu* (Delhi: Penguin, 1991), xix. For more on the British use of Manu, see pp. xviii, lviii–lx. Doniger makes a similar point in *The Hindus: An Alternative History*, 315.

[29] Doniger with Smith, "Introduction," lx.

[30] That kinship and family ties were discursively produced and were realized in concrete terms is now well established in scholarship. See Malavika Kasturi, *Embattled Identities, Rajput Lineages and the Colonial State in Nineteenth Century Colonial North India* (New Delhi: Oxford University Press, 2002). Kasturi analyzes the reconstitution of the family and martial masculinities amongst elite lineages in British India, against the backdrop of colonial ideologies, political culture, and material realities. Focusing on the period between 1860 and 1940, she examines the intersecting interests of a north Indian religious sect, the Dasnamis, and the Anglo-Hindu laws to show how ascetic communities refashioned their genealogies through property disputes mediated by colonial laws; how the relationships within the family of the Dasnami sect, comprising men, their female companions, and children were validated through rights of ownership and inheritance of property. Malavika Kasturi, "'Asceticising' Monastic Families: Ascetic Genealogies, Property Feuds and Anglo-Hindu Law in Late Colonial India," *Modern Asian Studies* 43, no. 5 (September, 2009): 1039–1083.

[31] Indrani Chatterjee, "When 'Sexuality' Floated Free of Histories in South Asia," *Journal of Asian Studies* 71, no. 4 (November 2012): 945–962, here 952, citing Judith Walsh, *Domesticity in Colonial India: What Women Learned When Men Gave Them Advice* (Lanham, MD: Rowman & Littlefield, 2004). For monastic lineages, see Indrani Chatterjee, *Forgotten Friends: Monks, Marriages, and Memories of Northeast India* (New Delhi: Oxford University Press, 2013).

almost always the oldest male member, married or unmarried, who held the highest patriarchal authority

Indian mythology is replete with stories of filial piety. Despite myriad versions of the Indian epics, the persuasive and coercive roles that fathers played in the lives of children are evident in the basic storylines. For example, in *The Ramayana* (ca. 300 BCE–300 CE), the hero Rama went into exile with his wife and younger brother to honour his father's words, to demonstrate his commitment towards his father. Similarly, in *The Mahabharata* (ca. 400 BCE–400 CE), a first-born prince renounces his throne and takes a vow of celibacy to enable his royal father to marry the woman the latter loved, thus earning the name Bhisma, the "utterer of a terrible vow." As the story of *The Mahabharata* unfolds, Bhisma remains the "patriarch" of the entire lineage of the Pandavas and the Kauravas, whose fight over who is the legitimate heir to the kingdom Bhisma gave up led to the Bhagavad-Gita's climactic battle at Kurukshetra.[32] Bhisma thus serves as an example not only of the power fathers had over their children but also the ways in which fatherhood is claimed by or ascribed to men with little or no genetic relationship to their "children."[33]

It is instructive to note that Indian populist literature frequently portrays fathers, biological or not, as victims of their own passions and involvements. In contrast, women as mothers, daughters, wives, and sisters in epics and popular literature are depicted as strong and determined.[34]

---

[32] For a summary and discussion of the story of Bhisma, a patriarch who is not the biological father see Jayatri Ghosh, "Satyavati: The Matriarch of the Mahabharata," in *Faces of the Feminine in Ancient, Medieval, and Modern India*, ed. Mandakranta Bose (New Delhi: Oxford University Press, 2000), 19.

[33] An extreme example of obedience to father is represented in the character of Parashurama, the ax-wielding incarnation often referred to as "Rama with an Ax." A son of an inter-caste couple, his Brahman father was the priest Jamadagni and his Kshatriya mother, the Princess Renuka. Parashurama beheaded his mother to follow the command of his father. As one version of the story went, when father Jamadagni suspected Renuka of her erotic desire for another king, he ordered their son Parashurama to cut off his mother's head, and the son complied. Satisfied by his son's obedience, when Jamadagni wanted to reward Parashurama with a boon, Parashurama begged him to bring his mother Renuka back to life. Parashurama also requested that "no one would remember her murder, that no one would be touched by the evil." Later, to avenge the death of his father, Parashurama killed the whole race of male Kshatriyas (twenty-one successive times) and filled five lakes with their blood. The story attests to Brahmanical dominance and appealed to the Brahmin writers of the Puranas. As Wendy Doniger pointed out, Parashurama, through his acts of killing the Kshatriyas, acted more as a Kshatriya than a Brahmin. Wendy Doniger, *The Hindus: An Alternative History* (New York: Penguin Books, 2000), 489. Doniger also noted that Parashurama does not appear as an avatar in *The Mahabharata*.

[34] Swapna Banerjee, "Debates on Domesticity," *History Compass* 8, no. 6 (2010): 455–473.

Even the male protagonists of the populist *Mangal Kabyas*,[35] an important genre of precolonial Bengali literature from the fifteenth-sixteenth centuries, that narrated an intricate play of human, animal, and divine forces, were much less developed as characters than their female counterparts. These popular representations of filial relationships serve as important indices of everyday life, as history in precolonial South Asia had a much more fluid, literary form that was narrated in the "dominant genre of a particular community, located in space, at a given moment in time."[36]

In Bengal, stories and "injunctions" reveal the strong connection between *pita* (father) and *pitritantra* (patriarchy), their embeddedness in property relationships and claims to inheritance for primarily male offspring. It is important not to conflate fatherhood (*pitritvo*) or masculinity (*purushotvo*) with patriarchy (*pitritantra*). One must also note here that property inheritance is only relevant to fatherhood for people who own property—for people who do not own land or do not have accumulated capital, the property cannot have been central to fatherhood. In her discussion on the broader context of Hindu traditions and modern law, Vasudha Narayanan cited examples of court cases of disputes between biological heirs and spiritual heirs over ownership of property. Those cases involve wrangling over the category of father.[37]

According to a common Hindu worldview, it is in the stage of the householder or *garhasthya*, and hence as a husband and *father* (emphasis mine), that a man attains material and sexual gratification through "'intimacy' based on shared work as well as on sensuality and procreation."[38] The Hindu view of *garhasthya* or domesticity upholds that "[H]e only is a perfect man who consists of three persons united, his wife, himself, and his offspring."[39] The sociologist T.N. Madan also showed that some of the prominent writers of the *dharmashastras*, the texts on codes of conduct,

---

[35] David Curley, *Poetry and History: Bengal Mangal Kabya and Social Change in Precolonial Bengal* (New Delhi: Chronicle Books, 2008).
[36] Velecheru Narayan Rao, David Shulman, and Sanjay Subrahmanyam, *Textures of Time: Writing History in South India 1600–1800* (New Delhi: Permanent Black, 2001), 4.
[37] Vasudha Narayanan, "Renunciation and Law in India," *Religion and Law in Independent India* (1993): 279–291. I thank Dr. Katherine Ulrich for alerting me about this reference.
[38] Patrick Olivelle, ed., *Gṛhastha: The Householder in Ancient Indian Religious Culture* (New York: Oxford University Press, 2019).
[39] Sudhir Kakar, "Setting the Stage: The Traditional Hindu View and the Psychology of Erik H. Erikson," in *Identity and Adulthood*, ed. Kakar (New Delhi: Oxford University Press, 1979), 8. Kakar quotes from *The Laws of Manu*, G. Buhler, trans. *Sacred Books of the East*, vol. XXV (Oxford: Clarendon Press, 1886), 335.

or scriptures considered the stage of the householder as the most important and valid stage in human life.[40] But, as the case of Bhisma shows, the biological relationship was not always required to make one a father.

As I discuss below, adoption was common, and families subscribing to different monastic lineages and religious traditions often attributed "fatherhood" to the spiritual mentor or *guru*.[41] Indrani Chatterjee systematically traces the gradual decline and the "ever-attenuated forms" of a vast swath of monastic teachers—Buddhist, Vaishnava, Shaiva, Tantric, and Sufi in northeast India—who contributed well into the 1800s varieties of social labour to the broad-based organization of collective life of the subcontinent. My book demonstrates that the new leadership role of the fathers can be discerned as a morphing of that guru model, and it did not represent a sharp break with the past. By figuratively assuming the guru-status, educated men as imaginary fathers wrote and published for children and their parents to raise India's future generation.

The history of the father in South Asia is yet to be written, and it is certainly not the goal of the present book. Obviously, the traditional roles of the father and the concept of fatherhood did not appear overnight but were rather constructed—and contested—in a wide variety of contexts, drawing on sources like the *Laws of Manu* and traditional tales like the *Ramayana*, and changed from one generation to the next. It was rare, however, for fathers to exist without being imbedded in a nexus of patriarchal authority and property relations.

Fathers as Property Owners

The basis of patriarchal authority for colonial subjects in states like Bengal, which remained the seat of British power from 1757 through 1911, was bolstered by British adoption of Hindu and Muslim legal systems, which were defined by property relations and rights of inheritance.[42] For the

---

[40] T.N. Madan, *Non-renunciation: Themes and Interpretations of Hindu Culture* (New Delhi: Oxford University Press, 2004).

[41] Chatterjee, Forgotten Friends; Kasturi, "'Asceticising' Monastic Families," 1039–1083.

[42] For more on marriage and rights of Indian men and women, see Bina Agarwal, *A Field of One's Own: Gender and Land Rights in South Asia* (Cambridge: Cambridge University Press, 1994); *Gender and Legal Rights in Landed Property in India* (New Delhi: Kali for Women, 1999); Flavia Agnes, *Law and Gender Inequality: The Politics of Women's Rights in India* (New Delhi: Oxford University Press, 1999); "Women, Marriage and Subordination of Rights," in

Muslim laws that the East India Company inherited, the colonial jurists produced a body of knowledge based on what they believed to be the "rules" created by clearly defined Islamic texts, such as the *Hedaya*.[43] The British viewed the Muslim family as a collection of individuals with established contracts. But the Hindu family was viewed as a joint unit based on British interpretation of Hindu laws regarding succession and property rights. H.T. Colebrook's seminal text, *Two Treatises on the Hindu Law of Inheritance* (1810), which helped standardize the emerging Anglo-Hindu laws, distinguished between two schools of thought evolving out of commentaries from the same body of *smriti* literature of ancient India.[44] The "Bengal" school based on Jimutavahana's *Dayabhaga* assigned the highest legal rights to the father as the sole owner of all property, ancestral and personal.[45] In contrast, Vijnanesvara's *Mitakshara* formed the basis of Banaras school and was followed all over India barring Bengal and Assam. In the *Mitakshara* system ancestral property belonged to the family collective or coparcenary, and it was only sons who were coparceners from birth. In contrast, the *Dayabhaga* system ensured that family members could enjoy access to the ancestral property but neither male nor female heirs had rights to the ancestral property until after the death of the father or the extinction of father's ownership for social, cultural, or political reasons.[46] Upon the father's death property rights were passed on to the widow and to male and female heirs following order of succession. The *Dayabhaga* system, although slightly favourable to women

Subaltern Studies XI: Community, Gender, and Violence, eds. Partha Chatterjee and Pradeep Jaganathan (New Delhi: Permanent Black, 2000); "Economic Rights of Women under Muslim Personal Law," *Economic and Political Weekly* 31, no. 2832 (October 1996); Srimati Basu, *She Comes to Take Her Rights: Indian Women, Property, and Propriety* (Albany: SUNY Press, 1999); *Trouble with Marriage* (Berkeley: University of California Press, 2015); G. Arunima, *There Comes Papa: Colonialism and the Transformation of Matriliny in Kerala, Malabar, c. 1850–1940* (Hyderabad: Orient Longman, 2003); Mytheli Sreenivas, *Wives, Widows, and Concubines* (Bloomington: Indiana University Press, 2008); Samita Sen, "Crossing Communities: Religious Conversion, Rights in Marriage, and Personal Law," in *Negotiating Spaces: Legal Domains, Gender Constructs, and Community Concerns*, eds. Flavia Agnes and Shoba Venkatesh (New Delhi: Oxford University Press, 2012).

[43] Eleanor Newbigin, *The Hindu Family and the Emergence of Modern India: Law, Citizenship, and Community* (Cambridge: Cambridge University Press, 2013), 35.

[44] Newbigin, *The Hindu Family*, 36–37.

[45] For the *Dayabhaga* system, see Ludo Rocher, *Jimutavahana's Dayabhaga: The Hindu Law of Inheritance in Bengal* (New York: Oxford University Press, 2002). For a feminist reading of the same text see Manomohini Dutta, *Inheritance, Property, and Women in the Dāyabhāga* (Ph.D. Dissertation, University of Texas, Austin, 2016).

[46] Eleanor Newbigin, *The Hindu Family*, 36.

in comparison to the Banaras school, still gave fathers and elderly male members unrestricted authority over ancestral property and family members.[47]

The paternal authority being strongly tied to economic relationships, particularly as established by colonial law, the importance of biological fathers was related to changing property rights.[48] But, in India, a father's occupation or income was not the sole indicator of the family's economic or social status. A father's brother or father could be the salient person for the determination of the family status.[49] Restructuring of the land-revenue system and shifting practices in judicial arrangements under different regimes of power often determined the claims of property rights of individuals. In early modern India, until the mid-nineteenth century, adoption was a common practice in ruling families without male heirs. At the same time, there was also a growing masculinization of property rights that deprived widows of their claims to property.[50] Heirs were adopted from within the larger family, which made the production of sons less important. With Lord Dalhousie's introduction of the "doctrine of lapse" (1848) that claimed princely states without male heirs would go over to the colonial state, more legal emphasis was put on biological connections.[51] Property rights and obligations of males were further complicated by processes of urbanization, migration from rural to urban set-ups, and the development of new professional, educational, and financial institutions under the colonial regime. Among both Hindus and Muslims, familial conflicts with parental authorities, both mothers and fathers, gave rise to nucleated households. With the diffusion of familial responsibilities and obligations, specific meanings ascribed to gender,

---

[47] Narendra Subramanian, *Nation and Family: Personal Law, Cultural Pluralism, and Gendered Citizenship in India* (Stanford: Stanford University Press, 2014).
[48] See, for instance, the case of Kerala where matriliny was replaced by patriarchal control, as described in Arunima, *There Comes Papa*.
[49] Bernard Cohn, "Recruitments of Elites in India under British Rule," in *Essays in Comparative Social Stratification*, eds. Leonard Plotnicov and Arthur Tuden (Pittsburgh: University of Pittsburgh Press, 1970), 143.
[50] Rochisha Narayan, "Widows, Family, Community, and the Formation of Anglo-Hindu Law in Eighteenth-Century India," *Modern Asian Studies* 50, no. 3 (2016): 866–897.
[51] Newbigin argues that the Fundamental Rights enshrined in the Indian Constitution far from being "neutral" were deeply anchored in the late colonial political economy. The citizen-subject of the Indian Constitution was tied to the ascriptive categories of gender and religion and the power structures governed by Hindu law. Eleanor Newbigin, "Personal Law and Citizenship in India's Transition to Independence," *Modern Asian Studies* 45, no. 1 (2011): 7–32.

age, and status became critical for the upwardly mobile community in nineteenth-century India.[52]

Analogous to the polysemic and complex nature of Indian families in which fathers operated, fatherhood too was conceived in multiple ways.[53] Recent scholarship has recognized that it is impossible to disassociate the Indian family and its affective connections from the lineages and operation of the state.[54] The ethos of familialism, pervading the link between state power and the often-conflictual family relations widely prevalent in the early modern era, was also "subject to manipulation and management."[55] While it was common for the king to adopt the stance of the father and demand filial loyalty from his subjects, the subjects too looked up to him as dependent "children" seeking care, protection, and support.[56] If metaphors of family and its "usable affect" were appropriated by rulers and the state as important tools to mobilize its subjects, actual families too, argued Sumit Guha, manoeuvred their relationships and positioned "individuals in new social roles for given political ends."[57] As the constitution of families and the construction of states were implicated in each other, even in the later period, the political-economic and socio-cultural ramifications of the colonial state impinged upon Indian men. With its pervading discourse of paternalism, the colonial state embarked on a path of reform and legislation to "civilize" its native subjects. As the reforms were carried out on institutional and socio-cultural levels, Indian men under colonial subjection self-consciously asserted their masculine authority through daily practices of fatherhood at home and in the public sphere. The increasing proliferation of print culture allowed educated Indian men to carve out an epistemic space and envision a pedagogy that would equip the next generation with a new tool to combat the changing

---

[52] Indrani Chatterjee, ed., *Unfamiliar Relations* (New Delhi: Permanent Black, 2004), 17.
[53] For polysemic nature of Indian families see Vatuk, "'Family' as a Contested Concept," 161–191.
[54] Andre Wink, *Land and Sovereignty in India* (Cambridge: Cambridge University Press, 2007).
[55] Sumit Guha, "The Family Feud," in *Unfamiliar Relations*, ed. Chatterjee, 76.
[56] See for instance, Gautam Bhadra, "The Mentality of Subalternity: Kantanama or Rajdharma," in *Subaltern Studies Reader, 1986–1995*, ed. Ranajit Guha (Minneapolis: University of Minnesota Press, 1997), 63–99.
[57] Guha, "Family Feud," 78. For more on the tension between state, family, and children see Sumit Guha, "Did the British Empire Depend on Separating Parents and Children," *Not Even Past* (blog). 24 January 2020. Available at https://notevenpast.org/did-the-british-empire-depend-on-separating-parents-and-children/.

world. As products of new colonial education, fathers endowed with new sensibilities became harbingers of new modernity and influenced the contours of parental relationship.[58]

Fathers as Interlocutors and Teachers

My story of fathers and children is about intersections and entanglements produced at the crossroads of the British empire, the colonial state, the activities of the European missionaries,[59] and the private–public lives of educated Indian males who acted as leaders in literary, political, and social movements.[60] Far from being a homogeneous entity, the fathers I study represented a hegemonic social formation who were caught in the middle.[61] Comparable to other parts of India, such as Surat in Bombay presidency, the terrain of urban landscape in nineteenth-century Bengal displayed contrasting social and political scenarios bound up with a changing configuration of power.[62] The Western-educated professional community (*shikshita madhyabitto*) of fathers reacted to the dissolute life-style of a new comprador class, broadly termed as the *babus*, who were also fostered by the colonial economy and gained social power and wealth in the new urban environment.[63] A series of satires in the early nineteenth century—*Naba-babu Bilash* (1825), *Dooti Bilash* (1825), and *Naba-Bibi Bilash* (1822)—captured the profligate lifestyle of this new

---

[58] Among the vast body of literature on South Asia a few selected examples are: Arjun Appadurai, *Modernity at Large* (Minneapolis: University of Minnesota Press, 1998); Mushirul Hasan, *Modernity and Nationalism* (New Delhi: Oxford University Press, 2009); Peter Robb, *Empire, Identity, and the India: Liberalism, Modernity, and the Nation* (New Delhi: Oxford University Press, 2006).
[59] For European missionary intervention in lives of children see Karen Vallgårda, *Imperial Childhoods and Christian Mission: Education and Emotion in South India and Denmark* (London: Palgrave Macmillan, 2015).
[60] For more on Bengali domesticity and private-public lives of Bengali men and women see, Sambuddha Chakravarty, *Andare-Antare: Unish Shatake Bangali Bhadramahila* (Calcutta: Stree, 1995).
[61] For an interesting discussion of interstitial location of middle-class leaders in a different context see Jennifer Riggan, *The Struggling State: Nationalism, Mass Militarization, and the Education of Eritrea* (Philadephia: Temple University Press, 2016).
[62] For a study of power hierarchy and response by colonial elites in the city of Surat in Bombay presidency, see Douglas Haynes, *Rhetoric and Ritual in Colonial India: The Shaping of a Public Culture in Surat City, 1852–1928* (Berkeley, California: University of California Press, 1991).
[63] Sinha, "Introduction," *Colonial Masculinity*, 5–7.

urban social group and represented the growing tension between the existing folk and the emerging elite cultures.[64]

Concomitantly, the middle-class fathers also distanced themselves from the poor and the uneducated who abandoned their children and were unable to provide them with education or economic sustenance. The critique that the leaders voiced was not targeted to specific caste, class, or religious groups but rather it aimed to cure the ills of prevalent social evils practised by a segment of the population.[65] The Western-educated leaders particularly reacted to the age-old practices of a section of the Brahmin community, the *kulins*, who traversed the landscape of rural-urban Bengal. The movements that the leaders spearheaded against polygamy, child marriage, and the advocacy of widow remarriage pivoted on the denunciation of the depraved practices of the *kulin* (derived from a Sanskrit word meaning good family) Brahmins of Bengal. The *kulin* Brahmins, owing to their special privilege in caste ranking and marriage rules in Bengali Hindu society introduced by King Ballal Sen in the twelfth century, indulged in multiple marriages (the numbers ranging from two to eighty) and were notorious for deserting and neglecting their children and wives.[66] In his proposal to ban polygamy, Iswarchandra Vidyasagar, the foremost social reformer of his day, included a lengthy tirade against *kulin* Brahmins as irresponsible fathers and dissolute husbands, arguing that their unnecessary power in the caste Hindu society needed to be curbed.[67]

This social reality was further complicated as the leaders were caught in a complex tangle of hierarchy and humiliation with the British who, alluding to decrepit social mores, regularly derided the male members of the Bengali middle class as dandy and effeminate. The social distinctions

---

[64] Sumanta Banerjee, "Marginalization of Women's Popular Culture in Nineteenth-Century Bengal," in *Recasting Women: Essays in Colonial History*, eds. Kumkum Sangari and Sudesh Vaid (New Delhi: Kali for Women, 2006; first published, 1989).

[65] In late colonial Bengal Dalit leaders launched social, religious, and literary movements that resonated concerns similar to those expressed by the upper caste reformist Hindu leaders. See Sekhar Bandyopadhyay, *Caste, Protest, and Identity in Colonial India: the Namasudras of Bengal, 1872–1947*, 2nd enl. ed. (New Delhi: Oxford University Press, 2011).

[66] Aishika Chakraborty, "Gender, Caste and Marriage: Kulinism in Nineteenth-Century Bengal," in *Intimate Others: Marriage and Sexualities in India*, eds. Samita Sen, Ranjita Biswas, Nandita Dhawan (Kolkata: Stree, 2011), 35–65.

[67] Iswarchandra Vidyasagar, "Bohubibaha Rohit Hoya Uchit Kina Etodbishoyok Prostab ('Proposal on Whether It Is Justified to Ban Polygamy' [1828])," in *Vidyasagar Rachanabali*, Vol. 2, ed. Tirthapati Datta (Calcutta: Tuli Kalam, 1994), 840–916.

and distancing from the different segments of the society that the *bhadralok* fathers claimed was complicated by notions of respectability and masculinity ushered in by a host of indigenous and foreign elements. It is this specific historical moment that makes the study of fatherhood so powerful—the conjuncture when the role of colonized men was shaped and transformed in many ways. What this book unravels is the process of becoming the father, the instantiation of fatherhood endowed with a moral guardianship and its investment in new cultural capital, the children. By tracking the literary and pedagogic moves, I suggest that the registers of masculinity for Indian men shifted over the long nineteenth and twentieth centuries.

My work documents change over time—the domestic culture under colonialism was undergoing a drastic transformation almost ushering in a "revolution," not so much in materializing a structural change but in reconstituting familial relationships when the role of the biological father, just like mothers and children, attained heightened importance in a burgeoning middle-class culture.[68] By foregrounding the experiences at home and their extension in the public realm of educational reforms, I explore the leadership roles of fathers as patriarchs of the family and of the community and eventually, of the nation and beyond. The "enunciative" and "performative" aspects of fatherhood, representing shifting sets of ideas and practices over time, revealed ambivalent and conflicted sensibilities of the colonized subjects on the one hand, and the latter's bid for hegemony over women, children, servants and other subaltern groups, on the other.

In the course of the nineteenth century, "fathers" from the educated middle class (*bhadralok*), both in their biological capacity and as reformers and ideologues, engaged in educational movements and social reforms to make their women and children part of a progressive modernity. As a new social formation, they emerged as an emotional community displaying altered sensibilities in setting up a home, providing

---

[68] Steven Mintz and Susan Kellogg, *Domestic Revolution: A Social History of American Family Life* (New York: Simon and Schuster, 1989) The book offer a comprehensive history of American family life from 1620 to the 1980s documenting transformations among different ethnic groups, Puritans, Native Americans, and African Americans. My use of the term "domestic revolution" is inspired by the work of Mintz and Kellog but the Indian scenario does not exactly correspond to the American.

economic support, ensuring protection, and in training their progeny with "appropriate" virtues of girl- and boyhood—values similar, but by no means identical, to the middle class in Victorian England.[69] While direct references to fathers were invisible in periodical literature, as Claudia Nelson also documents in the case of Victorian and Edwardian England (1837–1901), fathers were a lot more visible within middle-class homes.[70] The elite Indian patriarchy not only deployed different tactics of control for the "new woman" but it also mobilized itself and its imagined community of children to vindicate themselves before their colonial "masters" and to establish their hegemony in the charged political culture. The hegemony however was never complete owing to its differentiation, bias, and exclusionary practices but efforts of domination continued.[71] In their selective appropriation of the virtues of Victorian manhood, members of the Indian intelligentsia, by the turn of the century, offered a critique through a brisk cultural production of literature and an alternate scheme of education intending to challenge the colonial system.

For educated Indian men, children became the enabling agents. The various debates, deliberations, and interrogations around children from 1850s through 1930s created institutional and experimental spaces, such as schools, reformatories, inquiry commissions, and children's literature, a conglomerate that Satadru Sen termed the "juvenile periphery."[72] For the fathers, the "new child" like the "new woman," was a fleeting, unstable, and usable category—defined and appropriated literally and figuratively in different ways—contingent on its gender and socio-economic status. The spatiotemporal dynamics of children traversed both the home and the world thus demonstrating that a strong ideological divide between the private and the public exists only—like all reified categories—in theory, while on the ground reality was a much more complex interlayering, overlapping, and contesting set of contexts. In designing a

---

[69] John Tosh, *A Man's Place: Masculinity and the Middle Class in Victorian England* (New Haven, CT: Yale University Press, 2007).

[70] Claudia Nelson, *Invisible Men: Fatherhood in Victorian Periodicals, 1850–1910* (Athens: University of Georgia Press, 1995).

[71] The notion of "dominance without hegemony" is drawn from Ranajit Guha's "Discipline and Punish," in which he argued that in the imperial-nationalist context, neither the colonial state nor the indigenous elites had hegemony over the subaltern population. Ranajit Guha, *Dominance Without Hegemony* (Cambridge, MA: Harvard University Press, 1997), 100–151.

[72] Satadru Sen, "A Juvenile Periphery: The Geographies of Literary Childhood in Colonial Bengal," *Journal of Colonialism and Colonial History* 5, no. 1 (2004).

new curriculum of education these men responded to the exigencies of their personal life. Worried to provide the best education for their children, which was not imparted in schools set up by colonists, each leader was compelled to conceptualize a new pedagogical model and enforce cultural practices that were hybrid in nature. Focusing on the new pedagogy designed by iconic leaders like Tagore, Gandhi, and Nehru, my study makes a vital point that these men had dismissed the earlier colonial critique of "effeminate Bengalis" by transferring masculinity from physical strength to moral education, the latter stressing freedom of mind, courage, bravery, and filial piety.

Shorn of any direct reference to fathers, recent scholarship on children in India demonstrates that the new ideas of childhood and the perceived role of children were critical to the running of the colonial state and for the articulation of cultural and national identity in India. Works investigating educational curriculum,[73] different genres of vernacular literature,[74] imperial legislations,[75] labour policies and various

[73] For educational curriculum see, Sudipa Topdar, "The Corporeal Empire: Physical Education and Politicising Children's Bodies in Late Colonial Bengal," *Gender and History* 29, no. 1 (April 2017): 176–197; "Duties of a 'Good Citizen': Colonial Secondary Textbook Policies in Late Nineteenth-Century India," *South Asian History and Culture* 6, no. 3 (2015): 417–439; Catriona Ellis, "Education for All: Reassessing the Historiography of Education in Colonial India," *History Compass* 6 (December 2008); Sarada Balagopalan, "An Ideal School and the Schooled Ideal: Educational Experiences at the Margins," in *Educational Regimes in Contemporary India*, eds. P. Jeffrey et al. (New Delhi: Sage Publications, 2005).

[74] For cultural production of vernacular literature and children see PradipBose, "Sons of the Nation: Child Rearing in the New Family," in *Texts of Power*, ed. Partha Chatterjee (Minneapolis: University of Minnesota Press, 1995), 118–144; Sibaji Bandyopadyay, *Bangla Sishu Sahityer Chhoto Meyera* (Kolkata: Grasshoppers, 2014); *Gopal-Rakhal Dvandasamas* (Kolkata: Papyrus, 1991); Gautam Chando Roy, "Childhood Conditions: Moral Education in Early 20th Century Bengal," *History* [Journal of the Department of History, Burdwan University] 7, no 1 (2005); "Swadeshikal, Swadeshbodh O Bangla Shishusahitya," in *Shatabarser Aaloy Bangabhanga*, ed. Debabrata Ghose (2005); "Themes of 'National' Identity in Bengali Children's Literature, c.1880–c.1920: A Note," *Journal of History* [Mahisadal Raj College], 1 (2005); Nandini Chandra, *The Classic Popular: Amar Chitra Katha, 1907–1967* (New Delhi: Yoda Press, 2008); Ruby Lal, "Recasting the Women's Question: The Girl-Child/Woman in the Colonial Encounter," *Interventions* 10, no. 3 (2008): 321–339. Shobna Nijhwan, *Women and Girls in the Hindi Public Sphere: Periodical Literature in Colonial North India* (New Delhi: Oxford University Press, 2012); "Hindi Children's Journals and Nationalist Discourse (1910–1930)," *Economic and Political Weekly* 39, no. 33 (2004): 3723–3729. Tanika Sarkar, "Caste, Sect, and Hagiography: The Balakdashis of Early Modern Bengal," "The Child and the World: Rabindranath Tagore's Ideas on Education," *Rebels, Wives, Saints: Designing Selves and Nations in Colonial Times* (Calcutta: Seagull Books, 2009).

[75] Ishita Pande, "'Listen to the Child': Law, Sex, and the Child Wife in Indian Historiography," *History Compass* 11, no. 9 (September 2013); "Coming of Age: Law, Sex, and Childhood in Late Colonial India," *Gender and History* 24, no. 1 (April 2012); "Sorting Boys and Men: Unlawful Intercourse, Boy-Protection, and the Child Marriage Restraint Act in Colonial India," *Journal of the History of Childhood and Youth* 6, no. 2 (January 2013): 332–358.

institutions[76] highlight colonial legislation that impinged on the lives of men, women, and children. Informed by these works but departing from the focus on the colonial state and institutions, my book examines the practices of everyday life of native fathers and children enacted both at home and in the public domain of print culture. It traces the points of intersection between British policies and educated Indian males, the latter formulating their response through a series of discourses that evinced new forms of knowledge, awareness, and a self-reflexive critique. By engaging with literary and scientific sources, my attempt is to investigate the multiple ways "child" as a category (and the related ones of "boy" and "girl") entered divergent discourses and how different notions of childhood were imagined and appropriated by the native intelligentsia, the "fathers," to articulate their own identities.[77]

The Many Worlds of Indian Children and Childhood

Children and childhood, as subjects of inquiry, straddle different academic domains. Childhood Studies in postcolonial India emerged at the intersection of two related experiences: the colonial past and the Euro-American dominance of the academic culture in the postcolonial period.[78] The moral legitimacy of British rule lay in rescuing and reforming the subject population, including children and women, and in leading them to the path of civilization and progress. The liberal-utilitarian principles of the colonial state, based principally on ideas of James Mill (1773–1836), premised its superiority by dismissing indigenous ideas

---

[76] For labour policies and institutions see Emma Alexander, Sarada Balagopalan, and Satadru Sen.

[77] For historical, social, and literary constructions of childhood in India see Anto Thomas Chakramakkil, "The Polemics of Real and Imagined Childhood(s) in India," *International Research in Children's Literature* 10, no. 1 (2017): 74–88. For debates on whether there was an Indian childhood, see Olga Nieuwenhuys, "Is There an Indian Childhood?," *Childhood* 16, no. 2 (2009): 147–153; "Keep Asking: Why Childhood? Why Children? Why Global?," *Childhood* 17, no. 3 (2010): 291–296; "Global Childhood and the Politics of Contempt," *Alternatives: Global, Local, Political* 23, no. 3 (July–September 1998): 267–289.

[78] Nieuwenhuys, "Is There an Indian Childhood?" Also, see Zazie Bowen and Jessica Hinchy, "Introduction: Children and Knowledge in India," *South Asian History and Culture*, Vol. 6, Issue 3 (July 2015) pp. 317–319. Zazie Bowen and Jessica Hinchy, eds. *Children and Knowledge, Contemporary and Historical Perspectives from India.* (New York: Routledge, 2019).

and practices of childhood as archaic, inadequate, and barbarous and by adopting a paternalistic position of a "good father" to guide its immature and primitive subjects.[79] On the other hand, the postcolonial state's failure to successfully deal with children's issues aggravated by global economic factors such as the oil crisis of the 1970s, lead to an increasing intervention by international organizations such as UNICEF, the ILO, and the World Bank to drive quantitative research on Indian children. Important works on policy issues and legal studies were produced.[80] Anthropological studies brought alive lived experiences of children by conducting place-based research on mothers and children in rural settings.[81]

To salvage Indian childhood from its homogenized and numerical representations, the earliest conceptual engagement came from psychoanalysts such as Sudhir Kakar who, in his now-classic study, contextualized Hindu infancy and childhood through a close examination of societal roles, traditional values, kinship networks, and customs.[82] Kakar's analysis, though valuable for its time, mainly focused on the dominant view of the Brahmanical culture deeply embedded in the hierarchical ordering of castes. The worldview it projected was based on the *Manusmriti*, the classical Hindu text, which positioned the child at the bottom of the social order side by side with the low castes, slaves, servants, the old and the sick, newly-married and pregnant women. However, children along with the pregnant woman, the old and the sick were to be protected whereas lower castes and others who violated caste rules would be meted harsh punishment. Kakar also notes that Ayurveda demarcated childhood from the period of conception to the time when the child attained adulthood. Each period was marked by rituals and they gradually ensured the separation of the child from the mother, leading to his assimilation to

---

[79] James Mill, *The History of British India*, 1st ed. (London: Baldwin, Cradock and Joy, 1817). For Mill's biography see, Bruce Mazlish, *James and John Mill: Father and Son in the Nineteenth Century* (New York: Basic Books, 1975).

[80] Myron Weiner, *The Child and the State in India* (New Delhi: Oxford University Press, 1994, 4th imprint [1991]); Asha Bajpai, *Child Rights in India: Law, Policy, and Practice*, 2nd ed. (New Delhi: Oxford University Press, 2006).

[81] Ronald Preston Rohner and Majushri Chaki-Sircar, *Women and Children in a Bengali Village* (Hanover, NH: Published for University of Connecticut by University Press of New England, 1988).

[82] Sudhir Kakar, *The Inner World: A Psycho-analytic Study of Childhood and Society in India*, 2nd ed. (New Delhi: Oxford University Press, 1981).

the larger life of the community. Kakar comments that these stages are echoed in the different ritual ceremonies, such as *namakarana* (naming) performed within a month of the child's birth to *annaprashana* (when the child is given solid food) to *upanayana*, the sacred thread ceremony for upper-caste boys that marked the end of childhood, signalled the step-by-step transition to adulthood. But the socialization process described in those texts neither captured the complexity nor presented the experiences of girls or children of lower socio-economic groups.[83] While Kakar's insights are valuable for pointing towards how the child was constructed by high-caste male interlocutors, this is only a partial picture.

In a seminal article tracing the psycho-social origin of childhood, Ashis Nandy posited, "[T]here is nothing natural or inevitable about childhood. Childhood is culturally defined and created; ... there are as many childhoods as there are families and cultures, and the consciousness of childhood is as much a cultural datum as patterns of child-rearing and the social role of the child."[84] According to Nandy, political and psychological forces in a specific context enable the "concept of childhood and the perception of the child to be shared and transmitted."[85] His frame of reference for analysing Indian childhood adhered closely to the British characterization of the Indian subject population as "half savage and half child" who required the guidance of the civilized Western cultures. Engaging with the Western model that recognizes the child as an invention and an instrument of modernity,[86] Nandy invoked four different "uses" of the child and childhood in the modern worldview: the child as a "projective device," "a screen as well as a mirror";[87] childhood as a "dystopia for the modern world";[88] childhood as a "battleground of

---

[83] Kakar, *Inner World*, 204–207; see also the discussion in Vasanthi Raman, "The Diverse Life-Worlds of Indian Childhood," in *Family and Gender: Changing Values in Germany and India*, eds. Margrit Pernau, Imtiaz Ahmad, and Helmut Reifeld (New Delhi: Sage Publications, 2003), 84–111. Vasanthi Raman, "Politics of Childhood: Perspectives from the South," *Economic and Political Weekly* 35, no. 46 (November 11–17, 2000): 4055–4064.

[84] Ashis Nandy, "Reconstructing Childhood: A Critique of the Ideology of Adulthood," *Traditions, Tyranny and Utopias: Essays in the Politics of Awareness* (New Delhi: Oxford University Press, 1987), 56.

[85] Nandy, "Reconstructing Childhood," 56.

[86] Phillippe Ariès, *Centuries of Childhood: A Social History of Family Life* (New York: Vintage, 1965; original 1960); Lloyd DeMause, ed., *The History of Childhood* (Baltimore: Johns Hopkins Press, 1974).

[87] Nandy, "Reconstructing Childhood," 63.

[88] Nandy, "Reconstructing Childhood," 65.

cultures";[89] and finally, the mystification of the idea of childhood than "the idea of the child" by societies wedded to principles of reason and consumerism. Every age produced its own myth of the "obligated progeny sacrificing his life to right real or imaginary wrongs done to his parents or to his parent's generation."[90] Nandy's "child," like Kakar's, is very stable, an undifferentiated and monolithic category with no reference to caste, class, gender, region, or religion, all of which demarcated childhood in India. Nandy's child is an instrument in the hands of the adults. In his "reconstruction of childhood," the diverse worlds of Indian children are utterly missing.

While a comprehensive history of the multiple childhoods of India is beyond the scope of this book, a few examples of variations found in different castes, classes, tribes, and religions will show something of the diverse worlds of childhood, thus better positioning this book to explicate the manifold fathers of those children. The differing realities of children from the less privileged background are best garnered from testimonies in autobiographical writings. The stigmatized identities of a child, girl or boy, from the lower castes are evident in numerous autobiographical writings of Dalit writers. S.K. Thorat of the Mahar caste noted that "[A]n untouchable child, particularly in a village is subjected to a stigmatized identity from the time he begins to walk and to touch things and people. When he innocently enters the village temple or a caste Hindu household, or touches someone, he is reprimanded either by his parents or by the caste Hindus."[91] On another level, the Brahmanical order legitimized the monopoly of knowledge only for the upper-caste groups and barred the acquisition of knowledge by lower castes and women. Despite the postcolonial state's commitment to affirmative action for Scheduled Castes and Scheduled Tribes, the discrimination continued to persist, as evinced by the Dalit woman writer K. Pawde's attempt to learn Sanskrit in the post-independence years.[92] The reflection of Kancha Ilaiah, a member of

---

[89] Nandy, "Reconstructing Childhood," 65.
[90] Nandy, "Reconstructing Childhood," 68.
[91] See for example S.K. Thorat, "Passage to Adulthood," in *Identity and Adulthood*, ed. Sudhir Kakar (New Delhi: Oxford University Press, 1979).
[92] K. Pawde, "The Story of My 'Sanskrit'" in *Subject to Change: Teaching Literature in the Nineties*, ed. Susie Tharu (Hyderabad, India: Orient Longman), cited in Raman, "The Diverse Life-Worlds of Indian Childhood," 96.

the Sudra Kurumma community of Andhra Pradesh in southern India, could be instructive here:

> [o]ur childhoods were mutilated by constant abuse and by silence... For hundreds of generations the violent stoppage of the entry of the written word into our homes and our lives nipped our consciousness in the very bud. Even after schools were opened to us because of independence or *swaraj*,... the school teacher was against us, the textbook language was against us. Our homes have one culture and the schools have another culture.[93]

Another example that dissolves the monolithic Indian child comes from one of India's many tribal communities. Whereas the patriarchal basis of the Sanskritic tradition lay in its emphasis on the earth as the womb and the male "seed" (semen) in the formation of the child's (male) personality, evidence from the matrilineal community of the Garos in Meghalaya suggests a contrary picture.[94] The Garos treasure the birth of a girl child and privilege it more than the birth of a boy. Garo society does not harbour any notions of illegitimacy with regard to children, and their paternity is entirely social and not tied to biological connection. The girl child is absolutely critical in the continuity of the household. In case of an absence of a girl child in a family, there is provision for adoption to ensure continuity of the household.[95] In fact, there are many other tribal and semi-tribal groups whose worldviews on children and their socialization vary sharply from that of the Brahmanical model and remind us to avoid essentializing children (not to mention their fathers).

One final example of the variations on the child is drawn from the experiences of Muslims in India. As in the Garo case, the concept of illegitimacy is rare in Islamic law. It emerges only on occasions when a child is born of parents who cannot be married to each other—the father is

---

[93] Kancha Ilaiah, *Why I Am Not a Hindu*, cited in Vasanthi Raman, "The Diverse Life-Worlds of Indian Childhood," 95.

[94] A recent study indicated the low status of girls in one community of Varanasi by showing that the birth of a girl child is celebrated by merely 2% of all families the research surveyed. S. Ananthalakshmy and M. Bajaj, "Childhood in Weavers Community in Varanasi," in *Socialization of the Indian Child*, ed. D. Sinha (New Delhi: Concept, 1981), cited in Raman, "The Diverse Life-Worlds of Indian Childhood," 96.

[95] Raman, "The Diverse Life-Worlds of Indian Childhood," 98.

non-Muslim or the couple have prohibited degrees of relationship with each other. If paternity is established by the doctrine of *ikrah* or acknowledgement, there is a "presumption in law that the mother and father are married to each other." However, in the South Asian context, Goonesekere argues, the concept of the illegitimacy of a non-marital child was a colonial construct except in Islam.[96] The Hanafi School of Islamic law that dominates the subcontinent affirms that a child born out of a marital relationship has some legal relationship with the mother.[97] Furthermore, the Hanafi law asserts that "a child is considered totally incapable till the age of seven." After turning seven "he can participate in legal acts with the interdiction of the guardian or *wali* to ensure the interests of the minor child." Interdiction, however, is only possible up to a certain age. In Islamic law a child has the "right of inheritance, to custody, to shelter, religious education and a fixed share of inheritance (with the daughters getting half the share of that of the sons) and it was the duty of the parents to ensure that the child's needs were satisfied."[98]

There exist multiple worlds of experiencing, codifying, and conceptualizing childhood in the South Asian context, and explicating all these worlds is beyond the scope of this project. The plurality of experiences however compels us to situate children and childhood—and thus fathers and fatherhood—in the larger context of community, caste-class-tribe, kin-group, family, and religion.[99] In more recent years the United Nations' 1989-Convention on the Rights of the Child that claimed to impose a universal model of childhood across the globe and especially for the children of the South provoked sharp reactions among scholars studying childhood in India.[100] Sarada Balagopalan and Olga Nieuwenhuys, among others, raised critical questions and demonstrated the collusion of the postcolonial state and the global Nongovernmental Organizations in constructing Indian childhood as a series of "fundable

---

[96] S. Goonesekere, *Children, Law and Justice: A South Asian Perspective* (New Delhi: Thousand Oaks; London: Sage Publications, 1997).
[97] Raman, "The Diverse Life-Worlds of Indian Childhood," 98.
[98] Raman, "The Diverse Life-Worlds of Indian Childhood," 102.
[99] Childhood's long genealogy in Indian history and culture makes it redundant to engage in the debate generated by Ariès's thesis that childhood was "an invention" of the seventeenth century and its rebuttal by subsequent scholars. Ariès, *Centuries of Childhood*; Lloyd DeMause, ed., *The History of Childhood* (Baltimore: Johns Hopkins Press, 1974).
[100] Vasanthi Raman, "Politics of Childhood: Perspectives from the South," *Economic and Political Weekly* 35, no. 46 (November 11–17, 2000): 4055–4064.

issues."[101] Questioning the silences and the universalist model of progress propagated by the West, Balagopalan repeatedly alerted us about the criticality of the continued effects of the colonial past on the present lives of children in the South.[102] The rising scholarship on children in the past two decades has successfully dislodged the binaries between the fetishized Indian child waiting for rescue and the reification of an idealized child rooted in its frozen past.[103] In contrast, the new works projected the social imagery of the child who was not a victim but an active participant in the unfolding of the Indian modern.[104]

My work dwells on the imagination and construction of modern childhood by the educated literati fathers of colonial Bengal and beyond. It shows that these literati fathers were imagining childhood as a battleground and children as active agents of change. Children's agency here was not necessarily confined to decision-making and creative interpretation of existing practices. The dynamism of the father-children relationship and the changing norms that my work unfolds restore children in their multiple, daily interactions without necessarily foregrounding their autonomous, decision-making selves.[105] The moral ideological vision of the fatherly leaders I discuss extended beyond the immediate contours of their family and hence purported to be all-encompassing, blurring obvious caste-class, religious, and in some instances, gender divides. An against-the-grain reading of that discourse reveals that the target audience was primarily the members of the upwardly mobile, upper-caste *bhadralok* community. But the ideological narratives did not *overtly* (emphasis mine) exclude any particular segment of the population, such as the lower castes, lower classes, or Muslims. In fact, as studies of Dalit narratives from Bengal make clear, while life-experiences of growing up as a Dalit child were very different from that of a "normal" child of upper-caste

---

[101] Nieuwenhuys, "Is There an Indian Childhood?"
[102] Sarada Balagopalan, "Childhood, Culture, History: Redeploying 'Multiple Childhood,'" in *Reimagining Childhood Studies*, eds. Spyros Spyrou, Rachel Rosen, and Daniel Thomas Cook (London: Bloomsbury, 2019), 23–40.
[103] See for example, Oishik Sarkar and Debolina Dutta, "Beyond Compassion: Children of Sex Workers in Kolkata's Sonagachi," *Childhood* 18, no. 3 (2011): 333–349.
[104] See footnotes 64, 65, 66 for the current scholarship on children.
[105] On an astute reading of "agency" and "responsibility" of children see Balagopalan, "Childhood, Culture, History."

and class, the authors did not see an "apparent conflict" between ideals of Dalit religious and literary leaders and the Hinduism as it was practised in the households and the villages of Bengal. Neither did Dalit ideology and customs conflict with the reformism of the urban Brahmos and the Baptist Christian missionaries. Dalit leaders such as Harichand Thakur, the founder of the Matua sect and a contemporary of Rammohun Roy, preached monotheism and spread the messages of Vedanta.[106] Dalit children and fathers, although circumscribed by their caste positions, valued the ethos of a modern era as advocated by the dominant reformers.

Ravaged by the challenges of modernity and a brutal critique of degeneracy by the colonial state, educated parents, writers, and leaders imagined children as an embodiment of a universal individuality who were fit to be modern citizens of a burgeoning nation. The new progeny would be vitalized through new modes of pedagogy that enshrined new moral values of self-respect and freedom, especially from the bondage of colonial rule. The discourse on childhood not only talked about the imperilled child carrying the traits of the pre-modern past but it also delineated a path of recovery and regeneration. Through the child the native leaders imagined the impact of the colonial rule upon themselves; through the child, they also endeavoured to redeem and liberate themselves. The pedagogical models they envisioned were not restricted only for their own biological children but for the imaginary community of the freedom fighters and the future generation. In a restricted way, "the child and the adult came to stand for each other."[107] More than the child, this book underscores the role of male adults as parents, as hegemons, whose attitudes towards their own and an imaginary body of children were instructive in comprehending children and ideas of childhood.[108]

---

[106] Pramatha Ranjan Thakur, *Atmacharit ba purbasmriti [Autobiography or Old Memories]*, (Thakurnagar: Matua Mahasangha, 1994), 119, cited in Sekhar Bandyopadhyay, "Texts of Liminality: Reading Identity in Dalit Autobiographies from Bengal," in *Memory, Identity and the Colonial Encounter in India: Essays in Honour of Peter Robb*, eds. Upal Chakrabarti, Sanjukta Ghosh, and Ezra Rashkow (London and New York: Routledge, 2018), 91–109; 97.

[107] Satadru Sen, *Colonial Childhoods: The Juvenile Periphery of India, 1850–1945* (Cambridge: Cambridge University Press, 2012; first published, London: Anthem, 2005), 7.

[108] For the emphasis on adult attitudes in understanding children see Carolyn Steedman, *Strange Dislocations: Childhood and the Idea of Human Interiority* (Cambridge, MA: Harvard University Press, 1998).

The Historiographical Terrain

In the wake of Thomas Laqueur's (1990) lament that "we lack a history of fatherhood" and John Tosh's (1999) assertion that of all the qualifications for masculine status, fatherhood was the one least talked about in Victorian England, historians of Western Europe and North America redressed the balance by tracking traces of fathers and fatherhood in art, literature, and public debates in the Western world and particularly in nineteenth-century England.[109] Scholars recognized the connections among manhood, masculinity, and paternity, tracing their origins to Christianity and even earlier periods.[110] The pioneering series of *A History of Private Lives* (5 volumes) meticulously delineated the ascendancy of the "private" from the ancient pagan culture to the present and the implication of the home, family, and domestic life in the evolution of the Western "modern." The nineteenth century, following the French Revolution, was the golden age of private life when the individual, fortified by reason, political conviction, and existential values emerged with supreme confidence. Michelle Perrot argued that as "figurehead of the family as well as of the civil society," the father dominated the history of private life in nineteenth-century Europe and his authority was established in all possible ways by law, philosophy, and politics.[111]

Historians of South Asia, on the contrary, despite their serious intervention in the history of masculinity and the multifaceted politics of patriarchal domination, have not explored the question of fathers and

---

[109] Thomas W. Laqueur, "The Facts of Fatherhood," in *Conflicts in Feminism*, eds. Marianne Hirsch and Evelyn Fox Keller (New York: Routledge 1990), 205–221; John Tosh, "Father and Child," in *A Man's Place* (New Haven/London: Yale University Press, 1999), 79; Trev Lynn Broughton and Helen Rogers, *Gender and Fatherhood in the Nineteenth Century* (London: Palgrave Macmillan, 2007).

[110] Valeria Finucci, *The Manly Masquerade: Masculinity, Paternity and Castration in the Italian Renaissance* (Durham, NC: Duke University Press, 2003).; Margaret L. King, *The Death of the Child Valerio Marcello* (Chicago: University of Chicago Press, 1994.

Peter Stearns, *Be a Man: Males in Modern Society* (Holmes & Meier, 1990); John Tosh, *Manliness and Masculinities in Nineteenth-Century Britain* (New York: Pearson, 2005); *A Man's Place: Masculinity and the Middle-Class Home in Victorian England* (New Haven, CT: Yale University Press, 2007). For a comprehensive history of the material and ontological connection between private-public lives, see Michael McKeon, *The Secret History of Domesticity: The Public, Private, and the Division of Knowledge* (Baltimore: Johns Hopkins Press, 2005).

[111] Michelle Perrot, ed., *A History of Private Life: From the Fires of Revolution to the Great War*, trans. Arthur Goldhammer (Cambridge, MA: The Belknap Press of the Harvard University Press, 1990), 167.

fatherhood. Mrinalini Sinha argued that Indian colonial history has "enormous potential for developing adequately contextualized histories of masculinity in which masculinity itself is understood as constituted by, as well as constitutive of, a wide set of social relations." Masculinity and femininity, that is to say, cannot be confined solely within its supposedly "proper" domain of male–female relations.[112] Colonial masculinity was constitutive of a symbiotic relationship between the "manly" Englishman and "effeminate" Bengalis/Indians,[113] a perception fostered by the official British community and internalized by the colonized Indian literati.[114] A corrective to Sinha came immediately from Rosalind O'Hanlon, who, based on her study of precolonial north Indian martial cultures among Muslim nawabs, alerted us that the British were not the first to use masculinity in the way Sinha and later scholars suggested, that is, "in establishing hierarchies and affirming identities." O'Hanlon urged that to understand men as "gendered beings" we must explore what "psychic and social investments sustain their sense of selves as men, at what networks and commonalities bring men together on the basis of shared gender identity, and what hierarchies and exclusions set them apart."[115] Subsequently, as the scholarship came into its own, studies on masculinity in India were undertaken in the realm of public, national, imperial, precolonial and colonial contexts.[116] The literature on this topic is large and growing and has dismantled the notion of gender-binaries but those themes are beyond the purview of the current work.[117]. Let us return to a discussion of those that are relevant to this study.

---

[112] Mrinalini Sinha, "Giving Masculinity a History," *Gender and History* 11, no. 3 (1999): 445–460.
[113] Sinha, *Colonial Masculinity*.
[114] John Rosselli, "The Self Image of Effeteness: Physical Education and Nationalism in Nineteenth-Century Bengal," *Past and Present* 86 (1980): 121–148.
[115] Rosalind O'Hanlon, "Issues of Masculinity in North Indian History: The Bangash Nawabs of Farrukhabad," *Indian Journal of Gender Studies* 4, no. 1 (1997): 1.
[116] For studies of masculinity in ancient India see John Powers, *A Bull of a Man: Images of Masculinity, Sex, and the Body in Indian Buddhism* (Cambridge, MA: Harvard University Press, 2009) and Jarrod L. Whitaker, *Strong Arms and Drinking Strength: Masculinity, Violence, and the Body in Ancient India* (New York: Oxford University Press, 2011).
[117] A good summary and critique of the literature on masculinity from a sociological perspective is found in Radhika Chopra, "Muted Masculinities: Introduction to the Special Issue on Contemporary Indian Ethnographies," *Men and Masculinities* 9, no. 2 (2006): 127–130; Sanjay Srivastava, ed., *Sexual Sites, Seminal Attitudes: Sexualities, Masculinities and Culture in South Asia* (New Delhi: Sage Publications, 2004); Radhika Chopra, Caroline Osella, and Filippo Osella, eds., *South Asian Masculinities: Context of Change, Sites of Continuity* (New Delhi: Women Unlimited, 2004).

British and Bengali men, the main target of the attack, forged their manliness in relation to one another, not just through opposition but through shared values as well.[118] Educated Indians resisted stereotypes by incorporating hegemonic forms of masculinity, such as body-building and muscular strength.[119] Several works focus on bodily anxieties of the Indians, especially the educated Bengali population who offered a counter-narrative through their investments in body-building, martial arts, and various sports, from wrestling and football to adoption of indigenous folk dances that encompassed an all-round development of the "male" body and mind.[120] In the wake of fundamentalist Hindu nationalism, the notion of Hindu manhood became a subject of serious exploration illuminating how the indigenous masculinity of "warrior monk" and "Hindu soldier" was derived from and in relation to the hegemonic masculinity of the British imperialists who claimed a superior moral status and their legitimacy to rule.[121] Invoking past and present imaginings, engaging with Anglo-Hindu laws the connection among masculinity, asceticism, and Hinduism has been highlighted as well.[122] Elite and subaltern (*dalit*) masculinities (and femininities) are both being explored along with their hegemonic manifestations among the upper echelons of society.[123] Furthermore, the role of nineteenth-century colonial

---

[118] For a recent study of nationalist Bengali men as "revolutionary terrorists," see Durba Ghosh, *Gentlemanly Terrorists: Political Violence and the Colonial State in India, 1919–1947* (Cambridge: Cambridge University Press, 2017).

[119] Joseph Alter, "Celibacy, Sexuality, and the Transformation of Gender into Nationalism in North India," *Journal of Asian Studies* 53 (1994): 45–63; *Moral Materialism: Sex and Masculinity in Modern India* (Delhi: Penguin Books, 2011); Indira Chowdhury, *The Fragile Hero and Virile History* (New Delhi: Oxford University Press, 2001).

[120] Sayantani Adhikary, "The Bratachari Movement and the Invention of a 'Folk-Tradition,'" *South Asia: A Journal of South Asian Studies* 38, no. 4 (2015): 656–670; Amitava Chatterjee, "An Introduction" to "Body, Men, and Sports: Construction of Masculinity in Bengal," *Cultural Cartographies of Media: Exploring Media Spaces and Digital Cultures* (DigiMagazine) http://mltspaces.blogspot.com/2014/12/evolution-of-colonial-bengali-identity.html (accessed on September 5, 2016).

[121] Subho Basu and Sikata Banerjee, "The Quest for Manhood: Masculine Hinduism and Nation in Bengal," *Comparative Studies of South Asia, Africa and Middle East* 26, no. 3 (2006): 476–490; Sikata Banerjee, *Make Me a Man: Masculinity, Hinduism, and Nationalism in India* (Albany: State University of New York Press, 2005).

[122] William Pinch, *Warrior Ascetics and Indian Empire* (Cambridge: Cambridge University Press, 2006); Chandrima Chakraborty, *Masculinity, Asceticism, Hinduism: Past and Present Imaginings of India* (New Delhi: Permanent Black, 2011); Kasturi, "'Asceticising' Monastic Families," 1039–1083.

[123] Charu Gupta, "Feminine, Criminal, or Manly? Imaging Dalit Masculinity in Colonial North India," *Indian Economic Social History Review* 47, no. 3 (July/September 2010): 309–342; "Anxious Hindu Masculinities in Colonial North India: Shuddhi and Sangathan Movements," *CrossCurrents* 61, no. 4 (November 2011); Radhika Chopra, "Invisible Men: Masculinity,

educational reforms promoting masculinity around religious-communal identities has also been tracked.[124] While all of this scholarship informs the pages to follow, I seek to address the significant lacunae in the literature on South Asian masculinities: that fathers are an important historical category and that fatherhood as a conceptual tool is central to the construction of masculinity.

By leaving out the question of fatherhood, the framing principles of masculinity under current South Asian scholarship has actually ignored one of the most important constituents of masculinity. If "[M]asculinity acquires its meanings only in specific practices," as Sinha has claimed, I propose to look into the dynamics of father–child relationship, both at home and beyond the home, that acted as an autonomous site for parallel assertions of authority and manhood of the colonial subject.[125] By situating fathers at home and attending to their concerns that transcended private–public dichotomy, I extend Antoinette Burton's argument that the home acts as much an archive for reclaiming the history of men as it does for women.[126] It was not just women who dwelt in the archive of the home; home was a fecund ground for men as they imagine themselves as fathers and sons through memories, recollections, and projections into the future.

The only historical studies on fatherhood and to a lesser extent with children comes from psychoanalysts and scholars of Indic literature.[127] The latter demonstrate the conflict between Indian God Shiva and

Sexuality and Male Domestic Labour," *Men and Masculinities* 9, no. 2 (2006): 152–167; "From Violence to Supportive Practice: Family, Gender and Masculinities," *Economic and Political Weekly* 38, no. 17 (April 26–May 2, 2003): 1650–1657. Also, Radhika Chopra, ed., *Reframing Masculinities: Narrating the Supportive Practices of Men* (Hyderabad: Orient Longman, 2006); Radhika Chopra, Caroline Osella, and Filippo Osella, eds., *South Asian Masculinities: Context of Change, Sites of Continuity* (New Delhi: Women Unlimited, 2004).

[124] Parna Sengupta, *Pedagogy for Religion: Missionary Education and the Fashioning of Hindus and Muslims in Bengal* (Berkeley: University of California Press, 2011).

[125] For a more nuanced understanding of masculinity see Peter Jackson, "The Cultural Politics of Masculinity: Towards a Social Geography," in *Transactions of the Institute of British Geographers*, New Series, 16, no. 2 (1991), 199–213.

[126] Antoinette Burton, *Dwelling in the Archives: Women Writing House, Home, and History in Late Colonial India* (New York: Oxford University Press, 2003).

[127] Kakar, *Inner World*; Ashis Nandy, *Intimate Enemy: Loss and Recovery of the Self Under Colonialism* (New Delhi: Oxford University Press, 1983). Psychologists also pay attention to fathers and fathering. See J. Roopnarine and P. Suppal, "Kakar's Psychoanalytic Interpretation of Childhood: The Need to Emphasize the Father and Multiple Caregivers in the Socialization Equation," in *Childhood, Family and Socio-cultural Change in India: Reinterpreting the Inner World*, ed. D. Sharma (New Delhi: Oxford University Press, 2003), 115–137.

the elephant-headed Ganesha (Shiva's son) as a parallel to the myth of Oedipus that Freud appropriated for analysing human psychological dynamics.[128] The triangular relationship among father (Shiva), mother (Parvati), and son (Ganesha), with the son's aggressive contest with the father over access to or possession of the mother, are comparable in both the stories of Oedipus and Ganesha. However, contrary to Oedipus, in the Indian context, the father (here Shiva) is not killed by the son (Ganesha), but the father (Shiva) himself decapitates the son (Ganesha) and then revives him by giving him a new (elephant) head that symbolized castration. To quote A.K. Ramanujan, in India "[I]nstead of son's desiring mothers and overcoming fathers (e.g. Oedipus). we have fathers suppressing sons ... and mothers desiring sons."[129] Furthermore, instead of the fundamentally tragic ending of the Oedipus myth that leads to the exile from the mother, the story of Ganesha concludes "with his restoration and a new beginning in which relations between parents and child are reconciled." As Courtright pointed out, "[I]conographically he (Ganesa) is most often represented with his father, or father and mother together, but seldom with his mother alone."[130] While these psychoanalytical studies have less historical import for our purposes here, I want to draw attention to the aspects of affection, disciplining, control, anger, fear, and reconciliation that were all exhibited in the paternal behaviour of Shiva and were translated into practices of mortal fathers in colonial India.

The current scholarship's amnesia with fatherhood can possibly be explained by the ubiquitous presence and naturalization of paternal authority in gods, *gurus* (spiritual mentors), elders, family patrons, kinship authorities, and biological and genealogical fathers. The image of biological fathers as distant and removed from the daily lives of children[131] could further attest to the reluctance to include the father as a cornerstone of patriarchy. In contrast to the apathy towards the father, historical literature has given attention to mothers and wives as the cornerstone of an ideal Indian family.[132] In the nineteenth-century woman question, the

---

[128] Paul B. Courtright, "Fathers and Sons," in *Vishnu on Freud's Desk: A Reader in Psychoanalysis and Hinduism*, eds. T.G. Vaidyanathan and Jeffrey J. Kripal (New Delhi: Oxford University Press, 1999), 137–146.

[129] Quoted in Courtright, "Fathers and Sons," 138–139.

[130] Courtright, "Fathers and Sons," 139.

[131] Sudhir Kakar, *Identity and Adulthood* (New Delhi: Oxford University Press, 1981).

[132] On role of "new women" and re-constitution of the household see Swapna M. Banerjee, "Re-constituting the Household: Defining Middle-class Domesticity in Colonial Bengal—the

influence of Victorian ideology loomed large in the minds of reformers and ideologues.[133] The effects of Victorian ideologies on men who envisioned the new ideals of their women and children, however, received scant attention. The literature overlooks the conjoined hierarchical nature of the family relationship—the father and a husband mediated by the presence of a child, in most cases. My work recuperates the subjecthood and positionality of educated Indian fathers—their receptivity to given ideals from the West, their creative assimilation of certain principles and their translation into everyday practices. I examine the roles of fathers not merely as providers and nurturers but also as situated in a diachronic relationship of power that enabled them to assert their subject positions. More importantly, I emphasize the significance of vernacular education as "the theater of greater intellectual and artistic originality."[134]

Maintaining a distinction between manliness (*purushotvo*) and patriarchy (*pitritantra*), my study delineates the ways ideas and practices of fatherhood (*pitritvo*) informed and constituted Indian patriarchy (*purushtantra*). As evident from the scriptures (discussed earlier), pedagogic texts and sermons (chapters 2, 3, 5), the manliness of Hindu men demanded proper fulfilment of filial obligations that included obedience to parents and duties towards spouse, children, and extended family members.[135] To this the nineteenth-century reformers and ideologues added strength of character and moral training through a new pedagogical emphasis. The way masculinity was defined and valorized for Indian men can be best exemplified by Rabindranath Tagore's reverential reference to Iswarchandra Vidyasagar as the *purush singha* (lion man).[136] Tagore noted, "The chief glories of [Vidyasagar's] character was neither his compassion nor his learning, but his invincible manliness and imperishable

---

Mistress and the Servant," in *Men, Women, Domestics: Articulating Middle-Class Identity in Colonial Bengal* (New Delhi: Oxford University Press, 2004). See Chapter 3 for a discussion on motherhood.

[133] For the influence of colonies on British families and interpenetration of cultures, see Elizabeth Buettner, *Empire Families: Britons and Late Imperial India* (Oxford: Oxford University Press, 2004).

[134] Sudipta Kaviraj, *The Invention of Private Life: Literature and Ideas* (New York: Columbia University Press, 2015), 17.

[135] See Dipesh Chakrabarty, "Family, Fraternity, and Salaried Labor," in *Provincializing Europe: Postcolonial Though and Historical Difference* (Princeton, NJ: Princeton University Press, 2000), 214–236.

[136] Tagore and Vidyasagar, two luminaries from colonial Bengal, are subjects of discussion in Chapters 5 and 2.

humanity."[137] Masculinity of Indian men was neither determined by "possessive individualism" nor was it solely a question of military service, public performance, debates, and contestations that were performed in the arena of overt politics of the colonial state. Masculinity manifested in practices of everyday life and it worked through inhabiting certain roles and positions contingent on relational and kinship hierarchy—caring for and commanding subaltern members and showing respect to superiors. I argue that in late colonial India educated Indian men's quest for moral guardianship was an expression of their masculinity that poured through their emotions of affection and love; disciplining and punishment; and through a novel vision of education of their desire. At the same time, the lived practices of the fathers under discussion testified to the making and strengthening of reigning patriarchy.

The history of fatherhood takes us to the heart of a debate that has rocked the field of South Asian women's and gender history in the past decades. Referring to the lull that came over issues concerning women in the late nineteenth century, Partha Chatterjee provocatively argued that the nationalists and ideologues had resolved the "women's question" at the turn of the century by relegating it to the private sphere, the sphere of the home, the inner spiritual domain. He argued that the male reformers subjected their "new women" to second patriarchy by transposing and relocating their issues to the domestic domain. For Chatterjee, "the story of nationalist emancipation" is one that of "betrayal," as nationalism "conferred freedom only by imposing at the same time a whole set of new controls"—by defining "a cultural identity for the nation only by excluding many from its fold."[138] Chatterjee's astute formulation of the second patriarchy however does not allude to the process of how this patriarchy was constituted through different relationships. Neither did he problematize the complex domain of the "domestic" and the "private sphere." Feminist scholars taking exception to such a formulation challenged Chatterjee by demonstrating not only the organic nature of the household and its deep connection to state formation and the political economy but has also shown women's own agency in

---

[137] Rabindranath Tagore, "Vidyasagarcharit," *Rabindrarachanabali*, vol. 2 (Kolkata: Visvabharati, 1997), 782. The excerpt is from a lecture delivered in 1895.
[138] Partha Chatterjee, "The Nation and Its Women," *The Nation and Its Fragments* (Princeton, NJ: Princeton University Press, 1993), 154.

articulating their grievances and demands before the colonial state.[139] In her sharp retort to Chatterjee, Tanika Sarkar offered a more nuanced conception of the colonial patriarchy and the role of the Hindu males in a familial set up. Highlighting the complex reality of a subjugated political-economy under a restrictive colonial regime, Sarkar identified the crises that prompted Indian reformers and ideologues to engage with the "women's question." Limited opportunities of employment, criticisms from the missionaries and the Utilitarians about the degraded status of Indian women, and the blatant racism of the colonial administration threatened the morale of the educated Indian males, particularly the Bengalis. In the last quarter of the century, those who were involved in the administration and were claiming rights for participation in governance were further dismissed by the colonial officials as "effeminate" and "feeble" and hence not fit for self-rule.[140] Educated Indian males had succumbed to this criticism and had internalized it to an extent; but, they retaliated in different ways. The Hindu middle-class householder, the *karta* (husband and father), displayed an auto-critique and exhibited an anxiety concerning the social position of his women and about his own moral standing. The Indian intelligentsia engaged in a "convoluted critical exercise" questioning both Indian traditions and customs as well as its colonial connections. "They expressed more doubts about its own convictions than resolutions of issues related to its women."[141] The role of the *karta* as the Hindu husband and householder has been tracked in recent researches;[142] what still demands investigation is the plural and unstable category of the *karta* as the father who wrote and enforced rules within and outside families and whose identity was hinged on construction of different aspects of masculinity. Thus, in further complicating the current debate, my work resurrects the forgotten category of the father as a lynchpin of a dominant indigenous culture.

One of my major contentions is that the intelligentsia, to articulate their autonomous epistemic space as fathers in a "motherland" that they were trying to recuperate from foreign domination and control, appropriated

---

[139] Indrani Chatterjee, *Unfamiliar Relations; Forgotten Friends*; Padma Anagol, *The Emergence of Feminism in India, 1850–1920*. (London: Ashgate Publishing, 2015).
[140] Sinha, *Colonial Masculinity*.
[141] Sarkar, *Hindu Wife, Hindu Nation*.
[142] Sarkar, *Hindu Wife, Hindu Nation*; Kasturi, "'Asceticising' Monastic Families."

children as social imaginaries.[143] "Social imaginaries" is a concept developed by Charles Taylor extending Benedict Anderson's ideas of a nation as an "imagined community."[144] Social imaginaries represent a broad understanding of the ways a given people imagine their collective social life. The imaginaries include values, institutions, laws, and symbols common to a social group through which the latter imagine itself as part of a whole. The process of imagining children by the male intelligentsia in the period involved simultaneous imagining of their subject position as "fathers," articulating new and deconstructing older subjectivities. The rather gendered and exclusionary nature of this discourse through which both fathers and children were imagined reveals the culturally imposed identity of fathers and children and the process of formulation of an alternate road to progress, modernity, and a new nation. By focusing on the real and imagined communities of fathers and children, the study investigates ways by which Indian masculinities were constituted through various patriarchal practices such as the new literature that upheld different morals for the future generation.

The pedagogical exercises of the new generation of fathers included the writing of primers, school textbooks, and a vast array of literary and

---

[143] For discussions on notions of motherland as envisioned by the Indian intelligentsia see Sugata Bose, "Nation as Mother: Representations and Contestations of 'India' in Bengali Literature and Culture," in *Nationalism, Democracy and Development*, eds. Sugata Bose and Ayesha Jalal (New Delhi: Oxford University Press, 1997), 50–74. Also see Sugata Bose, *The Nation as Mother and Other Visions of Nationhood* (New Delhi: Penguin Random House Publishing, 2017); Sumathi Ramaswamy, *The Goddess as the Nation: Mapping Mother India* (Durham, NC: Duke University Press, 2010); Mrinalini Sinha, *Specters of Mother India: The Global Restructuring of an Empire* (Durham, NC: Duke University Press, 2006).

[144] Charles Taylor, *Modern Social Imaginaries* (Durham, NC: Duke University Press, 2007). Taylor conceptualized social imaginary in seeking to specifically understand multiple modernities in the West. The contexts and cultural forms such as the economy, the public sphere, and self-governance that characterized his social imaginaries were rather different from what existed in the non-Western colonies. Taylor's notion of social imaginaries rested on the separation of the state from political society. According to Taylor, for a modern democratic state in the West to be the "bulwark of freedom and the locus of expression of its citizens," the state itself must be imagined by its citizens for its legitimacy (Taylor, *Modern Social Imaginaries*, 192). But the question of citizenship was contested in India under British regime. The British colonial state in India was willing to confer subjecthood on Indians but it did not recognize them as citizens, as Partha Chatterjee and others pointed out. Chatterjee argued that the citizens of the colonized Indian nation were thus configured in the familial domain of its communities rooted in their precolonial and pre-capitalist past. For Chatterjee's take on Taylor and on notions of civil and political society, see Partha Chatterjee, "Communities and the Nation," in *Nation and Its Fragments*, 220–240. My work tends to destabilize the division Chatterjee proposes between the home and the world. Taylor's concept is useful for us as it involves explaining the way imagination figured in the construction of major institutions, representations, and practices. Taylor, *Modern Social Imaginaries*, 23.

scientific periodicals, and they attained culmination in the hands of prominent and not-so-prominent leaders. These men took upon themselves the responsibility of educating the future generation, but their mission remained restricted and unfulfilled—not only were their respective curricula ineffective but more importantly, their endeavours failed to reach the majority of the population. The literate community who were concerned with the new generation had a hegemonic aspiration: their educational projects competed with colonial ones. Most of the men who sought to reform the next generation formed their pedagogical goals and curricula in—and often against—two specific systems of patriarchal ideology. The first consisted of traditional Indian views of fatherhood, including the spiritual/symbolic father-gurus. The second had perhaps an even more powerful impact: the colonial educational system, which inculcated a specific notion of masculinity and fatherhood as it sought to form colonial subjects. One may note in this instance that the period that Indrani Chatterjee described as "when 'sexuality' floated free" already had subsided among the hegemonic middle class of colonial India by the mid-nineteenth century, and they were gripped by notions of gender-binaries and heteronormativity.[145] Many of the fathers delineated in the following chapters actively sought to frame not colonial subjects, but citizens of a new nation who embodied new forms of masculinity and femininity. A few words, by way of background, about the basic contours and expectations of the colonial educational system will be in order here.

Colonial Education

The first official intervention of the colonial government in Indian education came with the Charter Act of 1813. Fuelled by the arguments of parliamentarians and evangelical missionaries like Charles Grant (1746–1823) and William Wilberforce (1759–1833) in England and Governor-Generals like Minto (1806–1813) in India, the Company for the first time put on its agenda the aim of educating Indian people.[146] Towards that

---

[145] Indrani Chatterjee, "When 'Sexuality' Floated Free of Histories in South Asia," *Journal of Asian Studies* 71, no. 4 (November 2012): 945–962.
[146] For significance of the Charter Act of 1813 in spread of colonial education see Gauri Viswanathan, *Masks of Conquest: Literary Study and British Rule in India*, 25th year ed.

goal, it allocated one hundred thousand rupees and gave the missionaries a free hand to spread education and Christianity among native people. The Act advocated the revival and promotion of the knowledge of science and literature and was aimed at the encouragement of the learned natives in India.[147] Thus the earliest schools under Company administration were set up by the Christian missionaries in the presidencies of Bengal and Bombay, and in the Punjab. The missionaries had to rely on the knowledge of the native experts for translation and writing of textbooks. The Act thus provided the native intellectuals in Bengal and elsewhere an opportunity, albeit limited, to engage with the educational movement through literary endeavours.[148] Within a few decades the three reports (1835–1838) by William Adam, a Unitarian missionary and ardent abolitionist, who was encouraged by the pioneering Indian social reformer Rammohun Roy to inquire into the status of education, indicated that the number of students under domestic instruction was almost nine times higher than those attending public schools.[149] The average age of admission to a public elementary school was eight years and that of leaving was fourteen years.[150]

The education system developed by missionaries, colonial administrators, and indigenous leaders was formed amid a struggle between the

(New York: Columbia University Press, 2014). Also see J.P. Naik and Syed Nurullah, *A Student's History of Education in India (1800–1973)*, 6th rev. ed. (Delhi: Macmillan, 1974 [1945]).

[147] Some of the regular textbooks on modern South Asia provide a lucid history of colonial education, its embeddedness in multiple cross-currents of colonial experiments, and its impact on different communities and groups. See Sekhar Bandyopadhyay, *From Plassey to Partition: A History of Modern India* (Hyderabad: Orient BlackSwan, 2004); Ishita Banerjee-Dube, *A History of Modern India* (New York: Cambridge University Press, 2014); Sugata Bose and Ayesha Jalal, *Modern South Asia: History, Culture, Political Economy*, 3rd ed. (London/New York: Routledge, 2011); Thomas Metcalf and Barbara Metcalf, *A Concise History of Modern India*, 3rd ed. (New York: Cambridge University Press, 2012).

[148] Swapna Banerjee, "Children's Literature in Nineteenth Century India: Some Reflections and Thoughts," in *GRAAT* (Groupe de Recherches Anglo-Américaines de Tours, 2007), 337–351.

[149] William Adam, *Adam's Reports on Vernacular Education in Bengal and Behar with a Brief View of Its Past and Present Condition, Submitted to Government in 1835, 1836, and 1838; With a Brief View of Its Past and Present Condition* (Calcutta: Home Secretariat Press, 1868). The contemporary cities of Kolkata and Mumbai were known in the colonial period as Calcutta and Bombay. Throughout this book, I have retained the spelling of the sources for both cities and the names of individuals. Thus, colonial-era British publications use Calcutta, Bombay, Behar, and so forth, while for Bengali-language publications, I transliterate the spelling of the original, providing in brackets the alternative spelling in cases—like Thakur [Tagore]—were the Anglicized spelling is likely to be more familiar.

[150] Syed Nurullah and J.P. Naik, *A History of Education in India* (Bombay: Macmillan & Co. Ltd., 1951), 23.

effort "by non-Indians to impose a cheap imitation of the British educational system on India and the desire of the people of the country to create a new system to meet their own peculiar needs and problems."[151] The British claim that colonial rule was a "pedagogical enterprise for the improvement of India" was met with a two-pronged nationalist response—it acknowledged the benefits of English education that raised them from "the torpor of ages" and it simultaneously pointed out its limited scope and inadequacy for reaching out to the larger population.[152] The Western-educated middle class all over India had long engaged in pedagogical experiments from the early years of the nineteenth century. Working closely with the colonial state and the missionary educators, Bengali male reformers, such as Iswarchandra Vidyasagar (1820–1891), Akshay Kumar Dutta (1820–1886), and Bhudev Mukhopadhyay (1827–1894), among others, had written primers and manuals and had deliberated on the nature of education to be imparted to native students.

Matters came to a head with the British politician and writer Thomas Babington Macaulay's famous *Minute of Education* in 1835 that replaced Persian with English as the official language of instruction in India. With a strong Utilitarian justification and denouncing Indian languages and literature, Macaulay claimed that "of all foreign tongues, the English tongue is that which would be the most useful to our native subjects."[153] Backed by a sizeable section of the native population who realized the importance of promoting Western-style learning, Macaulay's *Minute* was followed by two other official proclamations, Wood's Despatch (1854) and the Hunter Commission (1882), which laid the blueprint for the colonial education system.

Intending to spread Western knowledge and science at all levels, Wood's Despatch introduced schemes of grants-in-aid to schools and training of all teachers for schools receiving government aids. This allowed the colonial government the right to inspect and assert greater control over education. After the Rebellion of 1857–1858 and the transfer of power from the Company Raj to the British Crown (1858), the colonial government became increasingly wary of missionary education verging

---

[151] Nurullah and Naik, *History of Education*, xiv.
[152] Sanjay Seth, "Vernacular Modernity: The Nationalist Imagination," in *Subject Lessons: The Western Education of Colonial India* (Durham/London: Duke University Press, 2007), 159.
[153] Thomas Babington Macaulay, *Minute of Education*, 1835.

on conversion. It launched the first Education Commission under Sir William Hunter in 1882 and its Report announced that the government would not delegate Western-style education to the missionaries; rather, it would create its own department of education with state subsidies.[154] My focus in this volume is on fathers whose activism, writing, and parenting took place in a context of—and often pointedly directed against—such state interventions in education and family life.

Education from the early nineteenth century thus became a pathway for educated native men to work hand-in-hand (or hand-against-hand, in some cases) with the missionaries and the colonial government. This also gave them the opportunity to create their epistemic space as moral guardians of the younger generation. By 1880–1890, the native literati not only launched vernacular literature for children (as described in chapter 2) but also took the active initiative in education programmes. In 1881–1882, Indians conducted the majority of the secondary and primary schools in British India (except Burma): 1,341 secondary schools and 54,662 primary schools were administered by Indian managers as opposed to 757 secondary and 1,842 primary schools run by non-Indians.[155] In Bengal, for example, Dwarkanath Tagore, along with other votaries of modern education, made significant donations for the promotion of schools and institutions, including the establishment of the Calcutta Medical College.[156] Towards the last quarter of the nineteenth century, the schools were endowed with state power and education became the site of "colonial governmentality."[157] The schools were not only designing curricula and introducing new subjects, they were bent on creating subjectivities and regulating native populations through a range of disciplinary practices. The school's main subjects of reform were males, with age unspecified, and dissemination of education among women followed a different trajectory.[158]

---

[154] Sudipa Topdar, "Duties of a Good Citizen: Colonial Secondary School Textbook Policies in Late Nineteenth-Century India," *South Asian History and Culture* 6, no. 3 (2015): 417–439.
[155] Nurullah and Naik, *History of Education*, 260.
[156] Sengupta, *Pedagogy for Religion*.
[157] Sanjay Seth, "Governmentality, Pedagogy, Identity: The Problem of the Backward Muslim in Colonial India," in *Beyond Representations: Colonial and Postcolonial Constructions of Indian Identity*, ed. Crispin Bates (New Delhi: Oxford University Press, 2006), 55–76.
[158] Geraldine Forbes, *Women in Modern India* (Cambridge: Cambridge University Press, 2007). For the education of Muslim women, see Gail Minault, *Secluded Scholars: Women's Education and Muslim Social Reform in Colonial India* (New Delhi: Oxford University Press,

This book maps the literary activism of educated natives and cultural and political icons like Tagore, Gandhi, and Nehru who resisted the colonial system of education by offering an alternative model. The colonial school systems that produced different kinds of childhoods have received significant attention in recent years, but the indigenist contribution that remained outside the periphery of the state-initiated pedagogy still remains to be unearthed.

Scope of the Book

The objective of the book is twofold: to trace the figuration of the child in multiple discourses produced by the indigenous literati—the "fathers"—in pedagogic literature, children's magazines, scientific journals, autobiographies, essays, and correspondences; and, to produce at the same time a contextualized study of the culture of fathers and children, noting its changing dimensions. In other words, my purpose is to try to determine if a historical study of the connection between the father and the child, each with their own agency, might affect masculinity studies and even national history. The child—a contentious subject of discussion and yet a repository of ideas and visions—is for the father a way of asserting manhood through his ideas, behaviour, and action as a patriarch of the household and as an architect of the nation.

Foregrounding the familial context and the thrust of new moral education emphasized outside of the official school curriculum, this book relies on different genres of literature that best captured the worldviews of the educated fathers. The focus on reformers and activists as fathers and their private–public lives underlines the book's attention to a select demographic segment at the exclusion of others, such as the working-class. It also determines the selective choice of sources. It has stayed away from the vast repertoire of children's literature and their maestros (such as Bibhutibhushan Bandyopadhyay, Abanindranath Tagore, Upendrakishore Ray Chaudhuri, Lila Majumdar, Sukumar Ray, Satyajit Ray, and many others) and privileged those figures who espoused

1999); Sumit Sarkar and Tanika Sarkar, eds., *Women and Social Reform in Modern India: A Reader* (Bloomington: Indiana University Press, 2008).

socio-political causes and were moved by a reformist and pedagogic mission through the early years of the nineteenth and the twentieth centuries. The book also eschews the vast world of fictional literature produced by female and male writers that captured vivid imageries of fathers from all walks of life.

The book treats the "fathers" as imperial social formations whose identities were forged at the intersection of global historical processes—not only were they products of colonial governance, several of them also travelled West and were grappling with translating ideas of freedom and democracy in their personal lives.[159] Well into the third decade of the twentieth century they remained "subjects" of a colonial government and not free citizens; from the 1870s they had started offering resistance particularly through different genres of vernacular literature. By assuming a position of authority, the Indian/Bengali literati—as fathers and moral guardians—imagined children, an unstable and gendered category, as a free body of citizenry. To become free citizens the male children ought to be redeemed from their precarity and deficiencies through an alternate system of pedagogy; the girl children were trained to be mothers and wives. The charge of effeminacy that was systematically levelled against the Bengali *babus* by the British was to be vindicated by the former's assumption of power through moral leadership; by raising a new generation of children through reformed education that creatively assimilated ideas and practices of the West and the East; and more importantly, by infusing the notion of masculinity with the cultivation of mind that was without fear. *Pourush* or manhood was not squarely confined to physical strength and a masquerading spirit in the public domain but it also involved character-building and fulfilling responsibilities at home and towards family members; filial piety; devotion and obedience to familial authority; physical and moral restraint; and reasoned decision-making as educated, rational beings constituted the crux of masculinity. In other words, the fathers were engaged in an ethical foundation of a national community strongly anchored at home.

---

[159] Tapan Raychaudhuri, *Europe Reconsidered: Perceptions of Europe in Nineteenth Century Bengal* (New Delhi: Oxford University Press, 1989); Simonti Sen, *Travels to Europe: Self and Other in Bengali Travel Narratives* (Hyderabad: Orient Blackswan, 2005).

Fathers and children were connected by a new sense of governmentality, the governmentality that was transferred to the realm of the home and the nation as a larger family. The colonial state deployed technologies of governmentality that denied its colonial subjects the right to citizenship. The colonial state classified and enumerated the subject population into different demographic segments and deployed them for different governmental purposes such as education, public health, and others.[160] The fathers that I examine belong to the community who were actively involved in questions of education from the early nineteenth to the mid-twentieth century until India was liberated from British colonial rule in 1947 and even afterwards. From a select body of literary sources, I demonstrate the diverse ways fatherhood or moral guardianship was asserted by Indian males. I read the different acts of fatherhood as a counter-narrative produced by intersecting ideas, forces, and differential power relationships unleashed in a colonial situation.

My purpose is not to understand fatherhood according to the timeless Indian archetypes, as suggested by Kakar, or to confine them within the Victorian parameters illustrated by John Tosh and others.[161] In my attempt to study fatherhood as a process, we will find representations of all these templates and perhaps more. True, the behaviour and concerns displayed by Indian fathers in the late colonial era resonated with that of Victorian men. As products of colonial culture, they were influenced by Victorian ideology and appropriated them selectively and imaginatively, similar to the fashion they adopted for their women. But what is crucial to recognize is the difference in contexts between Victorian and Indian men. Educated Indian men, who asserted their authority as fathers, both in public and private realms, were subjugated by a colonial state and were stung by its stringent critique. Through affective investments and building of cultural capital, the educated males, the fathers, vindicated their masculinity and reclaimed themselves as subjects in their own right.

---

[160] Partha Chatterjee, *The Politics of the Governed: Popular Politics in Most of the World* (New York: Columbia University Press, 2004). For a more recent discussion of governmentality of children spanning the colonial and the postcolonial period, see Sarada Balagopalan, *Inhabiting 'Childhood': Children, Labour and Schooling in Postcolonial India* (New York: Palgrave Macmillan, 2014).

[161] A detailed study specifically of the ideology of fatherhood would be a great contribution to the literature, but the aim of my book is to describe fatherhood more broadly.

By attending to a set of (gendered) practices and ideologies, my work demonstrates how educated Indian men claimed their subjectivities and agencies as fathers. By appropriating the figure of the child, not just as victims but as functionaries of change, the fathers empowered their patriarchal authorities. They forged their identities through an articulation of alternate modernity based on new cultural and pedagogical practices. The futurity of India lay with children; despairing over the present, the hopes were recast in terms of a new generation.

The book deploys the analytic of imagination to configure the many ways an unspecified body of children were addressed by the dominant literati fathers. Simultaneously, it pairs the lived experiences of the male leaders to demonstrate the contradictory worlds they straddled. Unsettling the boundaries of the home and the world, this book is a study of multi-layered power-relationship that inflected subjective identities of Indian men with relation to an imagined community of children. It tracks not so much the lives of children but the ways the ideas of a class-specific and gendered childhood were appropriated and mobilized by the hegemonic literati inhabiting a colonial state. At the heart of this discourse lay implicitly or explicitly the question of a free citizenry based on ideals of self-reliance and self-determination, however, limited and unrealized in actuality.[162] The burgeoning ideas of the early reformers such as Vidyasagar and Keshub Sen crystalized in the pedagogical innovations of Tagore as a visionary and a humanist and found resonances in Gandhi and Nehru as well. But none of the leaders were perfect fathers or successful educators. In fact, all major leaders discussed in the book had vexed relationship with their children and often with their own fathers. Their everyday practices as biological fathers and intergenerational relationships only disclose their limitations; yet, they harboured a global vision for the future generation. In the process of unravelling the struggle, what becomes apparent are the ambivalence and contradictions that beset the virtual fathers of modern India, a hallmark that underscored subjects of modernity in any other context.

---

[162] For discussion on citizenship see Engin F. Isin, *Citizenship after Orientalism: Transforming Political Theory* (Houndmills, Basingstoke, Hampshire: Palgrave Macmillan, 2015).

The Chapters

Following this Introduction's location of fathers and children in India's long past through the colonial era, Chapter 2 juxtaposes a few eminent real-life sons and fathers versus their life as social reformers and literary leaders in nineteenth-century Bengal. The chapter details how starting with the establishment of the Calcutta School Book Society in 1817, educated Indian men like Iswarchandra Vidyasagar (1820–1891), Keshub Chandra Sen (1838–1884), Rajendralal Mitra (1823/24–1891), Sivnath Sastri (1847–1919) and others aided missionary and colonial endeavours in production of school textbooks, illustrated journals, and translations of European literature in vernacular languages. It also draws on the lives of nineteenth-century reformers to highlight the contradictions that riddled their private–public selves. Their everyday practices in personal life as fathers and sons did not match with their public crusade for social reforms and improvements in the lives of children and women. The aim of the chapter is to reveal the multiple subject positions of the fathers contingent on different layers of authority and subordination within the family and in the public realm. Engaging with Dipesh Chakrabarty's ideas of the birth of the modern subject in colonial India, the chapter offers insights into the paradoxical and interstitial location of middle-class fathers as hegemonic and subaltern subjects.[163]

Chapter 3 explores the enunciative roles of writers trained in medical professions who acted as gatekeepers for an emerging nationalist culture. Positioning male and female children differently in various pedagogical and scientific discourses, they envisaged a moral pedagogy laced with prescriptions for raising healthy children and a robust nation. From the second half of the nineteenth century, native intellectuals, especially medical practitioners, detected a crisis in moral character and national health. They expressed their views in a series of Bengali scientific journals such as *Swasthya*, *Chikitsha Sammilani*, and *Onubeekshan*. Although mainly targeting the male child, this literature, in its lengthy discussions on child marriage, sexuality, national, and public health, impinged on the girl child as well. In this material, the child was imagined in a variety of capacities—as hapless victims, as subjects of reform, as aggressors and

---

[163] Dipesh Chakrabarty, "Family, Fraternity, and Salaried Labor," in *Provincializing Europe*.

as perpetrators of moral and sexual crimes, as well as signifiers of the hopes for a new nation. This chapter makes two important claims: first, by showing the different ways the child was imagined and appropriated in the new literature, it argues that the intelligentsia conceived the child, a highly gendered category, as the new social imaginary as Charles Taylor outlined. It also bears out what Nita Kumar and Sarada Balagopalan indicated in their works: the child was never conceptualized independently; there was no "absolute" childhood in colonial and native discourses of the Indians.[164] Second, it again unfolds the inherent contradictions and ambivalence of the Bengali literati as a modern subject.

To look into the idea of the performance of fatherhood in everyday life, Chapters 4 through 6 examine letters, memoirs, and autobiographies of men and women. In these sources, one hears the voices of children and of fathers as they define or as they defy the cultural norms. New sensibilities are being produced. Despite the "constructedness" of personal narratives, they are nonetheless excellent sources for making the connection between ideological discourses and lived reality. I explore the emotional landscape of love, affection, anger, disciplining, fear, and punishment displayed in the performance of fatherhood as a sign of masculinity forged within the familial—but also colonial familial—domain. Current historical scholarship is grappling with the question of emotion as a tool for crossing the boundaries between public and private, personal and collective.[165] Chapter 4 claims that a critical investigation of children–father relationships sheds light on both the existing cultures of childhood and the emerging national culture in late colonial India. The performative aspects of fatherhood were constitutive of gender-specific practices of masculinity, and fatherhood acted as a cornerstone of Indian patriarchy. The praxis of fatherhood enables us to document the entanglement of the history of affect with the history of power. It also allows us to "simultaneously interrogate, and engage with, the age, class and gender-based hierarchies within the households to work with conflict."[166] Building on cumulative evidence from personal narratives, this chapter reconstructs

---

[164] Nita Kumar, *The Politics of Gender, Community, and Modernity: Essays on Education in India* (New Delhi: Oxford University Press, 2011); Balagopalan, *Inhabiting Childhood*.
[165] Nicole Eustace, Eugenia Lean, et al. "AHR Conversation: The Historical Study of Emotions," *American Historical Review* 117, no. 5 (2012): 1487–1531.
[166] Indrani Chatterjee, *Unfamilar Relations* (New Delhi: Permanent Black, 2004), 16.

the different facets—the venerable, the affectionate, the ambivalent, the disciplinarian—that characterized the modern father.

Chapters 5 and 6 follow the life-works of the three iconic public figures, Rabindranath Tagore, Mohandas Karamchand Gandhi, and Jawaharlal Nehru—respectively addressed as Gurudev (mentor), Bapu-ji (father), and Chacha (uncle) in close quarters—who reflected substantially on children in national and international contexts.[167] These three leaders displayed close involvement as "modern" fathers at home and were also committed to greater public good that compelled them to engage with questions of education, inclusive of but beyond their own children. In many ways, they echoed the concern of the contemporary educationists and reformers; but more importantly, they departed from the earlier pedagogical models and established their new ones for the future generation evincing a transition from tentative contestations with the colonial government of the earlier decades to more self-confident moves constitutive of a new nation.[168]

Chapter 5 devotes itself to Rabindranath Tagore, an iconic figure of Indian modernity, as a father and an educator and his conceptualization of an alternate education and masculinity. Drawing on Tagore's everyday experiences, the chapter demonstrates the tangled relationship between his domestic reality and his public commitment to social justice and education. With Bengal as a take-off point, Chapter 6 offers a comparative picture of India by scrutinizing the efforts of Mohandas Karamchand Gandhi (1869–1948), and Jawaharlal Nehru (1889–1964). Gandhi was committed to a new model of basic education (*nai talim*), one involving self-help but rejecting "modern" scientific training; Jawaharlal Nehru, the foremost nationalist leader and the first prime minister of independent India, rewrote world history (*Glimpses of World History,* 1934) by writing to his daughter Indira (who would later also become the prime minister of

---

[167] There were other influential figures around the same period who also experimented with alternate pedagogical systems. Girjashankar Badheka or Gijubhai (1885–1939) from Gujarat, for example, introduced the Montessori system in India in 1920. See Meera Ashar, "... And What Can We Learn from That: Learning and Instruction in Gujarati Folk Stories," *South Asia History and Culture* (forthcoming).
[168] See Manu Goswami, "Colonial Pedagogical Consolidation," in *Producing India: From Colonial Economy to National Space* (Chicago: University of Chicago Press, 2004), 132–153 for the demands and contestations on national education forged by indigenous leaders with the colonial state.

India) from behind bars where he spent a substantial part of his adult life. With the publication of these letters, Nehru positioned himself not just as the father of Indira, but as the father of the nation. Nehru was influenced by Tagore and Gandhi, but differing from both of them, he implemented educational policies that he deemed fit for the newly independent nation-state. Unlike Gandhi, Tagore and Nehru never claimed themselves as "fathers" of the larger public, but their private–public concern with training the future generation certainly earns them a claim to virtual fatherhood of the larger population. They were not only fathers at home but were "fathers" of the nation, although their fatherhood remained limited, restricted, and unfulfilled in both the private and the public realm. Tagore, Gandhi, and Nehru had their specific hegemonic aspirations to mobilize children as citizens of a new modernity who would challenge and escape the injustices of colonial domination. They emphasized the shaping of the mind (soul control) over the control of the body (crowd control).[169] But their mobilization remained incomplete as they themselves were restrained by their class-caste status and conceptualizations of childhood and education.

My hope in writing this book is to open up the categories of father and fatherhood for further interrogation and reveal the heterogeneous practices that constituted it at a specific historical moment when educated Indian men were faced with the twin pressure of colonialism and nationalism. By underscoring knowledge and social identities produced at the intersection of colonial forces and native responses, this book tries to convey the conflicts and differences that existed within the indigenous population (class/caste, religious, ethnic groups) in articulating themselves in various societal roles. Through an exploration of the history of fatherhood, I attempt to demonstrate not only the tension of a burgeoning middle class, the stresses of unfulfilled dreams and ambitions of a fledgling nation, but also the tangled world of prophets and humanists, nationalists and reformers that transcended spatio-temporal boundaries of the home and the world.

---

[169] Ranajit Guha, "Discipline and Mobilize."

2
"Fathers" at the Crossroads
Literary Activism and Fatherhood in Nineteenth-Century Bengal

Pay close attention to studies (*lekhapora*) when you are young. Everyone loves you when you are educated...[1]

Never disobey your parents (*pita mata*). Always follow their advice. Never act otherwise. Parents will not love you if you do not listen to them.[2]

A good boy loves his parents dearly. He remembers all their instructions; never forgets them. He always executes whatever work the parents ask him to do; he never performs those acts that his parents forbid him to do.[3]

—Iswarchandra Vidyasagar

Every reading exercise in Iswarchandra Vidyasagar's primer *Varnaparichay* (part 2, 1855) tried to impress upon his young readers that filial piety and education (*lekhapora*) were the primary duties of being a responsible adult, and by default, one may argue, a good citizen in its early conceptualization. An ardent social reformer and a high-ranking official in the British educational system, Vidyasagar (See Figure 2.1), the iconic father of the Bengalis, echoed voices of educated and concerned fathers in colonial India. He made familial relations, particularly fulfilling obligations

---

[1] Iswarchandra Vidyasagar, *Varnaparichay*, part 2, *Vidyasagar Rachanabali*, ed. Tirthapati Datta, vol. 2 (Kolkata: Tuli-kalam, 2001 [1855]), 1262.
[2] Vidyasagar, *Varnaparichay*, part 2, *Vidyasagar Rachanabali*, 1263.
[3] Vidyasagar, *Varnaparichay*, part 2, *Vidyasagar Rachanabali*, 1264.

Figure 2.1 Ishwarchandra Vidyasagar

towards one's own parents, central to *santanér charitra gathan* (building characters of children).[4] Insisting that "parents will not love you if you do not listen to them," he made parental love conditional on children's behaviour. The emphasis on the reciprocal nature of the relationship commanding love and obedience from children to receive parental affection made children and parents both active agents (See Figures 2.2, 2.3, 2.4, 2.5 for Vidyasagar's parents, wife and son).

A principal paternal obligation of the nineteenth-century Indian reformers was educating and mobilizing children in the desired direction that intersected with and differed from the proffered model of the colonial state. Bengali reformers fulfilled that obligation by authoring vernacular texts and literature for children that captured their "competing

---

[4] For more on *santanér charitra gathan* as a new discourse see Pradip Kumar Bose, "Sons of the Nation: Child Rearing in the New Family," in *Texts of Power*, ed. Partha Chatterjee (Minneapolis: University of Minnesota Press, 1995).

Figure 2.2 Bhagabati Devi (Vidyasagar's Mother)

desires and imaginations."[5] Ascribing symbolic fatherhood to these reformers, this chapter maps the agentiality and subjecthood of "fathers" by tracing their intervention in the field of children's literature and pedagogy.[6] The reformist authors reflected on their state of being in the

---

[5] Dipesh Chakrabarty, "Family, Fraternity, and Salaried Labor," in *Provincializing Europe: Postcolonial Thought and Historical Difference* (Princeton: Princeton University Press, 2000), 207.

[6] I use both "agentiality" and "agency" in mapping the subject-positions of men I am describing in this chapter. By agency of the fathers I meant individuals who intervened and took an active role to produce particular effects. As my course of argument through the book will make clear I invoke the word "agentiality" after Bo Sträth and Peter Wagner's discussion of reflexivity, historicity, and agentiality: how individuals "relate reflexively to their being-in-the-world" and how they collectively use their "capacity for reflexivity such that they can critically relate to their history and give themselves new orientations in the present." Sträth and Wagner define reflexivity as the "human ability to, by means of imagination, step out of the immediate present and to imagine other possible worlds, or partial worlds. Historicity refers to the translation of such imagination into time, by means of which the present can be distinguished from a past that was different and from a future that may be different. Agentiality refers to the belief that human action may contribute to bring a particular different future about." Bo Sträth and Peter Wagner, *European Modernity: A Global Perspective* (London: Bloomsbury, 2017), 31, 197.

Figure 2.3 Thakurdas Bandyopadhyay (Vidyasagar's Father)

world, and by critically relating to their past, they oriented themselves in the present. Rooting for values inherited in the past, the leaders used imagination to escape the immediate present and visualize a different future. The agentiality of the leaders lay in their locus of struggle, in familial and extra-familial colonial arenas, and in their bid to change the future.[7] *Bhadralok* fathers in nineteenth-century Bengal inhabited a complex grid of power, and their identities were constantly constituted within a network of overlapping spheres including what has been characterized as the "public" and the "private." Bengali men who penned the earliest children's literature in the region held multiple subject positions: they were sons themselves, as well as fathers, authors, public speakers, government agents, government antagonists, and activists. As members of a

---

[7] For an excellent reference on literary history of this period see Stuart Blackburn and Vasudha Dalmia, *India's Literary History: Essays on the Nineteenth Century* (New Delhi: Permanent Black, 2004).

Figure 2.4 Dinamayi Devi (Vidyasagar's Wife)

"modern" professional community, the fathers, caught between different layers of authority and subordination, held contradictory positions when it came to exerting their subjecthood and agency.

The "middleness" of the Bengali middle class as a colonial elite has been written about at length. Their social agency as modern individuals and as architects of a new nation has been explained by the way they reconciled simultaneously their dominant and subordinate positions at home and in the world.[8] Departing from the stories of reconciliation and underscoring the lack of boundaries between the familial and the public, I focus on these leaders' simultaneous practices of "manhood" as biological fathers and as moral guardians of a larger community of children. The ambivalence and contradictions in their literary activism and daily

---

[8] Partha Chatterjee, "The Nation and Its Elite," in *The Nation and Its Fragments* (Princeton: Princeton University Press, 1993), 35–75.

Figure 2.5 Narayan Chandra Vidyaratna (Vidyasagar's Son)

practices provide a complex understanding of the paradoxical location of middle-class fathers as a hegemonic and a subaltern subject.

As the colonial state assumed the role of the adult and relegated the colonized to the position of the child, the goal of the British was to educate the Indians in "new ways of acting and thinking," to "civilize" them and to train them as "citizens."[9] To disseminate education in a foreign land and in vernacular languages, the British rulers and the missionaries had to rely on native experts, typically men of property and status. Since the establishment of the Asiatic Society (1784) and Fort William College (1800), educated Bengali men actively worked with the government in publishing and printing.[10] Their participation was formalized with the

---

[9] Krishna Kumar, *The Political Agenda of Education: A Study of Colonialist and Nationalist Ideas* (New Delhi: Sage Publications, 2004), 27–30. One must recognize here the limited conception of the term "citizen" or citizenship as conceptualized by the colonial state. Chapter 3 discusses more on question of nascent citizens.

[10] Anindita Ghosh, *Power in Print* (Delhi: Oxford University Press, 2006).

Charter Act of 1813, which allocated 100,000 rupees for the revival and promotion of the knowledge of science and literature and encouraged the involvement of the learned natives.

The early missionary efforts to translate and write textbooks for children also counted on indigenous support. The Baptist missionaries of Serampore, a suburb of Calcutta, fostered vernacular literature among the masses with the goal that the latter could read the Bible one day. Their very first periodical *Digdarshan* (1818), edited by the missionary John Clark Marshman, appeared as a "set of advice for the youth" and covered a wide range of topics—geography, agriculture, lifesciences, physics, and "discoveries" of countries such as the Americas. Their main contributors, however, were the local intelligentsia, such as Rammohun Roy (1782–1833), the pioneering social reformer, who wrote several scientific articles for this journal.[11] As employees of the Company Raj, these men were "subaltern" to the European missionaries, educators, and officials. But the opportunity to participate in educational programmes for drafting textbooks and literature for native children provided the native literati a cultural and epistemic space to articulate their own ideas and visions, albeit under European direction and supervision.[12]

Following the transfer of power to the British Crown (1858) the cultural environment shifted drastically as the colonial state's policy towards the Indians underwent a transformation and became explicit in public practices and administration. From the 1870s the Indian leaders became less committed to the liberal reforms of the colonial government and publicly endorsed conservative values drawn from an "invented" Hindu past. As the Bengali elites demanded political rights through an emerging body of vernacular literature and organizations, the government's attitude towards this group was best represented in the colonial "discourse" that characterized Bengali men as "artificial" and "unnatural"—"effeminate *babus*" in contrast to the "manly Englishman." The British were

---

[11] For the reciprocal influence of Britain and India on each other through religion and print culture see Daniel White, *From Little London to Little Bengal* (Baltimore: Johns Hopkins University Press, 2013).

[12] For the involvement of the native literati in colonial education and reforms see David Kopf, *British Orientalism and the Bengal Renaissance: The Dynamics of Indian Modernization, 1773–1835* (Berkeley: University of California Press, 1969); Parna Sengupta, *Pedagogy for Religion* (Berkeley: University of California Press, 2011).

determined not to grant these "emasculated men" the authority to preside over matters relating to the colonial government, as it was evident in the Ilbert Bill controversy of 1882.[13]

It was in this contentious political environment that the native literati played a pioneering role in a new field of literature with their "imagined community" of children, a topic we will explore in depth in the next chapter.[14] South Asian historiography has copiously surveyed the role of social reformers' engagement with the "woman question" and "new woman" in nineteenth-century India. But the preoccupation of the same social reformers with children has gained less attention. I contend that one of the many ways the social reformers showed their engagement with the younger generation was through their intervention as fathers in the lives of their own children and their leadership as authors and editors in the field of children's literature. The native fathers, in fact, envisioned a "new child" parallel to the conceptualization of the "new woman."[15] The new child was an upper class and caste-based gendered category characterized by its specific training and education; it was primarily the male offspring of the educated middle class, from both the Hindu and the Muslim communities, who would be raised as a worthy citizen.[16] The didactic responsibilities displayed by the authors were comparable to the parental obligations claimed by the colonial state. In that sense, the authors also represented "new fathers" who were "traditional" in keeping a monopoly over important life decisions for their family members (as

---

[13] Mrinalini Sinha, *Colonial Masculinity* (Manchester: University of Manchester Press, 1997), 3–4.

[14] Benedict Anderson, *Imagined Communities: Reflections on the Origins and Spread of Nationalism* (London: Verso, 1983). Although Anderson's conceptwas challenged and problematized by Partha Chatterjee, the idea of imagined communities was adapted widely and creatively in the South Asian context. See Partha Chatterjee, *The Nation and Its Fragments* (Princeton: Princeton University Press, 1993).

[15] The "new woman" was distinguished from her uneducated, unrefined, traditional counterpart, the working-class woman, and the ultra-Westernized women of "wealthy parvenu families," Partha Chatterjee, "The Nation and Its Women," in *Nation and Its Fragments*, 116–134.

[16] The sources examined here came from the Hindus, although the readers could have been both Hindus and Muslims. For parallel developments in the Muslim community see Margrit Pernau, *Ashraf into Middle Class: Muslims in Nineteenth-Century* (Delhi and Oxford: Oxford University Press, 2013); David Lelyveld, *Aligarh's First Generation: Muslim Solidarity in British India* (New Delhi: Oxford University Press, 2003); "Young Man Sayyid: Dreams and Biographical Texts," in *Muslim Voices: Community and the Self in South Asia*, eds. David Gilmartin, Sadria Freitag, and Usha Sanyal (New Delhi: Yoda Press, 2013).

we will see later) but were "modern" in terms of instilling morals and responsibilities in the next generation through publishing literature and magazines.[17]

The direct reciprocity between print language and literature and the articulation of social identities in colonial India is now well recognized. Anindita Ghosh has argued that it was in the linguistic and literary developments that "the earliest struggles among competing social groups took place, even before these were played out in the political arena of the modern nation."[18] In attempting to historicize "modern" fathers in India, I suggest that given the preponderance of male writers (granted that they were more likely to be literate and had the means to get their works published), one of the seminal moments of virtual "fatherhood" can be traced to the emergence of the field of children's literature in Bengal. On one hand, I examine the hegemonic efforts of metaphoric fathers in pedagogical and intellectual activities for children; on the other, I underscore their compromised location as fathers and sons and the undermining of their ideological positions. Their affective gestures and moral responsibilities towards wives and girl-children unfolded in unpredictable and contradictory ways as they yielded to domestic and extra-domestic pressures.

This chapter investigates the period from the establishment of the Calcutta School Book Society in 1817 to 1900, the period that marked the emergence of Bengali children's literature under native leadership until the field came into its own in the early twentieth century. It pays close attention to primers and periodicals that provide a substantial body of evidence to trace native initiative in pedagogy and literature.[19] While scholars have paid attention to Bengali fictional prose in the nineteenth

---

[17] For the class-specific nature of the literature under discussion and its critique see Gautam Chando Roy, "Science for Children in a Colonial Context: Bengali Juvenile Magazines, 1883–1923," *British Journal of History of Science*, Themes 3 (2018): 43–72.

[18] Anindita Ghosh, *Power in Print*, 3; Tithi Bhattacharya, *The Sentinels of Culture: Class, Education, and the Colonial Intellectuals of Bengal (1848–85)* (New Delhi: Oxford University Press, 2005).

[19] Parna Sengupta has focused on school textbooks and object lessons designed by the *bhadralok* members of the Department of Public Instruction (DPI) as indices of native resistance to and disregard of missionary education. She demonstrated the close connection between the spread of missionary education in Bengal and the self-fashioning of Bengali *bhadralok*, both Hindus and Muslims, along religious lines, during a period of half a century—from Charles Wood's educational Despatch in 1854 to the beginning of the twentieth century. Sengupta, *Pedagogy for Religion*.

century, early literature for children has not been explored yet.[20] The origins of Bengali children's literature, which included both pedagogic texts and other forms of realistic and imaginary writings, date back to the establishment of the Calcutta School Book Society in 1817.[21] The term *shishu sahitya* or children's literature, however, came into vogue much later when it was first coined in 1899 by an eminent Bengali thinker, educator, and science-writer, Ramendrasundar Tribedi (1864–1919).[22] It will not be an exaggeration to claim that the emergence of children's literature as a genre was closely linked with the reigning social and legal issues, such as restricting child marriage and polygamy, along with passing the Age of Consent Act (1891), which revolved around defining the legal age at which a child could marry or consummate a marriage.[23] The turmoil surrounding a "child" not only called for vaguely defining an age range for the child but it also demanded mediation of the colonial state and the native interlocutors to "rescue" and educate the child. The educational programmes that ushered in the field of children's literature were thus launched to train and reform the child who would display different sensibilities and represent a "civilized" body of future citizenry. We will map the role of the Indian intelligentsia as fathers through an examination of the early phases of the development of children's literature in Bengal. In particular, we will highlight the activities of Iswarchandra Vidyasagar, Keshub Chandra Sen, and Sivnath Satsri in promoting children's education in vernacular languages and the conflicted positions they inhabited in personal lives.

---

[20] For early fictional prose in nineteenth-century Bengal see Hansa Herder, "The Modern Babu and the Metropolis: Reassessing Early Bengali Narrative Prose (1821–1862)," in *India's Literary History: Essays on the Nineteenth Century*, eds. Stuart Blackburn and Vasudha Dalmia (New Delhi: Permanent Black, 2004), 358–401.

[21] Bani Basu, compiler, *Bangla Shishusahitya: Granthapanji* (*Children's Literature in Bengali: A Catalog*) (Kolkata: Bangiya Granthagar Parishad, 1962). In 1962 the Indian Library Association adopted a unanimous resolution for compiling a bibliography of children's literature in India. Following this initiative, the government of West Bengal adopted a plan for creating a catalogue of children's literature in the regional Bengali language. The result was a 500-page long bibliography of children's literature in Bengali covering the period from 1818 to 1962. The data presented here, unless otherwise stated, are from that compilation.

[22] Khagendranath Mitra, *Shatabdir Shishu-Sahitya* (Kolkata: Pashchimbanga Bangla Academy, 1999 [1958]), 138.

[23] Ishita Pande, "'Listen to the Child': Law, Sex, and the Child Wife in Indian Historiography," *History Compass* 11, no. 9 (September 2013); "Coming of Age: Law, Sex, and Childhood in Late Colonial India," *Gender and History* 24, no. 1 (April 2012); "Sorting Boys and Men: Unlawful Intercourse, Boy-Protection, and the Child Marriage Restraint Act in Colonial India," *Journal of the History of Childhood and Youth* 6, no. 2 (January 2013): 332–358.

The Burgeoning Field of Children's Literature and the Native Intelligentsia

Bengali intelligentsia played a key role in the Calcutta School Book Society (1817), inaugurating the first phase of children's literature. An institution founded jointly by European Orientalist scholars, missionaries, and educated Indians, both Hindus and Muslims, the Calcutta School Book Society was established with the objective of supplying cheap textbooks in vernacular languages to schools and *madrasas* in and around Calcutta. The Society accelerated the production of texts for children, apparently for both boys and girls, and also gave educated natives, well versed in English, Sanskrit, Persian, and Bengali, an agency in the new system of pedagogy.[24] Experimenting with new prose styles, the Calcutta School Book Society mainly published school textbooks and works on moral pedagogy, lacking variety in their contents.[25] The three active Indian members, Radhakanta Deb (1784–1867), Tarinicharan Mitra (1772–1837), and Ram Comul Sen (1783–1844), all social conservatives and opposed to colonial intervention in social matters such as the abolition of *sati* (1829), were instrumental in the Society's first publication *Neetikatha* (*Moral Tales*, 1818), a compilation of eighteen moral tales comprising of translations of Aesop's fables and other Arabic tales.[26]

The watershed moment in the field of children's literature, marking its second phase in 1847–1891, coincided with the pedagogical intervention

---

[24] For more on the Calcutta School Book Society see N.L. Basak, "Origin and the Role of the Calcutta School Book Society in Promoting the Cause of Education in India," *Bengal Past and Present* 78 (January–June 1959): 41; Brian Hatcher, *Idioms of Improvement: Vidyasagar and Cultural Encounter in Bengal* (Delhi: Oxford University Press, 1996); Kopf, *British Orientalism*, 184–187; Parna Sengupta, *Pedagogy for Religion*, 40–41. For activities of the Calcutta School Book Society with regard to children's literature see Sibaji Bandyopadhyay, "Shiksha o Adhunikata-r Pawth," in *Gopal-Rakhal Dwandwa Samas* (Calcutta: Papyrus, 1991), 78–191.

[25] The first illustrated magazine for children, *Paswabali* (*Animal Tales*) came out from the School Book Society in 1822. *Paswabali* had an interesting bilingual format: the English text appeared with its Bengali translation on the opposite page. Each issue of *Paswabali* focused on a particular animal (such as lion, bear, elephant, tiger, cat, rhinoceros, and hippopotamus) with its picture on the cover.

[26] Tarinicharan Mitra was the native secretary of the Calcutta School Book Society until 1831. Radhakanta Deb was a committee member at its formation. Radhakanta Deb and Tarinicharan Mitra were engaged in various educational activities at government-established colleges and institutions, such as the Fort Williams College in Calcutta. Ram Comul Sen was a scholar, writer, and bibliographer who held different positions with the colonial government. His grandson Keshub Chandra Sen was a foremost leader of the Brahmo Samaj and would be a pioneer in children's literature. For more on the trio, see David Kopf, *British Orientalism*, 184–187.

of Iswarchandra Vidyasagar.[27] Vidyasagar, the noted humanist–scholar–educator, known for his concern for women, children, and the oppressed, was deservedly regarded as the virtual father of Bengal. Following his campaign for widow remarriage in the mid-1850s, Vidyasagar's popularity soared so high that a folk-composer, Dasarathi Ray, described him as "the master of the Bengalis, and of the [East India] Company as well." Based on an observation of another poet, Brian Hatcher noted that Vidyasagar became "the patriarch of modern Bengal." In his background and experience, Vidyasagar was distinctive from the elite and affluent Bengali reformers: he came from an indigent Hindu family, but by virtue of his superb intellect and administrative skills he rose to top official positions in the colonial educational apparatus. He was among the few native reformers who straddled three worlds: his rich middle-class compatriots, the poor natives (*daridra athacha bhadralok*), and the higher echelons of British administration and officials.[28]

In 1854, Sir Charles Wood, the President of the Board of Control of the East India Company, sent a Despatch to Lord Dalhousie, the then-Governor-General of India, urging the Company Raj to bolster its effort to educate its colonial subjects. Among its many recommendations to establish an education department in every province and set up universities in Calcutta, Bombay, and Madras modelled after the University of London, it also advocated that natives be trained in their vernacular languages.[29] Following the Despatch, the Department of Public Instruction in Bengal was established and it increased the hiring of native experts: the chief among them were the two stalwarts, Iswarchandra Vidyasagar (1820–1891) and Bhudev Mukhopadhyay (1827–1894), who played critical roles in the academic curriculum in Bengal.[30] Vidyasagar, in particular, introduced a strong vernacularist element and signalled a new direction in children's literature and pedagogy.

---

[27] For an astute assessment of Vidyasagar see Asok Sen, *Iswar Chandra Vidyasagar and His Elusive Milestones* (Kolkata: Riddhi, 1977).
[28] Hatcher, *Idioms of Improvement*, 5.
[29] Sengupta, *Pedagogy for Religion*, 31–35.
[30] For more on Bhudev Mukhopadhyay see Parna Gupta, *Pedagogy for Religion*, 41–49; Satadru Sen, "The Conservative Animal: Bhudeb Mukhopadhyay and Colonial Bengal," *Journal of Asian Studies* 76, no. 2 (2017): 1–19; Tapan Raychaudhuri, *Europe Reconsidered: Perceptions of Europe in Nineteenth Century Bengal* (New Delhi: Oxford University Press, 1989).

Vidyasagar's pedagogy evinced his fatherly concern to broaden the social basis of the native intelligentsia—to advocate mass vernacular education that would be "more democratic than precolonial Brahmanical culture."[31] He bridged the gap between the traditional pandits and the Westernized, English-educated intelligentsia by bringing together Orientalist, Anglicist, and Vernacularist positions and introducing significant changes in each of them.[32] He made a break with the past missionary and government endeavours that sought to "civilize" and eventually proselytize the natives. His vernacular educational curriculum introduced history, geography, ethics, and natural philosophy in the form of elementary sciences as well as "morality" tales strongly infused with bourgeois and Brahmanical norms.[33] *Varnaparichay*, the most popular Bengali primer to date, introduced children to the world of the Bengali alphabet while at the same time teaching them a binary world of good (expressed via a character named Gopal) and evil (his foil, Rakhal) based on a morality that depended on acquiescence to parental authority but devoid of any poetic imagination or freedom.[34]

Vidyasagar's "idioms of self-improvement" emphasizing discipline, rigour, and control were supplemented by his legendary devotion to parents that he demonstrated in his own personal life (See Figures 2.2 and 2.3).[35] He displayed exemplary deference to both parents but the overwhelming influence of his father coloured every important decision made in his life.[36] For minor acts of disobedience as a child and a student, he endured tremendous physical chastisement from his father. To comply with his father's wishes, he married at an early age despite his personal reluctance. To honour his father's preference he declined a government post and opened a *tol* (school) in his village; when resigning from one government position to opt for another, he ensured that his father's well-being was not jeopardized and his brother had a secure source of

---

[31] Sumit Sarkar, "Vidyasagar and Brahmanical Society," in *Writing Social History* (Delhi: Oxford University Press, 2009), 246–247.
[32] Sumit Sarkar, "Vidyasagar and Brahmanical Society."
[33] Brian Hatcher, "Bourgeois Pedagogy and Nitisastra," in *Idioms of Improvement*.
[34] For the publication history of *Varnaparichay* and its stark representation of binaries between "good" and "evil," see Sibaji Bandopadhyay, *Gopal-Rakhal Dwandwa Samas* (Calcutta: Papyrus, 1991), 135.
[35] Hatcher, "Bourgeois Pedagogy."
[36] As a young boy he once undertook the most daring task of swimming across a rising river to see his mother. Indramitra, *Vidyasagarer Chhelebela* (Calcutta: Ananda Publishers, 1971).

employment.[37] Accordingly, in his texts for children, Vidyasagar pressed for total submission to parents and dedication to a secular form of education, the two fundamental requirements that promised success in a colonial society.

Vidysagar's pedagogy and ideological moorings have attracted significant scholarly attention but what remains to be addressed is his public acknowledgement of family values, especially conformity to the authority of parents and teachers that brought the domain of "home" to the realm of pedagogy and print culture.[38] His definition of an archetypal good boy (Gopal) in *Varnaparichay* part 1 was determined by his devotion to parents: "Gopal is a very good boy. He does everything that his parents (*pita-mata*) ask him to do."[39] It was followed by a list of activities that Gopal performed in daily life, the different kinds of *karmas* that Dipesh Chakrabarty alluded to in a different context to explain the sentiment of the prenationalist Indian patriarchy.[40] Gopal, the "good" boy, never transgressed the expected norms. In contrast, Rakhal did not obey his parents. He did whatever he wanted to do (*jathechhachar*), an idea also invoked by Chakrabarty to explain different notions of freedom in India and Europe.[41] In contradistinction to Gopal, Rakhal engaged in tantrums all day; he quarrelled and fought with his younger siblings. His parents had a hard time tackling him. Vidyasagar emphasized that Rakhal loved nothing more than playing; but he fought with everyone at play, invoking the wrath of his school-teacher (therefore surrogate father), *gurumahashay*, who reprimanded him all the time. Rakhal lost his books, and his father would have to replace them four times in the period of a month. The first part of *Varnaparichay* concluded with the cautionary note: "Nobody loves Rakhal. No boys should be like Rakhal. If someone followed in the footsteps of Rakhal, one could never be educated."[42] It

---

[37] Indramitra, *Karunasagar Vidyasagar*, 2nd rev. ed. (Kolkata: Ananda Publishers, 1992). Sumit Sarkar, *Writing Social History*, 226. Hatcher, *Idioms of Improvement*.

[38] Obedience to parental authority is an important parameter in understanding the history of children and childhood. On obedience and children in the American context, see Peter Stearns, "Obedience and Emotion: A Challenge in the Emotional History of Childhood," *Journal of Social History* 47, no. 3 (Spring 2014): 593–611.

[39] Iswarchandra Vidyasagar, "Varnaparichay, part 1" in *Vidyasagar Rachanabali*, vol. 1, ed. T. Datta (Calcutta, 2001), 1259–1260.

[40] Dipesh Chakrabarty, *Provincializing Europe*, 220.

[41] Dipesh Chakrabarty, "Postcoloniality and the Artifice of History: Who Speaks for 'Indian' Pasts?," *Representations* 37 (Winter 1992): 14.

[42] Vidyasagar, *Varnaparichay*, 1260.

was not just controlled behaviour but complete submission to the dictates of parents and teachers that was the lynchpin of success that Vidyasagar advocated for a modern individual. In contrast to the "possessive individual" of the West whose coming of age was contingent on the supposed death of the father, the male citizenry of Vidyasagar derived strength through adherence to parental authority.[43]

Vidyasagar's virtual fatherhood involved disseminating what constituted the right kind of education. In contrast to his own intrepid and mischievous childhood, which often infuriated his father, Vidyasagar left no room for frolic and spontaneity in the pages of his primer.[44] Playfulness was posited as an anathema to hard work, discipline, and rigour—the three essential attributes to succeed in life. In part 2 of *Varnaparichay*, Vidyasagar pronounced in no uncertain terms the horrific consequences of defying those moral virtues. He concluded the second part of the primer with a dark portrait of an orphan boy who was sentenced to death for stealing.[45] To hammer home the temerity of this youngster, Vidyasagar presented the readers with a rather startling scenario: on the eve of his execution when the accused met his aunt, his primary caregiver, he bit off her ears in vengeance, blaming her that she did not deter him from the path of wrong-doing.

It is ironic that "Karunasagar," the "Ocean of Sympathy," the other epithet that Vidyasagar enjoyed for his unparalleled kindness and compassion (*sahridayata*), invoked such a gory and harsh picture for his student-readers.[46] A combination of several overlapping factors have been cited to explain Vidyasagar's extreme position with the question of wrong-doing: the socio-political constraints of the colonial government, Brahmanical paternalism, influences of puritanical ideas of industry and his childhood learning of the *neetisastras* that he imbibed as a student.[47]

---

[43] For elaboration of this idea of the modern individual in the colonial Indian context see Dipesh Chakrabarty, *Provincializing Europe*.
[44] For Vidyasagar's intrepid childhood, see Indramitra, *Vidyasager Chhlebela* (Kolkata: Ananda Publishers, 2002).
[45] *Vidyasagar Rachanabali*, vol. 2, ed. T. Datta (Calcutta, 2001), 1274–1275. Also see Sumit Sarkar, *Writing Social History*.
[46] For *sahridyata* or compassion characterizing Vidyasagar as a modern man see Dipesh Chakrabarty, "Domestic Cruelty and the Birth of the Subject," in *Provincializing Europe*, 117–148.
[47] For these different ideas see Hatcher, *Idioms of Improvement* and Sumit Sarkar, *Writing Social History*.

The striking point however was that Vidyasagar, as a pedagogue, depicted a violent scenario to generate a sense of filial duty and compassion among students.[48] Through his strict moral pedagogy, he ensured that the future generation could avoid the pitfalls while accumulating new cultural capital to navigate their lives.

Vidyasagar's emphasis on unquestioned deference to parents and family were also evident in his other works for children, namely, *Kathamala* (1864; a translation of seventy-six stories from Aesop's Fables) and *Neetibodh* (*Idea of Justice*). In *Neetibodh* he elaborated the reasons for being respectful towards parents, siblings, and other family members:

> When we were young and helpless, our parents worked hard and took so much trouble and care to feed, nourish, and nurture us. Had they not bestowed their affection and compassion on us, we would have perished long ago. Therefore, it is our principal duty (*pradhan dharma*) and bounden responsibility (*oboshyokartabya karma*) to be grateful to them, to love and respect them, to try our best to satisfy them and care as much as we can about their wellbeing and welfare. If we cannot fulfill their requests and demands, we fail to perform our role as sons.[49]

His "moral pedagogy" was symptomatic of his paternalism and his embeddedness in familial relationships.[50] His pedagogy invoked not the motherland but real-life parents. His desired education exhorted biological parents and children's obligations towards them. As a public educator in the service of the colonial government, Vidyasagar emphasized the centrality of parents in rearing of children. When authority of men in the public sphere was curtailed by the colonial government, he upheld the authority of fathers and parents at home. He urged young readers to worship parents as living gods and goddesses. Challenging the colonial critique of the "unwholesome" practices of Indian homes, Vidyasagar

---

[48] This literary strategy of using descriptions of extreme violence to invoke compassion in the audience/readers had a long history in Indian literature, stretching back at least to the Mahabharata (ca. 400 BCE to 400 CE) and codified in classical Sanskrit literary criticism. Though Vidyasagar shifted the violence to the individual (Rakhal against his aunt, the state against Rakhal), rather than the wholesale slaughter of the epic.

[49] Iswarchandra Vidyasagar, "Neetibodh," in *Vidyasagar Rachanabali*, vol. 1, ed. T. Datta, new ed. (Calcutta, 2001), 1320.

[50] Hatcher, "Vidyasagar's Moral Pedagogy," in *Idioms of Improvement*, 162–188.

"FATHERS" AT THE CROSSROADS 67

asserted native parents as role models and established them as sovereign, autonomous individuals. His texts provided him an agency to produce new knowledge and claim the subjecthood of Indian parents, both as fathers and as mothers. The directives to children, however, flowed in a gendered narrative where the male child only featured as the protagonist for fulfilling filial obligations.

For a reformer like Vidyasagar who led a life-long crusade to uplift women, it is ironic that his primers and texts for children did not include a single girl character. Woman only appeared in the guise of the mother when he referred to *pita-mata* (fathers–mothers, parents) to evoke moral responsibilities for children. *Pita* (father) was the commander; but *mata* (mother), although revered, needed to be protected. The exclusion of the girl-child from his pedagogy signalled his ideological bias. Even for him the girl-child, representing the "new woman," was to be reared and trained as an ideal mother and wife; she needed to be rescued from social evils but was not conceived of as an independent citizen-subject. Vidysagar fostered an attitude towards women that soon became a part of the nationalist ethos—India was conceived as the motherland and women became "mothers" of the nation, an imagery that invoked redeeming of Bharat Mata's (Mother India) lost status by her patriotic "sons."[51]

This dichotomy in behaviour was also apparent in Vidyasagar's personal life. Renowned for his profound affection and concern for young widows and women, he was instrumental for the passage of the Widow Remarriage Act (1856) by the colonial government. He waged battles against oppressive social practices involving child marriage, marital injustices, arranged marriages, prohibition of education for women, and the horrors and cruelty of young Hindu widowhood.[52] He championed a new conjugality based on mutual consent of two partners and the union of two adult minds and bodies.[53] But in his personal life, he did not enjoy a companionate marriage; neither did he attempt to educate his illiterate wife, Dinamayi Devi (See Figure 2.4). Dinamayi Devi operated behind the scene and spent her life in Vidyasagar's ancestral village taking care

---

[51] Sumathy Ramaswamy, *The Goddess and the Nation: Mapping Mother India* (Durham: Duke University Press, 2010).
[52] Iswarchandra Vidyasagar, "Balyabibaher Dosh" ("Evils of Child Marriage") [1850] in *Vidyasagar Rachanabali* (Kolkata: Tuli Kalam), 678–685.
[53] Sumit Sarkar, "Vidyasagar and Brahmanical Society," in *Writing Social*, 261–262.

of her in-laws.[54] He devoted significant time, energy, and money to conducting widow marriages. Despite stiff opposition from family and society but with consent from his only son Narayan Chandra (See Figure 2.5), he arranged the latter's marriage with a young widow, performing the ceremony with "great eclat."[55] However, later his relationship became so embittered for his son's supposed waywardness that he disowned him publicly. As a son Vidyasagar never challenged his father. By the same token, as a father, he demanded the same uncompromising allegiance from his biological and imagined body of children. Furthermore, Vidyasagar acted somewhat helplessly when his daughter returned home as a young widow. Initially, he imposed upon himself the same restrictions that his daughter was subjected to. But there were no indications of him asking his daughter to refute the stringent social customs that were imposed on her as a young widow.[56] He fought vehemently to end unjust practices afflicting the widows; was instrumental in bringing about the legislation for widow remarriage (1856); and advocated a number of reforms to improve their lot—but he desisted from implementing any of those reforms in his closest quarters.

As scholars pointed out, Vidyasagar had to negotiate with native society and the constraints of colonial government to attain his ends. As an important official in colonial administration, Vidyasagar had the active support as well as restrictions of a foreign government; as a key representative of the Bengali intelligentsia, he could not afford to alienate the backing of the Brahmanical society to which he belonged. The intense pressures from both sides coloured his stance. My purpose of culling these contradictory evidence from his life is not just to expose his inconsistencies but to bring to the fore the complex matrix in which he operated. A highly respected dignitary in colonial administration, Vidyasagar, nonetheless, was in a subordinate position to British state officials. Throughout his life he pushed back and reacted sharply to racial and other forms of discrimination practiced by the colonial government. His pedagogical texts registered a counter-hegemonic move by bringing to the fore native parents and championing their authority over modern subjects. Deeply reflexive

---

[54] Sumit Sarkar, "Vidyasagar and Brahmanical Society," 277.
[55] Subal Chandra Mitra, *Isvar Chandra Vidyasagar: A Story of His Life and Works* (Kolkata: New Bengal Press), 535.
[56] Indramitra, *Isvar Chandra Vidyasagar*, 393.

of his present predicament, Vidyasagar's agentiality involved invoking values that were intrinsic to his native culture. His renewed emphasis on morality poised his readers, an imaginary body of children, for a better future. Children became the enablers to stake his claim for native subjects as parents (read fathers). But a gap remained between his vision as a reformer and his everyday practice as a biological father.

The Post-Vidyasagar Era: Native Literary Leadership in Periodicals for Children

"In our wretched country not too many people think about the worthiness of knowledge and building characters of *boys and girls* ... To fulfill that objective *Sakha* is being born"[57] (emphasis mine). This proclamation by the editor of a children's magazine encapsulates a major concern of the Indian literati in late nineteenth-century India. In contrast to Vidyasagar's gender bias, several editors and authors of early children's periodicals tended to include both girls and boys as their audience. The native writers in the post-Vidyasagar era privileged children as agents of change. Their preoccupation with the new generation embodied the moral guardianship characteristic of responsible fathers. Inspired by Europe and early missionary activities yet intending to go beyond Western influence, children's periodicals, a new literary genre in late nineteenth-century Bengal, became the major vehicle for articulating an alternate pedagogical vision of the putative fathers.[58] Between 1818 and 1900 no less than fifty Bengali periodicals were published for children.[59] According to Krishna Kumar, for children in colonial times a "more vital education, as a process of reconstructing worthwhile knowledge and disseminating it, was taking place under the auspices of magazines and literature."[60]

---

[57] From the children's magazine *Sakha*. Cited in Bani Basu, *Bangla Shishusahitya*, p. "thirty-four" of preface. (The preface spells out the page numbers.)

[58] For a more detailed study of children's literature see my "Children's Literature in Nineteenth-Century India: Some Reflections and Thoughts," in *Stories for Children, Histories of Childhood/Histoires d'enfant, histoires d'enfance*, vol. 2, GRAAT Journal 36, eds. Rosie Findlay and Sébastien Salbayre (Tours: Presses universitaires François-Rabelais, 2017), 337–351; now in open access at http://books.openedition.org/pufr/4974?lang=en.

[59] Khagendranath Mitra, *Shatabdir Shishu-Sahitya*, 3.

[60] Kumar, *Political Agenda of Education*, 133.

Bengali authors in this period balanced between the missionary goals of the British editors of the earlier publications, such as those of the School Book Society, and their wish to preserve an arena in which their own authority remained paramount.[61] The periodicals launched by the Indian leaders attempted to expand the mind of their readers by acquainting them with the history and culture of the larger world. The writers, while conforming to the basic models of the periodicals launched by the missionaries, envisioned its readers as "citizens of the world" and not "model subjects of the British Empire." From the last quarter of the nineteenth century, as the colonial government tightened its control and surveillance over educational curriculum of Indian schools, the native literati, predominantly Brahmos, launched magazines devoted exclusively to children.[62] Their intended audience, were not distinguished along class, caste, or religious lines, although the major consumers were children of the educated literati, many of whom were Brahmos. No wonder, literary critics, who made a distinction between school texts and children's literature, identified the decade of the 1890s as the period marking the beginning of children's literature in Bengali.[63] Again, this was the decade of intense debates on issues related to child marriage and the age of consent. An imaginary child was therefore central in the minds of reformers-writers. By heralding the field of children's literature, the leaders and ideologues played an avant-garde role in mobilizing children and imparting to them their desired form of education.[64] A new child addressed via a new literary genre enabled them to reclaim their own sovereign subjecthood that suffered humiliation under colonial domination and critique. This

---

[61] Kumar, *Political Agenda of Education*. For elaboration of this point and also for the social significance of magazines in molding children, see Gautam Chando Roy, "Science for Children in a Colonial Context: Bengali Juvenile Magazines, 1883–1923," *British Journal of History of Science*, Themes 3 (2018): 43–72.

[62] For children's magazines in Hindi see Nandini Chandra, *The Classic Popular: Amar Chitra Katha, 1907–1967* (Delhi: Yoda Press, 2008); Shobhna Nijhwan, *Women and Girls in the Hindi Public Sphere: Periodical Literature in Colonial North India* (New Delhi: Oxford University Press, 2012); "Hindi Children's Journals and Nationalist Discourse (1910–1930)," *Economic and Political Weekly* 39, no. 33 (2004): 3723–3729; Ruby Lal, "Recasting the Women's Question: The Girl-Child/Woman in the Colonial Encounter," *Interventions* 10, no. 3 (2008): 321–339; Nivedita Sen, *Family, School, and Nation: The Child and the Literary Constructions in 20th-Century Bengal* (Delhi: Routledge, 2015).

[63] Khagendranath Mitra, *Shatabdir Shishu-sahitya*; Hatcher, *Idioms of Improvement*.

[64] For more on children's literature see Supriya Goswami, *Colonial India in Children's Literature* (New York: Routledge, 2012).

juvenile audience—the future generation—the fathers hoped, trained differently, would be free from such kind of subordination.

The thrust of the native publications was to inculcate among their readers a desire to learn and to develop a sense of responsibility towards their own country (*swadesh*). The first monthly for youth *Gnanodoy* (*Dawn of Knowledge*, 1831),[65] edited by Krishnadhan Mitra, was emphatic about the younger generation's *vidyotparjon* or acquisition of knowledge, an emphasis we noticed in Vidyasagar's primer as well.[66] In its twenty issues, *Gnanodoy* covered ethics, history, and geography; traced Indian history from antiquity; and chronicled the rise and fall of Muslim rule in the subcontinent. But more importantly, it included histories of China, Greece, and Rome thus placing India on par with other ancient empires. *Abodhbandhu* (*Friends of the Innocent*, 1866), edited by a medical doctor Jogendranath Ghosh and an eminent poet and writer Biharilal Chakrabarty, marked a distinct departure from the missionary or the colonial efforts. Suffused with a spirit of patriotism, *Abodhbandhu* wanted to build children's character, provide them with entertainment, and help the country.[67] The mission statement was conveyed through a poem, marking the first issue of the magazine:

> *Swadesh-er je prokare hote pare hit*
> *Sadhyamoto chesta kora sobar uchit.*
> *Til somo heno kaaj Jodi mon-e loy,*
> *Tothacho nirosto thaka, jukti-jukto noi;*
> *Ki jani sohosro majhe jodi kono jon*
> *Samanya shey kshudro karje upokrito hon.*[68]

---

[65] *Gnanodoy* referred to its readers as *juba-byaktigon*, meaning the youth.
[66] The School Book Society showed its encouragement to *Gnanodoy's* editor Krishnadhan Mitra by purchasing fifty copies of this magazine with the purpose of distributing them among its most meritorious students. Khagendranath Mitra, "Patrika Prasanga: Unobingsha Satabdi 1818–1900," in *Shatabdir Shishu-Sahitya 1818–1918* (Kolkata: Monomohan Mukherjee, 1999 [1958]), 9.
[67] The famous poet, educator, and visionary Rabindranath Tagore, in his childhood, first got a taste of vernacular poetry and French novels translated into Bengali from the pages of *Abodhbandhu*.
[68] *Abodhbandhu* (*Friends of the Innocent*), a monthly periodical, eds. Jogendranath Ghosh and Biharilal Chakrabarty, vol. 1, no. 1 (Falgun, 1273 B.S. [1866]). *Abodhbandhu* also published articles on poor condition of women and Indian family life that reflected a critical evaluation of the social system. But it also alluded to its fleeting audience who were not just children.

> If there's a way one's own country can be helped
> One must try to do one's best
> If in one's mind a small task is conceived
> It is not justified to take a backseat
> It is possible, perhaps one in a thousand
> Will benefit from that small deed.

The twin objectives of enlightening children's minds and preparing them for a future were secured through fostering patriotism and opening the floodgate of knowledge that bridged the local and the global through introduction to new disciplines and tidings of the world. The training in this new direction was deeply anchored in family values rooted in respect towards one's own parents. The picture, however, gets more complicated when we foreground the agentiality of the editors-fathers and probe their interiority based upon available public records. An examination of Bengali children's periodicals with a closer attention to the life-worlds of two key Brahmo social reformers, Keshub Chandra Sen and Sivnath Sastri, will make our case clear.

Keshub Chandra Sen (1838–1884), the Pioneer of Children's Magazine

One of the chief exponents and a pioneer of magazines devoted *exclusively* to children was the Brahmo leader and social reformer Keshub Chandra Sen (See Figures 2.6 and 2.7),), widely known for his crusade against oppressive social norms, particularly those related to women.[69] Inspired by Protestant Christian virtues and with a zeal for reformed Hinduism, Keshub Sen was held dearly both by the progressive Bengalis in Calcutta and the British in London.[70] Sen's public career as a social and religious reformer overshadowed his engagement with children

---

[69] For historical studies of Keshub Sen, see John A. Stevens, *Keshab: Bengal's Forgotten Prophet* (London: Hurst Publishers, 2017); Meredith Borthwick, *Keshub Chunder Sen: A Search for Cultural Synthesis* (Kolkata: Minerva Publishers, 1977).

[70] Sen's popularity in England could be gleaned from the title of one of his lectures: "The living God in England and India: a sermon preached by Baboo Keshub Chunder Sen, in Mill-Hill Chapel, Leeds, on Sunday August 28th, 1870." For more on his social standing in England, see Stevens, *Keshab: Bengal's Forgotten Prophet*.

"FATHERS" AT THE CROSSROADS 73

Figure 2.6 Keshub Chandra Sen

through educational and institutional reforms. He launched the first fortnightly children's magazine *Balakbandhu* (*Friend of Boys*) in 1878. The title *Balakbandhu* (*Friend of Boys*) could be illusive and raise questions about whether Sen had girls as his audience.[71] It is instructive to note that in Bengali it is customary to use the overarching male gender to subsume

---

[71] The first children's periodical edited by a woman, Jnadanandini Devi, was called *Balak* (*Boys*), and thus likewise evinced the gender bias for its readership. *Balak* came out in 1885 from the illustrious Tagore family of Jorasanko, Calcutta. A family magazine dominated by the writings by Rabindranath Tagore, it covered the same range of topics—science, history, geography, poems, travels, riddles, and plays. The serialized play "Heyali" written by Rabindranath Tagore was perhaps the first play written for children in Bengali. Despite its high quality, *Balak* did not

Figure 2.7 Jaganmohini Devi (Keshub Sen's Wife. Courtesy: Collection of Professor Geraldine Forbes)

females under it. The term *chhelebela* (literally, boyhood) thus extends to both boys and girls.[72] Sen was wedded to the causes of girls, especially their education. He opened a school for girls where he sent his own daughter, Suniti Devi, and invited Mary Carpenter from England to help improve education of Indian girls.[73] Given his predilections, Sen possibly had children of both sexes in his mind as his readers.

Balakbandhu's objective was to disseminate scientific and general knowledge that children would devour with pleasure.[74] Grandson

---

thrive long as a children's magazine; it merged with *Bharati*, also a publication from the Tagore family, and catered more to adult readers.

[72] Women writers like Punyalata Chakrabarty titled their memoirs as *Chhelebelar Dinguli* (*Days of Childhood*, 1958).

[73] Geraldine Forbes, "Education for Women," *Women in Modern India* (Cambridge, UK: Cambridge University Press, 1996), 43.

[74] For alternate genres of Bengali children's literature drawn mostly from indigenous popular culture see Giuseppe Flora, "On Fairy Tales, Intellectuals and Nationalism in Bengal (1880–1920)," *Alla Revista Degli Studi Orientali*, Vol. LXXV, Supplement No. 1 (2002): 7–84.

of the social conservative Ram Comul Sen who was involved with the Calcutta School Book Society in the early nineteenth century, Keshub Sen surpassed his grandfather's zeal for progressive social reforms. He also marked a departure from the moral pedagogy of the earlier writers by introducing within the eight pages of *Balakbandhu* poems, fictions, articles, riddles, and mathematical puzzles that children would enjoy. Humorous and thought-provoking, it invoked morality by inserting a Sanskrit *shloka* in a dialog box. Every issue included a poem written typically by a boy that gave agency to the child. The child-poets were represented by the first and last initials of their names and the school they attended but their age was not mentioned. *Balakbandhu* also published serialized stories. From its twentieth issue it covered "national and foreign news" that included news about children. Its conscious effort to educate its readers in the art of writing "correct" Bengali prose, acknowledged and carried forward Vidyasagar's legacy.[75]

Keshub Sen's paternalism, especially extending over girls, was not just limited to his leadership in the emerging field of children's literature. In collaboration with the colonial government, he was instrumental for the passage of the Marriage Act of 1872, also referred to as the Act III of 1872.[76] The Act III that he initiated, specifically targeting the Brahmo community, designated the specific age of marriage—fourteen for girls and eighteen for boys—and it also aimed to formalize Brahmo marriages. Breaking away from the earlier generation of Brahmo leadership, Sen brought a new dynamism to the religious-cum-social movement by infusing its theology with social activism. He urged the Brahmo leaders to abandon their Hindu caste ties and rituals and allow women in leadership roles. Sen's radicalism already generated a split with the earlier generation of the Brahmos; it was further brought to a head by his complicated involvement in marriage reforms and his own failure to live up to its ideals. The marriage law not only drove a wedge between the Brahmos and the orthodox Hindu community but it also led to a

---

[75] Fortnightly *Balakbandhu* became a monthly from December 15, 1881, but stopped publication shortly thereafter. It came out as a fortnightly again in 1886; in 1891 it started coming out in its new edition. Khagendranath Mitra, *Shishu-Sahitya*, 19.

[76] Rochona Majumdar, *Marriage and Modernity* (Durham, NC: Duke University Press, 2009), 177. For an earlier history of colonial intervention in native marriage practices and its criminalization see Samita Sen, "Offences Against Marriage: Negotiating Customs in Colonial Bengal," in *A Question of Silence: The Sexual Economies of Modern India*, eds. Mary E. John and Janaki Nair (New Delhi: Kali for Women, 1998), 77–110.

break-up within the Brahmo community itself as Sen conducted the marriage of his minor daughter, Suniti Devi (1864–1932, m. 1878).[77] Incidentally, it was the same year when he launched *Balakbandhu*. There may not be a direct correlation between the marriage of his daughter and his initiative to launch the periodical, but it was apparent that matters related to children (boys and girls), their well-being and education, occupied his mind.

The marriage that Keshub Sen conducted between his 13-year old daughter Suniti Devi (See Figure 2.8) and the minor prince of Cooch Behar, Nripendra Narayan (1863–1911), in 1878 was hardly a private affair.[78] It drew national and international attention for Sen's controversial stand and became the single most important event in causing the divisions within the Brahmo Samaj, leading to the foundation of two distinct schools of Brahmoism—the Sadharan Brahmo Samaj led by Sivnath Sastri[79] and the Navabidhan or the New Dispensation spearheaded by Sen. According to Suniti Devi, who recorded a vivid description of the way her marriage was negotiated, the marriage was not the idea of her father. Her father was rather surprised by the repeated insistence of the Government and the representatives of the state of Cooch Behar who urged that the marriage of the prince and Suniti Devi would be most desirable.[80] The state of Cooch Behar was a princely state that came under the close supervision of the British Crown when king Nripendra Narayan, the bridegroom (Sen's son-in-law), was a 10-month-old. He grew up under British protectorate and to salvage the "prince" from the "evil and backward" condition of the state of Cooch Behar, the British

---

[77] For the controversy surrounding Keshub Sen and his daughter's marriage see Majumdar, *Marriage and Modernity*, 185. For a father's responsibility in conducting a daughter's marriage, see Tanika Sarkar, "A Pre-history of Rights: The Age of Consent Debate in Colonial Bengal," in *Hindu Wife, Hindu Nation* (New Delhi: Permanent Black, 2001), 226–249. Aishika Chakraborty, "Contract, Consent, Ceremony: The Brahmo Marriage Reform (1868–1920)," *Journal of History* [Department of History, Jadavpur University, Kolkata], vol. 26 (2008–2009), 1–32..

[78] For the diverse responses the marriage created among different sections in England and India, see John A. Stevens, "Marriage, Duty, and Civilization: Keshab Chandra Sen and the Cuch Behar Controversy in Metropolitan and Colonial Context," *South Asian History and Culture* 7, no. 4 (2016): 401–415.

[79] The name of Sivnath Sastri has been spelt in different ways: Sivanath, Shibnath, Sibnath. I use the "Sivnath" that was used in his autobiography, *Atmacharit*.

[80] The most vivid description of the circumstances leading to the marriage comes from the daughter's autobiography: Sunity Devee, Chapter 3: "My Romance," and Chapter 4: "My Marriage," *The Autobiography of an Indian Princess* (London: J. Murray, 1921), 42–67.

"FATHERS" AT THE CROSSROADS 77

Figure 2.8 Suniti Devi (Daughter of Keshub Chandra Sen)

quickly took charge of educating him. When the British finally decided to send him to England for a short training, the queens, the "mothers" of the prince, urged that they would only permit him to go if he married prior to his departure. The British protectors of the state approached Sen to find a suitable match, "an accomplished wife" for the prince so that the fallen, ignorant state of Cooch Behar, given to polygamy, superstition, intrigue, and oppression, could be salvaged.[81]

The insistence of the paternalistic role of the colonial state and its commitment to protect its princely subjects seemed to have swayed Keshub Sen. Sen defended his action pointing out that he did not initiate the match or the proposal and that he complied with the British request by regarding it as coming from "Providence." Sen claimed that he was not

---

[81] For an incisive reading of British and Indian marriage laws see Nandini Chatterjee, "English Law, Brahmo Marriage, and the Problem of Religious Difference: Civil Marriage Laws in Britain and India," *Comparative Studies in Society and History* 52, no. 3 (2010): 524–552.

coveting the wealth or the social position of the Raja. "As a private man I should not have acted as I have done." He urged that he acted not merely as an individual father but as a "public man," a loyal subject of the British, pressed by the "weighty" interests of a State. Sen definitely saw in the "packaged" proposal of the British the opportunity to spread Brahmoism in a backward state. Also important was his consideration of living up to the ideal of the "manly" gentleman that had been bestowed on him by the British in India and in London. While the critics of Sen questioned his moral rectitude, his defenders set forth a series of justifications in defense of his act. Scholars have offered an array of explanations for Sen's motives, but the crucial point here is the paradox that characterized Sen's public-private life. His action established his authority and prerogative as a father; but it contrasts notably with his identity as a public leader and metaphorical father championing a higher age of marriage and education for girls. Suniti Devi, in her *Autobiography*, voiced a strong defense for her father, but she also noted that she was opposed to marriage at that young age and that she was pulled out of her school to be married to the prince.[82] Furthermore, echoing the sentiment of the time, she indicated that obeying the commands of parents constituted the chief obligation of children. She thus happily agreed with the decision of her father and led a successful married life.

In Between Keshub Chandra Sen and Sivnath Sastri

Notwithstanding the anomalous position of fathers, the period between Keshub Chandra Sen and the other Brahmo leader, Sivnath Sastri, was marked by the significant production of juvenile magazines, which also contained exhortations to parents. Promodacharan Sen, the editor of *Sakha* (*A Male Friend*, 1883) had a fall-out with his father upon his conversion to Brahmoism. But echoing similar sentiments as Vidyasagar did, Sen proclaimed that "*Sakha will carry both the advice of parents*

---

[82] For an extensive account of the marriage and the negotiation process between Keshub Sen and the colonial state, see Devee, *Autobiography of an Indian Princess*.

and impart the education provided by the teacher"[83] (emphasis mine). He combined in *Sakha* the didactism of parents with the pedagogical mission of school-teachers, a conjoined role stressed by other educational leaders like Bhudev Mukhopadhyay as well.[84] With that spirit in mind he ensured that the young readers were made aware of the conditions of peasants, the working classes, and the poorer sections of society. *Sakha's* objective was clear: it would redress the imbalance of colonial education by disseminating knowledge and building "characters of boys and girls," thus explicitly including girls as its subject of reform.[85] *Sakha's* wide readership was evident from the remark of Bankim Chandra Chattopadhyay (1838–1894), the doyen of Bengali literature, who applauded *Sakha's* editor for bringing out a magazine that gave pleasure not only to young boys and girls but to the "grey-haired elderly," as well.[86]

Sakha (See Figure 2.9), was the first most beloved children's periodical in Bengali. Aesthetically distinctive for its high-quality wood-carved illustrations and printing, *Sakha* pioneered in publishing biographies of international leaders, again extending the legacy of Vidyasagar who authored *Charitabali* (*A Collection of Biographies*, 1856) chronicling biographies of important individuals in history. In the debut issue of *Sakha*, Promodacharan Sen authored the first Bengali children's novel, "Bhim-er Kapal" ("The Fate of Bhim"). The novel, serialized over ten subsequent issues, built around a youth called Bhim and his sojourn from rural to urban Bengal, a theme replicating the spatial transition that many middle-class boys experienced at that time.[87]

Emerging in the era of rising anti-colonial sentiments (the Indian National Congress would be founded in 1885), *Sakha* became a vehicle for introducing children to political themes. In the pages of *Sakha* the fathers preached patriotic feelings and not obedience to the Raj. An ardent nationalist, Bipin Chandra Pal (discussed in Chapter 4), also disowned by

---

[83] From the children's magazine *Sakha*. Cited in Bani Basu, *Bangla Shishusahitya*, p. "thirty-four" of preface.
[84] Parna Sengupta, "The Schoolteacher as Modern Father," in *Pedagogy for Religion*, 81–101.
[85] Bani Basu, *Bangla Shishusahitya*, p. "thirty-four" of preface.
[86] Aruna Chattopadhyay, ed., *Sakha, Sakha o Sathi* (Calcutta: Bangabani Printers, 2002), 1.
[87] Promodacharan Sen, "Bhim-er Kapal," *Sakha*, year #1 (January–October 1883); Aruna Chattopadhyay, *Sakha, Sakha o Sathi*, 19–44.

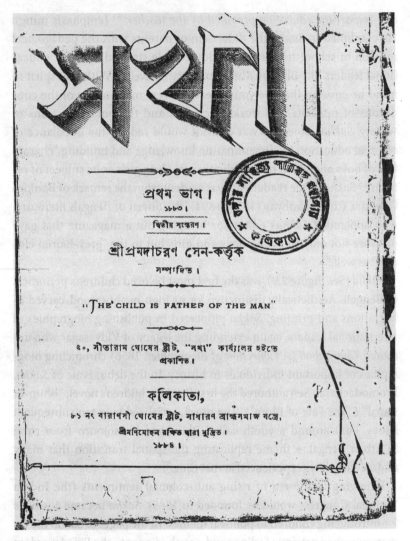

Figure 2.9 Cover page of the magazine *Sakha* [https://digi.ub.uni-heidelberg.de/csss/Sakha/Sakha_Vol_01.pdf]

his father for embracing Brahmoism, brought home to the young readers of *Sakha* the plight of nationalist leaders like Surendranath Banerjee and the political injustices of the colonial government. Bipin Chandra Pal concluded his essay, "Surendra-Babu-r Karabash" ("The Imprisonment of Surendra-Babu"), urging:

Boys and Girls! Please learn to shed a drop of tear for your wretched motherland! One day you will purify the Indian prisons; one day your hardship will end the impoverishment of your country. One day your nation will be proud of you.[88]

Sakha's front cover, stating, "[T]he child is Father of the Man," (See Figure 2.9) delineated the influence of Christianity and the magazine's paternalistic mission conveyed through the metaphor of the father and the child. Moreover, the editors regretted that the young readers were so encumbered by school curriculum that they could not do justice to *Sakha*. So, in the second year of *Sakha*, the editors tried to facilitate the readers by laying down strict rules on how to read the magazine.[89] They organized the content thematically according to the order of importance and insisted that the young readers should read each of the items time and again. *Sakha's* table of contents offered a variety of topics and were listed as follows:[90]

(i)	Fiction (e.g. "Bhim-er Kapal")
(ii)	Advice (e.g. "Who is Rich?" "Smoking")
(iii)	Descriptions (e.g. White Bear)
(iv)	New Knowledge about Science (e.g. presented as "Thakurdada-r Galpa" or "Grandfather's Tales")
(v)	Biographies (e.g. David Hare, Keshub Chandra Sen)
(vi)	Poems
(vii)	Riddles/Puzzles
(viii)	Miscellaneous

The variety of topics fuelled children's imagination; yet, instructions on how to read the magazine intended to control the minds of its readers. A modern father, in his capacity as a writer, reformer, or parent, only allowed limited freedom for his offspring. As we witnessed, Iswarchandra Vidyasagar and Keshub Sen, both votaries of individual freedom and

---

[88] Bipin Chandra Pal, "Surendra-Babu-r Karabash," *Sakha*, year #6, June 1886, 88–91. Aruna Chattopadhyay, *Sakha, Sakha o Sathi*, 69–72.
[89] Khagendranath Mitra, 3–4.
[90] Aruna Chattopadhyay, *Sakha, Sakha o Sathi*, 276–277.

reason, were not only compromised as fathers but the "independence" they granted their children was highly restrained.

Sakha entered a new phase with the premature death of its 26-year-old editor Promodacharan Sen in 1885. In 1894, *Sakha* merged with another leading periodical, *Sathi* (*Companion*) edited by Bhubanmohan Ray and came to be known as *Sakha o Sathi* (*Friend and Companion*). From its inception in 1893, *Sathi* took a bold and distinctive stand. Perhaps as a backlash against authoritarian patriarchs, Jogindranath Sarkar, one of *Sathi's* principal contributors, hailed the readers as "brothers and sisters" and announced *Sathi's* non-didactic stance. Addressing its readers as siblings and not children could be in tandem with the rising sentiment against the authoritarian, paternalistic state as well. Shorn of any advisory motives it claimed *not* (emphasis mine) to have "a cane" or "rebuke" for children. *Sathi's* objective was pure joy.[91] By consciously denying itself the moral high ground, *Sathi* introduced an element of lightness and joy in children's literature.[92] This element of joy would be carried forward by *Mukul*, another leading children's magazine under the aegis of the eminent social reformer, Sivnath Sastri. Joy as a goal of education is a theme we will revisit with Chapter 5's discussion of Rabindranath Tagore.

Sivnath Sastri and the Blossoming of Children's Literature

The most successful and long-lasting children's magazine in the last decade of the nineteenth century, *Mukul* (1895) flourished under the editorship of Sivnath Sastri (also known as Sivanath, Shibnath, or Sibnath; 1847–1919) a Brahmo leader dedicated to alleviating societal wrongs. *Mukul* meaning *Bud*, to bloom, represented the "blossom of knowledge,

---

[91] Bani Basu, *Bangla Shishusahitya*, p. "thirty-five" of preface. For a detailed study of *Sakha*, *Sakha o Sathi*, see Aruna Chattopadhyay, *Sakha, Sakha o Sathi*. It is important to note that *Sakha o Sathi* was also the first children's magazine to introduce advertisements in its pages.

[92] It was in *Sakha* and then in *Sakha o Sathi* that most of the later writers for children—Upendrakishore Raychaudhuri, Trailokyanath Mukhopadhyay, Dwijendranath Basu, Nabakrishna Bhattacharya, Bipin Chandra Pal, Bhubanmohan Ray, Jogindranath Sarkar, Ramendrasundar Tribedi, Sivanath Sastri, and women writers like Hemlata Debi—made their debut in writing.

"FATHERS" AT THE CROSSROADS 83

of love, of human flowers" and attracted contributions from all leading intellectuals of the period—Rabindranath Tagore, Jagadish Chandra Bose, Ramananda Chattopadhyay, Ramesh Chandra Dutta, Ramendrasundar Tribedi, among others.[93] The latter's contribution to *Mukul* attested to their commitment to issues related to a younger generation. Sivnath Sastri from the outset defined the readership of *Mukul*: "*Mukul* is not really meant for young children. It is meant for the age-group who are between eight–nine and sixteen–seventeen," clearly suggesting the burgeoning youth population.[94]

Mukul displayed a unique trend for its time by privileging the agency of its young readers while following the same genres and style of its predecessors. As editor, Sivnath Sastri (See Figures 2.10 and 2.11) engaged with its readers by responding to their questions with wit and humour. *Mukul*, like *Balakbandhu*, also published children's works. In its second year (*Jaishtha* issue), *Mukul* published a poem called *Nodi* (*River*) by an eight-year-old boy. This boy was none other than the maestro of children's literature in Bengali, Sukumar Ray, the son of Upendrakishore and the father of the famous film-maker Satyajit Ray, who would launch Bengal's most outstanding children's magazine *Sandesh* in 1913.[95] Like *Sakha*, *Mukul* also earned praise from contemporary newspapers. *Indian Mirror* hailed *Mukul* as "an exceedingly nice little paper, full of interesting and instructive subjects" modelled along the lines of *Boy's Own Annual*, an annual compendium of *The Boy's Own Paper* (1879–1967), a story-paper published by Religious Tract Society in England to instil Christian morals among teenage boys. For the first time for a children's magazine, *Mukul* changed its cover design from time to time.[96] The cover illustrations

---

[93] Bani Basu, *Bangla Shishusahitya*, p. "thirty-five" of preface.
[94] There were a few writers like Jogindranath Sarkar and Nabakrishna Bhattacharya who wrote poems for the younger age-group.
[95] For more on Sukumar Ray and his family see Chandok Sengoopta, *The Rays Before Satyajit: Creativity and Modernity in Colonial India* (New Delhi: Oxford University Press, 2016); Supriya Goswami, "Trivializing Empire: The Topsy-Turvy World of Upendrakishore Ray and Sukumar Ray," in *Colonial India in Children's Literature* (New York: Routledge, 2012), 135–168; Emily K. Bloch, *Making Sense of Nonsense: A Contextual Study of the Art of Sukumar Ray* (Ph.D. dissertation, University of Chicago, 2013); "Questions of Identity in the Nonsense Literature of Sukumar Ray," in *Identities: Local and Global*, eds. Kailash C. Baral and Prafulla C. Kar (Delhi: Pencraft International, 2003), 249.
[96] For cover illustrations of *Mukul*, go to http://www.bengalichildrensbooks.in/Mukul.php (accessed on September 9, 2017).

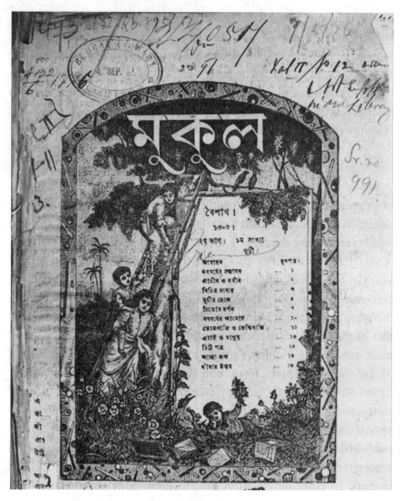

Figure 2.10   Cover page of the magazine *Mukul* [http://www.bengalichildrensbooks.in/Mukul.php]

included both boys and girls signalling a more inclusive audience. More interestingly, several of the covers had the picture of Queen Victoria as the empress, suggesting both loyalty to the Crown and the subaltern status of the magazine editors[97] (See Figure 2.12).

---

[97] A few other periodicals, such as *Anjali* (1898), *Kusum* (1898), and *Prakriti* (1900) came out after *Mukul*. *Prakriti*, carrying the subtitle "under the supervision of students" was particularly important for being the first children's magazine to include works by Bengali Muslims, like Mojammel Haq and Abdul Karim. Khagendranath Mitra, *Shatabdir Shishu-sahitya*, 37.

"FATHERS" AT THE CROSSROADS   85

Figure 2.11 Sivnath Sastri

Sivnath Sastri was distinctive in his editorship of *Mukul*. Not only did he clearly define his youth audience but as evident from the cover illustrations, he also targeted girls as well as boys. Illustrations of Queen Victoria and children paying their homage to her alluded to the political culture of the time: pictures of the Queen Mother often appeared in adult, especially women's, magazines as well; the goal of incipient nationalism was to build bold, patriotic citizens who were still loyal subjects of the British empire and not necessarily members of an "independent" nation-state. Sastri, as the editor, was not troubled by his subaltern status to the Queen Mother, but he objected to wrongful subordination of native subjects by colonial officials.[98] Even when he was a young student Sastri had protested such wrongful treatment.[99] The magazine provided him a cognitive space to rear righteous citizens outside the control of the colonial state.

---

[98] The idea of India as an independent nation-state free from colonial rule would emerge in the course of 1930s.

[99] Sastri noted in his autobiography an interesting episode of him not yielding to the wrongful command of his school inspector, Mr. Woodrow, to take off his shoes. Sivnath Sastri,

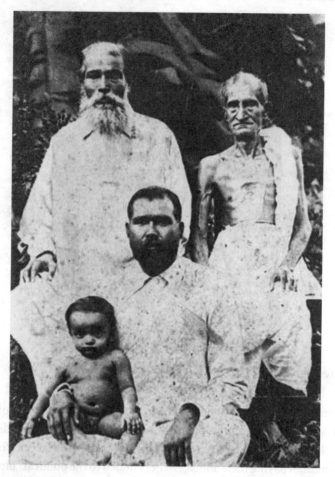

Figure 2.12 Four Generations of the Sastris (Courtesy: Archives of the Centre for Studies in Social Sciences, Kolkata)

Sastri was not simply a literary activist. He was a leader and the official biographer of the Brahmo movement who originally followed Sen but later became his sharpest critic following the controversy surrounding the marriage of Sen's daughter. A student of Vidyasagar's in Sanskrit College, Sastri was deeply committed to social causes; held important administrative positions in colonial schools; gave up government service

Atmacarit Autobiography of Sivnath Sastri, trans. Suniti Devi, ed. Nisith R. Ray (Kolkata: Rddhi India, 1988), 44–45.

to devote himself full-time to organize the Sadharon Brahmo Samaj; and was instrumental in establishing a girls' school, the Brahmo Balika Shikshalaya, where he sent his daughters for education. He did not envision girls' education as different from boys, a point over which he had a difference of opinion with Keshab Chandra Sen, originally his mentor, who prescribed a very specific kind of education for women, something we will discuss in Chapter 4. Sastri was an extremely reputable reformer and an eloquent preacher of the Brahmo religion, a person who lived "a new kind of intensely modern life." His life, as Sudipta Kaviraj noted, was both "saintly" and "rationalistically modern."[100]

Sastri was always favourably disposed towards girls—as a child and as an adult he deeply cared for his sisters; he mourned the death of his younger sister Unmadini until his own end. Growing up he also cared for young girls close to his age-group in his neighbourhood.[101] Yet Sastri harboured a deep inconsistency in his personal life. To respect *pitriajna*, the command of his father, he was compelled to undergo a second marriage under very peculiar circumstances. Following the custom of his high-caste community, Sastri was first married at age 13 to Prosonnomoyee, a girl of comparable high-caste status but of less "erudite reputation."[102] This became a source of conflict within his family, particularly for Sastri's father. Following a trivial incident, the father, in Sastri's absence, decided to send the wife back to her natal family and persuaded Sastri to marry again. Sastri, despite much protest and resentment, yielded to his father's command and married Birajmohini, his second wife, "sometime in 1865."[103] By Sastri's admission, "for want of acquaintance" he did not develop "any attachment" to his first wife; but he "felt deeply for her" as he could see a "great injustice was being done to her for some paltry offence of her people." Sastri further explained, "I was old enough to form a strong opinion against bigamy but I was so used to unquestioning obedience to my father that I did not dare to speak out my mind to him."[104]

---

[100] Sudipta Kaviraj, "The Invention of Private Life: A Reading of Sibnath Sastri's *Autobiography*," in *Telling Lives in India: Biography, Autobiography, and Life History*, eds. David Arnold and Stuart Blackburn (Bloomington: Indiana University Press, 2005), 85.
[101] Sastri, *Atmacharit*, 33.
[102] Sastri, *Atmacharit*, 91.
[103] Sastri, *Atmacharit*, 48.
[104] Sastri, *Atmacharit*, 47.

Struck with remorse, Sastri's "heart bled to think that an innocent girl was drawn into the whirlpool to live a life of misery forever."[105] But he was powerless before his father.

Repentant and disturbed, Sastri moved closer to the Brahmo movement and embraced it whole-heartedly in 1869 to address social injustices, such as polygamy and lack of girls' education. After joining the Brahmo Samaj, Sastri brought back his first wife into his family. Since he never lived with his second wife and the marriage was not consummated, he tried to arrange a remarriage for 14-year-old Birajmohini, but the latter strongly resisted such a proposal. After she lost her parents, she finally came to live with Sastri in 1872 but the two never cohabited in the same house until the death of Prosonnomoyee, Sastri's first wife.[106] Sastri recorded his uneasiness with his bigamous status and the way he dealt with the problematic situation. The father–son relationship that demanded absolute obedience and conformity soon exploded as his father disowned Sastri following his official conversion to Brahmoism. As Sastri noted, for eighteen to nineteen years his father did not speak with him or see his face.[107] These ruptures in filial relationship concerning conversion to Brahmoism were not uncommon among the educated middle class in late colonial Bengal.[108]

Sastri was himself an affectionate father. As a modern father he noted the birth of his five children: four daughters—Hemlata (1868. See Figure 2.13), Tarangini (1870), Suhasini (1873), youngest Sarojini who died in 1877—and son Priyanath (1871). However, he never directly mentioned with which wife he had these children. It was only when reporting the ailing health of his first wife that he mentioned the pre-mature birth of their second daughter, Tarangini. Like a good husband, Sastri was all praise for his first wife, Prosonnomoyee. In a collection of essays reminiscing about people who he admired most and who influenced his life, Sastri fondly mentioned both his father and his first wife, Prosonnomoyee.[109]

---

[105] Sastri, *Atmacharit*, 48.
[106] Sastri, *Atmacharit*, 88.
[107] Sastri, *Atmacharit*, 74.
[108] Falling out with fathers upon conversion to Brahmosim and loosing inheritance were common in colonial Bengal. Rammohun Roy, the founder of the Brahmo movement, was disowned by his father of all property rights for his conversion to Brahmoism. Other examples will follow in the book. .
[109] Matching his children's date of birth with the period of his co-residence with the two wives could give some indication who the birth-mothers were, but this needs more research and is not really germane to my argument.

Figure 2.13 Hemlata Devi (Daughter of Sivnath Sastri; Courtesy: Collection of Professor Geraldine Forbes)

Sastri's deep allegiance to paternal authority put him in a compromised position in his private life. Acutely aware of the hierarchies that children inhabited and as the "father" of a minority religious community over which he presided, Sastri propagated the agency of the young population. Not only did he address a youth group as opposed to younger children, he published works of the juvenile writers, as an editor responded to their letters, and made them active learners through various types of intellectual involvement. The children in the later Brahmo magazines like *Sakha*, *Sathi*, and *Mukul* were in the driver's seat and more than just subjects of pedagogy that Vidyasagar envisioned.

These contradictory episodes from the lives of nineteenth-century leaders lead to a complicated understanding of the nexus between the dominant patriarchy, social, cultural, family norms, and in some instances, overt or tacit interventions of the colonial state. For our purposes, they underscore the situatedness of *bhadralok* fathers and sons and the maze of hierarchy and subordination that they traversed. It is not a stretch to assume that these anomalies were not specific to the three leaders but were common to other men as well. The instances discussed testify to the unrestricted authority of fathers in conventional and reforming Indian households; simultaneously, they also capture the enigmatic characteristic of the reformers in reconciling their public agenda with private practices.

The location of the Bengali middle-class male was such that he was in a position of authority in one context and in a position of subordination in another. Such a sliding position in familial and extra-familial hierarchies signals something more than their hybridity coalescing the Western modern with indigenous sensibilities.[110] So, how do we connect the ideological production of knowledge in the public realm with the contradictory performativity of father–child relationship in private lives? How do we bridge the gap between the conflicted experiences of the historical actors at home and their dissemination of public knowledge and service? Partha Chatterjee explained that the indigenous elites, subjected to the "rule of colonial difference" and excluded from the decision-making process in the political realm, forged "a new sphere of the private in a domain that was marked by cultural difference: the domain of the "national" was defined as one that was different from the "Western." Rejecting the conception of universal humanity, the new subjectivity of the educated Indians rested on "particularity and difference."[111] Chatterjee's analysis of the new subjectivity of the colonial literati is instructive for understanding the "middleness" of the colonial elites, but he assumed the "home" as monadic units impervious to outside influences. This chapter, in contrast, by paying parallel attention to the apparently irreconcilable private and public, have tried to juxtapose the familial and the political to bring out the permeability of the two.[112] To offer a more variegated picture of elite fathers, I located them at the crossroads of intersecting trajectories: the compelling pressures of community, family, kinship, social and political obligations, and the demands and criticisms of a colonial state.

---

[110] Homi K. Bhaba, *Location of Culture* (New York: Routledge, 1994).
[111] Chatterjee, *The Nation and Its Fragments*, 74–75.
[112] For the lack of boundaries between the familial and the public, see "Introduction," Indrani Chatterjee, ed., *Unfamiliar Relations: Family and History in South Asia* (New Brunswick, NJ: Rutgers University Press, 2004), 35.

The experiences in family life were accompanied by new literary practices like children's literature that vindicated the leaders' struggle with their modern selves. The content and ideas of literary production provided the middle-class fathers with a sense of selves; allowed them to "organize and interpret their world;" and also establish their ideological hegemony.[113]

The contexts of the Bengali/Indian "modern" and its different institutions and practices such as marriage and property rights tend to explain the contradiction that resided in the heart of Indian patriarchy.[114] The leaders were reformers but not revolutionaries. Dipesh Chakrabarty invoked the different cultural norms and rituals that distinguished the "modern" man in India from his European counterparts. In Chakrabarty's example, pre nationalist Indian men's devotion (*bhakti*) towards their fathers and forefathers and their daily ritualistic practices flouted the archetype of the modern Western individual rooted in his property rights. If Lockean ideas of the coming of age of the modern individual was based on emergence of private property and a supposed "death" of the father, "the Bengali desire for a modern patriarchy," Chakrabarty argued, was "predicated on a rejection of the model of the 'possessive individual' of Lockean thought."[115] Chakrabarty thus urged scholars to explore the modern subject in India through their involved histories of competing desires and imaginations rather than "rationalizations" of their "interests and power."[116]

The nineteenth century was by no means the golden age of children's literature in Bengal, but the literary productions for children acted as a palimpsest in which the new concerns of the Bengali fathers were registered. The reform-minded fathers expressed their creative desire to mobilize children as a body of citizenry by expanding their cognitive world and raising their awareness, driving home the need for self-improvement and character-building. Children's journals under native

---

[113] Himani Bannerji, *Inventing Subjects: Studies in Hegemony, Patriarchy and Colonialism* (London: Anthem Press, 2001), 12.
[114] Majumdar, *Marriage and Modernity*, 24; Mytheli Sreenivas, *Wives, Widows, Concubines: The Conjugal Family Ideal in Colonial India* (Delhi: Orient Blackswan, 2009). Tanika Sarkar, *Hindu Wife, Hindu Nation*, 226–249. Eleanor Newbigin, "The Codification of Personal Law and Secular Citizenship: Revisiting the History of Law Reform in Late Colonial India," *Indian Economic and Social History Review* 46, no. 1 (2009): 121–144.
[115] Dipesh Chakrabarty, "Family, Fraternity, and Salaried Labor," in *Provincializing Europe*, 218.
[116] Dipesh Chakrabarty, "Family, Fraternity," 217.

leadership became the early repositories of nationalist ideas and sentiments, as evident in the writings of Bipin Chandra Pal and others. Furthermore, the literary movement also aimed to refine and modify the Bengali language, cleansing it of its rustic vulgarity. In the early twentieth century children's periodicals in Bengali reached its zenith with the publication of *Sandesh* (1913) edited by Sukumar Ray, who first wrote in the pages of *Sakha*.

Conclusion

Located at the crossroads of intersecting cultures and practices, educated Bengali fathers inaugurated a field of vernacular literature, especially for children, made possible by the new print culture. Literature, particularly in the context of Bengal, was crucial for the understanding of modernity because it dealt with experience. As Sudipta Kaviraj asserted, while history or standard social theory approach experiences from outside, through aggregate processes, "literary works explore them from inside," capturing "how it feels to live when modern history happens."[117] I argue that the hegemonic aspirations of the *bhadralok* fathers could be mapped along the burgeoning field of imaginary literature that targeted a larger linguistic and cultural community of the new generation. As major interlocutors they assumed the role of moral guardians for an incipient nation but often failed to inculcate the same sense of morality in their own children. Vidyasagar, after all, rejected his son for "waywardness" and that suggests that he was unsuccessful in arousing in him the sense of morality he professed for others. Gandhi, as we will see later, also had the same struggle with his eldest son.

Specific moments of fathers and children displaying authority and subalternity, anger, ambiguity, subordination, on the one hand, and taking on leadership roles in a new public culture, on the other, add another dimension to the question of colonial masculinity that we will explore further in the subsequent chapters. For colonial masculinity need not always

---

[117] Sudipta Kaviraj, *The Invention of Private Life: Literature and Ideas* (New York: Columbia University Press, 2015), 4.

be studied in agreement or conflict with the colonial state played out in the public arena. Ideas and practices of paternity also acted as the site for assertion of manhood that diffused the interference of the colonial state. Strengthening one's body, nurturing a martial culture, or acquiring the knowledge of English as a language of power were not the only means for Indian men to respond to the colonial critique.[118] The ideals of masculinity, as contemporary thinkers like Bankim Chandra Chattopadhyay proclaimed, rested on "self-respect, justice, ethical conduct, responsibility, and enlightened leadership,"[119] all of which were articulated in the pages of the children's periodicals. Masculinity was defined in everyday practices, in important decision-making for children and family, and in disseminating the native literati's "education of desire."[120] The education that the Bengali fathers promoted through new literature invoked a new subjectivity for their readers and championed them as harbingers of a new nation, a process akin to the role of children's literature for the Victorian middle class.[121] But instead of scaling child-father relationship only in terms of distance, intimacy, protection, provision, and tyranny,[122] I trace the agency and agentiality of Bengali middle-class men as fathers

---

[118] Sikata Banerjee and Subho Basu, "The Quest for Manhood: Masculine Hinduism and Nation in Bengal," *Comparative Studies of South Asia, Africa and Middle East* 26, no. 3 (2006): 476–490; Shefali Chandra, "Mimicry, Masculinity, and the Mystique of Indian English: Western India, 1870–1900," *Journal of Asian Studies* 68, no. 1 (February 2009): 199–225; Indira Chowdhury, *The Fragile Hero and Virile History* (Delhi: Oxford University Press, 2001); John Rosselli, "The Self Image of Effeteness: Physical Education and Nationalism in Nineteenth-Century Bengal," *Past and Present* 86 (1980): 121–148; Shefali Chandra, *The Sexual Life of English: Languages of Castes and Desire in Colonial India* (Durham, NC: Duke University Press, 2012).
[119] Partha Chatterjee, *Nation and Its Fragments*, 71.
[120] The expression "education of desire" has gained prominence after Ann Laura Stoler's book, *Race and the Education of Desire: Foucault's History of Sexuality and the Colonial Order of Things* (Durham, NC: Duke University Press, 1995). Stoler invoked Michel Foucault's notion of desire as "embodying productive and generative properties" in tracing how sexual desire was incited by regulatory discourses of the Dutch colonizers in the Indies. Stoler borrowed from Nancy Armstrong's ideas of "desire" for eighteenth- and nineteenth-century Britain. Armstrong discussed British middle class's desire for education, their "programs for cultivating the heart" of those "who were to embody the triumph of middle-class culture." Stoler, *Race and the Education of Desire*, 109. I am using the expression after Armstrong. Nancy Armstrong, *Desire and Domestic Fiction: A Political History of the Novel* (London: Oxford University Press, 1987), 15.
[121] For fathers as educators in nineteenth-century England, see Valerie Sanders, "'What do you want to know about next?' Charles Kingsley's Model of Educational Fatherhood," in *Gender and Fatherhood in the Nineteenth Century*, eds. Trev Lynn Broughton and Helen Rogers (London: Palgrave Macmillan, 2007).
[122] John Tosh, "Father and Child," in *A Man's Place: Masculinity and the Middle-Class Home in Victorian England* (New Haven: Yale University Press, 2007), 79–101.

to their own children and as metaphorical fathers through their pedagogical endeavours beyond the confines of their homes.

Straddling an interlocking relationship of subalternity and dominance, the patriarchs displayed the ambivalence and contradiction that riddled the life of modern fathers and sons. The subjects of Bengali modernity engaged in "multiple and noncommensurable practices" that were "distinctly nonmodern by standards of modern political thought."[123] The adjacency of the private–public worlds of these men underscores the continuum between the home and the world—the compromised location of sons and fathers within the multigenerational extended family were concurrent with their zeal to become moral guardians to educate children in an alternate pedagogy different from that of the colonial state and academic institutions.

What is significant in this literature, running parallel to the dominant discourse on women, is reclaiming children as valid subjects. The production of children's magazines acknowledged children as agents, agents who read, do puzzles, and cajole their parents into buying the magazine for them. The native champions of children's literature were none other than the reformist leaders who were also the architects of the "new woman," a "new family," and the "new nation." In their discourse on family and women, children played an equally significant role. Just as the modern patriarchy subjected their women to new ideological parameters, for children too they granted limited autonomy: children representing the new citizenry were subjected to a "restrained freedom" and they were compelled to adhere to the strict disciplinary regime and norms of the patriarchal family.[124]

The vignettes of private lives and the public literary career of the leaders demonstrated the intersections of macro-political forces and everyday practices that reformers and writers were negotiating, experiences that shaped their masculine and fatherly identities, an aspect that we will explore more in depth in the subsequent chapters. Paternalistic masculinity was manifest through owning responsibilities and charting an imaginary territory of pedagogy and literature. But masculinity in the form

[123] Dipesh Chakrabarty, "Birth of the Subject," in *Provincializing Europe*, 144.
[124] Satadru Sen, "Remembering Robi," in *Traces of Empire: India, America, and Postcolonial Cultures: Essays and Criticism* (Delhi: Primus Books, 2014), 58–74.

of asserting one's will was always compromised and controlled by elderly family members, especially fathers. Fatherhood as a process of manhood in colonial India involved not just declaration of authority; it also included subordination to various familial and extra-familial forces, as well. The process of rethinking a new culture of childhood and fatherhood by Indian men was fraught with tensions and challenges from colonial mediations and familial interventions. The nineteenth-century fathers thus need to be conceptualized in their different subject positions with which non-bourgeois, non-individualistic practices of subjectivity intersected.[125] The inconsistencies manifested not only in personal lives but also in the literary outpourings, which despite their best efforts to address both girls and boys, remained gendered at the end.

I have explored Vidyasagar, Sen, and Sastri as representative examples to make a much wider claim: these nineteenth-century leaders, with their failings and limitations, navigated a difficult terrain to lay the foundation of the nationalist movement and a robust field of literature, both of which gathered significant momentum in the early years of the twentieth century. As visionaries and reformers, they were crucial for shaping the minds of the future generation. By infusing the literary career of these "founding" fathers with their personal details, this chapter has offered a more nuanced understanding of the "vicissitude of nineteenth-century fatherhood," as Broughton and Rogers have pointed out in a different context.[126] Instead of looking at literary history and familial experiences in terms of collaboration and resistance, this chapter highlighted the simultaneity of constantly negotiated and fractured experiences in a localized, here familial, trajectory and the specific cultural conjuncture that defined the contradictory modern of colonized subjects as fathers.

---

[125] Sen, "Remembering Robi."
[126] Trev Lynn Broughton and Helen Rogers, "Introduction," in *Gender and Fatherhood in the Nineteenth Century*, eds. Broughton and Rogers (London: Palgrave Macmillan, 2007), 20.

3
Fathers in a Motherland
Children as Social Imaginaries in the Scientific Literature of Nineteenth-Century Bengal

There is indeed a close relationship between body and mind. If the mind is not as healthy and fit as the body, there is no sound health. Control of mind is as necessary as rejection of unrestricted diet, cleanliness of body, and tidiness of clothes you wear.... Cleanliness (*porichhonnota*) of mind is absolutely necessary like a clean body, it is as essential as noble thoughts and right diet.

Swasthya, 1899[1]

... so that girls and boys can extend their knowledge as they read their periodicals as part of their games or even as story books; *so that the youth can put aside sensually exciting texts and take interest in useful things, so that the aged can engage in serene discussion of good things ...*

Editor Rajendralal Mitra, *Bibidhartha-Sangraha*[2]

The fatherly concern for "*santaner charitra gathan*" or building the character of children stressed a new moral order encompassing proper training of mind and body crucial for building a robust national culture.[3] The emphasis on filial piety and patriotism in the juvenile literature that we traced in the previous chapter was supplemented by an urgency on

---

[1] *Swasthya (Health)* 2, no. 6 (1305 B.S. [1898]): 145. The title page of *Swasthya* read as follows: "A Bengali Monthly Journal of Health and Sanitation (in English), Edited by D.D. Gupta, M.B. *Late Civil Surgeon, Kuch-Behar.*" The italics were in the original. The journal was published from Kolkata by Victoria Press. It cost Re. 1.00.

[2] *Bibidhartha-Sangraha*, 1851. Cited in Bose, *Health and Society in Bengal*, 15.

[3] In 1912 Satischandra Chakrabarti wrote a pedagogical text on formation of characters of children called *Santaner Charitra Gathan*. For an extensive discussion of this influential text see Pradip Kumar Bose, "Sons of the Nation: Child Rearing in the New Family," in *Texts of Power*, ed. Partha Chatterjee (Minneapolis: University of Minnesota, 1995), 118–144.

Fathers in a Motherland. Swapna M. Banerjee, Oxford University Press. © Oxford University Press India 2022. DOI: 10.1093/oso/9789391050245.003.0003

bodily care, health, and character. Working from a position that Indian children were suffering from a lack of physical and psychological well-being, Bengali professionals trained in medicine and other scientific fields attributed the decline to a variety of natural and societal causes.[4] As a remedy they advocated purity of mind, strong body, controlled diet, and cleanliness.

Interestingly, this emphasis on children's education and character strongly resonated the ideas expressed in John Locke's *Thoughts Concerning Human Education* (1692). Locke proclaimed: "A sound mind in a sound body, is a short, but full description of a happy state in this world. He that has these two, has little more to wish for." He further stated: "I imagine the minds of children as easily turn'd this or that way, as water it self: and though this be the principal part, and our main care should be about the inside, yet the clay-cottage is not to be neglected." Finally, his advice: "The consideration I shall here have of health, shall be, not what a physician ought to do with a sick and crazy child; but what the parents, without the help of physick, should do for the preservation and improvement of an healthy, or at least not sickly constitution in their children. And this perhaps might be all dispatch'd in this one short rule, viz. *That gentlemen should use their children, as the honest farmers and substantial yeomen do theirs*."[5] (emphasis mine) Although there is no direct evidence whether the nineteenth-century Bengali writers were "deriving" their thoughts from seventeenth-century Locke's dictum, the scientific literature published between 1880 and 1900 evince the early efforts of the

---

[4] For more on the growing literature on science, medicine, and race in colonial India, see David Arnold, *Colonizing the Body: State, Medicine, and Epidemic Disease in Nineteenth-Century India* (Berkeley: University of California Press, 1993); Rachel Berger, *Ayurveda Made Modern: Political Histories of Indigenous Medicine in North India, 1900–1955* (London: Palgrave Macmillan, 2013); Irfan Habib and Dhruv Raina, eds., *Social History of Science in Colonial India* (Delhi: Oxford University Press, 2007); Mark Harrison and Biswamoy Pati, eds., *The Social History of Health and Medicine in Colonial India* (London/New York: 2011); Deepak Kumar, *Science and the Raj* (Delhi: Oxford University Press, 2006); Projit Bihari Mukharji, *Nationalizing the Body: the Medical Market, Print, and Daktari Medicine* (London: Anthem, Press, 2009); Ishita Pande, *Medicine, Race, and Liberalism in British Bengal: Symptoms of Empire* (London/New York: Routledge, 2010); Gyan Prakash, *Another Reason: Science and Its Imagination in Modern India* (Princeton, NJ: Princeton University Press, 1999).

[5] John Locke, *Some Thoughts Concerning Education* (1692); John W. Yolton and Jean S. Yolton, eds. (Oxford, UK: Clarendon Press, 1989). The specific quotes are from *Internet Modern History Sourcebook*. https://sourcebooks.fordham.edu/mod/1692locke-education.asp (accessed on February 15, 2020). India did not have a seminal text like Jean-Jacques Rousseau's *Emile, or On Education* (1762) that acted as a blueprint for future pedagogy for all of India.

medical practitioners, ingeniously combining ideas of the West with their own long-lost past, to craft ideas of nascent citizens. Albeit gendered, the would-be citizens had to be able-bodied and informed, and the process of shaping such citizens became more pronounced in the twentieth century in Bengal and other parts of India .

Empires produce subjects, not citizens. Yet, the story is not as simple and linear in the long history of British empire-building in India. In the later decades of the nineteenth century, threatened by the Indian intelligentsia's anti-colonial offensive, the British produced textbooks like *The Citizen of India* (1897) for the school curriculum to disseminate "state feeling" and the duties of a good citizen. Soon thereafter in the early twentieth century, the Boy Scouts movement (1908) under the leadership of Baden-Powell was launched as well.[6] The pedagogy of the native literati, whether through voluntary associations or through independent literary movements, was part of a larger exchange of ideas that was global in nature. As scholars have shown, the new educational movement of the natives creatively assimilated influences of Victorian and Edwardian England with knowledge and practices of India's plural pasts.[7]

The term "citizen," as *nagarik* or *odhibasi*, did not appear in the Bengali scientific literature of the late-nineteenth-century. Citizenship, still a nebulous concept for the colonized population, was *assumed* through the ascription of certain attributes—physical, ethical, and moral—that would make the subjected population fit for self-rule. As a bio-moral concept, citizenship was thus imagined in diverse ways, both by the native literati and the colonial state as a potentially emancipatory concept. Similar to Victorian and Edwardian England, the ideals of citizenship for the indigenous leaders included healthy body and character; discipline, duty, and obedience, rather than specific rights and privileges.[8] At different points in history, "becoming a citizen" entailed "either an extension of the status to more persons or a liberatory dismantling of hitherto existing

---

[6] Sudipa Topdar, "Duties of a 'Good Citizen': Colonial Secondary Textbook Policies in Late Nineteenth-Century India," *South Asian History and Culture* 6, no. 3 (2015): 417–439; Carey Anthony Watt, *Serving the Nation: Cultures of Service, Association, and Citizenship in Colonial India* (Delhi: Oxford University Press, 2005).

[7] Harald Fischer-Tiné used the term "creative translation" in the article cited previously. Dipesh Chakrabarty too has referred to the process of "translation."

[8] For similar processes in nineteenth-century England, see Watt, *Serving the Nation*, 50.

structures of oppression which were replaced by more egalitarian and inclusive structures."[9]

Kathleen Canning and Sonya O. Rose posited citizenship as a multi-dimensional concept and argued that it needed to be understood in "both discursive and experiential dimensions." Invocation of citizenship "might enunciate visions or claims of those formally excluded from citizenship. Citizenship was experienced by subjects, that is both by historical actors and by those subjected to various instances of power." "Actors in different historical situations appropriate these subject positions in order to challenge, redefine, or honour the boundaries of citizenship."[10] Drawing on Canning and Rose, this chapter explores the multiple ways the writers, i.e. the colonized subjects, imagined themselves and imagined children—a gendered yet otherwise undifferentiated category in terms of caste, class, and religion—as a new body of citizenry—who were both victims and agents of change.

In the new genre of scientific literature addressing young adults and educated parents, "children" and "youth" were implicit categories imagined by the bilingual intelligentsia. While print-capitalism facilitated this imagination of children in a "homogeneous" time to borrow Benedict Anderson's phrase, the literati imagined a future that was influenced by the modular ideas of European modernity but rooted in its Indian past and in that sense recognizably distinct from the West.[11] Children acted as "social imaginaries" on whose bodies and minds new ideas of health and regeneration were inscribed.

---

[9] For a discussion of the emancipatory potential of citizenship and its gendered dimension, especially in India, see Anupama Roy, *Gendered Citizenship: Historical and Conceptual Explorations* (Delhi: Orient Longman, 2005), 3. For a more recent take on citizenship and a postcolonial critique of the dominant Western notions of citizenship see Isin Engin, *Citizenship After Orientalism: An Unfinished Project* (New York: Routledge, 2014). Particularly instructive for us in the volume are the articles by Aya Ikegame, "Mathas, Gurus and Citizenship: The State and Communities in Colonial India" and Ranabir Samaddar, "The Heterogeneous World of the Citizen."

[10] Kathleen Canning and Sonya O. Rose, "Introduction: Gender, Citizenship and Subjectivity: Some Historical and Theoretical Considerations," *Gender and History*, 13, no. 3 (November 2001): 427–443.

[11] For the role of print capitalism in imagining a community, see Benedict Anderson, *Imagined Communities* (London, Verso: 1991). Partha Chatterjee offered a rebuttal to Anderson's theory and emphasized the "rule of colonial difference" that underscored the imaginations of indigenous elites of colonized countries like India and Africa. Partha Chatterjee, *The Nation and Its Fragments* (Princeton, NJ: Princeton University Press, 1993), 4–13.

What does it mean, to claim children acted as "social imaginaries"? Charles Taylor coined the phrase social imaginary to indicate "the ways people imagine their social existence, how they fit together with others, how things go on between them and their fellows, the expectations that are normally met, and the deeper normative notions and images that underlie these expectations."[12] For Taylor, social imaginary is "not a set of ideas; rather, it is what enables, through making sense of, the practices of a society."[13] He adopted the term "imaginary" to focus "on the way ordinary people "imagine" their social surroundings" which is not expressed in theoretical terms but through images, legends, and stories. In contrast to social theory, which often could be the prerogative of a minority intellectual community, social imaginary is shared by a large section of the population. Social imaginary conveys "a common understanding that makes possible common practices and a widely shared sense of legitimacy."[14]

Taylor's concept of social imaginary is particularly instructive for explaining the invocation of children in the literature discussed in this chapter—the imaginings represented the common understanding and shared concerns of colonial subjects, both elite and non-elite, and their claim for legitimacy within its linguistic community (the Bengalis) and before a colonial government. Spearheading a new literary genre, men in the medical profession displayed an overwhelming engagement with children to ameliorate the latter's dismal state of being and to project children as beacons of hope for a reformed future. While children and youth were defined by the politics of the texts in which they were represented, they became an important vehicle for the Bengali literati to imagine a collective social life in the face of strident criticism of the colonial state.[15] The paternalistic concern of the writers was therefore not confined to their biological children and kin relations but also extended to the juvenile population and their roles in an incipient nation.

Fatherly responsibility in nineteenth-century India typically entailed breadwinning, protecting, and nurturing, as well as physical and moral

---

[12] See previous note.
[13] Taylor, *Modern Social Imaginaries*, 2.
[14] Taylor, *Modern Social Imaginaries*, 23.
[15] For children being defined by the politics of the texts see Indrani Chatterjee, "Introduction," in Chatterjee, ed. *Unfamiliar Relations* (New Brunswick: Rutgers University Press, 2004), 3–45.

care for children, not only of one's own but also the younger members of an extended, multi-generational family. But in the changing socio-cultural landscape of the late colonial era, over and above familial responsibilities, educated fathers as interlocutors assumed the moral guardianship of raising, protecting, and guiding the younger generation at large. Harking on loss and degeneration, they perceived children in different crisis situations and offered possible means of remediation. This chapter examines the trope of loss and regeneration in late nineteenth-century Bengali scientific journals and interrogates the multiple ways the "fathers" imagined children in this new literature.[16] In this new discourse boys and girls, irrespective of their caste, religious, and socio-economic backgrounds, were conceived as victims and as agents of change. Frequently invoked in discussions of health, hygiene, and sexuality, the predominantly Hindu writers configured children in three different guises—girl-children as hapless victims of unjust social practices and mothers;[17] boy-children as would-be "citizens" constituting the future generation; and male youths engaged in excessive sexual practices causing national degeneration. All three positions of children required remediation; but they were also granted agency, however, mediated, in specific moments of their mobilization. The harnessing of children as enabling agents signalled a counter-hegemonic effort by the intelligentsia to articulate their autonomous epistemic space as fathers in a "motherland" that they were trying to recuperate from foreign domination and control.

Scholars in different fields have long demonstrated the connection between health and national regeneration. Modern medicine and its implication in the formation of colonial subjects have been explored in depth in recent South Asian history.[18] In colonial contexts, the scholarship emphasized the importance of the body as zones for political-economic

---

[16] For a discussion of imagination and loss as a sign of modernity see Sumathi Ramaswamy, *The Lost Land of Lemuria: Fabulous Geographies, Catastrophic Histories* (Berkeley: University of California Press, 2004).

[17] Girls, also imagined as sexual aggressors, did not figure in the scientific literature I surveyed. For more on that theme, see Ishita Pande, *Medicine, Race, and Liberalism in British Bengal: Symptoms of Empire* (New York: Routledge, 2010).

[18] Pande, *Medicine, Race*; Pradip Kumar Bose [Pradipa Basu], ed., *Health and Society in Bengal: A Selection From Late 19th-Century Bengali Periodicals* (New Delhi: Sage Publications, 2006). Also, in Bengali, Pradipa Basu, ed., *Samayiki: Purono Samayikpatre-r Probondha Sankalan, Bijnan o Samaj 1850–1901*, Vol. 1 (Kolkata: Ananda Publishers, 1998). *Samayiki* is a compendium of nineteenth-century periodicals in Bengal. Bose and Basu are the same person; the editor uses Pradipa Basu for Bengali works and Pradip Kumar Bose for English ones.

domination and cultural control. It also pointed out the ways bodies were imbued with meanings and acted as a source of knowledge and power.[19] In the case of colonial India, the literature reveals a consensus that in the field of knowledge-production there was a dialogue between the colonial state and its native subjects, although the playing field was by no means level.[20] Sudipa Topdar has documented the centrality of children's bodies in formation of imperial pedagogical ideologies and the indigenous response.[21] This chapters taps the pedagogic material that preceded the records Topdar investigated in her work. This is a new body of literature that circulated outside of the school curriculum and aimed to promote scientific knowledge in the last quarter of the nineteenth century. The authors, mostly doctors trained in Western medicine, were lesser-known activists than the ones discussed in the last chapter. But they were instrumental in disseminating corporeal science to a lay audience. The male professionals who wrote took upon themselves the task of educating their fellow natives, parents (fathers and mothers) and young adults, who were not well versed in English and Western sciences.[22] The goal of the editors was "that common people have easy access to knowledge, so that the trader and the shopkeeper can learn about the world … "[23] The literati's use of vernacular to disseminate new knowledge constantly appropriated familial relations and the crises that they were faced with. For the professional experts, the road to a better future rested with the new generation—in recovering the health and psyche of children and young adults, both conceived in gendered terms but rooted in home.

---

[19] Kathleen Canning, "The Body as Method? Reflections on the Place of the Body in Gender History," *Gender and History* 11 (1999): 499–513. Tony Ballantyne and Antoinette Burton, eds., *Bodies in Contact: Rethinking Colonial Encounters in World History* (Durham, NC: Duke University Press, 2005).

[20] Mark Harrison, *Climates and Constitution: Health, Race, Environment and British Imperialism in India 1600–1850* (New Delhi: Oxford University Press, 1999), 59.

[21] Sudipa Topdar, "The Corporeal Empire: Physical Education and Politicising Children's Bodies in Late Colonial Bengal," *Gender and History* 29, no. 1 (April 2017): 176–197.

[22] Outside of Bengal, in the early decades of the twentieth century there was a proliferation of a new scientific literature called *santati-sastra* (lit. "the science of progeny" or "progeniology") that instructed newly-married middle-class couples on how to produce mentally and physically perfect children. Santati-sastra differed from classical eugenics as pioneered by Franics Galton and its readaptation by Indian eugenicists. Rather, it drew on sources such as Ayurveda, *ratisastra*, and theories of heredity developed by a mid-nineteenth century American phrenologist. See Luzia Savary, "Vernacular Eugenics? *Santati-Śāstra* in Popular Hindi Advisory Literature (1900–1940)," *South Asia: Journal of South Asian Studies* 37, no. 3 (2014): 381–397.

[23] *Bibidhartha-Sangraha*, 1851. Cited in Bose, *Health and Society in Bengal*, 15.

John Tosh has shown how manliness in late nineteenth-century England was constituted outside of the home—there was a conscious effort to divorce masculinity from Victorian domesticity, and club, adventure, and sports life for bourgeois men flourished as never before.[24] In the colonial situation, where Indian men were routinely subordinated in the public realm and disparaged for their supposed frailty, lack of sportsmanship, and disinclination towards adventure, the family and its constitutive members became the domain to reclaim masculine and patriarchal authority in an indirect way.[25] The home not only provided comfort, succour, and refuge, it also became the playground for articulating masculine identities as authoritative fathers and to inscribe those attributes and ideologies onto the male progenies to equip them as modern subjects. The boundary between the home and the world was porous as concerns of public culture articulated in the print media were channelized to manage familial situations and reform familial practices.[26]

Age-old social customs such as child marriage, widow burning, and lack of education for women reflected family practices that plagued nineteenth-century Bengal. The criticism by the colonial state that described India as the land of dirt, disease, prejudice, and superstition and its native males as frail, weak, unscientific, lethargic, effete, and sexually predatory made the prevalence of these practices a crisis. From the 1880s, the eugenicist argument of the British, blaming child marriage as the cause for the Hindus ranking in the middle in "the scale of nations," gained ground.[27] The vernacular periodicals, which became the principal means of reformulation and dissemination of scientific ideas and knowledge of educated male elites, thus echoed the colonial critique and

---

[24] John Tosh, *A Man's Place: Masculinity and the Middle-Class Home in Victorian England* (New Haven, CT: Yale University Press, 2007), 7.

[25] This is not to deny the importance of sports and various forms of physical culture that gained currency among Indian males to assert their masculinity. See James Mills and Satadru Sen, eds., *Confronting the Body: The Politics of Physicality in Colonial and Postcolonial India* (London: Anthem Press, 2004).

[26] For a parallel development in England in the late nineteenth and the early twentieth century when informal education focused on building character of its future citizens was conducted at home, see Stephanie Olsen, *Juvenile Nation: Youth, Emotions and the Making of the Modern British Citizen 1880–1914* (London: Bloomsbury, 2014).

[27] David Arnold, *Colonizing the Body: State, Medicine and Epidemic Disease in Nineteenth-Century India* (Berkeley: University of California Press, 1993), 283; Harald Fischer-Tiné, "From Brahmacharya to Conscious Race-Culture: Victorian Discourses of 'Science' and Hindu Traditions in Early Indian Nationalism," in *Beyond Representation*, ed. Crispin Bates, 241–269.

conflated the crisis in national health and physical debility with child marriage and other social issues. Funded by the government's Vernacular Literature Committee and printed by the Baptist Missionary Society, the first illustrated Bengali periodical *Bibidhartha-Sangraha* on science, health, and "national regeneration" (the last term described in Bengali as *jatiya punurujjiban*) published a "proposal" in 1854. The article "Bibaha-Bishayak Etoddeshiya Kuprotha" ("The Unjust Practices of Marriage in this Country"), delineating the deleterious practices of child marriage in India,[28] heaped vituperative criticism on crude marriage practices among the Bengali Hindus. The Bengali author blamed lack of education for such practices as child marriage and mourned its pervasive ill-effects on the national culture. Invoking a visual imagery of repugnance and horror, the proposal cited the horrendous impact of child marriage on conjugal life and physical health; untimely and inappropriate incitements in children's minds interrupting education and retarding growth; death of the first child leading to the loss of family lineage; and finally, gruelling poverty culminating from all the aforementioned factors. The authors cited both boys and girls as victims of unjust social practices and of undiscerning and short-sighted parents. Drawing attention to the sad state of young widowers and widows, the proposal proclaimed the right of both, particularly that of the girls, to remarry. The equal treatment of boys and girls in specific scenarios and the empathy for girls/women was symptomatic of the reformist socio-cultural climate of the time when liberal reformers like Iswarchandra Vidyasagar, in spite of their caste-class bias, were owning parental responsibilities and empowering children through an able body and mind.[29] The publication of this essay on child marriage in *Bibidhartha Samgraha*, the periodical launched by the joint initiative of the colonial state, the missionaries, and the Bengali reformers with the avowed "ambition" of "educating 'native' people in modern systems of knowledge," signalled the urgency of the subject matter in colonial Bengal. The political culture of Bengal at that time, particularly the crusade against child marriage and widowhood, informed discussions of the editor Rajendralal Mitra (1822–1891), an eminent educationist and

---

[28] *Bibidhartha-Sangraha*, ed., Rajendralal Mitra, Vol. 3, no. 32 (Kartick, 1776 sakabda [1854]). Reprinted in Basu, *Samayiki*, 162–165.
[29] For the caste-class bias of Vidyasagar, see Asok Sen, *Iswar Chandra Vidyasagar and His Illusive Milestone* (Calcutta: Riddhi, 1977).

scientific-literary scholar of the time. The raison d'être for this literary intervention insisting on changes in everyday practices was embedded in the intellectual climate in which science was introduced in the colony and the response it evoked among its native practitioners, the "fathers," calling on the future generation to revive and save a "nation" in its making.

Introduction of Science in the Colony and the Native Interlocutors

The introduction of science in the colony was fraught with tension and contestation between the colonial state and the educated natives.[30] The "fathers" of education in Bengal worked against a British attitude that sought to downplay science, particularly the technical subjects that ensured the power of the Raj, in favour of the humanities, for pragmatic as well as racist reasons. Indeed, some British officials were hostile towards any education. The British law-member Thomas Babington Macaulay, who was instrumental in introducing English as the official language and western-style education in India in 1835, asserted that the government did not owe its subjects anything at all, "least of all a share in the reconstruction of their educational systems."[31] He detested science and advocated a purely literary curriculum for India. A contemporary British journal proclaimed Macaulay's view that "more useful knowledge is to be gained from the study of one page of Bacon's prose, or Shakespeare's poetry, than from a hundred pages of Euclid."[32] In 1854, F.J. Mouat, the

---

[30] The spread of science in India could be traced back to Section 43 of the Charter Act of 1813, which granted one lakh (hundred thousand) rupees to be spent on education that would introduce and promote "the knowledge of sciences among the inhabitants of the British India." The Act of 1813 also lifted the blanket ban on missionaries in and around Calcutta and allowed them to forge ahead in their propagation of religion and education. With regard to science, it did not specify whether it would spread indigenous or European science among the inhabitants but perhaps expected a fusion of the scientific and medical techniques of the East and the West. Showing an awareness of the local techno-scientific traditions, in 1824 the Committee of General Instruction, Bengal, reported "the arithmetic and algebra of the Hindus lead to the same result and are grounded on the same principles as those of Europe." However, within a decade such attitude was immediately replaced by radically different views of British law-members like Thomas Babington Macaulay whose largely unfounded contempt towards India's learning and education became the blueprint for future course of action. See Deepak Kumar, *Science and the Raj, 1857–1905* (Delhi: Oxford University Press, 1997), 48.
[31] Thomas Babington Macaulay, "Minute of Education," cited in Kumar, *Science and the Raj*, 49.
[32] Kumar, *Science and the Raj*, 49.

then Secretary to the Council of Education, Bengal, felt that the study of literature was "'more conducive to the improvement in the strength and tone of mind' than 'a particularly exclusive mathematical education.'"[33] The privileging of natural philosophy and literary studies by the colonial government thus delayed the introduction of natural science in India.[34] Even Wood's Despatch on Education in 1854 did not pay any attention to science education in the colony. The British administrators' indifference towards science education in India underscored their fear that the spread of education would undermine Britain's claim to superiority to govern India.[35] Nonetheless, a growing need for apothecaries, medical or hospital assistants, surveyors, and mechanics to serve the emerging medical, survey, and public works department called for training local youths rather than hiring technical staff from abroad.[36] Emphasis was more on applied sciences, promoting geology, mechanical innovations, such as telegraphs, and land surveys. Based on land surveys, the British instituted major land reforms such as the Permanent Settlement (1793) in Bengal and the Ryotwari Settlement (1820) in Madras to maximize revenue—but they still made no effort towards introducing agricultural sciences that would lead to improvement in agriculture and hence revenue production.[37] While self-interest led to the introduction of some, primarily applied, sciences in the education curriculum of India, Raj administrators were for the most part reluctant to advocate for indigenous education on par with that offered in Britain. The Bengali literati would work to rectify this, thereby positioning themselves as "fathers" to their readership.

---

[33] Kumar, *Science and the Raj*, 49
[34] Kumar, *Science and the Raj*, 49
[35] *The Bombay Quarterly Magazine*, 1, 2 (Jan. 1851): 10, cited in Kumar, *Science and the Raj*, 51.
[36] For a contemporaneous account from the Muslim point of view see Syed Mahmood, *History of English Education in India, 1781–1893* (Aligarh: M.A.O. College, 1895). Also see David Lelyveld, "*Naicari* Nature: Sir Sayyid Ahmad Khan and the Reconciliation of Science, Technology and Religion," in *The Cambridge Companion to Sir Sayyid Ahmad Khan*, eds. Yasmin Saikia and Raisur Rahman (Cambridge: Cambridge University Press, 2018).
[37] For a comparative study of different land tenure systems introduced by the British see Md Hamid Husain and Firoj High Sarwar, "A Comparative Study of Zamindari, Raiyatwari and Mahalwari Land Revenue Settlements: The Colonial Mechanism of Surplus Extraction in 19th-century British India," *Journal of Humanities and Social Sciences* 2, no. 4 (September–October 2012): 16–26.

The Asiatic Society in Calcutta, founded by William Jones in 1784, acted as the major centre of scientific research in eighteenth-century India.[38] It was purely a European-male-dominated institution with no participation of women—European women were yet to arrive in any significant number in the colony, and it was uncommon among Indian women at that time to attend public institutions of learning—and until 1829, they accepted no Indians. For its approximately two thousand readers, the Asiatic Society brought out important journals, such as *Gleanings in Science* and *Calcutta Journal of Natural History*. The *Calcutta Journal* even wanted to establish an Indian Association for the Advancement of Natural Science after the model of the British Association for the Advancement of Science.[39] However, the advancement of science in the colonies was discouraged by colonists on the basis of a repeated condemnation that Indians were not fit for the study of sciences, especially natural sciences.[40] This characterization of the Indians for their unsuitability for scientific learning ran parallel with the caricature and stereotype of the Bengalis for their frail body and feeble-mindedness, in short, their "effeteness," and a lack of "courage, independence, and veracity."[41] Rosselli argued that from 1870 onwards, educated Bengalis had more or less conceded that they were "liliputian in size and weak in constitution."[42] No wonder, the editor of *Bibidhartha-Sangraha,* Rajendralal Mitra (whom we quoted previously and will discuss later subsequently), as the first Indian president (1885) of Asiatic Society, echoed British sentiments of decay and stressed the urgency of national regeneration.

---

[38] The Asiatic Society was later followed by the Literary Society in Bombay in 1804, the Literary and Scientific Society in Madras in 1818, and the Calcutta Medical and Physical Society in 1823. The first two became branches of the Royal Asiatic Society in London founded in 1825. Exclusionary in their policies, these organizations served mainly as clubs for European men. Kumar, *Science and the Raj*, 55.

[39] Kumar, *Science and the Raj*, 55–57.

[40] For more on science see Irfan Habib and Dhruv Raina, eds., *Social History of Science in Colonial India* (Delhi: Oxford University Press, 2007); David Arnold, *Science, Technology and the Raj, The New Cambridge History of India*, vol. 3, part 5 (Cambridge: Cambridge University Press, 2000).

[41] See John Rosselli, "The Self-Image of Effeteness: Physical Education and Nationalism in Nineteenth Century Bengal," *Past and Present* 86, no. 1 (1980): 121–148; Mrinalini Sinha, *Colonial Masculinity: The 'Manly' Englishman and the Effeminate Bengali in the Late Nineteenth Century* (Manchester, UK: Manchester University Press, 1995); Indira Chowdhury, *The Frail Hero and Virile History: Gender and the Politics of Culture in Colonial Bengal* (Delhi: Oxford University Press, 2001).

[42] Rosselli, "Self-Image of Effeteness," 123.

While the bio-politics of the colonial state had castigated the Indians, particularly the Bengalis, as the racialized "other" unfit to govern themselves, the native intellectuals as moral leaders launched their own movements against this pervasive imperial ethos. Having internalized this criticism and owning the stereotypes, trained Indian doctors and professionals in scientific fields responded by forming organizations and publishing literature that disseminated the need for an active physical training and education, especially for children. Whereas the missionaries and the colonial state targeted Indian men, the latter in turn focused their attention on children who would constitute the new body of citizenry. As printing gained currency in Bengal, a significant branch of vernacular periodicals, some addressed to parents and others to the younger generation, appropriated children and youths as subjects of reform, emphasizing the latter's need to be educated in science, health, and medicine.

The initiative taken by the Bengali literati in promoting science among their younger reading public was evident from the scale of vernacular publications on science in the last half of the nineteenth century. The missionary Reverend James Long's *Descriptive Catalogue of Bengali Works* (1855) listing science-related Bengali publications between 1800 and 1896 and other sources give us a sense of the proliferation of scientific literature of the period. Between 1875 and 1896 there were 776 texts in Bengali on different branches of Science—472 on medical science, 180 on mathematics, and 124 on general sciences.[43] The number of scientific texts in Bengali represented one-third of the total number of texts produced all over India during that period. The numbers certainly attest to the proliferation of Bengali print culture in all its varieties and forms.[44] Most of these works were translations of original texts in English; but it

---

[43] The importance of science, specifically that of medical science, can be gleaned from James Long's *Descriptive Catalogue of Bengali Works* (1855) which provides us with a list of science related publications in Bengali between 1800 and 1852: Mathematics – 5, Geometry – 1, Geography – 8, Maps – 7, Medical Science – 17, Natural Science – 13, Physics, Chemistry, and Astrology – 11. Between 1853 and 1867 this scientific literature increased in both numbers and variety: Texts on Mathematics jumped to 20, Geometry – 10, Medical Science – 46, Physics – 12, Chemistry – 38, Maps – 5, Life Science – 8, Applied Science – 3, Natural Science – 2, and Agricultural Science – 10. Around the same time there were 8 texts published on Ayurveda and 6 texts on Astrology. Basu, *Samayiki*, 16.

[44] See Anindita Ghosh, "Literary Bengali and Low-Life Print Culture in Colonial Calcutta: Revisiting the 'Bengal Renaissance,'" *Economic and Political Weekly* 37, no. 42 (October 2002). Also, *Power in Print: Popular Publishing and the Politics of Language and Culture in a Colonial Society, 1778–1905* (Delhi: Oxford University Press, 2006).

is significant that these specific body of scientific texts were chosen for translation. The examples were modified and selected carefully to make the material intelligible to Indian readers without any or much background in science.

An important public space where the Bengali literati freely articulated their concerns with public health, hygiene, and medicine were the newly-established societies, associations, and clubs (*sabhas* and *samitis*). Educated men in nineteenth-century Bengal firmly believed that the production and exchange of ideas and practices, particularly among the scientific community, was facilitated more by societies such as the associations of doctors rather than scientific laboratories and institutions.[45] Several organizations founded between 1830 and 1840 promoted the culture and acquisition of knowledge and science and published journals.[46] The vernacular periodicals acted as principal organs for disseminating knowledge to reach out to the common people. A leading association, the Society for the Acquisition of General Knowledge (1838–1843), founded by the followers of the early nineteenth-century radical reformist group, the Young Bengal, had two hundred members by 1843 and launched attacks on many existing social conditions including the treatment of women. Often under attack by the colonial state for their supposedly seditious activities,[47] the clubs and associations provided the intellectual "fathers" an outlet to freely discuss and debate a wide variety of subject matters (in vernacular) without foreign intervention.[48]

The publications, activities, and membership of these predominantly male clubs revealed aspirations for a renewed and reformed Bengali culture—not only were the editors, writers, and members quite young in age (between twenty and thirty), the deliberations of the clubs also focused on male youths. For example, an eminent writer and versatile scholar,

[45] Bose, *Health and Society in Bengal*, 14–16.

[46] Some of the organizations of that period were Jnansandipan Sabha, Bijnandayini Sabha, Sarbatattvadeepika Sabha, Jnaanchandradaya Sabha, Sadharan Jnanoparjika Sabha, and Tattvabodhini Sabha, the last being particularly important.

[47] For example, in February 1843, Raja Dakhinaranjan Mukherjee (1814–1898), an orator and social reformer, delivered the address "Present Conditions of the East India Company's Courts of Judicature and Police under the Bengal Presidency." According to the contemporary newspaper *Bengal Harkaru*, this lecture "was interrupted by the Principal of the Hindoo College, on the grounds of its seditious and treacherous tendency." See Parna Sengupta, *Pedagogy for Religion*, 282.

[48] Pradipa Basu, ed., *Samayiki: Purono Samayaik Patrér Prabandha Sankalan*, vol. 1: *Bijnan o Samaj* (1850–1901) (Calcutta: Ananda Publishers, 1998), 13–15.

Akshay kumar Dutta (1820–1886), who edited *Tattvabodhini Patrika* (1843–1932), a long-running periodical produced by the Brahmo association Tattvabodhini Sabha, disseminated scientific ideas in accessible language for a broad, general readership. Under the title of *Bijnan* or *Bijnan Barta* ("Science" or "Scientific Information"), it regularly published articles on geology, zoology, physics, and anthropology.[49] The topics discussed and the intended readership of these magazines gestured towards a futurity contingent upon the preparedness of the younger generation to face the challenges of a new modernity ushered in by the hegemonic colonial state. The role of these societies and literature in the making of Indian national culture is well recognized in scholarship. What still demands attention was the role of the male protagonists wielding literary leadership as moral custodians and the way they imagined the younger male generation who embodied their hope as the new citizenry.

While native intelligentsia used the categories of "child" and "youth," official discourse elided the latter. The blanket category of "child" dominated official discourse, so that youth as an important demographic segment in nineteenth-century India was lost in the labyrinth of legislation grappling with issues of child marriage and oppressive social practices. The constituents of the "child" category were differentiated by gender: when the Child Marriage Restraint Act (1929) was finally passed by the colonial government, mainly at the insistence of the natives, it declared the child to be a person who, if a male, is under eighteen years of age and, if a female, is under fourteen years of age. This "incontrovertible"[50] official definition of the child eliminated the category of youth and curtailed girls' childhoods, revealing the paternalistic and patriarchal attitude of the colonial state referring to minor native subjects. The native intelligentsia, on the contrary, and as the following section demonstrates, deliberated on the "ages" of children and the intersection of child and youth-hood in different socio-temporal realities. The question of youth in colonial India, with its gendered dimensions, therefore, has

---

[49] *Tattvabodhini Patrika* (1843–1932) was noteworthy for its broadmindedness in representing an amalgamation of ideas from the pre-colonial past and the present, without ruffling sentiments of people belonging to different castes, creeds, and religions. Rajendralal Mitra, another stalwart in the field of education, worked with Dutta as part of *Tattvabodhini Patrika*'s editorial board between 1848 and 1850.

[50] Ishita Pande, "Coming of Age: Law, Sex, and Childhood in Late Colonial India," *Gender and History* 24, no. 1 (April 2012).

to be mapped upon an emerging and shifting terrain that was battling a number of social, political, and cultural forces and was contingent upon caste, class, ethnicity, region, and space.

Children and Youth as Subjects of Reform

Intending to educate and inform a wider audience, Rajendralal Mitra, the editor of the journal *Bibidhartha-Sangraha* exhibited his fatherly concern to mould and redirect the predictable natural tendencies among young readers. The juvenile population's urge to read "sensually exciting texts" had to be countered by the more fruitful knowledge produced in the newly launched journal; the existing body of "sensuous" vernacular literature had to be replaced by more refined texts on science and ethics to mold and inform children and keep them on track. Thus, despite the consternation of the experts promoting a reformed vernacular prose and scientific terms in English, Mitra chose to advocate new ideas in simple, colloquial Bengali to reach out to the widest possible audience. The chief targets were the young adults and their parents who subscribed to the newly minted journals and were responsible for bringing up the juvenile population. Mothers, in particular, were specially addressed for ensuring a healthy body of citizenry.[51]

At a time when the perceived frailty, precocity, and sexuality of native bodies called for intervention by the colonial state, Indian interlocutors mobilized their Western knowledge in vernacular languages to enunciate on issues of physical culture, health, and marriage. The first step in the process was to further educate parents and young adults alike. At least eighteen Bengali scientific periodicals were published between 1866 and 1899 with the objective of acquainting common people with Western medical science.[52] In translating the data and other related contents from different branches of medicine the vernacular periodicals attempted to

---

[51] The popularity of *Bibidhartha-Sangraha* among the educated Bengalis was evident from the reminiscences of Rabindranath Tagore (1861–1941), the intellectual stalwart, who recounted in his memoirs the way he, in his teens, eagerly waited to receive a copy of *Bibidhartha-Sangraha* from his elder brother's collection. Bose, *Health and Society in Bengal*, 16. Rabindranath Tagore, "Jivansmriti," in *Rabindra Rachanabali*, vol. 9 (Kolkata: Visva-Bharati, 1989), 452.

[52] For a complete list of Bengali medical journals published in the second half of the nineteenth century see Pradip Bose, *Health and Society*, 21.

reduce the knowledge gap among the educated community who, however, lacked proficiency in English. But the process was fraught as debates ensued over what language the new scientific knowledge was to be disseminated in and more importantly, on the question of the validity of indigenous "local" versus Western "universal" knowledge in the fields of medicine. Educationists like Mitra argued that the "translation of Western scientific terms into Indian languages can never be slavishly literal."[53] The "translocation and translation of Western science in the Indian context" led to a "displacement of both Indian culture and Western science" and there emerged a knowledge and culture that was a "hybrid" of both.[54]

The process of new knowledge production by imaginary fathers was not just intrinsic to late-nineteenth-century Bengal. In other parts of India Hindu reformist organizations such as the Gurukul Kangri of Punjab also appropriated and assimilated a scientific discourse of "conscious race culture" (eugenics) and environmentalism betraying a direct influence of Victorian and Edwardian England. The trope of degeneration and decline that marked the writings of the Indian writers was also rampant in mid-nineteenth-century Great Britain, those ideas being particularly reinforced by Darwin and Spencer.[55]

Two scientific journals, *Chikitsha Sammilani* (1884–1894) and *Swasthya* (1898–1902), concerned with questions of national health, captured a sense of restlessness and unease over myriad social issues troubling nineteenth-century Indians. *Chikitsha Sammilani* (See Figure 3.1) was one of the earliest and unique medical journal in Bengali that included different sections on the three dominant medical disciplines in India—allopathy, homoeopathy, and Ayurveda. The editors and contributors of this journal were well-known practitioners of these three branches who discussed diseases and their symptoms, particularly those of children, and the lines of treatment to be offered; they also reviewed health and health-education policy of the government and championed the idea of introducing Ayurveda as a discipline in the medical institutes.[56] *Swasthya* (See Figure 3.2), edited by Durgadas Gupta, was a

---

[53] Rajendralal Bose, *A Scheme for the Rendering of European Scientific Texts in India*, cited in Bose, *Health and Society in Bengal*, 17.

[54] Bose, *Health and Society in Bengal*, 17.

[55] Harald Fischer-Tiné, "From Brahmacharya to Conscious Race-Culture: Victorian Discourses of 'Science' and Hindu Traditions in Early Indian Nationalism."

[56] Basu, *Samayiki*, 686–687.

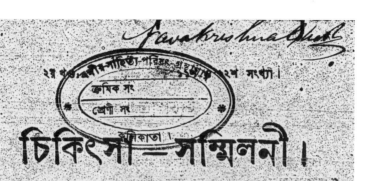

Figure 3.1 Cover page of *Chikitsha-Sammilani*

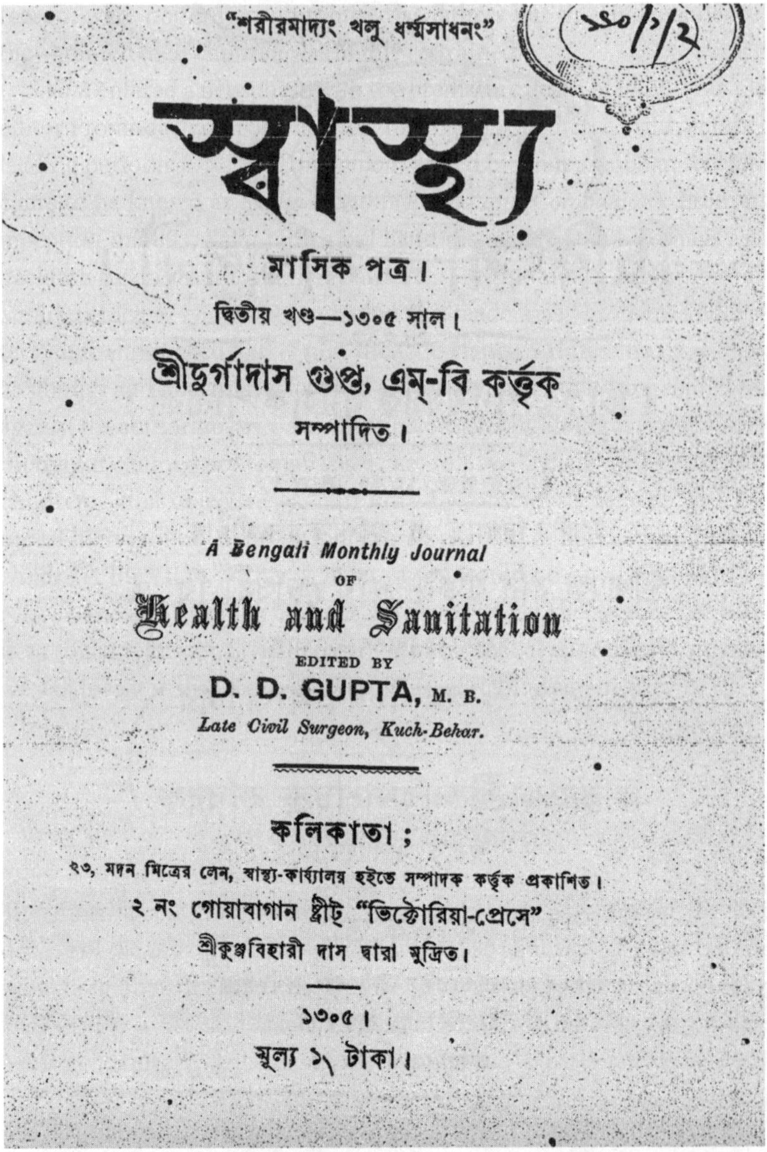

"শরীরমাদ্যং খলু ধর্ম্মসাধনং"

স্বাস্থ্য

মাসিক পত্র।

দ্বিতীয় খণ্ড—১৩০৫ সাল।

শ্রীদুর্গাদাস গুপ্ত, এম্-বি কর্ত্তৃক
সম্পাদিত।

A Bengali Monthly Journal
OF
Health and Sanitation
EDITED BY
D. D. GUPTA, M. B.
Late Civil Surgeon, Kuch-Behar.

কলিকাতা ;

২৩, মদন মিত্রের লেন, স্বাস্থ্য-কার্য্যালয় হইতে সম্পাদক কর্ত্তৃক প্রকাশিত।
২ নং গোয়াবাগান ষ্ট্রীট "ভিক্টোরিয়া-প্রেসে"
শ্রীকুঞ্জবিহারী দাস দ্বারা মুদ্রিত।

১৩০৫।

মূল্য ১৲ টাকা।

Figure 3.2 Cover page of *Swasthya*

monthly periodical on health and medicine, in which doctors and medical practitioners regularly wrote about hygiene, health, diseases, and their treatments. One of the major contributions of this periodical was to bring into public view the acute picture of the outbreak of plague in Calcutta and Bombay.[57] The authors in these journals launched their discussion from a sense of "lack," and "national degeneration" that needed to be addressed. An acute anxiety with physical debility and moral corruption was inscribed on the bodies of male and female children imagined in different contexts. New regimes of discipline, self-control, and nutrition were formulated by appropriating the minds and bodies of children. The authors attempted to strike a balance between their newly acquired knowledge of Western science and careful assimilation of the canons of traditional Indian medicine.

Whereas the colonial state defined adulthood for its gendered subjects along specific ages—eighteen for males and fourteen for females—the fathers of the educated community imagined their children as "would-be citizens" through more nuanced stages of life. *Vishak Darpan*, "[A] monthly Magazine of Medicine in Bengali" (co-edited by a Muslim and a Hindu doctor), published a lengthy essay by the London-trained doctor Jogendranath Mitra demarcating the period of infancy (*shaishab*) between the date of birth and two years; youth (*koumar obostha*), a phase that never appeared in colonial legislation, divided into two phases—from age two to eight and from eight to fourteen-fifteen.[58] The article dwelt on the biological growth of children, from the weight at birth to successive gains; the formation of different organs; the functions of different glands; common diseases, their treatment, and cures; dietary specifications; and administration of drugs and medicines. While this engagement evinced the native experts' mastery of human physiology and their zeal to inform the lay public, their emphasis on bodily care and bodily functions of children and the simultaneous training of their minds demonstrate the many ways the Bengali intelligentsia imagined their

---

[57] Bose, *Health and Society in Bengal*, 279.
[58] "Shaishab o Koumar Obostha-y Sharirik Bidhan o Kriya-r Bisheshattva," in *Vishak-Darpan, A Monthly Magazine of Medicine in Bengali*, eds. Maulavi Ahiruddin Ahmed and Debendranath Ray, vol. 6 (July 1896–June 1897), 230–241.

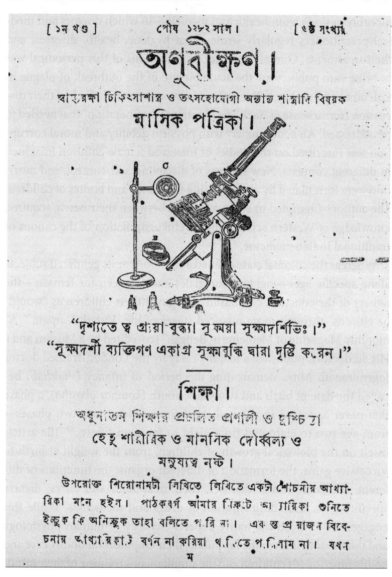

Figure 3.3 Cover page of *Onubeekshan*

children as the future citizenry. They envisioned a moral order inhabited by male citizens of healthy mind and body and females as mothers of the nation. The question of women being citizen-subjects remained amorphous in the literature of the period.

Women as Mothers: Subjects of Pedagogy

At the heart of this medical discourse lurked the question of gender as a constitutive element in articulating differences.[59] Beset with the trauma of child marriage victimizing girl-children and in turn, paralyzing the nation, the intelligentsia's anxiety with the well-being of the future generation shifted to the roles of mothers.[60] *Swasthya, A Bengali Monthly Journal of Health and Sanitation*,[61] (See Figure 3.2) constantly urged the care of the child by describing the newborn (*sodyoproshuto shishu*) as the most vulnerable and even more helpless than animal cubs. Mothers' hearts were so full of affection because they had to take care of these utterly dependent infants.[62] Several articles on home, the housewife, child-rearing, vegetarian and non-vegetarian diets, particularly diets of widowed women, clearly established women as *Swasthya*'s targeted readers. With women as their pedagogical subjects, the male authors gave all-round instructions on breast-feeding, illnesses, and maternal responsibilities in lengthy essays such "Matristonyopayee Shishur Palon Bidhi" ("Rules of Rearing Breastfeeding Infants"), "Shishu-r Peera" ("Illness of Children"), and "Chhele-r Oshukh o Mata-r Gnyatobyo" ("What a Mother Should Know about a Sick Child"). While the term "shishu," possibly designating the first two years of life, was not segregated along sex,

---

[59] For socialization of girl children see Jasodhara Bagchi, Jaba Guha, Piyali Sengupta, *Loved and Unloved: The Girl Child in the Family* (Kolkata: Stree, 1997). Jasodhara Bagchi, "Socializing the Girl Child in Colonial Bengal," *Economic and Political Weekly* 28, no. 41 (October 9, 1993): 2214–2219. For comparable experiences of Bengali Muslim girls see Sonia Nishat Amin, *The World of Muslim Women in Colonial Bengal, 1876-1939* (Leiden: Brill Press, 1996); Asha Islam Nayeem and Avril A. Powell, "Redesigning the Zenana: Domestic Education in Eastern Bengal in the Early Twentieth Century," in *Rhetoric and Reality: Gender and the Colonial Experience in South Asia*, eds. Avril A. Powell and Siobbhan Lambert-Hurley (New Delhi: Oxford University Press, 2006), 50–81. Asha Islam, Nayeem, "How to Educate the Girl Child? Financing Female Education in Colonial Bengal," in *Readings in Bengal History: Identity Formation and Colonial Legacy*, eds. Asha Islam Nayeem and Aksadul Alam (Dhaka: Bangladesh History Association, 2017), 179–202. For Muslim women outside of Bengal see Margrit Pernau, "Noble Women, Courtesans, and Women's Moral Reforms," in *Ashraf into Middle Classes* (New Delhi: Oxford University Press, 2013).

[60] Sexuality was another major theme that inflected the understanding of the women in colonial literature. But sexuality of the girl-child was not the concern of the writers I studied. For a study of female sexuality as a key to social and political thought in eastern India, see Durba Mitra, *Indian Sex Life: Sexuality and the Colonial Origins of the Modern Social Thought* (Princeton: Princeton University Press, 2020).

[61] This subtitle appeared in English in the title page of the journal.

[62] "Sodyoproshuto Shishu ('The New-Born')," *Swasthya, A Bengali Monthly Journal of Health and Sanitation* 2, no. 5 (1898): 114–116.

women occupied two contra-distinct positions in this new discourse: as mothers who needed education in human physiology for the successful raising of children; and as chaste, Hindu widows whose strict regimen of diet and life-style were worth emulating. Without any specific reference to the girl-child, girls were imagined as the "mother" of the nation.[63]

This positioning of women came out in a more convoluted narrative, full of inconsistencies and contradictions, of the scientific writers whose fatherly concern with girl-children was manifest in questions related to marriage. Echoing the concerns of the earlier publications such as those in *Bibidhartha-Sangraha* (mentioned earlier) denouncing child marriage for its ill-effects on society, in 1888 Dr Pulinchandra Sanyal, the editor of *Chikitsa Sammilani* (See Figure 3.1), wrote an extensive essay called "Bibaha Bichaar" ("Scrutinizing Marriage Practices") pointing out the intimate connection between marriage and national health.[64] The article began with a strong denunciation of child marriage, whether it was performed in infancy or prematurely in youth and the ill-effects it bore on Indian society. His premise echoed the conservative sentiments of the time that marriage was chiefly meant for procreation and perpetuation of the race. Under-developed bodies and reproductive organs of male and female juveniles were bound to produce weak progenies who would perish very quickly. Likewise, children produced by advanced-aged couples would also meet with a similar fate. Possibly engaging with the reigning question of the 1880s—the age of marriage and its consummation, both of which demanded attention from the colonial state—the author reflected on the appropriate age of marriage through meticulous scrutiny of reproductive behaviour in myriad species of plants and animals and from varied human cultures from around the world. His deliberation was only to presage his more forceful rejection of Western influence on Indian culture. In discussing fulfilment of sexual urges among different species, Dr Sanyal claimed that the practice of artificially satisfying sexual desires through "unnatural" means (presumably alluding to masturbation) was prevalent, particularly among men

---

[63] For the specific nature of women's education see Bharati Ray, Collected and Edited. *Nari o Poribar: Bamabodhini Patrika (1270–1329 Bangabda)* (Kolkata: Pustak Bipani, 1999).

[64] Pulinchandra Sanyal, "Bibaha Bichaar," *Chikitsa Sammilani* (1294–1295 B.S. [1888]), reprinted in Bose, *Health and Society in Bengal*, 166–187. Dr. Pulinchandra Sanyal was the editor of the journal *Chikitsa Sammilani* between 1887 and 1890.

and women in the West, and was now spreading among young Indians. Ironically, his remedy for such inimical practice was the age-old Indian custom of child marriage, sanctioned by authoritative texts that acted as a guard against such "disastrous" social consequences among its natives. In *Bibidhartha-Sangraha* (1854) Rajendralal Mitra had strongly denounced child marriage and advocated for equal protection of girls and boys; in the late years of the nineteenth century, authors like Sanyal reversed such progressive social claims and defended archaic social practices to fulfil their own hegemonic aspirations.

Defying the influence of the West but also contradicting himself, Dr Sanyal urged that child marriage was not harmful to the human race and that it would not obliterate the Indians. Eliding his own negative bias towards girls he, in fact, claimed to speak on behalf of them by proclaiming that Indian girls did not have the ability to choose their own husbands and that since "time immemorial" they willingly played second fiddle to their husbands/men. Relegating the girl-child to a perpetual secondary position, Sanyal claimed that the marital age for boys should be raised: it was after all men who shouldered the main brunt of household responsibilities. Again, undermining his own position, Sanyal urged that typically, Indian men were not married underage; often they were capable of making their own decisions. However, men should weigh their decisions carefully before committing themselves to marriage. Full of generalities and contradictions, the article concluded by strongly condemning the West, defending child marriage, and championing a patriarchal culture.[65] In his dense narrative, the girl-child was unable to make choices and assert agency; but, she was capable of being a sexual partner, bearing children, and becoming the mother of future citizens. Nonetheless, in these chauvinistic imaginings, the girl-child both in her abilities and inabilities occupied a significant position.

---

[65] This conservative and contradictory rhetoric was not new in the last quarter of nineteenth century Bengal. Tanika Sarkar identified this group of orthodox, professional, urban estate-holders of considerable influence in Calcutta as "revivalist-nationalist" who deployed an overtly nationalistic rhetoric to defy any form of colonial intervention in Hindu domestic sphere. Also, the Native Marriage Act of 1872 was met with a storm of controversy and the conservative resistance opened up the space for discussion of Hindu conjugality in the public domain. Tanika Sarkar, "Conjugality and Hindu Nationalism: Resisting Colonial Reason and the Death of a Child-Wife," in *Hindu Wife, Hindu Nation: Community, Religion, and Cultural Nationalism* (Delhi: Permanent Black, 2001), 191–225. Rochona Majumdar, *Marriage and Modernity: Family Values in Colonial Bengal, 1870–1956* (Durham: Duke University Press, 2009).

In the volatile socio-political culture of late nineteenth-century Bengal, there also prevailed a counter-narrative that argued against child marriage. While *Swasthya* and *Chikitsa Sammilani* included essays from both sides, several essays in *Swasthya* challenged the conservative opinion defending child marriage. They ascribed the ill-health of Bengalis to child marriage and argued that marriage and national health were inextricably connected. Refuting the claim that child marriage was prevalent in ancient India, one writer urged its readers to be mindful of the age of marriage. With a strong recommendation of age twenty-five to forty for males and under thirty-five for women, the essay even called for government intervention to determine and enforce marital practices. Exclaiming "Like father, like sons," the article cited the research of several European scholars that demonstrated age and physical health of fathers affected the health of children and hence of the nation.

Worries about marriage age and age of consumption, procreation, and national health were recurrent themes in *Swasthya*.[66] One article argued that the birth of a girl-child resulted in worries among parents—first about her looks and then about procuring dowries for her marriage. With the advent of a boy, parents worried about his education and then his ability to earn his livelihood. Underscoring parental worries, it pointed out that fathers of both boys and girls were driven by financial considerations in negotiating marriages: a son's father wanted to extract maximum dowry from the brides; a girl's father looked for a bargain in selecting sons-in-law. The writer also urged fathers to check the family medical history of the bridegrooms to prevent deformities and illness in the future offspring.[67]

In this patriarchal discourse surrounding children and health, the value of girls rested on being mothers and for bringing revenue to their in-laws, although the last part was never discussed openly in those journals.[68] The conservatives buttressed their views by claiming that girls

---

[66] Writers in this magazine also linked dowry with national health. A dowry-death from the early years of the twentieth century that continued to attract national attention in contemporary India was that of Snehalata Mukhopadhyay, who committed suicide to save her father from paying an inordinate amount of dowry for her marriage. For more on Snehalata, see Rochona Majumdar, *Marriage and Modernity*, 54–90.

[67] *Swasthya* (Aswin–Kartick 1308 B.S. [1901]), reprinted in Basu, *Samayiki*, 190.

[68] For recovering subjectivities of girl children in literature see Barnita Bagchi, "Cheery Children, Growing Girls, and Developing Young Adults: On Reading, Growing, and

were not opposed to early marriage and that such practice was not adverse to their life. The slightly liberal version that opposed child marriage spoke not for the girls' own mental and physical well-being, but rather worried that early childbirth by premature bodies would produce weak offspring and hence unhealthy citizens.[69] Furthermore, although the state of motherhood was celebrated, mothers were not placed in any decision-making capacity. At the end girls/women were imagined for producing healthy "children" (male) to constitute the future nation. The affect and bodily care of the future nation were both delegated to women although they were given very little power in real life. The genre of scientific literature signalled a shift—what started with a chronicling of India's unjust practices of child marriage and widowhood later got entwined with a critique of the debilitating characteristics of India's male youth and young adults. The girl-child surfaced in questions related to child marriage, only to quickly "sublimate" into a wife and mother.[70]

Motherhood as the obligatory function of the woman was also emphasized in the leading periodicals for women—*Antahpur, Bamabodhini Patrika, Mahila*, and *Paricharika*.[71] Upholding family as the societal cornerstone, the predominantly male editors and authors of these magazines envisioned a reformed domesticity with special emphasis on child-rearing and motherhood—qualities constituting an ideal mother (*adarsha mata*) and a good housewife (*sugrihini*).[72] The "new woman"

Hopscotching Across Categories," Working Papers id:1993, eSocialSciences (https://ideas.repec.org/p/ess/wpaper/id1993.html (accessed on December 3, 2019).

[69] Tanika Sarkar, *Hindu Wife, Hindu Nation* (New Delhi: Permanent Black, 2001) Ruby Lal, "Recasting the Women's Question: The Girl-Child/Woman in the Colonial Encounter," *Interventions* 10, no. 3 (2008): 321–339.

[70] For *Bamabodhini Patrika* and education of women see Krishna Sen, "Lessons in Self-Fashioning: 'Bamabodhini Patrika' and the Education of Women in Bengal," *The Victorian Periodicals Review* 37, no. 2 (Summer 2004): 176–191. Tanika Sarkar, Geraldine Forbes, Ruby Lal, Ishita Pande, Rochona Majumdar among others have written about this fleeting presence of the "girl-child" in discussions and debates on child marriage and the passage of the Age of Consent Act in 1891.

[71] See Meredith Borthwick, *Changing Role of Women in Bengal 1840–1905* (Princeton, NJ: Princeton University Press, 1984); Partha Chatterjee, *The Nation and Its Fragments* (Princeton, NJ: Princeton University Press, 1993); Tapan Raychaudhuri, "Love in a Colonial Climate: Marriage, Sex and Romance in Nineteenth-Century Bengal," in *Perceptions, Emotions, Sensibilities: Essays on India's Colonial and Postcolonial Experiences* (Delhi: Oxford University Press, 1999); Tanika Sarkar, *Hindu Wife, Hindu Nation* (New Delhi: Permanent Black, 2001); Judith Walsh, *Domesticity in Colonial India: What Women Learned When Men Gave Them Advice* (New Delhi: Oxford University Press, 2004).

[72] Walsh, *Domesticity in Colonial India*.

(*bhadramahila*), embodying selected virtues of the Victorian lady and the chaste, Hindu female was expected to subscribe to the new domestic ideology: "it's a shame, that not a single woman has been able to rise up to the qualities of an ideal mother... that is why Bengali society is not witnessing domestic peace, purity, harmony, and prosperity. Mother is the presiding deity (Goddess Lakshmi) of the home, the peace-keeper and care-giver for all ... "[73] Several articles while exalting the role of women as mothers, discussed how harmful it was for underage girls to be mothers and for the children born who were "deprived of the guidance of an educated and capable mother due to the latter's lack of education."[74] While this was one of the few spaces where there was an actual concern for girls, and their health and happiness, from male authors, the conception of women as wives, mothers, and caregivers obliterated any attempt to position them as children. In these early years of print culture, the few women who wrote and contributed to these journals also veiled their desires behind the roles of wives, mothers, and daughters. They emphatically echoed the same sentiments as men upheld. The youthful presence of frolicking girl-children was never emphasized by men or the few women who published, a point that we will explore further below.[75]

The Male Child and Youth as the Future Citizens

The urgency for national regeneration that undergirded the writings of the medical professionals echoed a deep sense of loss. Deliberating on natural, local, and behavioural practices, an article in *Chikitsa Sammilani* emphasized that "[T]he belief that is currently nurtured by foreigners and many thoughtful, nationalist-minded Indians that people of this country are short-lived and weak is not completely unfounded." It attributed the causes of its degeneration to two sets of factors: (a) *naisargik* (natural and

---

[73] "Adarsha Janani" ("Ideal Mother"), *Bamabodhini Patrika* cited in Pradipa Basu, *Samayiki* (Kolkata: Ananda Publishers, 2009), 21, p. twenty-one. [Page number spelled out in original.].
[74] Bose, *Health and Society in Bengal*, 27.
[75] This point was made clear in Ruby Lal, *Coming of Age in Nineteenth Century India: The Girl-Child and the Art of Playfulness* (Cambridge: Cambridge University Press, 2012).

physical) or *sthaniya* (local); (b) *krome labdha dushita protha* (gradually acquired corrupt practices) or *prakritimulak* (behavioural). While explaining the natural factors such as air pressure and temperature that impact on human physique and strength and the way they could be altered through the change of locale for successive generations, the main focus of the article was on corrupt practices and behaviours undermining physical health. It suggested that those social ills could be remedied through determined effort [strong will] to change harmful cultural norms.[76] The principal reasons for the loss of health and character were attributed to child marriage; polygamy; unwholesome food; lack of exercise; drinking; masturbation; and sexual intercourse.[77] Paying close attention to the condition of women and sexuality, the writer called upon the expertise of European and American authorities, such as that of Dr R. Trall's *Sexual Pathology*.[78] The references to Western sources and harping on conditions of degeneration of male youths owing to natural and environmental factors testified to the strong influences eugenicist ideas of Victorian and Edwardian England had on these writers.

The desire to reform the health and mind of the youth population, to build and train their body and form their character signalled the early efforts of the Indian intelligentsia to claim the role of fathers and create active citizens, although these terms (father, citizen) were not directly invoked and remained rather implicit.[79] Missing in this literature were the questions of caste, class, religion, or sect. Its explicit and often lengthy discussion of sexuality alluded to an adult male audience. However, the main focus of the discussion was how to reform and remold the future generation of citizens—typically, male children.

---

[76] "Jatiya Daihik Punurujjiban" ("Regeneration of National Health") in *Chikitsha Sammilani* (Baishakh, 1292 B.S. [April, 1885]), reprinted in Bose, *Health and Society in Bengal*, 135–141.

[77] *Chikitsha Sammilani* (Baishakh, 1292 B.S. [April, 1885]), reprinted in Pradip Kumar Basu, *Samayiki*, 135–141.

[78] There are few if any details given about these Western doctors, making it difficult to identify them. Trall is one of the few exceptions; it is plausible that the author was invoking Dr Russell Trall (1812–1877), an American health reformer and physician, who emphasized hygiene, vegetarianism, and hydropathy as a cure to physical malfunction. See Bose, *Health and Society in Bengal*, 110 (footnote).

[79] See Carey Watt, "Education: The Making of Active Citizens in Mind and Body," *Serving the Nation: Cultures of Service, Association, and Citizenship in Colonial India* (Delhi: Oxford University Press, 2005), 130–170.

Diet and nutrition constituted one of the major areas of deliberation for the writer-fathers.[80] Combining elements from India's past as well as from the West, the authors merged instructions from Charaka and Sushruta, ancient Indian scholars, with the "British enthusiasm" towards diet and exercise. Several essays claimed that negligence towards diet was a primary reason for the lack of strength and "physical degeneration" among the Hindus. The "fathers" writing in *Chikitsha Sammilani* and *Swasthya* emphasized "portion control" when it came to intake of food. Reminding readers of the different food groups—protein, carbohydrate, and fat—and their implications for physical well-being, one article in *Swasthya* even included comparative charts showing how different kinds of individuals (healthy and active, healthy but inactive, "ill-nourished") expended their energy.[81] Once again the subject of concern was the youth, school-going male children between ten and eighteen years of age, and their diets. This specific age group, transitioning from youth to early adulthood (*Kaishor o joubanarambha*), the authors argued, represented an important stage in the human life-cycle for its massive physiological and psychological shifts. One author argued that consumption of nutritious food was urgent for the best fulfilment of physical and mental development. Lack of a healthy diet would lead to dismal adulthood for the upcoming generation because the body and mind would not be prepared to deal with the harsh, competitive reality they were faced with. In many ways, the author—anonymous like many in these publications, and so likely the journal editor—tried to establish the antagonistic connection between colonial rule and the youth population. Turning to parents who were charged with shaping the mind and body of their children, he complained, "parents in our country today are so bogged down with education of their boys and girls that they sometimes tend to neglect

---

[80] For the adoption and consumption of certain kinds of food and cuisine and their association with masculinity and self-articulation of the Indians see Parama Roy, "Meat-Eating, Masculinity, and Renunciation in India: A Gandhian Grammar of Diet," *Gender & History* 14, no. 1 (April 2002): 62–91; Utsa Ray, *Culinary Culture in Colonial India: A Cosmopolitan Platter and the Middle Class* (Cambridge: Cambridge University Press, 2015); Ray, "Consumption and the Making of the Middle Class in South Asia," *History Compass* 12, no. 1 (January 2014):11–19; and Ray, "The Body and Its Purity: Dietary Politics in Colonial Bengal," *Indian Economic and Social History Review* 50, no. 4 (October–December 2013): 395–421.

[81] "Ahaar-er Poriman" ("Diet Portions"), *Swasthya* (Jaishtha, 1307 B.S. [1900]), reprinted in Bose, *Samayiki*, 156–158.

the very important responsibility of feeding children properly."[82] He warned parents that their hastiness for children's education should not undermine or neglect the latter's physical health, as good health was indispensable for a bright future. After a series of instructions, the article encouraged Indian parents to follow a model diet chart adapted from a boarding school in England. What is interesting in this discourse was the writer-fathers' ambivalent relationship to the colonial rule: on the one hand, colonial education was blamed for excessive stress and physical debility of the younger generation; on the other, it was the British/Western diet and nutrition that were considered to be the model. He exhorted:

> English boys who attend boarding schools have a fixed time for their meals... In every aspect of life we imitate the British. Likewise, during student life if the diet and activities of our boys are restrained and regulated, it will be really beneficial for them.[83]

Saying this the writer provided a chart of the diet followed in English boarding schools. Although the essay broadly targeted a specific age group that represented the youth subsumed under the broad category of children, it mainly included the male population and elided the nurturance of the girl-child.

The unabashed discrimination between boys and girls was evident in the article "Pathyaboshthar Khadya" ("Diet for Students"), published in a subsequent issue of *Swasthya*. It specifically focused on boys between the ages of eight and twenty. It emphasized how a boy's body and mind developed until age twenty; a girl, on the other hand, would be "old" at twenty (*kuri-te buri*). A leading health journal trying to influence the nation thus revealed not only its gender bias but also the prevailing attitude towards girl-children. This essay further cautioned parents to be mindful of their sons' diet while nothing was said about their daughters: it urged parents not to subject boys to the pressure of modern education and sacrifice their health at the cost of intellectual excellence. Age twenty seemed to be an important benchmark as the writer insisted that knowledge could

---

[82] "Pathshala-r Chhele-der Ahaar" ("Diet for School Boys"), *Swasthya* (Karttick, 1307 B.S. [1900]), reprinted in Basu, *Samayiki*, 158–161.
[83] "Pathshala-r Chhele-der Ahaar," *Samayiki*, 160.

be acquired at any stage in life but proper development of physique and health could not be attained beyond twenty.[84] The elision of girls as the subject of bodily care and nutrition mirrored the same bias that pervaded the pedagogical literature as well. The differential treatment of boys and girls led to the latter's subordination to patriarchal values and norms. Able-bodied boys represented the prospective citizenry; but girls figured only as mothers and wives and were valued for their roles in social reproduction.

If fathers worried about the diet of a growing boy to build a healthy nation, they were further beset with concern over the sexual behaviour of the male youth population. The youth folded under the category of the "child," and an undefined segment in the colonial discourse, represented a specific demographic in the vernacular literature. The youths occupied a grey zone—they were repositories of hope as the future lay with them; they were also sources of despair because of their degenerate behaviour. Echoing the colonial critique of sexual excesses among the native males, the Bengali writers voiced the ominous peril of masturbation plaguing the youths.[85] The contrasting images of the youth as representing modernity and moral laxity was tied to the articulation of the middle-class self-identity based on class, caste, social, and cultural divides. The professional fathers, vying for power with the colonial state, consciously disassociated themselves from a section of the native population allegedly wallowing in decadence and decrepitude. They scripted their critique in satires, plays, poems, and novels that underscored the society's moral decay and illuminated the tension between existing folk and the emerging elite cultures.[86] Leading satirists wrote scathing accounts of the youth population who, as part of a new comprador class fostered by the colonial political economy, gained social power and wealth in the new urban environment and were invested in a *demimonde* culture of courtesans and prostitutes.[87]

---

[84] "Pathyaboshthar Khadya" ("Diet for Students"), *Swsasthya* (Agrahayan, 1307 B.S. [1900]), reprinted in Basu, *Samayiki*, 161–162.

[85] Sexual anxieties and sexual knowledge also became palpable concerns in early-twentieth-century Marathi periodicals. Srikant Botre and Douglas Haynes, "Sexual Knowledge, Sexual Anxieties: Middle-Class Males in Western India and the Correspondence in Samaj Swasthya, 1927–53." *Modern Asian Studies* 51, no. 4 (2017): 1–44.

[86] Sumanta Banerjee, *The Parlour and the Street* (Calcutta: Seagull, 1989).

[87] Sex work was so rampant in nineteenth-century Calcutta that Kaliprasanna Sinha's *Hutom Penchar Naksha*, a trenchant satire of the period, documented how even the illustrious and

Drawing on those social symptoms, medical practitioners from Bengal, who were engaged with socio-cultural debates raging over health and body, lamented that masturbation was assuming endemic proportion among youths and was sapping the foundation of a healthy nation.[88] Labelling masturbation as a contagious act among boys ranging between ages eight to fifteen, the authors listed how this unnatural (*anaisargik*) act of gratification destroyed intelligence, energy, enthusiasm; brought about behavioural changes such as irritation, lack of appetite, and poor performance in school; caused iron deficiency, quick ejaculation, erectile dysfunction, and a shrinking penis; ultimately, the ill-effects were manifested in several bodily and psychological symptoms from low-grade fever and low morale, to lack of interest in women and premature death.[89] Blaming the decline of India on her degraded youth culture, an article entitled "Bharat-er Obonoti" ("Degeneration of India;" author unknown) in the journal *Onubeekshan* (See Figure 3.3), urged fathers, mothers, teachers, guardians, and social reformers to arise, awake, shake off the awkwardness, and take control of the situation by openly forbidding young children from this heinous act. It implored that restraining the youth was the only way to lift India out of the mire; India was ruined by these deleterious practices—her only hope lay with her future generation—only the strength and intelligence of the young generation could bring about an end to the distress and suffering of the poor motherland.[90] Interestingly, in contrast to the author who took English boarding school food as the dietary model, this article ended with a prescription of diet drawn from Ayurveda that was suitable for young boys; it also pointed out the limitation of British treatment and medicine for specifically Indian cases.[91]

"respectable" members of the *bhadralok* society, such as Prince Dwarkanath Tagore, rented most of his forty-three houses in North Calcutta to sex workers.Kaliprasanna Sinha, *Hutom Penchar Naksha* (Calcutta, 1862), cited in S. N. Mukherjee, *Calcutta: Myths and History* (Calcutta: Subarnarekha, 1977).; Bhabanicharan Bandyopadhyay, *Kalikata Kamalalaya* (Calcutta, 1825).

[88] For explication of the connection among "marriage, masturbation and the government of self" see Pande, *Medicine, Race, and Liberalism in British Bengal*. See especially 170–177.

[89] Pyarimohan Sengupta Kaviraj, "Hastamaithun-e Balak o Naba Jubakgan," in *Chikitsha Sammilani* (1229 B.S. [1887]), reprinted in Basu, *Samayiki*, 227–229.

[90] *Onubeekshan* (Poush 1282 B.S. [1875]), reprinted in Basu, *Samayiki*, 229–231.

[91] For more on Ayurveda see Rachel Berger, *Ayurveda Made Modern: Political Histories of Indigenous Medicine in North India, 1900–1955* (London: Palgrave Macmillan, 2013); Projit Mukharji, *Doctoring Traditions: Ayurveda, Small Technologies, and Braided Sciences* (Chicago: University of Chicago Press, 2016).

The concerns of the print media were not entirely abstract, but echoed the authors' worries about their own bodies and those of their families. The worry with excessive sexuality of the younger generation and the conflation of early marriage of youth with the masturbation epidemic signalled an urgency on part of many or even most of the intelligentsia to internalize and respond to the colonial critique that blamed India's degeneration—and thus, implicitly or explicitly, the necessity of British rule—on its unwholesome social practices. Concern with the frail bodies of Indian/Bengali youth—attributed primarily to "unnatural" means of fulfilling sexual appetite fuelled by Western influence and to be countered with prescriptions from Charaka, the ancient authority on medicine—fanned masturbation to a level of national calamity.[92]

The anxieties of the authors about diet and sexuality of young males were resonant of parallel concerns both in other parts of India, such as in the reform movements of Gurukul Kangri in Punjab, as well as in Victorian and Edwardian England. What is strikingly different in the Bengali scientific discourse was the absence of advocacy of celibacy or *brahmacharya*, a theme that enjoyed preeminence in instructions of Gurukul Kangri. The medical practitioners of Bengal urged parental control, restrained behaviour, and wholesome diet of the rising youth population; but they did not put forward a prescription of *brahmacharya* which other nationalist organizations so ardently championed with a eugenicist logic.[93]

An analysis of this discourse helps unpack the worries that were ingrained in the subliminal presence of an undefined mass of children who were constantly brought to the fore through the idiom of crisis and for their redeeming power as the future generation. Yet, the apparent silence

---

[92] Since much of the debate in the pages of the Bengali medical journal ensued from letters written by anonymous readers/masturbators, repentant of their past actions, the authenticity of their accounts is open to doubt. In contrast, in Marathi periodicals, young middle-class men actively sought sexual advice and shared their sexual knowledge and anxieties with the editor, R.D. Karve, a major advocate of birth-control and sex education in western India. Also, contrary to the Bengali writers' condemnation of youth for their sexual excesses, the 1940s-print culture in western India widely circulated advertisements of sex tonics promoting middle-class men's sexuality and conjugal happiness. See , Srikant Botre and Douglas Haynes, "Sexual Knowledge, Sexual Anxieties: Middle-Class Males in Western India and the Correspondence in Samaj Swasthya, 1927–1953." *Modern Asian Studies* 51, no. 4 (2017): 1–44; Douglas E. Haynes, "Selling Masculinity: Advertisements of Sex Tonics and the Making of Modern Conjugality in Western India, 1900–1945," *South Asian Journal of South Asian Studies* 35, no. 4 (2012): 1–45.

[93] Harald Fischer-Tiné, "From Brahmacharya to 'Conscious Race Culture:' Victorian Discourses of 'Science' and Hindu Traditions in Early Indian Nationalism."

on issues of class, caste, race, ethnicity, and religion (particularly the absence of Muslim children, although Muslim women's bodies figured in the medicalized discourse of the Europeans) establish the imagined character of a homogenized body of children as a "potentiality rather than an actuality"[94]—who would grow physically, emotionally, intellectually to function as responsible adult citizens in a new nation. The engagement of the Bengali intelligentsia, both conservatives and progressives, with children and youth in Bengal was symptomatic of their concerns to shape the minds and bodies of India's would-be citizens, not to mention their own children. The rapid spread of print culture in the last quarter of the nineteenth century provided them with an outlet to air their views. This scientific literature became a vehicle for the native intelligentsia to display their courage to blame colonial rule for draining the vitality and health of India's youth. They showed the inadequacy of Western medical science for India and urged the colonial rulers to harness the resources and insights offered by Charaka, Sushruta, Ayurveda, Unani, and Kaviraji to make modern medicine effective for the Indian population. The new discourse on science and health, articulated in the public domain, provided the colonized literati with an opportunity to confidently assert their autonomy, sovereignty, and their differences with the West and produce their own forms of knowledge through a negotiation of the best of Western and Eastern methods and practices. But to mobilize their claims the native interlocutors had to appropriate the home and its members—namely, children and women.

Children in this generalized narrative were constantly hurled from the margins to the centre while their personhood and subjectivity were hardly brought to the fore. Children, as well as women, were viewed as the raw clay out of which to shape a new India. In this new cultural production of scientific literature, the indigenous male literati imagined themselves as moral guardians and also imagined children and women as both hapless victims and repositories of hope. Even if children and youths were not frail and degenerate across the board and even if the epidemic of masturbation and the repentant masturbator tropes were possibly made up (their authenticity remained questionable for Bengal)—the "fathers" would have "invented" them. The children and youths, in other words, were doubly imagined:

---

[94] Claudia Castañeda, *Figurations: Child, Bodies, Worlds* (Durham, NC: Duke University Press, 2002), 1–12.

imagined in the ordinary sense of being invented and imagined in the Anderson–Taylor–Chatterjee sense of being characters in a social imaginary. It is, of course, easier for one to demand "imaginary" youths to be reformed than to improve one's own character, or the character of one's actual children; and imaginary children are easier to manipulate in the creation of a new social imaginary than actual children would be. In this new discourse, there is an erasure of class, caste, and religion although the nature and language of discussion were almost prohibitive for ordinary people. Furthermore, the prescriptions on diet and daily living made it abundantly clear that the literature addressed the rising middle-class population.

To study the history of this specific genre of scientific discourse is not to emphasize a cause–effect relationship between the colonial critique and the colonized's response but to acknowledge the complicity and coexistence of both in a highly charged environment fraught with social and cultural tensions—the conflictive intersections where new forms of knowledge and subjecthood were produced and where children as ubiquitous subalterns were invoked as future citizens although remaining as undefined, liminal characters.[95] Evident was the incommensurability of the discourse where the "imagined community" of the future generation remained undefined at its best and exclusive at its worst.

Conclusion

This chapter aimed to recuperate the fatherly voice embedded in the scientific literature of late-nineteenth-century Bengal.[96] My attempt was to underscore the ambivalent authorship of the writers as "imagined" fathers and their appropriation of the category of children as social imaginaries to define a collective social identity. According to Benedict Anderson and subsequently qualified by Partha Chatterjee for the colonial context, "imaginings of nations" require "new tools and forms of imaginations—new

---

[95] Indra Sengupta and Daud Ali, eds., *Knowledge Production, Pedagogy and Institutions in Colonial India* (New York: Palgrave, 2011).
[96] The scientific literature discussed earlier has been extensively scrutinized in recent scholarship. See works by Projit Mukharji, Mark Harrison, Biswamoy Pati, Rachel Berger, Ishita Pande, Durba Mitra, and others cited previously.

imaginaries."[97] The social imaginary, an idea developed by Charles Taylor drawing on Anderson's "imagined community," is complex at any given time. It involves the "kind of normal expectations we have of each other, the kind of common understanding that enables us to carry out the collective practices that make up our social life."[98] Such understanding, which is "both factual and normative" also represents a "largely unstructured and inarticulate understanding of our whole situation … "[99] The social imaginary of nineteenth-century Bengalis encompassed an enormous range of ideas about health and hygiene, parents and children, bodies and minds while overlapping and contesting with social imaginaries held by Europeans and non-Bengali Indians. Though their social imaginaries cannot be precisely defined as "explicit doctrines," this chapter highlighted many of the themes and tropes that make up their imaginaries. Most centrally, it has been argued that in the genre of vernacular scientific literature, lying outside the official curriculum and colonial pedagogy, Bengali middle-class men appropriated children as new tools and forms of imagination for their own self-fashioning. The gendered notions of children in their multiple guises were both factual and normative: the notions gestured towards the *bhadralok* fathers' world of thinking who positioned themselves as reformers and visionaries capable of establishing acceptable norms for the juvenile population. Although never identifying themselves as fathers, the writers assumed paternalistic measures for the collective moral economy to redeem the future generation. Acutely aware of the alleged shortcomings afflicting the natives, they imagined children in various positions of precarity and power.

In the contested production of knowledge, I located the autonomy and authority of educated Indian males, not as subjugated subjects known for their physical frailty and intellectual disability but as caring and authoritative fathers who went beyond their mundane parental obligation of providing economic sustenance and protection. The new print culture provided the fathers with an avenue for achieving governance over bodies in their homes in a context where political self-governance seemed only a distant or future possibility in the public sphere. Contrary

---

[97] Craig Calhoun, "Nation and Imagination: How Benedict Anderson Revolutionized Political Theory," *ABC Religion and Ethics* (May 9, 2017) (http://www.abc.net.au/religion/articles/2017/05/09/4665722.htm (accessed on May 5, 2018).
[98] Charles Taylor, *Modern Social Imaginaries*, 24.
[99] Charles Taylor, *Modern Social Imaginaries*, 25.

to the argument that home and family represented a distinct sphere for Indian nationalists' self-articulation, my study demonstrates the multiple ways the domestic and the familial were deeply imbricated and manifest in public concerns. In the changing socio-cultural milieu this gender and class-specific literature for the Bengali middle-class signalled an "emotional frontier" for collective emotional formations of subjects as fathers and children, a theme that we will explore in the next chapter.[100]

The scientific discourse, emerging at the intersection of colonial and early nationalist politics, harboured the question of masculinity beyond the realm of public movements against colonial authority.[101] The Indian literati, who took part in this public debate on issues of health, hygiene, child marriage, and sexuality, simultaneously accepted and rejected the colonial politics of masculinity and paternity. They upheld themselves as male subjects endowed with the responsibility of bringing up healthy citizens. In the hierarchical organization of power with the colonial state at the apex, these native men positioned themselves as heads of household and as leaders of a burgeoning nation—the motherland that they were trying to recover from foreign domination. The trope of degeneration accepted the frailty of the current generation and in trying to remedy it, the educated community not only blamed the colonial government for such a state but also expressed their hegemonic aspirations to take control as male subjects.[102]

The "insistent figuration" of the "child" as future of the nation, made possible by the proliferation of print culture in late-nineteenth-century Bengal, played a constitutive role in the making of the domineering and the sanctimonious figure of the "father," who was actively constructing a moral universe centred on newly envisioned models of family, men, women, and children.[103] In the austere discourse of the "fathers," children

---

[100] For the concept of "emotional frontier" and emotional formations, see Karen Vallgårda, Kristine Alexander and Stephanie Olsen, "Emotions and Global Politics of Childhood," in *Childhood, Youth and Emotions in Modern History: National, Colonial, and Global Perspectives*, ed. Stephanie Olsen (London: Palgrave Macmillan, 2015).

[101] Mrinalini Sinha has analyzed four key moments—the Ilbert Bill controversy (1883–1884); the native volunteer movement (1885–1886); the Public Service Commission (1886–1887); and the Age of Consent Controversy (1891)—to explicate the politics of colonial masculinity. *Colonial Masculinity: The "Manly Englishman" and the "Effeminate Bengali" in the Late Nineteenth Century* (Manchester, UK: Manchester University Press, 1995).

[102] This point has been raised earlier by Tanika Sarkar, "The Hindu Wife and the Hindu Nation: Domesticity and Nationalism in Nineteenth Century Bengal," *Studies in History* 8, no. 2 (1992): 119–120. Also published in *Hindu Wife, Hindu Nation*.

[103] I borrowed the term "insistent figuration" from Castañeda.

of today would not only become the citizens of tomorrow but in their state of "becoming" adults they also became vessels for containing today's "wrongs"—early marriage, sexual excesses, moral and physical degeneration—thus absolving the fathers blamed for the same vices. In contrast, girl-children were turned into mothers of the nation. This transference of guilt to male children and the usurpation of agency from females were enabled by the configuration of the child in its making; in its inherent power to mutate, to transform, and hence amend and transcend its limitations in the future.[104] But the native experts' contested discussions on sexuality, child marriage, national health, and regeneration also appropriated children and their bodies as a public platform, as an impassioned battleground to reclaim their own stakes.

I argue that when the relationships of native masculinity to family, women, nation, and state were under scrutiny, the figure of the child became the enabling agent and the ground for challenging stereotypes and imagining an alternate universe.[105] The act of imagining and historicizing children, in both the imaginary, utopian past and an imaginary future empowered the male writers. The tremendous plasticity of children—the girl as the child-wife and mother of future progenies and the boy as citizen subject—provided the perfect medium for projection and articulation of the subjugated native's own self. In the local figurations of the gendered youth, thrust into the public space by the exigency of a colonial elite, were imbricated global concerns with progress, modernity, and the new nation. The blanket category of children, with its inclusions and exclusions, thus became one of the new "habitations of modernity," assailed by its vices but simultaneously produced, reshaped, and determined by modern powers in their circulation and production of knowledge.[106]

---

[104] For childhood as "an imperfect transitional state on the way to adulthood" see Ashis Nandy, "Reconstructing Childhood: A Critique of the Ideology of Adulthood," in *Traditions, Tyranny and Utopia: Essays in the Politics of Awareness*, ed. Nandy (Delhi: Oxford University Press, 1992).
[105] For the plasticity of children in the realm of Bengali literature see Satadru Sen, "A Juvenile Periphery: The Cartographies of Literary Childhood in Colonial Bengal," *Journal of Colonialism and Colonial History* 5, no. 1 (2004).
[106] Dipesh Chakrabarty, *Habitations of Modernity: Essays in the Wake of Subaltern Studies* (Chicago: University of Chicago Press, 2002).

4

Imagining Fatherhood

Representations of Fathers in Autobiographical Literature of Colonial Bengal

> For five years a son shall be treated with great tenderness. For ten years he shall be subjected to rigorous discipline. When he attains his sixteenth year the father shall treat his son as a friend.[1]

Bipin Chandra Pal (1858–1932), the eminent nationalist leader whom we briefly met in Chapter 2, commenced his autobiography with the above saying, proudly affirming that his father religiously followed the preaching of the ancient Indian scholar Chanakya, aka Kautilya, in bringing him up. "Up to my sixth year I was treated by my father almost as a young divinity." Bipin's every whim was satisfied, and nobody dared to restrain him. Much to the consternation of the father, Bipin's mother was the only exception to take the child to task.[2] The closeness was further reinforced as Bipin Pal (See Figure 4.1) recalled how his father had fed him with his own hands and they enjoyed food from the same platter; his father gave him his daily bath, and every night Bipin slept under the "protective embrace of his father."[3] Pal invoked fond memories of his father, showering love and affection on him to corroborate the sayings of the ancient text. The experience also attested to the "intense emotional ties between parents and children within the family," a practice that cemented "the new idea of childhood" that was produced by the ideological

---

[1] Bipin Chandra Pal, *Memories of My Life and Times* (New Delhi: UBS Publishers' Distributors, 2004 [1932]), 10. For a different reading of the relationship between Bipin Chandra Pal and his father, see Judith E. Walsh, "Fathers and Sons: The Second Generation," in *Growing Up in British India* (New York: Holmes and Meier, 1983), 113–130.

[2] Pal, *Memories of My Life*, 10.

[3] Pal, *Memories of My Life*, 10–11.

Fathers in a Motherland. Swapna M. Banerjee, Oxford University Press. © Oxford University Press India 2022.
DOI: 10.1093/oso/9789391050245.003.0004

Figure 4.1 Bipin Chandra Pal

discourses of nineteenth-century Bengal.[4] This "new idea" of childhood that dominated the pages of normative, pedagogical, and autobiographical literature, however, represented itself as an old one, seeking its affirmation and even reinventing an ancient Hindu ideal for the father-son (and father-children) relation that both challenged and complemented Western and Victorian notions of domesticity and child-parent relationships.

In the new normative discourse of late colonial Bengal, the family was conceived as an important domain where the child occupied the centre stage. Proclaiming that the family is a cornerstone of society and it ought to be reformed if society needed to change, the Bengali intelligentsia wrote profusely about an ideal family built around new notions of

---

[4] Pradip Kumar Bose, "Sons of the Nation: Child Rearing in the New Family," in *Texts of Power: Emerging Disciplines in Colonial Bengal*, ed. Partha Chatterjee (Minneapolis: University of Minnesota Press, 1995), 118–144, here 118, 119.

conjugality and roles of the "new woman" as a good wife (*sugrihini*) and an ideal mother (*adarsha mata*). Informed by Victorian norms of domesticity, the normative literature on family discussed conjugal relationships, wifely duties, motherhood, child-rearing, health, hygiene, and sexuality.[5] But, conspicuous by its absence is a discussion of what constituted an "ideal" father. A likely explanation for this elision could be the presumptive attitude of the male authors—they took their position of *paterfamilias* as "natural" and felt no necessity to spell out their roles. They assumed an auto-didactic stance as reformed sons, fathers, and husbands—the "new man"—who acquired different sensibilities through modern education and Western learning yet held on to their "traditional" pasts, as well. It was a process similar to the one these men pursued in envisioning the "new" woman: a creative assimilation of ideas from Victorian domesticity and a reinvented Hindu past, intervened by numerous concurrent forces. Even though educated Indian men associated themselves with the world of service outside the home, they were confident of their unquestioned authority in the family which acted as a source of refuge, comfort, and support for myriad afflictions they faced under the colonial regime.[6]

The construction of separate spaces and roles for men and women in colonial Bengal was part of a global process that resonated with experiences of Victorian and Edwardian England (1837–1901).[7] In the wake of changes unleashed by an industrializing society and an expanding empire, Victorian fathers seemed to be in a state of flux. The pivotal role of Victorian mothers as doyens of domesticity and caregiving was on the ascendance and the "cult of the home," which was the crux of a bourgeois family ideal, also became the pivot for the hegemonic masculinity. Although scholars rightly warn against confining fathers to specific stereotypes,[8] one can still discern four distinct "patterns" of fathers in Victorian England: the "absent" and "distant" father who, responding to the exigencies of economic demands and compelling cultural factors in

---

[5] "Bangla Patra-Patrika-i Griha and Paribar" ("The Home and Family in Bengali Periodical Literature") in "Introduction" to *Samayiki: Purono Samayikpatrér Probondho Sankalan*, vol. 2: *Griha o Paribar*, ed. Pradip Bose (Kolkata: Ananda Publishers, 2009), 13 *thirteen* (not page 13)

[6] Pradip Bose, "Sons of the Nation," 118.

[7] Judith Walsh, *Domesticity in Colonial India: What Women Learned When Men Gave Them Advice* (New York: Rowman & Littlefield Publishers, 2004).

[8] Trev Lynn Broughton and Helen Rogers, *Gender and Fatherhood in the Nineteenth Century* (London: Palgrave Macmillan, 2007).

mid-nineteenth-century England, led an itinerant life-style; the protective father involved in raising children on a day-to-day basis; the playful father who spontaneously engaged with children and expressed intense grief over the loss of offspring; and the "tyrannical father" who used corporal punishment to discipline the child.[9]

Although the context and subject positions of Indian fathers in a colonized state were vastly different from the Victorians, they also exhibited distance, protectiveness, playfulness, and "tyranny" in dealing with children. But the composite image of fathers from children's accounts renders a more complicated picture. In Bengali children's imaginings fathers were supreme figures of veneration, not necessarily as providers but as moral icons. The image of "*adarsha pita*" (ideal father), though not sanctified in advice manuals, ran parallel to that of the *adarsha janani* (ideal mother).[10] Narratives from daughters, because of their differential treatment and socialization, added another dimension to practices of fatherhood by demonstrating their affection, vulnerability, and ambivalence. A sub-theme that ran through most accounts were fathers as strict enforcers of discipline who took children to task for any violation of norms, expectations, and family honour. As a larger-than-life figure, a father's authority was never defied in public, the realm in which the personal narratives circulated. A father's act, however egregious, autocratic, and irrational, was ultimately justified. In children's reconstruction of memories of their fathers, even the severity of his punishment was mitigated by a "just" cause and the outpouring of affection by the father.[11] The trope of filial piety and culture of restraint constituted the making of the modern dynamic father. A father's role was not restricted to his capacity as the breadwinner and the provider. A father commanded unquestioned authority and demanded respect irrespective of his decision, judgement, and behaviour; his acts of training and disciplining attended by anger and abuse provoked by children's misdemeanour and disobedience were markers of his manliness. *Pitritwo* (paternity) was therefore an important vehicle for the expression of *purushotwo* (manliness and masculinity).

---

[9] John Tosh, "Father and Child," in *A Man's Place: Masculinity and the Middle-Class Home in Victorian England* (New Haven: Yale University Press, 2007), 79–101.

[10] For role of mothers in raising sons in a different context, see Margaret L. King, *Mothers and Sons: A History* (Lewiston, New York Edwin Mellen Press, 2014).

[11] On reconstruction of past and history see Sumit Guha, *History and Collective Memory in South Asia 1200–2000* (Seattle: University of Washington Press, 2019).

Virtues of fatherhood imagined by children were inextricably linked with notions of masculinity. That home was integral to masculinity as a social identity is well documented in historical literature. As John Tosh put it, the home was "the place both where the boy was disciplined by dependence, and where man attained full adult status as householder."[12] In India, both ancient and modern, scholars argued that the hierarchical relations at home, especially between men and women, acted as the microcosm of the political world or the state; any disruption or disorder in one tended to threaten the other.[13] One of the major components of masculinity (*purushotwa*) endowed in the character of the father (*pita*) was maintaining peace and order at home. A father established his rule at home through providing, protecting, controlling, decision-making, and training its younger members in gender-specific ways so that they were fit to lead adult lives. As we have already seen, expectations for girls and boys were different. Whereas both needed the care of nurturing parents, especially of mothers, girls were raised to fulfil maternal and wifely functions. Boys, on the other hand, had to be economically independent and live a life without deviating from family norms. The sons were expected to carry on the lineage and enhance the prestige of the family. Nurturing a gender-specific vision of childhood, fatherhood in its child-rearing practices nurtured both hopes and fears, a practice that is intrinsic to all patriarchal cultures.[14]

Although the normative texts described in earlier chapters did not typically include how to be ideal fathers, the salience of fathers is displayed in children's testimonies about the impact their own fathers had on them as children.[15] The majority of personal narratives, including autobiographies, memoirs, diaries, correspondences, and other "portraits from memory"[16] of Bengali middle-class men and women, begin with the father and the paternal heritage. Memoirs, such as the one by Bipin Chandra Pal (See Figure 4.1), narrate intimate moments with fathers and

---

[12] John Tosh, "Introduction: Masculinity and Domesticity," in *A Man's Place* (New Haven, CT: Yale University Press, 2007), 2.

[13] See works by Tanika Sarkar and Kumkum Roy.

[14] See Tosh, *A Man's Place*, 4.

[15] Satischandra Chakravarti's *Santaner Charitra Gathan* that Pradip Bose discusses in "Sons of the Nation" briefly discussed the role of fathers.

[16] Malavika Karlekar, *Voices from Within: Early Personal Narratives of Bengali Women* (Delhi: Oxford University Press, 1993), 12.

a rather distant mother.[17] In most of these writings, the male authors' own positions as fathers do not figure prominently, even when they had children at the time they penned their accounts; instead, they appear as sons.[18] While it is impossible to determine whether the reasons for this come from genre conventions, patriarchal expectations that fathers were the most important figures in the family, or the authors' individual psyches and relationships with their parents and children, the fact that such narratives share this tendency suggests the explanation is most likely due to both literary and cultural factors rather than individual whim.

The most direct images of strong and authoritative fathers emerge from autobiographical literature, in contrast to the normative texts that laid the ideological foundation of a family, the pedagogical texts emphasizing filial piety, and the scientific journals upholding the health and hygiene of an incipient nation. The autobiographical accounts also register the emotions and sensibilities revealed in everyday life.[19] As Brian Hatcher pointed out, autobiographies, as a literary genre, evolved at the intersection of profound changes in colonial Bengal and India.[20] According to Dipesh Chakrabarty, of the many "public and private rituals of modern individualism that became visible in the nineteenth century," autobiography was one of the four genres that flourished to express the modern self.[21] Maintaining a distinction among three modern literary forms—lyric poetry, realistic novels, and autobiographies—Sudipta Kaviraj

---

[17] For a study of Indian autobiographies in the colonial period see Judith Walsh, *Growing Up in British India: Indian Autobiographers on Childhood and Education under the Raj* (New York: Holmes & Meier, 1983). Walsh reiterates the psychoanalyst Sudhir Kakar's thesis that the mother is "omnipresent in the psyche of Indian men." However, the examples in her work demonstrate that adult children as autobiographers were critical of their mothers and also noted their distance with her. Walsh, *Growing Up in British India*, 19.

[18] We will notice an exception in the case of the polymath Rabindranath Tagore (Chapter 5) whose writings and correspondences included his children. His memoirs did not dwell on his children at all.

[19] For autobiography as a performative genre and the relevance of the term "autobiography" and "autobiographical" in the South Asian context, see Anshu Malhotra and Siobhan Lambert-Hurley, eds., *Speaking of the Self: Gender, Performance, and Autobiography in South Asia* (Durham: Duke University Press, 2015).

[20] Brian Hatcher, "Sanskrit Pandits Recall Their Youth: Two Autobiographies from Nineteenth-Century Bengal," *Journal of the American Oriental Society* 121, no. 4 (October–December 2001): 580–592.

[21] Dipesh Chakrabarty, "Postcoloniality and the Artifice of History," in *Provincializing Europe: Postcolonial Thought and Historical Difference* (Princeton: Princeton University Press, 2000), 34.

claims that the autobiography holds "a peculiarly significant place in the inauguration of new forms of social life" because it "describes and reflectively comments on real, not fictive, lives." True, in contrast to lyric poetry and novels, autobiographies are closer to real lives, but they are nonetheless narratives, and thus fictive in their own way. Autobiographies by Bengali writers display a type of imagined relationship; what adults recounted about their childhood relationship with their fathers was in some sense idealized, insofar as the authors stressed certain aspects of that relationship over others and included or excluded anecdotes accordingly. To stress an earlier point, most of the male authors were fathers at the time of writing their autobiographies, but the fact that their autobiographies did not emphasize their daily activities with their children is surely significant—either of the genre, or of their own relations with their children, or of their own relations with their fathers, or some combination thereof.[22]

By drawing on autobiographical narratives, this chapter attempts to explore how fathers were "imagined" by adult children, both men and women.[23] The narratives are not held as "authentic" but as mediums of representations, with all their complexities that offer myriad possibilities of reading and interpretation. The "imaginary father" in colonial Bengal was constructed amid a variety of contexts: the pedagogical (literary magazines), the scientific (journals), and, as described in this chapter, the autobiographical. At the same time, these fathers were constructed in dialogue with other imaginary figures. The imaginary figures that served as both inspiration and foils for the Bengali fathers include a number of contemporary constructions: British fathers (in India and abroad); Indian fathers from a range of caste and economic backgrounds; wives/mothers; and, of course, the imaginary sons and daughters, biological, and otherwise, that made these men fathers in the first place. But inspiration and foils also came from a "narrative" and a "reconstructed" past: the fathers of previous generations as well as the fathers of (a perhaps invented)

---

[22] For more on autobiography see Philippe Lejeune, *On Autobiography*, ed. P.J. Eakin and trans. Katherine Leary (Minneapolis: University of Minnesota Press, 1989). Sidonie Smith and Julia Watson, *Reading Autobiography: A Guide for Interpreting Life Narratives*, 2nd ed. (Minneapolis: University of Minnesota Press, 1989).

[23] For a discussion of life-histories in Indian history see David Arnold and Stuart Blackburn, *Telling Lives in India: Biography, Autobiography and Life History* (Bloomington: Indiana University Press, 2004).

Hindu "tradition."[24] The inspiration and foil came from the future, as well: the children who were the targets of these fathers' pedagogical interventions would someday be free citizens, and in turn fathers and mothers themselves—and this future, too, shaped how fathers and father-figures interacted with children.

The stories that people told about being fathers and being the children of fathers reflected sociocultural expectations for fatherhood as much as (or even more than) they reflect everyday practices. Although people's stories relate everyday practices, they are nonetheless narratives and thus reflect sociocultural mores about fatherhood (not to mention literary conventions) more than being a simple catalogue of daily events. As far as those depictions go, there are four tropes that recur: a tension between distance and intimacy; the importance of modern education, especially for boys (for girls, early marriages were deemed more important than education); obedience and fulfilling expectations of a patriarchal family throughout life, even after sons were married with families of their own; and enforcement of discipline and chastisement, the latter involving corporal punishment.

I interrogate if the "fathers" of the autobiographies were the same as or different from the fathers in the pedagogical and scientific literature. The fact that fathers appear in the narratives examined here as the fathers of the authors, rather than as the authors themselves, suggests that maybe those fathers were an older style—the "old father" as opposed to the "new father"—that the authors used as a foil for their own (new) type of fatherhood. The "fathers" of this chapter are also somewhat different because here we examine the voices of women and daughters reflecting on their fathers. Do the voices of women describe a different type of father than the voices of men—voices found in autobiographical literature, but also the voices of scientific and pedagogical literature? And how do the four recurring tropes listed previously compare/contrast to the tropes of the pedagogical and scientific literature? Do they reveal different aspects of the "imaginary father" than were revealed in the other genres? Were the fathers themselves social imaginaries of the adult male population? While obedience and education were the two values emphasized across the board, records of corporal punishment in personal narratives were a

---

[24] Sumit Guha, *History and Collective Memory*, 9.

new issue that did not directly surface in school textbooks and the periodical literature in Bengali.

The imaginings of fathers in personal narratives rested on memories. Memories intervened to conceptualize the roles of fathers.[25] But memories of fathers in the autobiographies were not commemorative in nature, that is to say, fathers were not "called to remembrance" by a ceremony, observation, or monumentalization. Rather, they came into play in the process of reconstructing stages of life—from infancy to adulthood as far as memory could reach. The imaginings of filial relationship bridged the gap between the rhetoric of textual literature and reality. In remembering and representing fathers, the personal narratives also offered the emotional landscape of parents and children. The act of remembering everyday life represented collective psychology that involved "not only feeling but also doing."[26] In the literary representation of fathers, we witness not only their ideas, beliefs, and conceptualizations of children but also the daily interactions expressing a range of feelings that were specific to their cultural norms and expectations.

Michael Roper has emphasized the importance of subjectivity and emotions while writing the social history of relationships such as that of the mother and the son.[27] Subjectivity and emotions are key to understanding filial relationships in the Indian context as well. The *bhadralok* fathers and children can be represented as "a group in which people have a common stake, interest, values, and goals," as "emotional communities,"

---

[25] The literature on imagination, memory, and history is enormous. For our purposes, Sumit Guha, *History and Collective Memory* and Indrani Chatterjee, *Forgotten Friends: Monks, Marriages, and Memories of Northeast India* (New Delhi: Oxford University Press, 2013) are particularly important. For the active role of imagination in making history, see Sumathy Ramaswamy, *The Lost History of Lemuria: Fabulous Geographies, Catastrophic Histories* (Berkeley: University of California Press, 2004). Dipesh Chakrabarty, "Nation and Imagination," in *Provincializing Europe* (Princeton: Princeton University Press, 2000), 149–179. Other relevant works are Stefan Berger and Bill Niven, eds., *Writing the History of Memory* (London: Bloomsbury Press, 2014); Giorgio Agamben, *Remnants of Auschwitz*, trans. Daniel Heller-Roazen (New York: Zone Books, 1999). Maja Zehfuss, *Wounds of Memory: The Politics of War in Germany* (Cambridge: Cambridge University Press, 2007).

[26] Rob Boddice, "The Affective Turn: Historicizing the Emotions," in *Psychology and History: Interdisciplinary Explorations*, eds. Cristian Tileagă and Jovan Byford (Cambridge: Cambridge University Press, 2014), 147–165.

[27] Michael Roper, "Slipping Out of View: Subjectivity and Emotion in Gender History," *History Workshop Journal* 59, no. 1 (2005): 57–72.

a term introduced by Barbara Rosenwein.[28] Nestled within the larger social community of the family, the interaction between Bengali fathers and children displayed varying emotional practices that were contingent on their socio-economic, cultural, and temporal standing. In the Indian context, Rajat Kanta Ray, emphasizing the centrality of personal narratives in exploring emotional history, further alerted us about the importance of *sthana* (place), *kala* (time), *patra* (dramatis personae) as the "crucial context[s] for understanding the precise meanings and expressions of human emotion."[29] The emotions of affection, anger, and despair expressed by the *bhadralok* fathers in their interaction with children thus need to be read in their specific situatedness (*sthana*), personality (*patra*), and the particular moment (*kala*) in the history of the Bengali "modern." Contact with new ideas of Western liberalism, urban professions,

---

[28] Barbara Rosenwein, *Emotional Communities in the Early Middle Ages* (Ithaca, NY: Cornell University Press, 2006), 25. Rosenwein described "emotional communities" the same as "social communities—families, neighborhoods, parliaments, guild, monasteries, parish church membership..." Scholars seeking to explore emotional communities attempt to "uncover systems of feeling: what these communities (and the individuals within them) define and assess as valuable and harmful to them; the evaluations that they make about other's emotions, the nature of the affective bonds between people that they recognize, and the modes of emotional expression that they expect, encourage, tolerate, and deplore." Rosenwein alerted us that "not only does every society call forth, shape, constrain, and express emotions differently, but even *within the same society* contradictory values and models, not to mention deviant individuals, find their place." Her work further showed how family was "a clear site of many sorts of emotions." Barbara Rosenwein, "Worrying about Emotions in History," *American Historical Review* 107, no. 3 (June 2002): 842. The context for Rosenwein's study is early Middle Ages in Europe and the community she was describing was decidedly distinct from that of South Asia. But her problematization of family as a major arena for diverse emotions proves instructive for modern Indian families and resonates with theories offered by experts on South Asia. See Margrit Pernau, "Studying Emotions in South Asia," *South Asian History and Culture*, 12: 2–3, (2021): 111–12.

[29] Rajat Kanta Ray, *Exploring Emotional History: Gender, Mentality and Literature in the Indian Awakening* (Delhi: Oxford University Press, 2003), viii. Ray explored emotions through literature and "not on the basis of the letters and diaries of contemporaries," which in the context of India are "not easy for the scholar to procure and utilize" given their "reticence" in intimate matters. The historian Tapan Raychaudhuri, however, drew on personal narratives to argue that altered conjugal relationships in colonial Bengal were suffused with a different kind of emotion emanating from the perceptions and sensibilities of the colonial era. Tapan Raychaudhuri, "Love in a Colonial Climate: Marriage, Sex and Romance in Nineteenth-Century Bengal," in *Perceptions, Emotions, Sensibilities: Essays on India's Colonial and Postcolonial Experiences* (Delhi: Oxford University Press, 1999), 65–95. Curiously enough, in their analysis of the mental world of nineteenth-century historical actors, both Ray and Raychaudhuri stayed away from engaging with the current historical literature on emotions that has significantly bolstered our understanding. Ray's work, in turn, is also given short-shrift in the emerging scholarship. William M. Reddy, *The Making of Romantic Love: Longing and Sexuality in Europe, South Asia, and Japan, 900–1200 CE* (Chicago: University of Chicago Press, 2012); Margrit Pernau, "Male Anger and Female Malice: Emotions in Indo-Muslim Advice Literature," *History Compass* 10, no. 2 (2012): 119–128, do not refer to Ray's works.

educational institutions, and ideologies, combined with the Indo-Islamic influences of the past, engendered altered sensibilities in men and women that were rooted in gendered subjectivities tethered to home.

The overarching theme that underscored the father–child relationship was that of veneration and a special kind of moral education that a father imparted to his children. We may recall here the way Vidyasagar and other indigenous educators in vernacular primers emphasized filial piety. Likewise, the scientific journals urged parents to monitor and raise their children. Whether a father was an eminent public figure, a patriarch riddled with contradictions, or a raging disciplinarian, the Indian father was always remembered with respect (*sroddha*) and devotion (*bhakti*). With all his limitations and strength, the Indian father was never denied or rejected by his children. The rule of the father prevailed, and his behaviour and emotions were a testament to the prevailing expectations of manhood and the hegemonic possibilities in the domain of the home and family. The different facets of a father—venerable, affectionate, ambivalent, and strict—were intertwined and dependent on one another. Among the hundreds of autobiographies written by men and women that relate experiences with fathers, only a handful are selected that document the archetypes. The specific examples will help bring out the characteristics of fatherhood in sharper relief.

The Venerable Father in an Aristocratic Household: Maharshi Debendranath Tagore of Jorasanko

An image of the venerable father who enjoyed considerable public presence emerge from the writings of the Tagore family of Jorasanko, Kolkata. The wealth of information shared by female and male family members through three successive generations of the aristocratic Tagore family offers a complex portrait of the "imaginary father," embodied in Maharshi Debendranath Tagore (See Figure 4.2), a father who traversed the public–private world and was venerated in *bhadralok* circles of colonial Bengal. The Tagores, as business partners with the British and through their leadership roles in new religious (Brahmo), cultural, and nationalist movements, acted as major trend-setters and culture-builders in colonial

Figure 4.2 Debendranath Tagore

India.[30] Furthermore, the "fathers," sons, and daughters of the Tagore family had a public presence and their activities blurred boundaries of the home and the world. Insights into their lives also shed light on the changing parent-child relationship in late colonial Bengal. As opposed to the ahistorical and monolithic description of Indian fathers as "invariably distant," the sources examined reveal a more nuanced picture.[31] The

---

[30] Blair B. Kling, *Partner in Empire: Dwarkanath Tagore and the Age of Enterprise in Eastern India* (Berkeley: University of California Press, 1976).

[31] Sudhir Kakar, *The Inner World: A Psycho-Analytic Study of Childhood and Society in India* (Delhi: Oxford University Press, 1981), 131.

remembrances of daily practices between fathers and children delineate changing emotions in father-child relations and corroborate that many of the suggestions of the pedagogic and scientific literature are put into practice. Remembrances also evince actions, namely, corporal punishment, not advocated in the literature.

Debendranath Tagore (1817–1905), son of Prince Dwarkanath, a leading business partner with the British, was a reformer and a foremost leader of the reformist Brahmo Samaj, a monotheistic religious association founded by Rammohun Roy in 1828. Popularly known as Maharshi (Great Saint), Debendranath was a product of the colonial culture. He first went to the school set up by Rammohun Roy, the ardent social reformer and votary of Western-style education; Debendranath then attended Hindu College, the earliest colonial institution of higher learning in Kolkata. As a leader of a reformist religion, Debendranath was caught in the throes of change—in his advocacy of monotheism, he drew from the Indic past and balanced it with reasoned judgement and conscience.

Although Debendranath led the life of a renouncer and a preacher, he still firmly controlled his family finances.[32] His father Dwarkanath died in London in 1846 and left a huge debt amounting to about a crore of rupees, while his assets were worth only about forty-three lakhs. Dwarkanath incurred the debt in the name of his firm but he safeguarded his family by securing part of his property in a trust. After Dwarkanath died, Debendranath, the oldest son, in consultation with his brothers, refused to avail themselves of the protection granted by the trust and placed "everything unreservedly in the hands of their creditors, till all their heavy liabilities were liquidated."[33] He not only paid back his father's debt, but he also paid the "heavy debts" that Debendranath's brothers Girindranath and Nagendranath incurred.[34] For his probity and filial commitment, he naturally earned the right to control family resources. He maintained extensive registers of wages and salaries of people employed on the estate

---

[32] As a staunch patriarch and an avid social reformer, Debendranath drew severe criticisms from later family members and posterity. Those criticisms are beyond the scope of this chapter as it focuses on the reconstructed and projected memory of Debendranath by his children and grandchildren.

[33] Satyendranath Tagore, "Introduction" to Debendranath Tagore, *Autobiography*, iv.

[34] Debendranath Tagore, *Autobiography*, 81.

and decided about expenses as well as distribution of his property among his children and other family members.

He was definitely not a representative of the "ordinary" Bengali middle class, but he served as a role model for the reformed community that he envisaged. As evident from his *Auto-biography*, he positioned himself as a public leader with a strong reformist zeal that he also brought to bear on his family life. The merging of his public concerns with domestic responsibilities makes him a seminal father figure, especially when he was remembered so extensively by his noteworthy daughters, sons, and grandchildren. Despite his stern, authoritarian ways which called for criticism, the reconstituted memories of his children and grandchildren projected him as a paragon of a venerable father, thus making him worthy of study.

Myriad accounts left by his children—daughters Saudamini Devi (1847–1920) and Swarnakumari Devi (1855–1932) and sons, Satyendranath (1842–1923) and Rabindranath (1861–1941) (See Figures 4.3, 4.4, 4.5), leading public figures and writers of nineteenth-century Bengal—convey the sombre emotions filled with awe and respect associated with childhood memories of their father. The accounts help us locate the importance of the father at home and his role as a pioneering leader of a religious-cum-social movement. The adult children's veneration of their father underscored as much his role as a social reformer as the patriarch, the *Babamahashai* (father) and the *Kartamashai* (head of the household) of the Tagore family. What also stands out is the emphasis that Debendranath put on educating his children.

The public persona of father Debendranath as a social and religious reformer was also important for his daughters: Saudamini Devi dedicated her life to taking care of her elderly father and the Tagore household,[35] while Swarnakumari Devi (See Figure 4.4), a celebrated writer, poet, musician, and social worker, proudly recorded the social activism of her father. In her short memoir *Shekele Kawtha* (*Tales from the Past*), Swarnakumari Devi dwelt mainly on the education and status of

---

[35] Saudamini Devi, *Pitrismriti o Anyanya Rachana*, ed. Sutapa Bhattacharya (Kolkata: De's Publication, 2010). Also see Abanindranath Tagore and Rani Chanda, *Gharoa* (Kolkata: Visvabharati Granthanbibhag, 1941), 50–60.

148 FATHERS IN A MOTHERLAND

Figure 4.3 Debendranath's children: Sons Satyendranath Tagore (standing in the middle) and Jyotirindranath Tagore (seated); daughters-in-laws, Jnanadanandini Devi (Satyendranath's wife; top left), Kadambari Devi (Jyotirindranath's wife, top right)

women of her generation and underscored her father's and elder brother Satyendranath's contribution to the cause. She claimed that if Rammohun Roy was the first to initiate religious reforms, her father pioneered the *social* (emphasis mine) reforms that fought for the education of women, eradication of child marriage, and advocated "civilized" (*sushabhya*)

Figure 4.4 Swarnakumari Devi (Debendranath's daughter)

attire for Bengali women.[36] She upheld the role of Debendranath as one of the few fathers in Bengal who sent their daughters to Bethune School, the first formal institution for girls set up by the colonial government in 1848. Swarnakumari averred that by initiating family members to the new principles of Brahmoism, Debendranath introduced a comprehensive education for all women in the Tagore household. He also removed idolatrous Hindu practices and particularly those that discriminated against women. All his daughters, including Swarnakumari, learned science and got trained in new and "improved" methods of learning taught by "pundits" and *memsahibs*, combining the best of the East and the West. Debendranath maintained strict supervision as to what his children were learning. He was opposed to mindless and mechanical forms

---

[36] Swarnakumari Devi, "Shekélé Kawtha," in *Shekélé Kawtha: Shatak Shuchona-i Meyeder Smritikawtha*, eds. Abhijit Sen and Abhijit Bhattacharya (Kolkata: Noya Udyog, 1997), 65.

Figure 4.5 Two Brothers: Rabindranath (left) and Jyotirindranath Tagore (right)

of learning: once, when he found out that the governess was making the girls copy what she wrote on a slate, he immediately dismissed her and breaking all conventions he assigned a better teacher, Ajodhyanath Pakrashi—"a male outsider in the women's quarters."[37] Swarnakumari regretted that whenever her father was away, the education of Tagore women within the household was neglected.

According to Swarnakumari, Debendranath even raised the age of marriage for girls of the Tagore family and scripted a new form of marriage. In 1868, Swarnakumari was married at age thirteen to twenty-seven-year-old Janakinath Ghosal, a strong-willed man who was disowned by his own zamindari family for endorsing Brahmoism and entering into this marriage with the daughter of a Brahmo leader. Age

---

[37] Chitra Deb, "Jorasanko and the Thakur Family," in *Calcutta, the Living City*, vol. I, ed. Sukanta Chaudhuri (Delhi: Oxford University Press, 1990), 66.

thirteen for Swarnakumari actually indicated a rather late age of marriage for Tagore girls! Instead of a Brahmin priest, Debendranath presided over the occasion following new rules of marriage that he designed. The description of the entire marriage ceremony with its new rituals and hymns was printed in *Tattvabodhini Patrika*, a periodical run under the aegis of Debendranath and the Brahmo community.[38] For Swarnakumari, her father Maharshi Debendranath was as important at home as he was for the wider public.

Satyendranath Tagore (1842–1923), Debendranath's second son, the first Indian Civil Servant (ICS),[39] a versatile scholar and an author, likewise stressed education as a key feature of his relationship with his father—although, unlike his sister, in his writings he did not stress Debendranath's advocacy for women's education. Satyendranath (See Figure 4.3) opened his autobiography noting that as a child he did not get close to the father. The father would call his children from time to time, testing them on their knowledge of Bengali and English and at other times, the children would go and sit in his gathering (*majlish*) where he delivered sermons to the family members.[40] On some days he would lecture especially for children, giving the advice to correct specific wrongs that he detected among them. His sermonizing continued through Satyendranath's adult life, even in his twenties, after he returned from England as an ICS.[41] The father cautioned him about the ills of Western culture and its blind imitation. Satyendranath noted that his father was known as a conservative but by his reckoning, he was a progressive by the standard of his time.[42]

---

[38] Abhijit Sen and Anindita Bhaduri, eds., *Swarnakumari Devi-r Rachana-Sankalan* (Kolkata: De's Publishing, 2000), 538. Swarnakumari had a successful marriage with Janakinath, who was a Theosophist and a founding member of the Indian National Congress (1885). More importantly, he was a signatory of the Marriage Act of 1872 that aimed to raise the age of marriage for girls and boys (especially for the Brahmos). It may be worth noting here that Swarnakumari and Janakinath's own daughter, Sarala Devi Chaudhurani (1872–1975), the fierce feminist and anti-colonial activist, got married late in her thirties.

[39] The Indian Civil Service (ICS) was created by the British Raj to carry on administration in the colony, and it recruited Indian members of certain backgrounds (typically elites) upon their completion of a rigorous examination conducted in England.

[40] Satyendranath Tagore (Thakura), *Amar Balyakatha o Amar Bombai Probash* (Kolkata: Indian Publishing House, Prantik Press, 1915), 1.

[41] Satyendranath Tagore was in his twenties when he was in England between 1862 and 1864 for his ICS examination and training.

[42] Satyendranath Tagore (Thakura), *Amar Balyakatha*, 3.

Filial devotion was so high that as "a humble tribute" to his father's memory, Satyendranath, along with his daughter Indira Devi, translated Debendranath's *Auto-biography* "in the hope that it may reach a wider circle of readers than the original could possibly command."[43] In his introduction to the *Auto-biography*, Satyendranath emphasized the achievement of his father as a spiritual leader of the Brahmo movement and as a paragon of moral virtues. For him, the autobiography was important not for any "stirring adventures or sensational incidents" but for its value in "being a record of the spiritual struggle of a noble soul" and "an illumined life struggling towards more light, and shedding its brilliance on all around."[44] Satyendranath could have been following genre convention to begin his memoir with an account of his father, notwithstanding the distance he felt with him; but his writings testified to the authority and respect Indian fathers enjoyed among children. Undoubtedly, his father's role as the Maharshi, the Saint, further enhanced his veneration among children.

Swarnakumari imagined her father as a champion of women, but her brother Satyendranath maintained reticence over their father's commitment to women's causes. Satyendranath was known for his active advocacy of women's issues. He was fuelled by John Stuart Mill's *Subjection of Women* (1869, first print) in England and became an ardent votary of women's equality and education in India. In 1859, Maharshi Debendranath arranged for Satyendranath to marry eight-year-old Jnadanandini Devi (1850–1951), who later became an iconic representation of the modern *bhadramahila* (respectable lady).[45] Jnadanandini (See Figure 4.3) grew up within the confines of the Tagore household and got educated in English and Bengali, showing that the Tagores' propensity for educating daughters extended to daughters-in-law.[46] As far as raising the age of marriage was concerned (as Swarnakumari Devi proclaimed), Debendranath held a double standard. He adhered to older norms of

---

[43] Debendranātha Tagore (Thākura), *The Auto-Biography of Maharshi Devendranath Tagore*, trans. from the Bengali by Satyendranath Tagore and Indira Devi (Calcutta: S.C. Sarkar and Sons, 1994); "Introduction," i.

[44] Debendranātha Tagore, *Auto-Biography of Maharshi Devendranath Tagore*, xvii.

[45] In her education, dress, manners, and ways Jnadanandini Devi represented the first "modern" Bengali woman. She was strong and confident; pioneered social reforms; and became the editor of *Balak* and *Bharati*, the two literary journals from the Tagore family.

[46] Indira Devi Chaudhurani, *Smriti-Samput*, vol. 1 (Santiniketan: Visvabharati), 2.

choosing very young brides (between eight and ten) for his celebrated sons but postponed the marriages of his own daughters until they were thirteen or so.

Satyendranath's autobiographical writings are significant as much for their silences as for what they say. Accounts by his own daughter, Indira, suggest that while Debendranath did agree to supervise the education of his son's child bride, there were limits to his willingness to accept a modern daughter-in-law. Satyendranath, according to his daughter Indira, encouraged his wife (Indira's mother)—whom he viewed as a companion and help-meet—to leave the Tagore household in Kolkata for first Bombay (Mumbai), and then even more radically, England. Indira reported that her pregnant mother, along with three little children (she herself among them, then three and a half years old), travelled alone to England and lived there by herself until her husband Satyendranath and brother-in-law Rabindranath joined her much later. Debendranath would have been a highly unusual man for his class and era had he not objected strenuously to such independence—but Satyendranath said nothing of it.[47] Satyendranath's and Swarnakumari Devi's focus on the public career of their father as a religious and social reformer obliterated the sharp division between the private and the public.

A more full-fledged paternal image of Debendranath emerged from the youngest of the fourteenth children, Rabindranath Tagore (1861–1941), the Nobel-laureate poet, writer, artist, musician, educator, and humanist.[48] In his *Reminiscences* he devoted an entire chapter to his father, capturing his earliest memories and echoing the same sentiment as his older brother:

> Shortly after my birth my father took to constantly travelling about. So it is no exaggeration to say that in my early childhood I hardly knew him. He would now and then come back home all of a sudden, and with him came foreign servants with whom I felt extremely eager to make friends.[49]

---

[47] Indira Devi Chaudhurani, *Smriti-Samput*, vol. 1 (Santiniketan: Visvabharati), 3–4.
[48] For the profound influence of father Debendranath on his son Rabindranath see Brian Hatcher, "Father, Son and Holy Text: Rabindranath Tagore and the Upanisads," *Journal of Hindu Studies* 4, no. 2 (2011): 119–143.
[49] Rabindranath Tagore, *My Reminiscences* (London: Macmillan, 1917), 67.

Figure 4.6 Rabindranath Tagore

Like his other siblings, Rabindranath (See Figure 4.6) never reached the immediate presence of his father and would only watch him from a distance from his hiding place at the head of the staircase. At the break of dawn, his father would sit on the roof, "silent as an image of white stone, his hands folded on his lap." When his father came home the entire house "filled with the weight of his presence."[50] He remembered everyone being dressed up, everyone being alert; and his mother supervising the cooking. He recalled that the children were asked to keep quiet lest they disturbed their father's peace. He remembered himself and the other children moving slowly, talking softly, and not even venturing to peek at the father.[51] Debendranath, indeed, maintained a distance from his children, who grew up under the regime of servants, but as noted by his children, he made sure that his children received a well-rounded education

---

[50] Rabindranath Tagore, *My Reminiscences*, 70.
[51] Rabindranath Tagore, *My Reminiscences*, 70.

in languages, arts, humanities, physical and biological sciences, sports, music, and (for the boys) wrestling.

As the youngest child (his other siblings were perhaps too old), Rabindranath alone had the privilege of enjoying the close company of his father when they both travelled to the Himalayas. A commanding personality with a meticulous eye to detail, Debendranath carefully chose and ordered for his son a "full suit of clothes" with a "gold-embroidered velvet cap."[52] Rabindranath reflected: "though nothing would induce him to put obstacles in the way of my amusing myself as I pleased, he left no loophole in the strict rules of conduct which he prescribed for me in other respects."[53] As much as Rabi enjoyed his freedom from his school in Calcutta, his trip to the mountains followed a "rigorous regime,"[54] waking up before sunrise to learn his Sanskrit declensions, taking a shower in ice-cold water, hiking up the mountain ridges with his father, singing devotional songs for him, and pursuing lessons in English, Bengali, and astronomy.[55] Debendranath entrusted Rabi with the responsibility of his cash box, not a meagre charge for an eleven-year-old. Negligence on Rabi's part would surely have earned him a reprimand. It may be instructive to note here that Debendranath, as a young boy, also received from his paternal grandmother, with whom he nurtured an especially close relationship, a cash box containing some money and other valuables.[56]

The distance between father and son recalled here was bridged in later life through mutual affection and favour. Rabindranath's own son, Rathindranath, had been familiarized with his father's memories of childhood, and the relationship with Debendranath: "My grandfather loved his youngest son and was delighted to discover unusual talent in him while still a boy. Probably for this reason he was very generous to him." While most of the male children stayed in the ancestral home of the Tagores in Jorasanko, Rabindranath was given the "most convenient and comfortable rooms in the family house" and when he was still dissatisfied with it, "grandfather helped him to build a separate house for himself."[57]

---

[52] Rabindranath Tagore, *My Reminiscences*, 67.
[53] Rabindranath Tagore, *My Reminiscences*, 78.
[54] Rabindranath Tagore, *My Reminiscences*, 101.
[55] Rabindranath Tagore, *My Reminiscences*, 89–91.
[56] Debendranath Tagore, *Auto-Biography of Maharshi Devendranath Tagore*.
[57] Rathindranath Tagore, *On the Edges of Time* (Kolkata: Visvabharati, 1958), 148.

It was customary for members of the Tagore family to live off of the extensive family estate and live in multiple residences that the family possessed in the province of Bengal. According to the grandson Rathindranath's reminiscence, Debendranath had entrusted Rabindranath with the management of his estates but he was such a "strict disciplinarian" that on the second of every month he wanted the accounts to be read out to him. "He would remember every figure, and ask awkward questions whilst the report was being read." Rabindranath had told his own children how he "used to be afraid of this day of trial, like a school-boy going up for his examination. We children would wonder why our father was so afraid of *his* father."[58]

The governing emotions that defined the relationship between Debendranath and his children were of extreme veneration leading to awe and fear. Despite Debendranath's proclaimed other worldliness, he was controlling and authoritative in the way he conducted himself at home and with others. Rabindranath mentioned several times that Debendranath stood out from his countrymen as he had a "well-defined code to regulate his relations with others and theirs with him." People "had to be anxiously careful" in their dealings with him.[59]

If the masculinity of Indian men was compromised as colonized subjects, influential men like Debendranath were "sovereign" in his familial set-up. He maintained his command over his family even when he was physically absent:

> On the occasion of any ceremonial gathering, at which he could not be present, he would think out and assign a place for each thing, the duty for each member of the family, the seat for each guest; ... After it was all over he would ask each one for a separate account and gain a complete impression of the whole for himself.[60]

The domineering impact of Debendranath, as the patriarch in charge of family resources, cast its spell on Rabindranath's conjugal life. To manage his father's estate Rabindranath was often stationed in various

---

[58] Rathindranath Tagore, *On the Edges of Time*, 148–149.
[59] Rabindranath Tagore, *My Reminiscences*, 77.
[60] Rabindranath Tagore, *My Reminiscences*, 77.

IMAGINING FATHERHOOD

places in eastern Bengal and Orissa, away from his wife and children, and he had very little freedom in manoeuvring his personal priorities. As much as Rabindranath, as a modern man, wanted to be in the company of his family, he still had to yield to the dictate of his father. In 1891, he wrote to his wife, Mrinalini Devi (1872–1902):

> If you are already on your way, I shall see you when I am in Calcutta this time. I shall try to arrange for you to come with me to Orissa.... *I have already told father what I want to do, I think he understands. I may get my way if I talk to him once or twice more – still it is best not to raise our hopes.*[61] (emphasis mine)

In several letters, Rabindranath expressed his desire to be close to his wife and children, but he was left completely at the discretion of his father. This domination of the father over the conjugal life of adult sons seems to have been a common experience. The fathers arranged marriages for both sons and daughters as we witnessed in many instances. We also gathered from the life of Sivnath Sastri (Chapter 2), a nineteenth-century Brahmo reformer and writer from Bengal, how his father forced him to abandon his first wife for tenuous reasons and marry a second time.[62] Despite generational differences, these instances exemplify the power of the patriarch, his veneration in the family, and the contingent nature of masculine authority, even as an adult son and husband. The hierarchical power structure in the family and the culture of deference to elders offset the generational conflict between fathers and sons that was emphasized in the Western context—the Lockean notion of the modern individual whose attainment of subjecthood depended on the "death" of the "absolutist" monarch. The abolition of kingship based on patriarchal principles in Western Europe threatened the paternal authority of the father in the family. The revolutionary principles of liberty, equality, fraternity called for more egalitarian relationships at home and especially between the father and the son, akin to the hierarchy in the monarchy.[63]

---

[61] Rabindranath Tagore, *Chitthi Patra*, vol. 1 (Kolkata: Visvabharati, 1966), 28–29, emphasis added.
[62] Shibnath Sastri, *Atmacharit* (Kolkata: Signet Press, 1952).
[63] Mary Jo Maynes and Ann Waltners, *The Family: A World History* (New York: Oxford University Press, 2012), 87.

But the Indians operated as subordinate subjects under a colonial regime and suffered scathing criticism for their lack of ability on various counts, especially as free citizens. In such a scenario, educated Indians, men and women, arguably laid a tremendous emphasis on the veneration of their paternal figures.

Although Debendranath's control over his adult children's movements interfered with their conjugal life, Rabindranath vouched that his father never stood in the way of his independence as a child. Debendranath was not deterred by the danger of his son making mistakes; he had not been alarmed at the prospect of his children encountering sorrow. As Rabindranath described, "He held up a standard, not a disciplinary rod,"[64] an expression closely akin to the Unitarian description of fathers.[65] The Brahmos had close ties with and were particularly influenced by the Unitarians and Debendranath was no exception.[66] Debendranath accorded "Supreme Authority" to "Reason and Conscience,"[67] in which one could see traces of the influence of post-Enlightenment ideas disseminated by the colonial regime. He allowed his sons to indulge in personal liberty but was careful enough to bridle their freedom. Unlike "distant" fathers, he represented the concerned yet controlling "modern" father, not only of his children but also of the Brahmo community. For him, his own children and family were as important as the other children and members of the Brahmo sect. Thus, he would give shelter to Keshub Chandra Sen and his family when Sen endorsed Brahmoism and was rejected by his family. Although Debendranath and Keshab would have a major fall out in later years leading to the split of the Brahmo Samaj, in a time of crisis when Debendranath housed them, the two families stayed together in perfect amity and harmony. Debendranath's umbrella-like leadership for his family and community personified and brought to life the concerns

---

[64] Rabindranath Tagore, *My Reminiscences*, 95.
[65] Broughton and Rogers, eds., *Gender and Fatherhood in the Nineteenth Century*, 18.
[66] Lynn Zastoupil, "Defining Christians, Making Britons: Rammohun Roy and the Unitarians," *Victorian Studies* 44, no. 2 (2002): 215–243; Peter van der Veer, *Imperial Encounters: Religion and Modernity in India and Britain* (Princeton: Princeton University Press, 2001). Debendranath vehemently opposed any direct Christian influence in his life and works and to defray missionary attacks on the Brahmos, he wrote *Brahmo Dharma Grantha* (Kolkata: Brahmo Samaj, 1848), a theistic manual of religion and morals.
[67] Debendranath Tagore, *Auto-Biography of Maharshi Devendranath Tagore*, iii.

Figure 4.7 Sarala Devi Chaudhurani

expressed by scientific writers and the literary activists for an imagined community of children.

In his children's and grandchildren's imaginings, too, Debendranath emerged as a public leader of a newly formed community and the patriarch. Even the fiery feminist and nationalist leader Sarala Devi Chaudhurani (1872–1945), daughter of Swarnakumari Devi, reminisced about her own birth by saying "yet another granddaughter was born to the *Maharshi*" (emphasis mine). Instead of any reference to her parents, she noted her arrival with respect to her illustrious maternal grandfather, Debendranath, the Maharshi. Sarala Devi's (See Figure 4.7) birth was not celebrated with fanfare, but the family made sure that they observed the birth rituals following the newly founded Brahmo religion.[68] Debendranath was the *Kartamahashai* (the head of the household) for

---

[68] Sarala Devi Chaudhurani, *The Scattered Leaves of My Life: An Indian Nationalist Remembers*, trans., ed., and introduced by Sikata Banerjee (Kolkata: Stree, 2011), 1.

his family, *Pitridev* (father-god) or *Pitrimahashai* (venerable father) for his children, *Kartadadamashai* (grandfather) for his grandchildren and *Maharshi* (Saint) for his community and the public. Despite the physical distance, his presence loomed large over his children, grandchildren, and the extended family.

Debendranath's grand-nephew, Abanindranath Tagore (1871–1951), the leading nationalist artist and writer, in his characteristic artistic spirit rendered the most intimate portrait of the Maharshi. Abanindranath established the aura of the revered *Kartadadamashai* (grandfather) through a vivid recounting of Debendranath's social interactions with friends and family. Abanindranath's attention to several humorous incidents, such as his interactions with an old friend and nephew Iswar Mukherjee, shed light on a more personable Debendranath.[69] Abanindranath also vividly recalled Debendranath's tremendous stature in the family as he meticulously presided over all important matters, especially finance. Even if he was away from important events like a wedding, he would provide detailed minutiae and guidance of how the ceremony would be performed.[70] Debendranath's glory was such that his children and grandchildren carefully shelved any defiance, anger, or love; instead, they paid their homage to the god-like image of the restrained *Maharshi*. They did not openly discuss (at least not in print) his control over the family estate and the way he conducted business in real life.

In his *Autobiography*, Debendranath also positioned himself as a leader of the reformed Brahmo community. His role as an imaginary father eclipsed his role as a biological one: He hardly recounted his own role as a father of fourteen children. He neither traced his paternal genealogy nor discussed the image of his father except only in the context of his death in England and the debt he left behind for posterity. Debendranath's *Autobiography* commenced with celebrating the memory of his paternal grandmother who left a profound spiritual influence on him. Debendranath projected himself as a spiritual leader, a man of principle and commitment who stood up to odds and challenged the convention that went against his faith. He daringly rejected Hindu

---

[69] Abanindranath Tagore and Rani Chanda, *Gharoa* (Kolkata: Visvabharati Granthanbibhag, 1941), 38–39.
[70] Abanindranath Tagore and Rani Chanda, *Gharoa*, 48.

rituals at the death of his father courting the displeasure of family and friends. Debendranath displayed characteristics, as his son Rabindranath emphasized, which were not "typically" indigenous, and he was not relaxed in nature. He gave his children the freedom to choose and make decisions on some matters; he delegated responsibilities, but not authority, to his children. He drew sustenance from traditional Indian roots from the Vedas and the Upanishads and selectively endorsed Western values of freedom, reason, and individualism that shaped his personal habits and behaviour. He birthed new parental practices based on newly acquired values and judgement—introduced children to a blended curriculum drawing from the East and the West. His children studied a wide array of subjects, from science and mathematics to music, Sanskrit, biographies, and classical literature. Wrestling or body-building was part of compulsory training for the boys. Discipline and rigour reigned supreme in his endeavours. But these aspects of his parenting, the awe and fear that he generated in everyone's minds, could be gleaned only from the reflections of his children remembering their childhoods. They were not apparent in his writing.

Fatherhood was an expression of manhood—through wielding authority and power over household members and resources. Debendranath's commanding position in his family spoke of his manhood—a status that he earned by virtue of his moral superiority as well as his ownership and management of economic and cultural resources. Brian Hatcher pointed out that Debendranath bequeathed a tremendous spiritual legacy for Rabindranath, and I may add, to his children, by introducing him/them to the wealth of Upanishadic thoughts, thoughts that Satyendranath, Rabindranath, and other children actively drew upon. Yet, as the children claimed, Debendranath's immense legacy for them, both spiritual and material, did not stunt their independence and growth. Satyendranath's modern lifestyle with his wife (See Figure 4.3) and children and Rabindranath's sermons to his students were clear testimony to their breaking away from the disciplinary and spiritual regime of their father.[71] In practices of daily life, too, both Satyendranath and Rabindranath turned out to be more affectionate and interactive parents, something that we can follow from the accounts of their children.

[71] Hatcher, "Father, Son and Holy Text," 136–137.

Indira Devi Chaudhurani (1873–1960), the only daughter of Satyendranath Tagore and co-translator of Debendranath's *Autobiography* with him, was a highly accomplished musician, author, and social activist and was especially close with her uncle Rabindranath. In the reminiscences of her childhood, she harped on playful and happier moments, both with her father and her uncle Rabindranath, especially during their stay in England. Like her aunt Swarnakumari, she remembered Satyendranath as a champion of women's rights and education and noted his fondness for British ways of life. Indira Devi's recollections are especially instructive because owing to her father's position as a civil servant, they lived in a nuclear household of parents and children, first in England, then in Bombay. Even when they moved to Kolkata, they lived in separate houses close to the missionary schools that she and her brother Surendranath attended.

Throughout her memoir, Indira Devi dwelt on moments explaining how she took after her father. A funny incident that she recorded provided a rare insight into Satyendranath. Indira Devi learned from her mother that initially Satyendranath was not too favourably disposed towards her because of her darker complexion. Child Indira Devi took "revenge" on him when she first saw him in England. She was used to seeing fathers of European children who were all white. When Satyendranath came to England to join his family and Indira Devi found him to be dark in comparison, she cried aloud, "That's not my papa" and hid behind the door. She jokingly noted that disowning children was quite common, but one rarely heard about "a daughter disowning her father."[72] Indira Devi also recalled many playful moments with uncle Rabindranath, who came with her father. He used to sing and teach funny "Hindi" songs for them; sang English songs as well; and read out to Indira and her brother Surendranath a book called *Helen's Babies*. Father Satyendranath supplied them with many English books—*Pilgrim's Progress, Don Quixote, Arabian Nights, Grimm's* and *Hans Anderson's* fairy tales.[73] Satyendranath was a disciplinarian like Debendranath; he urged on waking up early and following a strict routine—a trait that Indira Devi inherited from him. But he was much more relaxed with his children. On the contrary, it was his wife, Jnadanandini, who was more concerned with children's

---

[72] Indira Devi Chaudhurani, *Smriti-Samput*, 1:5.
[73] Indira Devi Chaudhurani, *Smriti-Samput*, 1:7–8.

education and activities. Overall, Indira enjoyed an intimate relationship with her father and uncles, and they did not seem to be controlling her as Debendranath did. As is well documented in her own writings and public record, Indira Devi remained close to her father and uncles through the last day of her life. More important to note is the fact that she was not subjected to child marriage. Her marriage at age twenty-five in 1899 with Pramatha Chaudhuri, an eminent journalist and writer, was not arranged by her father.

Practices of fatherhood in the Tagore family changed over the generations. Veneration prevailed but the awe-struck image of the domineering patriarch gave way to a closer and intimate relationship with fathers who nonetheless held important public positions. From this specific instance of the aristocratic and celebrated Tagores, let us now segue into the world of other *bhadralok* families where accounts, especially of women, provide deeper insights into more complicated and paradoxical practices of fatherhood.

Affectionate but Ambivalent Patriarchs: Daughters Recall Fathers

Accounts written by daughters from prominent families, noting the outpouring of affection from their beloved fathers, further affirm that the Indian or the Victorian stereotype of a distant, cold, and aloof father did not dominate actual relations between Bengali fathers and daughters in this period.[74] While the preference for sons as a cultural capital, for carrying on the family name, lineage, and social and economic security, is well known, daughters' remembrances harped on affection and attention they received from their fathers. No doubt, women who wrote their lives represented a privileged group who received necessary education to express themselves in writing. Barring a few exceptions such as Rassundari Devi whose memoir was more an act of devotion than self-writing or the actress Binodini Dasi who delivered a scathing criticism of *bhadralok* men, or Kanan Devi, who freely noted in her autobiography that

---

[74] For an insightful account of Bengali women and their relationship with fathers see Manisha Roy, *Bengali Women* (Chicago: University of Chicago Press, 1992 [1972]).

her mother was not legally married to her father,[75] most educated women who wrote conformed to the ideology of the *bhadramahila* (respectable lady) who did not challenge the patriarchy.[76]

In the world of autobiographies, men's and women's writings were distinguished for their characteristic structure and content: men's autobiographies were considered more political, whereas women's were more personal. South Asian women's autobiographies, it has been argued, often represent their collective selves and are not written just for themselves. They present an "almost imperceptible fusion or extension of the self and the other."[77] My reading of South Asian women's autobiographies suggests that they are characterized by an unbounded sense of self; they are assertive yet restrained; and are often marked by self-erasure, pointing to a long-standing culture of non-selfhood in the Indian subcontinent.[78] But those moments of self-erasure also allude to the hidden or obvious marks of power that shape their lives. By representing themselves in writing, the women autobiographers committed an act of power. Their individualism cannot be located in the binaries created by the "Self" and the "Other" but in the endlessly reproduced plastic kind of "self." As Marylyn Booth pointed out in a different context, "the authorial 'I' of women represented both an individual and collective identity."[79] In a hierarchical social structure, women told their stories differently. I argued elsewhere that women's self-writings were often more candid and caustic than their male counterparts, but when it came to representing their fathers, women adopted a more protective stance.[80] The trope of filial

---

[75] For Rassundari Devi, see Tanika Sarkar, *Words to Win: Making of a Modern Autobiography*, repr. ed. (Delhi: Zubaan Books, 2014). For Binodini Dasi see Rimli Bhattacharya, *My Story and My Life as an Actress* (New Delhi: Kali for Women, 1998). Kanan Devi, *Sabare Ami Nomi*, 1st ed. (Kolkata: M.C. Sarkar and Sons, 1974), 3.

[76] Conformity to dominant patriarchal ideology was common among educated women with feminist inclinations in early twentieth century. See, for example, the works of two prominent authors, Santa Devi and Sita Devi, daughters of the progressive writer-journalist-activist Ramananda Chattopadhyay. Nupur Chaudhuri, "Nationalism and Feminism in the Writings of Santa Devi and Sita Devi," in *Interventions: Feminist Dialogues on Third World Women's Literature and Films*, eds. Bishnupriya Ghosh and Brinda Bose (New York: Routledge, 1996).

[77] Malhotra and Lambert-Hurley, eds., *Speaking of the Self*, 10.

[78] Swapna Banerjee, "Baby Halder's *A Life Less Ordinary* – A Transition from India's Colonial Past?," in *Colonization and Domestic Service*, eds. Victoria Haskins and Claire Lowrie (New York: Routledge, 2014), 239–255.

[79] Malhotra and Lambert-Hurley, eds., *Speaking of the Self*, 10.

[80] Swapna Banerjee, *Men, Women, and Domestics: Articulating Middle-Class Identity in Colonial Bengal* (Delhi: Oxford University Press, 2004).

piety and veneration shrouded any public critique of the discrimination they faced as girl-children. However, daughters' memories captured the gender biases of *bhadralok* fathers and revealed their vulnerability and paradoxical behaviour.

For middle-class fathers, education and the character formation of children, and especially marital customs and practices, had a different implication when it pertained to daughters. Education and marriage stood in contradistinction to each other with respect to girls in late colonial Bengal.[81] As we saw in an earlier chapter, the Brahmo reformist leader Keshub Chandra Sen was embroiled in a major controversy surrounding the marriage of his daughter, Sunity Devee (also spelt Suniti Devi). A votary of the Marriage Act of 1872 that increased the age of marriage for Indian girls and boys, Sen arranged the marriage of his underage daughter with the Maharaja of Cooch Behar. Far from a critical stance on her father's position, Sunity Devee's memoir celebrated the contribution of her father towards women's causes: she described him as "one of the most remarkable men India has ever produced" and noted that he founded the Native Ladies' Normal School and a college for girls named after Queen Victoria. At the same time she also mentioned that her father maintained that "for a woman to be a good wife and a good mother is far better than to be able to write M.A. or B.A. after her name."[82] Sunity Devee defended her father's decision to marry her off by acceding to his ideology and the fact that he yielded to the pressure of the colonial government, as we discussed in Chapter 2. She recorded in meticulous

---

[81] For the "indelible imprints" fathers had on daughters, see the words of the editors of a recent anthology of daughters' reminiscences of fathers: "The first man in a daughter's life is her father, her introduction to the other sex. He is very special. The father-daughter relationship cannot be contained in definitions ..." To answer the question "what drew us and bound us to our fathers?" the daughters collectively agreed that what made the presence of fathers so compelling were "the qualities" that influenced them; "the values" they imbibed; or those that they "rejected." In the editors words, "the conflicting feelings of love and hurt, anguish, rage, and fear. The need for father's approval and the elation when we won it, the bewilderment of being let down, the wrench at parting." The fathers the book discussed came out of the period when India was undergoing a transition from British colonial rule to independence. For these fathers, "education was the means to power and status in society," but they were also challenged by contradictory ideas and conflicting emotions. Their Western education and "rationality" wrestled with "constrictions of custom and tradition," with "pressures from family and society in the bringing up of daughters." Priti Desai, Neela D'Souza, and Sonal Shukla, *Indelible Imprints: Daughters Write on Fathers* (Kolkata: Stree, 1999), xi—xiii.

[82] Sunity Devee, *The Autobiography of an Indian Princess* (London: J. Murray, 1921), 21. "Sunity Devee" is also spelled "Suniti Devi."

details how the affectionate father Keshub Sen broke the news to her that the Maharaja's family was coming to see her for marriage. Dedicated to her studies and unprepared for this abrupt decision (she had no prior knowledge about it), Sunity was devastated. But she complied with her father's discretion without a challenge and noted that she had a fulfilling married life.[83]

Despite facing odds, women offered a favourable picture of their fathers. Haimabati Sen (1866–1933), who recounted her life from being a child bride to a lady doctor, was frank enough to describe her landowning father Prasannakumar Ghosh as an alcoholic and given to licentiousness. Acknowledging that "[d]rinking and debauchery were ritual duties in those days" among zamindars, she spoke about the large-heartedness of her father and the kindness and generosity that made up for his vices.[84] Haimabati (See Figures 4.8 and 4.9) noted with great pride that upon her birth her "father was so pleased that he ordered celebratory music for an entire month and the house illuminated with wreaths of lamps." He commanded: "No one must describe my child as a girl. My daughter has no less rights than those which accrue to other people's sons." He looked upon Haimabati as his first-born son and declared in no uncertain terms that he would have "nothing to do with anybody who treated her with contempt" because of her gender.[85] He would even give her a male name, Chuni Babu (Mr Chuni).[86] She continued to be her "father's pet" until six or seven; dressed in boy's clothes she spent most of her time in the outer quarter of the house; and although as a girl-child she was not supposed to be educated, she had a high standing with one teacher to whom she gave her father's tobacco and delicious titbits of food.[87] Soon thereafter, unknown to the female members of the household who opposed the education of the girl-child, Haimabati's father arranged her education with a tutor.

Her mother, on the other hand, was so disappointed at her birth that she "took to her sick bed in sorrow and disappointment" and she spent

---

[83] Sunity Devee, *The Autobiography*, 48.
[84] Haimabati Sen, *"Because I Am a Woman": A Child Widow's Memoirs from India*, trans. Tapan Raychaudhuri, eds. Geraldine Forbes and Tapan Raychaudhuri (New Delhi: Chronicle Books, 2011), 6.
[85] Haimabati Sen, *Because I Am a Woman*, 9.
[86] Haimabati Sen, *Because I Am a Woman*, 10.
[87] Haimabati Sen, *Because I Am a Woman*, 11.

Figure 4.8 Haimabati Sen (Courtesy: Collection of Professor Geraldine Forbes)

her days in "tearful sorrow."[88] Haimabati recalled repeatedly the neglect she received from her mother. Equally fierce and ill-disposed were the other female members of the family. At the end, their wishes prevailed and nine-year-old Haimabati was married to a forty-five-year-old man. In the days immediately following the marriage, both at her natal home and at the in-laws', Haimabati frantically looked for her father. Breaking convention, her father came to see her at her in-laws in the first week of

---

[88] Haimabati Sen, *Because I Am a Woman*, 9.

168 FATHERS IN A MOTHERLAND

Figure 4.9 Haimabati Sen's family (Courtesy: Collection of Professor Geraldine Forbes)

her marriage; but customs and cultural practices stood in the way of getting her immediately out of the in-laws' home. Regretting how he yielded to social pressure and married his dear daughter off, Haimabati's father had to intervene shortly after the wedding to rescue her from the old and wealthy husband who Haimabati described as "a drunkard" and a "whore-monger."[89] Haimabati still had to go back to her in-laws and stay there until her husband died within a year when she was ten years old. This time, her father finally took her back but he himself died shortly thereafter.

In both scenarios of Sunity and Haimabati, fathers were remembered as affectionate and were favourably disposed towards daughters. But they were vulnerable to social and cultural pressures that revealed their double-position. Contrary to the popular conception that fathers favoured sons, several women noted how their fathers celebrated their birth. Shudha Mazumdar (1899–1994) began her memoir with an excerpt from her father's diary: "Wife brought to bed of a daughter ... The

[89] Haimabati Sen, *Because I Am a Woman*, 31.

Figure 4.10 Shudha Mazumdar Family Picnic (Courtesy: Collection of Professor Geraldine Forbes)

entry was dated 22 March, the year 1899 ... My advent had been important enough to be noted down by my father."[90]

Shudha's father, unlike Haimabati's, was an educated, westernized man from a landowning family in Bengal. He was a member of the Indian Civil Service and a staunch supporter of British rule. Shudha (See Figures 4.10 and 4.11) recalled that at a time when women's education was restricted, he set up a radical example by sending Shudha to a private missionary school, St. Teresa's Convent, much to the consternation of her mother who considered her husband's decision as "foolhardy and irresponsible."[91]

Shudha shared minute details about everyday interactions with her father. Shudha's father did not discriminate against her as a daughter: he would coax and feed Shudha the "forbidden" food like chicken cutlet cooked by his Muslim cook as he would also do with his sons. This reminds us of the kind of intimacy Bipin Chandra Pal described with his father in the opening of his autobiography. Generous and charitable by

---

[90] Shudha Mazumdar, *Memoirs of an Indian Woman*, ed. with an introduction by Geraldine Forbes (New York: M.E. Sharpe, 1989), 3.
[91] Mazumdar, *Memoirs of an Indian Woman*, "Introduction" by Forbes, xii.

170 FATHERS IN A MOTHERLAND

Figure 4.11 Shudha Mazumdar and her husband (Courtesy: Collection of Professor Geraldine Forbes)

nature, her father would sometime have Shudha accompany him in his afternoon outings. Dressed in her best outfit and a straw hat, it was an "ordeal" for Shudha as she would have "to sit still and bored" watching "passing streets and people" while her father was absorbed in his own thoughts.[92] The distance and awe that Shudha felt with her father were obvious from her description. Shudha portrayed his manliness by emphasizing his Anglicized manners, habits, and practices. The connection

---

[92] Mazumdar, *Memoirs of an Indian Woman*, 13.

between eating practices, knowledge of English, and masculinity have already been established by scholars.[93] He nurtured two hobbies—horses and health—that resonated with the rising trend of the westernized masculine culture. "In a specially built gymnasium, he exercised regularly and kept magnificent health in old age." He never ate the common food for the family: "He dieted according to every book on dieting, experimenting to discover what was best for him. His diet was composed, according to an English recipe book, of meat and fish—boiled, baked, or steamed—and vegetables."[94] Diet and exercise, which constituted healthy body and mind of a "man," characteristics that were discussed in the pages of scientific journals, were thus quintessential for the "man" that Shudha's father was. Despite his pronounced cultivation of manly characteristics, he, like most men of his class and era, agreed to marry his daughter off at age twelve, interrupting her education. He could not stand above family pressure and his double standard with respect to his girl-child was apparent. Shudha, like Sunity, was also fortunate to have a companionate-style, romantic marriage.

Monica Chanda (d. 1995), the mother of the celebrated feminist scholar Malavika Karlekar, daughter of one Indian Civil Servant and a granddaughter of another, devoted her memoir recounting her days of growing up (until marriage) under the close auspices of her father.[95] Each of the twenty-two short chapters in her memoir recalled memories of close interaction with her elite, westernized father, Jnanendra Nath Gupta. Her father too, like Sunity's, Haimabati's, and Shudha's, did not stake a claim for her education. Her daughter Malavika Karlekar in the "Editor's Note" wrote, "[I]t is interesting ... that despite their wide learning and commitment to education as an ideal, neither Monica's maternal grandfather, R.C. Dutt, an eminent member of the ICS, nor his son-in-law ... laid much store by girls' education ..." Monica travelled far and abroad with her father but regretted that her parents did not take her piano lessons or education seriously. Karlekar rightly noted, "Monica's life can be read

---

[93] For connection between masculinity and eating habits, see Paroma Ray, *Gender and History*; for the connection between Anglicization, knowledge of English language, and masculinity see Shefali Chandra.
[94] Mazumdar, *Memoirs of an Indian Woman*, 7.
[95] Monica Chanda, *Days with Dinko and Other Memories*, ed. Malavika Karlekar (Delhi: Archana Press, 2018).

as a metaphor, an icon of the encounters between cultures, where a father reared in the indigenous tradition and then acculturated into the ICS ethics with strict sexual division of labour, was avowedly against formal schooling for girls..."[96]

There were, however, exceptions to these archetypes. Two prolific women writers, Santa Devi (1893–1984) and Sita Devi (1895–1974), daughters of the famous writer, editor, journalist, and educator Ramananda Chattopadhyay (1865–1943) fondly reminisced about their progressive, affectionate father.[97] Ramananda Chattopadhyay (aka Chatterjee) (See Figure 4.12), a member of the Brahmo community and a close associate of the Tagores, gave leadership to three significant journals in colonial India—*Dasi* (1892–1897), *Prabasi* (1901–1970s), and *The Modern Review* (1907–1995). Ramananda was an ardent advocate of progressive social reforms and a sharp critic of colonial education and imperialist practices.[98] His daughter Santa Devi (See Figures 4.13 and 4.14) wrote a biography of her father, *Bharat Muktisadhak Ramananda o Ordho Satabdir Bangla* and then a memoir *Purvasmriti*,[99] whereas her sister Sita Devi (See Figure 4.15) wrote a memoir reminiscing about the memorable company of Rabindranath Tagore. Both sisters got their B.A. degrees and lived an active intellectual life (See Figures 4.12 and 4.13). Neither of them were victims of double-standards with regard to marriage or education. In *Purvasmriti* (*Memories of Past*), Santa Devi fondly noted early memories with her father, especially during their stay in Allahabad, UP, where they spent their early years. Her father being a Brahmo leader and editor of *Prabasi* and *The Modern Review*, their home was a hub of intellectuals and reformers, like Sivnath Sastri and others, from around the country. Ramananda was not an itinerant or distant father and was present in his family's everyday life. Santa Devi shared snippets of her memories—from going to Brahmo prayers (with father) every

---

[96] Malavika Karlekar, "Editor's Note," *Days with Dinko*, 4.
[97] For a biography of Ramananda Chattopadhyay see Kalyan Chatterjee, *Media and Nation-Building in Twentieth-Century India: Life and Times of Ramananda Chatterjee* (London/New York: Routledge, 2020).
[98] His open attack on colonial government, especially in the English-language periodical *The Modern Review*, caught the ire of colonial officials. For the reach of periodicals edited by Ramananda Chattopadhyay, see Samarpita Mitra, "Periodical Readership in Early Twentieth Century Bengal: Ramananda Chattopadhyay's Prabasi," *Modern Historical Studies* 47, no. 1 (2013): 204–249.
[99] Santa Devi, *Bharat Muktisadhak Ramananda o Ordho Satabdir Bangla* (Kolkata: De's Publishers, 2005; originally published by Prabasi Press, 1950); *Purvasmriti* (Kolkata: Thema, 2006).

Figure 4.12 Ramananda Chattaopadhyay

Sunday morning to her father assisting her with cooking when everyone fell sick in the family and 8-year old Santa had to take charge.[100] Certain incidents she related evinced the intimacy with her father: she was about ten years old and would often fall asleep in the open courtyard (as was the norm in northern India); when the rain came all of a sudden, her father would pick her up in her sleep and transfer her to the room.[101] Santa Devi, through her nostalgic reminiscences of a very rich and eventful life, finally averred that she never lost touch with her dear father as long as he was alive.[102] The underlying tensions and inconsistencies that

---

[100] Santa Devi, *Purvasmriti*, 19, 8, 39.
[101] Santa Devi, *Purvasmriti*, 39.
[102] Santa Devi, *Purvasmriti*, 88.

Figure 4.13 Two sisters, Sita Devi and Santa Devi (Ramananda Chattopadhya's daughters. Courtesy: Collection of Professor Geraldine Forbes)

often characterized father-daughter relationship were absent between Ramananda Chattopadhyay and his two daughters. .

Compared to the father-son relationship, which was often marked by power struggle, daughters' experiences with fathers offered a more variegated picture of the filial relationship and the compromised status of fathers. The *bhadralok* fathers were imbued with new ideas of modernity and progress hinged on Western-style education and manners, on the one hand; but on the other, a majority of them were committed

Figure 4.14 Santa Devi (Courtesy: Collection of Professor Geraldine Forbes)

to old-style community and family values, particularly relating to girls' education and marriage. Some of them overcame their gender bias and son-preference when they celebrated the birth of daughters and were willing to educate them, but a majority of them did not rise above their caste-class practices and were vulnerable to communal customs and social pressures. The memories of venerable fathers by both sons and daughters brought alive their ambivalence and tension. The rather generous and forgiving recounting of fathers by their daughters testified to the reality that the fathers, although vulnerable, were the ultimate

Figure 4.15 Sita Devi (Courtesy Collection of Professor Geraldine Forbes)

decision-makers and arbiters of "justice" at home. They were broad-minded to celebrate the birth of daughters and provide them with education; but they were vulnerable to social pressures, both at home and outside in the realm of colonial governance. Masculinity and manhood waged through authority and power over family members were always constructed by social norms, particularly when it came to a choice between daughters' education and marriage. The stories we have recounted here were narrated by conformist and obedient daughters; but there were examples of disobedient, risk-taking, and delinquent children from whose accounts we can recover the raging authority of fathers as strict disciplinarians.[103]

The Disciplinarian Father

Discipline and punishment constituted the backbone of the parent–child, especially father–child relationship. The biopolitics that were apparent both in colonial policies and scientific literature of the indigenous literati were also manifest in disciplining children through physical punishment. In discourses on the character formation of children, the body of the child occupied a special place as authors advocated that children disobeying parents should be met with severe physical consequences. Running contrary to Michel Foucault's emphasis on the body that was subjected by the modern regimes of power to internal discipline and self-control, the child's body in late colonial Bengal acted as a site of control.[104] If children rebelled against parents or family, they had to be subjected to bodily punishment because "proper character would emerge out of a subjected body."[105] Physical pain inflicted through punishment would act as an expiation to transform the character of children (and

---

[103] Indian fiction and cinemas, in different genres and languages, routinely depicted and still depict fathers as the unrelenting patriarch, as the arbiter and controller of the lives of their children. Parallelly, there was a re-imaging of father in Bengali fiction from the early-twentieth century that brings out their affable side. Rabindranath Tagore's *Gora* and *Noukadubi*, as well as Saratchandra Chattopadhyay's *Grihadaha*, *Sesh Prashna*, and other novels, upheld the image of an affectionate and caring father, mostly belonging to the reformist Hindu community, who doted on his daughter and dutifully endorsed her choice in marriage and other decisions of her life. The iconography of an affectionate and understanding father who was the daughter's friend, philosopher, and guide, was also evident in fiction penned by women authors. Ashalata Singha's *Amitar Prem* and *Jibandhara* along with Sita Devi's *Banya* are only a few examples of such paternal re-imagining. One may also note in this connection that the kind of filial attachment upheld by Tagore's short story, *Kabuliwala*, and the universality of the paternal experience emphasized by the proverbial phrase, "Seo Pita, Amio Pita" ("he is a father, I too am a father'), constructs fatherhood as an experience that cut across barriers of caste, class, religion, and ethnicity. Ashapurna Devi's *Pratham Pratishruti* and *Subarnalata* also register the shifting paradigms of the father-daughter-bond in a changing generational frame. A discussion of these literary works lies outside the scope of this project.
[104] For the biopoltics of the state and modern disciplinary regimes see Michel Foucault, *Discipline and Punish: The Birth of the Prison* (New York: Pantheon, 1978).
[105] Pradip Kumar Bose, "Sons of the Nation," in *Texts of Power*, ed. Partha Chatterjee (Minneapolis: University of Minnesota Press, 1995), 135.

students). As the personal narratives reveal, disciplining and punishment attended by anger and outrage took various forms: from corporal punishment and threats to disowning children, excommunication from families to depriving offspring of their ancestral property rights. Whereas lessons for children or the scientific journals advocated the well-being of children without any mention of physical punishment, the autobiographical texts left ample testimony to paternal rage and violence in regimenting children.

Iswarchandra Vidyasagar recorded many instances of bodily punishment he received from his father upon slightest deviation from his orders. Vidyasagar's father never failed to contain child Vidyasagar's stubbornness through scolding and beating.[106] After all, a child's character had to be "molded by domination and punishment."[107] Also, establishing physical prowess over subordinate subjects such as children and servants signalled authority and manhood. However, Vidyasagar, in his moral pedagogy, did not talk about the physical chastisement of children. But in his own position as a father, Vidyasagar took a strong moral stand and severed all connection to his son on grounds of ideological differences.

Sivnath Sastri, another social reformer we encountered in Chapter 2, noted the most severe form of corporal punishment he received from his father. His father was known for his harsh temperament and whims, a point we discussed earlier with regard to Sivnath's forcible second marriage. As a boy, Sivnath experienced the worst form of his rage that resulted in a severe beating. As Sivnath described, his devout Brahmin family followed strict disciplinary practices through generations. He remembered the ritual observances of his great grandfather and his intolerance of any deviation. Serious retribution for departures from prescribed norms was integral to the day-to-day running of the Sastri family. But nothing surpassed the rage of his father over slight lapses of behaviour. Once, as part of a family wedding celebration, Sivnath entered into an argument and then a physical fight with one of his cousins; subsequently, the cousin's mother reported the incident to Sivnath's father. The father was not ready to tolerate any misbehaviour by his son. It is worth sharing

---

[106] Iswarchandra Vidyasagar, "Vidyasagar Charit," in *Vidyasagar Rachanabali*, vol. 1 (Kolkata: Tuli-Kalam, 1997), 397.

[107] Bose, "Sons of the Nation," 134.

Sivnath's vivid recounting of the event as it brings home the complex family dynamics—the enormous power a father wielded over his child and family, the mother's opposition, and the child's compliance with the father's command. Anticipating the brutal response the incident would provoke, Sivnath's mother tried to hide Sivnath from his father, got rid of sharp sticks that his father might use, and even asked Sivnath to keep his head and face covered. But undeterred by the implorations of his wife and other relatives, Sivnath's father started hitting him with a heavy log. His mother stood like a "lifeless statue" and when the father looked at her, she sternly remarked, "You need not be afraid of me. I am not going to stand in your way. You can kill your son if you like." The father responded "alright" and continued to hit the child until he became unconscious. "After a few blows," wrote Sivnath, "the whole world seemed to whirl and I fell down senseless." His mother, fearing that her son must have died, left the house and lay "prostrate in a wood nearby." When Sivnath came to senses he found "two persons rubbing my body with turpentine and my father was helping them."[108]

From Sivnath's description of the whole incident, we get a sense of both the undisputed authority of his father as well as his own subjectivity: when his father initially sought him out from his hiding place to punish him, he asked Sivnath to keep quiet and not to cry while he went away to get the stick ready. Other family members, including his mother, asked Sivnath to run away but he replied, "I cannot go ... father has asked me to stand here." It was a clear sign of his observing *pitriajna*, the command of the father, which could be out of fear and the power he wielded over the child's mind. But after the incident, when his mother came back, Sivnath complained to her about the "injustice of the matter." The offence, he thought, was "slight" and "the punishment was heavy." It was at that time that he also noticed that his father was "rubbing his nose hard on the ground," signifying an act of penance vowing not to repeat a wrong deed that he committed. Since then his father promised, "not to raise his hand to strike any of us, even when he had the strongest provocation to do so."[109]

---

[108] Sivnath Sastri, *Atmacarit: Autobiography of Sivnath Sastri* (Kolkata: Rddhi India, 1988), 36.
[109] Sivnath Sastri, *Atmacarit*, 36.

The authority of fathers did not cease with children attaining adulthood. A major source of contention among adult sons and fathers in nineteenth-century Bengal was over the conversion from orthodox Hinduism to the reformed monotheism of the Brahmos. In fact, Sivnath Sastri, who always complied with the dictates of his father, finally fell out with him on grounds of religion. When his father forbade him to associate with the Brahmos or attend their prayer meetings, Sivnath held out firmly: "I have obeyed all your orders implicitly and will continue to do so in future. But please do not dictate me in matters touching my religious faith." Sivnath later found out that the answer hurt his father so deeply that he wept like a child and declared that his son was dead to him: "the son who disobeyed his parents and became a heretic was as good as dead."[110] This incident reminds us of the tremendous emphasis the pedagogical texts, such as those authored by Vidyasagar, placed on filial piety and obeisance to parental and familial authority.

Sastri's father was relentless in disciplining his son. When Sastri, fortified by a new faith and a new resolution, went home during the holidays, he asked his mother not to put him to his usual task of worshipping the family idols that his father worshipped. Hearing this, his father "burst into a blaze" and with a "cudgel in his hand," he asked his son to do his bidding. Sivnath, now in his late teens or early twenties, retorted firmly that he could not be compelled to do the work even if all his bones "would be drawn out one-by-one." His father trembling "with rage and anger" restrained himself this time and let him have his way.[111] Sivnath's father severed all relations with his son for eight years. But when Sivnath fell seriously ill and expressed his last wish to see his parents, his father (and mother) visited him in Kolkata and arranged a physician for him, but the father refused to enter his house. Despite his financial hardship during those eight years he never accepted any help from Sivnath but when the latter reached out "the poor Brahmin hastily collected whatever resources he could and came." "This large heartedness was one of his chief characteristics," reflected Sivnath.[112]

---

[110] Sivnath Sastri, *Atmacarit*, 50.
[111] Sivnath Sastri, *Atmacarit*, 51. Sivnath's autobiography recorded this incident as taking place between 1861–1867 and he was born in 1847. He was formally initiated to Brahmo Samaj by Keshub Chandra Sen in 1869. There could a possible miscalculation of the date when the incident took place.
[112] Sivnath Sastri, *Atmacarit*, 111.

By juxtaposing the impetuosity of his father unleashing brute force on the child and his simultaneously affable nature, Sastri's autobiography conveyed not only the power of his father as the patriarch *extraordinaire* but it also told the story of his tormented self—the power-structure he inhabited and the ambiguities and tensions that underscored his kin and family relations. His self-writing was not just the story of his own or that of a single person; it was "about the modern individual" of whom he was an example, as Sudipta Kaviraj has argued.[113] The melding of extraordinary sternness of fathers with their palpable affection characterized the younger generation's idealization and memorialization of fatherhood, fatherhood that exposed and facilitated (male) children to acquire Western-style education but did not allow them to question or transgress expected familial norms and ideological boundaries.

The brilliant orator, writer, and revolutionary nationalist Bipin Chandra Pal, with whose words we opened this chapter, devoted two chapters of his memoir to his father, delineating the depth of father-son relation and the triumph of paternal love. Comparable to Sivnath, Bipin suffered retribution from his father as he converted to Brahmoism during his college days in Kolkata. When Bipin refused to come home in rural east Bengal and rumours of his "apostasy" (i.e. conversion to Brahmoism) reached his father, the latter immediately stopped his remittances supporting him, expecting dire financial straits would force his son to turn around. When that failed, Bipin's father took the most drastic step in a fit of rage—he married again at the age of sixty-four in the hope of getting another son. Incidentally, Bipin's father never had another son, and Bipin explained: "He had placed on me his hopes of carrying on the family tradition. I was his only son. He had no brothers, and no nephews who could fill up my place in the family scheme. And it was this which drove him to marriage at this advanced age."[114]

Bipin wrote, "Immediately after his marriage, he sent me in a lump all the arrears of this half a year. In doing so, he wrote to me a long letter the contents of which I shall never forget as long as my memory lives. I did not preserve it. But I am able to reproduce it even after this long

---

[113] Kaviraj, *The Invention of Private Life*, 311.
[114] Pal, "Father and Son," *Memories of My Life and Times*, 250.

lapse of time almost word for word."[115] "Baring his wounded soul," "full of pathos," "subtle in its irony and its pathetic humour," this was the last letter Bipin received from his father and it "shut his door" against him. After about nine years the father relented on grounds of ill-health, and he wanted his only son and his family to be back in the ancestral village. The story that followed was one of "The Triumph of Fatherly Love," the last chapter in Bipin Pal's memoirs, relating how, in the short period his father lived after the reunion with his son, he whole-heartedly accepted Bipin and his family, particularly his wife, a former widow, on whom he bestowed all his paternal love and bodily care seeing her through a serious spate of illness.[116] Bipin Chandra Pal paid tribute to his father through the stories of his reconciliation and magnanimity. Conspicuous by their absence are any chapter on his mother, wife, or children.

Bipin Pal was most eloquent in elaborating his father's deep connection with him as a son. Like other parents of his generation, his father "devoutly prayed for a son who would continue the line of his ancestors and by his learning, wealth, social distinction and character, add fresh glories to the family history. His affection for me was something religious, if not spiritual."[117] By bringing up his son he was paying off a debt to the "unremembered line of his forbears"—*pitrireena* or the debt to the fathers. Along with the Hindu past, Pal invoked race and eugenics the same way the scientific writers did to promote a future body of citizenry. He explained the child-rearing process as "race preservation": to raise the male child in the "ways and wisdom of the race was an equally sacred obligation imposed upon every householder" and it constituted the debt to the gods or *deva-reena*:

> The *deva-reena* was "discharged by the preservation of the ancient rituals of the race, and *rishi-reena* or debt to the rishis, who were the repositories of the intellectual illumination and the ethical and spiritual ideals of the race ... these were the debts under the burden of which every Hindu was born, and for the due discharge of which he entered the marital life and became a householder ... Marriage and the rearing

---

[115] Bipin Chandra Pal, *Memories of My Life and Times*, 330.
[116] Bipin Chandra Pal, *Memories of My Life and Times*, 337–346.
[117] Bipin Chandra Pal, *Memories of My Life and Times*, 249.

of issue, particularly of male issues, were thus part of the religion of the Hindu householder of the higher and educated classes of the generation to which my father belonged. The idealism formed really the foundation of a highly developed science of *eugenics* [emphasis mine] in our society... He was consciously working to bring out the highest possibilities of my mind and body. He had also, quite naturally, his social ambitions.[118]

This lengthy quote illustrates that Bipin Chandra's defense of his father was no different from the ways children were imagined in the scientific periodicals. His evocation of eugenics to justify his father's behaviour signalled how he conceived the imaginary fathers of a future nation. He rationalized his father's action through a characteristic merging of a reinvented Hindu past explained through male householders' ritual debts to ancestors and the commitment to the present and future that included improvement of race as well as fulfilment of social aspirations. In making the case for his father, the intentionality of Bipin Chandra Pal was obvious. Despite differences and conflict, he placed his father above all questions and doubts. The father was the object of veneration; his intention, authority, and power remained unquestioned by the son.

But not all accounts of fathers and children were justified along lines of Hindu tradition and eugenics. There were instances when children positioned themselves as risk-takers and did not hedge their defiance challenging the raging authority of fathers. The writer-playwright-director Premankur Atorthi (1890–1964) in his multi-volume autobiographical novel *Mahasthabir Jatak* (3 vols., 1944–1954) offered a candid picture of his father. Premakur Atorthi, belonging to the rising middle class, did not claim heritage from a particularly illustrious family. Neither did he try to justify his father's behaviour as Pal did. His narrative portrayed a caring yet temperamental father. He recalled the memory of an exceedingly strict father who often flew into a rage and threatened that his son would "be beaten to death" for acts of disobedience. This image quickly switched to an over-bearing yet nurturing father who warmed up the milk and handed out the bowls to his three sons. He took his sons—nine, five, and four years old—for a walk in the streets of late-nineteenth-century

[118] Bipin Chandra Pal, *Memories of My Life and Times*, 248.

Calcutta and introduced them to the educational landmarks in the city. Unable to attain higher education owing to his adverse family situation, Atorthi's father instilled in his boys the values of hard work, studies, prayers, and discipline, hoping that they would bring his dreams to fruition.[119] The experiences between fathers and sons revealed an emotional intimacy where the father voluntarily shared his feelings and convictions. Atorthi chronicled not only the towering and generous personality of this whimsical yet high-minded father but also his frequent outbursts of uncontrolled anger, in which he subjected his sons to brutal corporal punishment for the slightest offense. We must note here that Atorthi did not have a female sibling, so it is hard to determine what his father's position would have been with regard to a girl-child. For Premankur Atorthi's father, shaming, strictness, and austerity were all part of the healthy rearing of children, imparting to the latter a superior, moral education. Atorthi's record did not document any sign of guilt or remorse that his father suffered from for his excessive anger; rather softness and comfort always came from the mother, a female relative, or a neighbour. Atorthi also noted similar experiences in school in the inhumane beating he received at the hands of a British teacher who supposedly took "great pleasure" in beating up native students.[120] The narrative chronicled many more delinquent behaviours by the author and his friends and their escapades from the brutality of corporeal punishment in school and at home. Unlike Debendranath or Rabindranath, he was not a leader who set norms for his family and followers, but he was determined to equip his sons with the necessary education and training so that they could lead a *bhadra* life. Harassed by the vagaries of life, Atorthi's father exerted his full-fledged masculine authority at home, particularly over his sons.

In most of the autobiographical narratives of this period, misbehaviour and disobedience of boys incited physical punishment from fathers and teachers. When men told stories about their childhood, the angry father administering corporeal punishment was a common trope. But despite being prone to anger and inflicting punishment on children, none of these fathers were portrayed as being as "tyrannical" as Tosh described

---

[119] Premankur Atorthi, *Mahasthabir Jatak*, vol. 3 (Kolkata: De's Publishing, 1964), 7–8.
[120] Premankur Atorthi, "Satyabadi" [One Who Always Says Truth]," *Mouchak* 15, no. 5 (1924 [Jyaistha, 1331 BS]), 66–72.

in the context of Victorian England.[121] At the end, the fathers overcame their anger and showered affection upon their sons. Their deployment of anger to exert authority was cultural but the lack of self-control was also a sign of their limitations.

Pitritwo (paternity) for these middle-class fathers was entrenched in their caste-class status, their religious-cultural community, and it was tied to the honour of the family. The instances of disowning sons for converting to the new religion of Brahmoism was not just a punishment for violating a father's belief system but it was also attached to the question of continuing family lineage and honour that the sons' transgressed by abandoning their ancestral religion. Sivnath's, Bipin's, and Premankur's fathers were not public figures like Debendranath Tagore. But they upheld their family values and aspired for the modern education ushered in by the colonial government. They were determined to equip their sons with the necessary education and training so that they could lead a *bhadra* life, but their children were also expected to adhere to conservative cultural norms. For daughters, over whose life the fathers and families had more control, the yardstick was pronouncedly different.

While bias towards sons and the behaviour meted out to them by fathers depicted a gendered reality, let us complicate the picture with reminiscences from a woman who defied her father. Leela Majumdar (1908–2007), an outstanding female author, especially for children, belonged to the versatile family of the elite Raychaudhuris, whose members through several generations made a pioneering contribution to the printing business and children's literature in colonial and postcolonial Bengal.[122] In her autobiography *Pakdandi* [*The Winding Road*], Leela Majumdar (See Figure 4.16) recalled that her childhood was spent in absolute bliss in the foothills of the Himalayas in north and north-eastern India. She wrote:

> [I]n spite of having the supreme sense of happiness and security, my father was very strict. He had no doubt that severe spanking was absolutely mandatory to raise healthy children. My father was prepared to sacrifice everything for us; but he roared out so loud at the slightest acts

---

[121] Tosh, *Man's Place*, 79–101.
[122] For Leela Majumdar's ancestral family, the Rays, see Chandok Sengoopta, *The Rays Before Satyajit* (Delhi: Oxford University Press, 2016).

Figure 4.16 Leela Majumdar

of disobedience that our hands and feet froze. As a matter of fact, *I never got along well with my father, and later in life we parted company forever.* Whatever it was, as a child I used to avoid my father, but at the same time I had great respect for him.[123] (emphasis mine)

Majumdar's father, like Sudha Mazumdar's and Monica Chanda's, was a representative of the successful Bengali middle class—he worked for the colonial government, was posted in different locales within India, and harboured sensibilities that constituted the *shikshito bhadralok sampraday* (educated respectable community). Leela Majumdar vividly recalled the intensity of the slap that her father inflicted on her when she chewed on a plum stone that she picked from his empty plate. She also recounted his superb physical strength, extraordinary courage, and sportsmanship, qualities that were highly valued by Indian males, especially in

---

[123] Leela Majumdar, *Pakdandi* (Kolkata: Ananda Publishers, 1986), 5–6.

the face of British criticism. Her uncle (her father's elder brother), who actually raised her father, also nurtured a similar belief towards spanking, but he spared the girls. Leela's father did not. Leela Majumdar narrated instances of playfulness that her father exhibited towards children; but the children never overcame the distance that grew out of extreme fear of their father's anger, temper, and punishment. Majumdar's expressions were bold and less inhibited perhaps because she had already lost connection with her father following her choice of marriage partner and also because of her family's lesser social standing relative to the Tagores.

In the Bengali sociocultural landscape, falling out with fathers on the grounds of choosing marriage partners and romantic love was a common experience among women and men.[124] The multitudes of instances bring home the autocratic and hurtful regimes of fathers. The semi-autobiographical novel *Na Hanyate* (*It Never Dies*) of the writer and social activist Maitreyi Devi (1914–1990), daughter of the well-known philosopher Surendranath Dasgupta (1887–1952), stands out in that respect.[125] *Na Hanyate* (*It Never Dies*), redolent of a lost romance and unrequited love, and which was penned as a response to the novel *Bengali Nights* by the Indologist Mircea Eliade (1907–1986), with whom the author had an affair, was exceptional in its critique of the author's father, who was renowned worldwide for his scholarship.[126] Raised in a liberal, upper-caste Hindu household, Maitreyi Devi, "a poet" and a "precocious" daughter of a philosopher, powerfully recreates her teenage romance (she was sixteen) with her father's Romanian student Mircea Euclid (the last name was changed from Eliade to Euclid), then twenty-three; when the secret love affair became known to the family, her father banished Mircea from their home.[127] Forty-two years later, when Maitreyi Devi re-lived that

---

[124] For extensive accounts of father-daughter conflict around "love marriages," see Aparna Bandyopadhyay, *Desire and Defiance: A Study of Bengali Women in Love, 1850–1930* (Hyderabad: Orient Blackswan, 2016).

[125] Maitreyi Devi, *Na Hanyate* (Kolkata:Manisha Granthalaya, 1974). English translation by Maitreyi Devi, *It Does Not Die* (Kolkata: Writer's Workshop, 1976). My references are drawn from Maitreyi Devi, *It Does Not Die: A Romance* (Chicago: University of Chicago Press, 1994).

[126] For an insightful commentary on the two novels and their authors, see Ginu Kamani, "A Terrible Hurt: The Untold Story Behind the Publishing of Maitreyi Devi." https://www.press.uchicago.edu/Misc/Chicago/143651.html (accessed on February 11, 2020).

[127] At the age of twenty she was married to a Bengali man, lived a fulfilling married life with two children, published poetry and prose, and wrote books on Rabindranath Tagore, her mentor (Gurudev). Later in life she founded an orphanage and engaged in social work.

unfulfilled romance, she also left a daring testimony to the brutality and double-standards of her father (and her family). Thus, she introduced her father as follows:

> My father was a very learned man. In fact, a versatile genius... He is well-known for his erudition and feared by many because of it. His scholarship is aggressive; he can easily reduce a person in argument to shambles; he is very fond of this game. Yet he has a hypnotic charm. People cling to him. His students are devoted to him and will go to any length to support him. He also loves them. But that is a different kind of love, there is no sympathy in it. He loves them for his own sake and not theirs. For example, he loves me not for me so much as for himself... My father is full of me, yet I know if I dare go against him the littlest bit he won't hesitate to crush me ruthlessly. My likes and dislikes are immaterial. I have to be happy at his command.[128]

This critical commentary on her father as an autocratic patriarch lingers through the novel in which "history and fiction... deftly mingled."[129] Thanks to her family's elite status, Maitreyi Devi grew up in a rich cultural milieu and enjoyed the illustrious company, including that of Rabindranath Tagore. But her father's social conservatism and intervention stood in the way of consummating her love. The pages of this autobiographical novel strongly registered her disenchantment and anger with her father as she candidly recorded his hypocrisy, extra-marital affair, and self-centredness.[130]

It is important to focus now on how children were positioned in the narratives. The "story-telling children" recounting austere, sanctimonious, and care-giving fathers were active constituents of the emotional expressions defining filial relationships. If anger was recalled as the

---

[128] Maitreyi Devi, *It Does Not Die*, 21–22.

[129] Gopal Bhowmik, *The Indian PEN Journal*, July 1975. Cited in Ginu Kamani, "A Terrible Hurt: The Untold Story Behind the Publishing of Maitreyi Devi." https://www.press.uchicago.edu/Misc/Chicago/143651.html (accessed on February 11, 2020).

[130] For the argument that in contrast to personal narratives, fictions that merged with autobiographies offered Bengali women an opportunity to reveal their interiority and inscribe themselves in imaginary characters see Aparna Bandyopadhyay, "Towards a History of Women in Love in Colonial Bengal." Paper presented at the International Conference on *Shifting Contours, Widening Concerns: Women's History, Historiography and the Politics of Historical Representation*, held at Research Centre for Women's Studies, SNDT Women's University, Mumbai, 11–13 February 2015.

dominant emotion among most fathers expressing power and control, the response that it elicited from children was that of fear. Yet fear alone could not keep the youthful impulses under control. Both Sivnath Sastri and Bipin Chandra, although dependent on fathers for financial support, chose to follow their heart when it came to matters of new religious belief and persuasion. Premankur Atorthi and Leela Majumdar were risk-takers in several instances—Atorthi's delinquent behaviour in school and Majumdar's choice of her marriage-partner as a young adult are pertinent examples. Maitreyi Devi took the refuge of literary imagination to defy all conventions and shame her celebrity father by revealing his "secrets." Disobedience of children challenged the ordained behaviour expected of them by their parents. By crossing the boundaries they were at risk of being subjected to brutal physical and moral chastisement, and in extreme scenarios, of losing their relationships with their fathers, as in the case of Sastri, Pal, and Majumdar. The adult children so frankly recorded the conflicts possibly because they were able to break away from the socio-economic control of their fathers.

The moral universe that the fathers created and the mothers adhered to subjected children to strict disciplinary codes. Violation of those norms established children as autonomous subjects exerting their agency, albeit exposing themselves to the risk of physical and moral consequences. But in the context of India, physical punishment of children by fathers was entirely within the range of permissibility. The dominance of the father, in particular, was established through disciplining both the mind and the body of the child. Physical punishment was considered therapeutic to remedy the ills that plagued the character, the "prison of the body."[131] The moral anxiety expressed in advice literature also sanctioned anger as a corrective to "deviant" behaviour and we witness its manifestations in child-father interactions.[132] The evidence presented in this chapter was not just intrinsic to colonial Bengal. Autobiographies from all across India, including those of Mohandas Karamchand Gandhi and Jawaharlal Nehru, recorded rage and anger of fathers. We may infer from this that filial fear, but also defiance, were defining experiences of colonial Indian

---

[131] Bose, "Sons of the Nation," 135.
[132] Pernau, "Male Anger and Female Malice."

childhood. Nonetheless, whatever was the defining emotion, they were garbed in overarching veneration.

Conclusion

Through an examination of self-writings of adult children, the chapter mapped the dominant modes of imagining fathers in their strengths and weaknesses—as supreme figures of veneration; as affectionate yet compromised and ambivalent personalities caught up in crossroads of familial and social pressures; and as strict disciplinarians demanding allegiance from recalcitrant or independent-minded children who pursued their own choice on personal matters such as religion and marriage. The records testified that adult children imagined their fathers irrespective of their role as economic providers. The varied moments of parental interactions demonstrated fathers' hold over children's minds and bodies. Memories of mothers recorded in the same sources rarely upheld them in positions of absolute authority. It was the father's decision to impart specific education to his children; it was his moral guidance that prepared them for the world; it was his decision to justify or not his daughters' marriages; the father appeared as the supreme dispenser of moral guidance, etiquette, and justice within the home. The ordinary practices with children captured the interiority of the fathers whose manhood was expressed in their own, autonomous, sovereign space of the home where they were freely able to express themselves, translating and transgressing the ideological paradigms of the normative and the scientific texts into lived reality.

The fathers of the autobiographies instantiate but also challenge the fathers of the pedagogical and scientific literature. Since in these narratives fathers were, by and large, the fathers of the authors, they were an older style—the "old father" as opposed to the "new father"—used as a foil for the authors' own (new) type of fatherhood. Another contrast comes from the fact that while the importance of education and obedience to the father's will were important both in pedagogical and in autobiographical literature, it is only in the latter that corporeal punishment dominates as the response to disobedience, violation of norms, or a failure to study.

The voices of women describe a different type of father than the voices of men. While daughters' autobiographical narratives at times echoed sons' narratives in stressing distance from fathers, they more frequently noted close and affectionate relations, belying the stereotype of a distant, cold, and aloof father. Although fathers were involved in daughters' education, in most cases early marriages for girls were deemed more important than continued studies, although that did not stop daughters from idealizing their fathers. Several daughters, like Sunity Devee, made a special effort to absolve their fathers of any blame. Finally, while some daughters reported that their fathers used corporeal punishment against daughters as well as sons, the physical aspects of disciplining were highlighted far more in men's narratives.

The intersection of varied sources that we examined through the chapters of this book provides a composite imagining of fatherhood. The autobiographical evidence reinforced by pedagogic and scientific literature evoked creative assimilation of indigenous values from the past and selective borrowing and adaptations of mores from Victorian and Edwardian England that repeatedly invoked obedience to patriarchal and parental authorities at home. The deferential tone of the autobiography while talking about fathers shrouded the injustices the authors faced as children. The liminality of child-selves was emphasized in lieu of deference to the father. The biggest caveat of personal narratives is their reliance on memory, which is always fragmented, discontinuous, selective, and often incomplete. Memory, whether individual or collective, is after all socially produced. Imagination played a significant role in this reconstruction.[133]

Once compliance with family values and community practices were fulfilled, children, who were looked upon as future citizens if male and wives and mothers if female were introduced to a gendered educational curriculum that bore influences of both Victorian and Edwardian England and an imagined Indian past. In adult children's imaginings, fathers were represented as sources of authority, but their authority was

---

[133] For memory and generational narration see Wulf Kansteiner, "Generation and Memory: A Critique of the Ethical and Ideological Implications of Generational Narration," in *Writing the History of Memory*, eds. Stefan Berger and Bill Niven (London: Bloomsbury Press, 2014), 111–134.

often challenged by risks that children took and decisions they made as young adults. The unpacking of various emotions recorded in father-child experiences revealed the nature of changes that filial relationship underwent in late colonial India. The writings discussed in the chapter also signalled the process that went into the making of the "new" man when domesticity became a motor for change.[134] Meanings attached to masculinity, such as respect, devotion, strength, courage, and uprightness, were inextricably linked to the virtues of fatherhood imagined by children.

The affective bonds between fathers and children were not new, but the changing practices of emotional intimacies in filial relationships debunk the stereotype of distant Indian fathers. The chapter has aimed to foreground a changing context in which the emotions of affection, anger, fear, and despair played out. If thought and emotion are embodied and only understood in their social context,[135] the emotional practices that this chapter recounted were embedded in specific social settings (*sthana*), at the specific historical moments (*kala*), and were performed by the specific individuals (*patra*) that Rajat Ray has emphasized in his works. The selective examples from the educated middle-class Bengalis demonstrate not just "collective feelings" but also a range of "collective practices" of child-rearing, and therefore also collective experiences of childhood and fatherhood that evolved through successive generations over a period of time.[136]

Male members of the Indian intelligentsia were as invested in the ideas and practices of fatherhood as they were instrumental in formulating new visions of women and motherhood. Indeed, as the narratives considered in this chapter suggest, for many educated Bengalis in this era, fathers were actually of far more interest than mothers, at least when it came to representing their lives to the public. The practice of fatherhood was an equally important component of the same patriarchy that had subjugated women to new ideological parameters at the close of the nineteenth

---

[134] Swapna Banerjee, "Debates on Domesticity and Position of Women in Late Colonial India," *History Compass Journal* [Blackwell Publishing, Oxford, UK] 8, no. 6 (2010): 455–473.

[135] Monique Scheer, "Are Emotions a Kind of Practice (And Is that What Makes them Have a History)? A Bourdieuian Approach to Understanding Emotion," *History and Theory* 51, no. 2 (2012): 193–220.

[136] See Boddice, "Affective Turn."

century.[137] The fathers, as literate members of the middle class, were at risk of criticism by the colonial government. But paternal expressions of love, protection, control, and discipline acted as an attribute and vector of colonial masculinity (*purushotwo*).

The emotional and physical practices of fatherhood translated the rhetoric of manhood into reality within the domain of the familiar and the intimate. By tracking the emotions of fathers and children, I have attempted to hint at a burgeoning culture that shaped their selves and world. The expressions of restraint, ambiguity, outrage, or exuberance with children disclose the dominant texts of the behaviour of fathers who defined and defied the norms in an altered colonial milieu. This is not to ascribe unrestrained power to the paterfamilias but to give those fathers due recognition as hegemonic subjects playing an active role in the micropolitics of everyday family life. Middle-class fathers and their children represented an "emotional community" that was constitutive of the reigning patriarchy, charting the "dominant norms of an emotional life" and new emotional possibilities for children.[138]

Fatherhood enabled Indian men to redeem their precariousness and exert their masculinity in the hierarchical power relationship with women and especially children in the negotiated space of the home. But these experiences, far from being universal, were contingent upon the specific contexts of marriage, social status (including economic class as well as caste), and institutions within which they were enacted. The pleasures, pangs, and anxieties of fatherhood were embedded in the larger political-economic and sociocultural forces that shaped the practices of everyday life, and of course, children's emotional upbringing.

---

[137] Chatterjee, "Women and the Nation."
[138] Reddy, *Navigation of Feeling*, 129.

5
Rabindranath Tagore
The Father and the Educator

We must find some meeting-ground, where there can be no question of conflicting interests. One of such places is the University, where we can work together in a common pursuit of truth, share together our common heritage, and realise that artists in all parts of the world have created forms of beauty, scientists discovered secrets of the universe, philosophers solved the problems of existence, saints made the truth of the spiritual world organic in their own lives, not merely for some particular race to which they belonged but for all mankind.

—Rabindranath Tagore[1]

The above quote embodies the holistic vision of Rabindranath Tagore (1861–1941), an iconic figure of Indian modernity, the poet-novelist-playwright and artist, an educationist, and a global thinker, whom we met in Chapter 4 as the son of the religious reformer Debendranath Tagore. Tagore's (See Figure 5.1) yearning for a universal meeting ground is traceable to his deep-seated frustration with the colonial education system with which he deeply engaged: "The basic complaint is that despite years of learning in the schools of the English, we have not been able to shed our student tags. We seem to have accumulated knowledge from the outside, but contributed nothing from the inside."[2] Tagore's despair and longing expressed here were rooted in his personal experiences as a child, as an

---

[1] Rabindranath Tagore, "An Eastern University," in *Creative Unity* (London: Macmillan, 1922); Cited as front-matter in Sabyasachi Bhattacharya and Ashoke Mukhopadhyay, ed., *The Common Pursuit: Convocation Addresses at Visva-Bharati, Santiniketan, 1952–1993* (Kolkata: Visva-Bharati, 1995).

[2] Rabindranath Tagore, "Asontosh-er Karan (1919)," in *Shikhsa* (Kolkata: Visvabharati Granthan Bibhag, 1990).

Figure 5.1 Rabindranath Tagore (1909)

adult, and as an important public figure. For an understanding of the context that gave birth to Tagore's intellectual philosophy one needs to visit his different stages of life as a student, as a father, and as an educator.

Reflecting on the future of Indian democracy in the face of growing religious fundamentalism, Martha Nussbaum offered a comparative assessment of Tagore, Gandhi, and Nehru. She claimed that all three "are in their own ways *fathers* of the kind of democratic pluralism that is in jeopardy in today's India" (emphasis mine).[3] Nussbaum argued that, despite their similarities in envisioning a united India free from caste divisions, religious hostilities, and age-old hierarchical practices, in their advocacy of women's empowerment and political equality as well as in their endorsing of religious pluralism and a secular state, they each differed in their conceptions of how to achieve and preserve democracy. Nussbaum

---

[3] Martha C. Nussbaum, "Tagore, Gandhi, Nehru," in *The Clash Within: Democracy, Religious Violence, and India's Future* (Cambridge, MA: Harvard University Press, 2007), 80–121, here 81.

added significantly to a new assessment of Tagore by asserting the relevance of his pedagogical model for India's democracy—"a public education that would nourish critical freedom" and advocate "a public poetry of humanity that would use art, emotion, and the humanities to craft a pluralistic public culture."[4] Nussbaum's invocation of fatherhood for Tagore, Gandhi, and Nehru reaffirms my attribution of paternity to the literary leaders and reformers of India: these men may have been flawed fathers (symbolic and real), but paternity nonetheless was a defining feature of their identity and leadership. This chapter and the next, with their focus on these three important leaders, underscore the connection between familial experiences and public practices, between fatherhood and an altered pedagogy in late colonial India. They also tease out the connection between *pitritwo* (fatherhood) and *pourush/purushotwo* (masculinity), a running theme that I delineate throughout the book.

Tagore, like his contemporaries, was a product of the nineteenth century who displayed sensibilities informed by post-Enlightenment European philosophies.[5] Scholars disagreeing with such a view have explained Tagore's distinctive thinking as drawing from indigenous roots and environment in addition to the European ideological influences.[6] The familial context that was integral to colonial modernities and was especially critical for Tagore's pedagogic endeavours calls for an investigation.[7] Even a recent essay on Tagore's meditations on love and interiority relies solely on his novels and poems at the exclusion of his intimate experiences.[8]

---

[4] Nussbaum, "Tagore, Gandhi, Nehru," 121.

[5] Michael Collins, *Empire, Nationalism and the Postcolonial World: Rabindranath Tagore's Writings on History, Politics, Society* (New York/London: Routledge, 2012). Partha Chatterjee, "Tagore's Non-Nation," in *Lineages of Political Society* (New York: Columbia University Press, 2011), 94–128; Satadru Sen, "Remembering Robi," in *Traces of Empire* (Chennai: Primus Books, 2014), 58–74.

[6] Sekhar Bandyopadhyay, "Rabindranath Tagore, The Indian Nation, and Its Outcasts," *Harvard Asia Quarterly* 15, no. 1 (2013): 34–39; Brian Hatcher, "Father, Son and Holy Text: Rabindranath Tagore and the Upanisads," *Journal of Hindu Studies* 4, no. 2 (2011): 119–143; Tanika Sarkar, "The Child and the World: Rabindranath Tagore's Ideas on Education," *Rebels, Wives, Saints: Designing Selves and Nations in Colonial Times* (Calcutta: Seagull, 2009).

[7] Dipesh Chakrabarty, "Family, Fraternity, Salaried Labor," in *Provincializing Europe* (Princeton: Princeton University Press, 2000); Partha Chatterjee, "The Nation and Its Women," in *The Nation and Its Fragments* (Princeton: Princeton University Press, 1993); Tanika Sarkar, *Hindu Wife, Hindu Nation* (New Delhi: Permanent Black, 2001).

[8] Sudipta Kaviraj, *The Invention of Private Life: Literature and Ideas* (New York: Columbia University Press, 2015).

My examination of Tagore emphasizes the role of the family and reconciles his familial experiences, especially his role as a son and a father, with his far-reaching goals as a protagonist of a new kind of education and human welfare.[9] Although it may seem ironic to scrutinize a "Myriad-Minded Man"[10] and an international figure like Rabindranath Tagore through the constraining prism of domestic and private life, I argue that it is crucial to situate Tagore in his family life in order to comprehend his public persona; that his familial experiences and his role as an institution-builder cannot be disentangled from each other. It was his personal experiences from child- to adulthood in the domestic as well as the public realm that informed and fuelled his reformist agenda. More importantly, Tagore bridged the gap between real and imaginary fathers we discussed in the previous chapters. In developing his new pedagogy, he transcended the boundaries between the home and the world and acted as a representative of the private–public man, who was deeply invested in children of his own and of others.

Tagore was distinctive in many ways when compared with the real and imagined fathers discussed in previous chapters. The plethora of his own works and the vast repertoire of writings on him offer a wealth of direct evidence on his pedagogy, thoughts, and actions. If the other interlocutors as imaginary fathers obliquely used children to develop a critique of the colonial education system, Tagore as a dedicated educator was a more forceful critic and directly focused on children, steering them through his reformed curriculum. His children were both real and imaginary—he had a lived experience of working with his own children and with unrelated students while he simultaneously envisioned a generation emboldened by his ideals and inspiration. Needless to say, imagination reigned supreme with Tagore. Contrary to his predecessors, for him, children and youth were not hapless victims embodying the ill-effects of the colonial system (Chapter 3). Rather, he identified a crisis in the forging of their identities: their distress was caused by a colonial education that

---

[9] Michael Collins, in his recent study, has emphasized the actualization of Tagore's philosophical positions, the reconciliation of his ideas with actions, an approach congruent with the one I take here; see Michael Collins, *Empire, Nationalism and the Postcolonial World: Rabindranath Tagore's Writings on History, Politics, Society* (New York/London: Routledge, 2012).

[10] Krishna Dutta and Andrew Robinson, *Rabindranath Tagore: The Myriad-Minded Man* (London: Bloomsbury, 1995).

alienated them from their roots. His criticism did not rest on the rejection of Western learning and thoughts. His remediation was an alternate pedagogy that would impart in vernacular language the best of Western knowledge and Indian tradition in an educational setting conducive for his students. Although criticized for his elitism and detachment from the masses, Tagore was a leader who was deeply committed to the upliftment of the grassroots population through education, putting him in the role of a metaphorical father to a broader community.[11] Furthermore, his educational model challenged the prevailing views of masculinity, as Tagore in his position of a symbolic father sought to reshape an incipient nation's children (mainly sons) into future citizens and hence, implicitly, offered a new view of fatherhood. His curriculum combining arts, music, dance, and poetry was geared towards attaining joy and freedom rather than prioritizing physical strength, emotional stoicism, job skills, and distant relationships with wives and children. He championed education for the sake of knowledge and enjoyment, free from the shackles of any proposed causes, including that of earning a livelihood.

Tagore's stages of life—from a restive child to a "father as educator"—bring into relief the intersectionality of his private self and public commitments. His life offers insights into the interiority of a "father" whose novel educational programmes challenged the detached nature of the existing model. The gnawing discomfort and the claustrophobic environment of British-run institutions that Tagore experienced as a child gave rise to his later critique of colonial education and translated into his efforts to reform the system, a system that he believed would cater not only to his own children but to children at large. By assuming the moral guardianship of a world inhabited by free citizens whose minds were "without fear" and their heads "held high," Tagore positioned himself as a "father."

The chapter builds on an amalgamation of sources—personal narratives, correspondences, essays, and addresses by Tagore, supplemented by remembrances of his children, relatives, students, and followers. We saw vignettes of his childhood experiences with his father in the last chapter. Here we draw further on his memories as a child and experiences as a father himself. In many ways Tagore could be regarded as the "new man" (parallel to

---

[11] See for example, Blanka Knotková-Čapková, *Tagore on Discriminations: Representing the Unrepresented* (Prague: Metropolitan University Prague Press, 2015).

the "new woman"), personifying virtues of a modern father celebrated in Victorian and Edwardian England and also emphasized in his father's theistic manual, *Brahmo Dharma Grantha*. The prior chapters have emphasized the intertwined relationship between *pitritwo* (fatherhood) and *purushotvo* (masculinity) by tracking everyday interactions and literary productions in various genres that imagined children and fathers in myriad positions of power and helplessness. The early reformers' discomfort with colonial pedagogy expressed in vernacular primers, normative texts, and scientific journals found a culmination in Tagore's direct attack on British education for disempowering Indians and in his alternate curriculum to fortify the future generation.

Tagore has been often criticized by fellow Bengalis for his bourgeois effeminacy. But his radical critique of colonial education and the daily practices defying conventional notions of manhood were largely overlooked in those assessments. His rejection of the geopolitical boundaries of the nation-state and emphasis on freedom, arts, and "public poetry" over muscular or militant nationalism challenged the dominant culture of masculinity. His paternalism embraced a "manliness" privileging moral, aesthetic, and spiritual sustenance over economic and political considerations. Tagore's intervention in educational movements and his simultaneous deep-seatedness in family offer us an opportunity to explore the role of fathers as mentors and thus the ways in which alternate notions of masculinity and patriarchy existed alongside dominant ethno-nationalistic forms.[12] Tagore's new definition of manliness and fatherhood nurtured freedom but also commanded compliance. His everyday experiences and activism demonstrated the importance of his family both as an enabling and a restrictive force and the tangled connections between his domestic reality and public commitment to social justice and education.

Attributing Rabindranath with an "imaginary" fatherhood, this chapter steers our gaze to his affective connections as a father and a public leader. Born into a wealthy family of colonial Calcutta, Tagore came from a strong patriarchal culture. His grandfather, Prince Dwarkanath (1794–1846), a "business tycoon" partnered with the British; and his father

---

[12] The work of Mrinalini Sinha, "Giving Masculinity a History," *Gender and History* 11, no. 3 (1999): 446, which suggests that masculinity in this period was not connected to gender-specific sex-roles but were "constitutive of social relationships," is suggestive here.

Debendranath (1817–1905), whom we met in the previous chapter, held immense power in the Bengali socio-cultural and religious milieu. Tagore's brothers held important government posts and contributed to various branches of arts and literature. Active involvement in nationalist, cultural, and educational movements made the Tagores the architects of a new colonial modernity.[13] Tagore's accomplishments determined his reception, particularly in the West, as a humanist and a critic. But his personal narratives, letters, and essays unveil his more "radical" side, as a rebel child and a visionary father.[14]

To reconcile the gap often placed between Tagore's towering [public] persona and his "private" experiences, I explore the ways his familial moments coalesced with and translated into his public practices as an educationist who created an edifice of modern Bengali childhood, widely endorsed by the educated middle class. Foregrounding his experiences as a student, a father, and an educator, I contend that Tagore's daily experiences as a child and a father followed by the transference of his affective concern to a larger body of children, in whom he tried to inculcate a new sense of selfhood through his unique education, was inflected with an alternate sense of manhood (*pourush/purushotvo*). His pedagogy, albeit limited in its success, empowered him as a virtual father with a distinct conceptualization of masculinity, one that defied colonial forms of domination. Tagore's educational vision evolved with his life and was an active, dynamic process. From the promotion of vernacular language to freedom of mind, to economic sustenance for the poor and the future generation, Tagore provided a well-thought-out direction for the community and the world.

From *Chhelebela* (Boyhood) to Manhood: Colonial Education and Family

Tagore's distaste for colonial education was rooted in his boyhood experiences. His memoir *Boyhood Days* opens up with the bustle and scurry that

---

[13] Krishna Kripalani, *Dwarkanath Tagore, A Forgotten Pioneer: A Life* (New Delhi: National Book Trust, 1981) Blair Kling, *Partner in Empire: Dwarkanath Tagore and the Age of Enterprise* (Berkeley: University of California Press, 1976).

[14] For the radicality of Tagore, see Sanjukta Dasgupta, Sudeshna Chakravarti, and Mary Matthew, eds., *Radical Tagore: Nation, Family and Gender in Tagore's Fiction and Films* (New Delhi: Orient Blackswan, 2013).

characterized his multigenerational urban household in "old Kolkata," but he presents his childhood as being full of ennui and languor during his regular study hours under the home-tutor.[15] With their study "illuminated by a *sej*, a lamp with a double wick in a glass bowl," Rabindranath painted his earliest experiences of learning at home:

> In that dim, flickering light, our tutor, Master-moshai,[16] taught us the First Book of Pyari Sarkar.[17] I would yawn, then become drowsy, and afterwards, rub my eyes to stay awake. I was repeatedly reminded that Master-moshai's other pupil, Satin, was a gem of a boy, extraordinarily serious about his studies; he would rub snuff in his eyes to ward off sleep. As for me? The less said the better. Even the terrible prospect of remaining the only illiterate dunce among all the boys would not keep me alert. At nine in the evening, half asleep, my eyes heavy with drowsiness, I would be set free.[18]

In these pronouncements by Tagore, one hears not only the agony of average Indian children overstudying but also the idealization of a quintessentially "good" student in the character of Satin. It also reminds us of the similar emphasis that Vidyasagar put on Gopal, the good boy and his love for studies, in his primer *Varnaparichay* (1855). It is difficult to ascertain if it was customary for affluent Bengali families to hire private tutors for training their children so early in life. But informal training at home, particularly for boys, was part of the colonial culture. By the time Tagore was growing up, primary schools had been set up by the colonial administration. The three reports (1835–1838) by William Adam indicated that the number of students under domestic instruction was almost nine times higher than those attending public schools.[19] The average age of admission to a public elementary school was eight years old, and that

---

[15] Rabindranath Tagore, *Boyhood Days*, trans. Radha Chakrabarty (London: Hesperus Worldwide: 2007 [1940]), 6.
[16] "Master-moshai" is the Bengali variant of the address for a teacher.
[17] Pyari Sarkar (1823–1875) was a textbook writer and an educationist in colonial Bengal.
[18] Rabindranath Tagore, *Boyhood Days*, 6.
[19] William Adam, *Adam's Reports on Vernacular Education in Bengal and Behar with a Brief View of Its Past and Present Condition, Submitted to Government in 1835, 1836, and 1838; With a Brief View of Its Past and Present Condition* (Kolkata: Home Secretariat Press, 1868).

of leaving was fourteen.[20] Female education, it should be noted, was almost non-existent.

It was not only Tagore's memories of his informal schooling at home but those of the Normal School that were "not the least sweet in any particular."[21] His earliest memories of Normal School was that of singing English verses, whose language was inscrutable to child Rabi: "Unfortunately the words were English and the tune quite as foreign, so that we had not the faintest notion what sort of incantation we were practising;..."[22] Much to the dismay of the British school authority, the verse failed to invoke any kind of cheerfulness among the boys. He noted that had he been "able to associate with the other boys, the woes of learning might not have seemed so intolerable. But that turned out to be impossible—so nasty were most of the boys in their manners and habits."[23] Neither did he cherish the memory of the teachers; their language was so "foul" that out of sheer contempt he refused to answer any questions he asked.[24] Tagore did not elaborate further on the manners and speech of fellow students or teachers, but they definitely hurt his sensibilities even as a child. He whiled away his free time in school sitting near a window overlooking the street and counting: "one year—two years—three years—; wondering how many such would have to be got through like this."[25]

Tagore's critical recollections of his school days brought home the nature and purpose of colonial education. The education system developed by missionaries, colonial administrators, and indigenous leaders was fraught with a struggle between the effort "by non-Indians to impose a cheap imitation of the British educational system on India and the desire of the people of the country to create a new system to meet their own peculiar needs and problems."[26] The British claim that colonial rule was a "pedagogical enterprise for the improvement of India" was met with a

---

[20] Syed Nurullah and J.P. Naik, *A History of Education in India* (Bombay: Macmillan, 1951), 23.
[21] Rabindranath Tagore, *My Reminiscences* (London: Macmillan, 1917;; Gutenberg ebook released in 2007), 33. http://www.gutenberg.org/files/22217/22217-h/22217.htm#Page_30 (accessed on March 20, 2016).
[22] Rabindranath Tagore, *My Reminiscences*, 33.
[23] Rabindranath Tagore, *My Reminiscences*, 34.
[24] Rabindranath Tagore, *My Reminiscences*, 34.
[25] Rabindranath Tagore, *My Reminiscences*, 34.
[26] Nurullah and Naik, History of Education in India, xiv.

two-pronged nationalist response—acknowledging the benefits of the English education that raised them from "the torpor of ages" and simultaneously pointing out its limited scope and inadequacy for reaching out to the larger population.[27] Western-educated middle-class people all over India had long engaged in pedagogical experiments from the early years of the nineteenth century. As we have seen, working closely with the colonial state and the missionary educators, Bengali reformers, pedagogical fathers such as Iswarchandra Vidyasagar (1820–1891), Akshay Kumar Dutta (1820–1886), Bhudev Mukhopadhyay (1827–1894), among others, had written primers and manuals and had deliberated on the nature of education to be imparted to native students.

As a rebel child, Tagore refused to comply with the demands of a colonial education system: "[S]o long as I was forced to attend school, I felt an unbearable torture."[28] Dwelling on his experiences in Normal School and Oriental Seminary, the schools that were run by the colonial officials and the missionaries, he reflected, "possibly my suffering was unusually greater than that of most other children. The non-civilized in me was sensitive; it had great thirst for colour, for music, for movement of life. Our city-built education took no heed of that living fact."[29] After dropping out of successive institutions, he finally gave up school at age fourteen, the year his mother died, and it was "through the joy" of his freedom that he "felt a real urge to teach himself."[30] Shorn of the restrictiveness of the formal school system, Tagore was nourished by the strong cultural environment at home. As a "living university," the Tagore household of Jorasanko exposed him to a confluence of European and Indian thoughts and literature—Shakespeare, Dante, Byron, Goethe, Shelley, and Keats on the one hand; classical Sanskrit dramas and poetry by Kalidasa et al., and modern works by Bankim Chandra Chattopadhyay, Biharilal Chakrabarty, and Michael Madhusudan Dutt, on the other. He was equally conversant with the different genres of folk literature and music through nursery rhymes,

---

[27] Sanjay Seth, "Vernacular Modernity: The Nationalist Imagination," in *Subject Lessons: The Western Education of Colonial India* (Durham/London: Duke University Press, 2007), 159.

[28] Rabindranath Tagore, "Talks in China (1925)," in *My Life in My Words*, ed. Uma Das Gupta (New Delhi: Viking, 2006), 94.

[29] Rabindranath Tagore, "A Poet's School," *Santiniketan Vidyalaya*, 20, cited in *My Life in My Words*, 64.

[30] Rabindranath Tagore, *My Life in My Words*, 69.

Baul songs, and Vaishnava literature and lyrics.[31] Furthermore, he imbibed the Upanishadic-inspired Brahmo ideals preached by his father.[32] In 1878, sixteen-year-old Rabindranath travelled to England with his elder brother Satyendranath and attended lectures in Law at University College, London. He returned to India without receiving a degree. A combination of his deep resentment of early schooling in Calcutta, the more liberal education at home, and then his experiences in England went into the making of his later academic programme and his stance as a pedagogic father.

But the young man was still subject to the control of his own father. As he transitioned to manhood, like most of the men and women of his status and era, Tagore's marriage was arranged by his father. Tagore at age twenty-two married eleven-year-old Bhabatarini, later known as Mrinalini Devi[33] (1872–1902), a bride selected by his father Debendranath following strict caste rules[34] (See Figure 5.2). At every stage of his career, he reckoned with his father's authority without confronting him. Tagore's awe and deference to his father could be explained by his *pitri-bhakti* or veneration of his father that we discussed in the last chapter. In his personal life, however, he registered a shift in his dealings with his own wife and children. In other words, while he did not explicitly reject the role and expectations of a dutiful son, he staked out a new position for himself as a "new father."

Rabindranath Tagore: The Intimate Father at Home

> On Sunday night, I felt my spirit leave my body to come and see you. I saw you sleeping on one side of the large bed, next to you were Beli and Khoka [their eldest daughter and son, Madhurilata and Rathindranath]. I caressed you and whispered in your ears,

---

[31] Kathleen O'Connell, *Tagore: The Poet as Educator* (Kolkata: Visva-Bharati, 2002), 44–45.
[32] Brian Hatcher, "Father, Son and Holy Text," 119–143.
[33] The Tagores had the practice of renaming their brides, who usually came from humble social backgrounds. Bhabatarini, Tagore's wife, was given the name Mrinalini.
[34] Dasgupta et al., *Radical Tagore*, 3.

Figure 5.2 Rabindranath and his wife Mrinalini (1883)

"*Chhoto-bou* [My Little Wife], please remember that on this Sunday night I left my body to come and see you. I shall ask you on my return from England if you saw me too." Then I kissed Beli and the baby, and returned.[35]

---

[35] Tagore, *Chitthi Patra*, 11–12. Tagore had five children : Madhurilata aka Bela (1886–1918); Rathindranath (1888–1961); Renuka aka Rani (1890–1904); Mira Devi (1892–1962); Shamidranath (1896–1907).

On board for his second trip to England in August 1890, Rabindranath wrote the previously mentioned letter to his wife, Mrinalini Devi. If Debendranath led an itinerant life to fulfil the leadership responsibilities of his religious community, Rabindranath, too, as a celebrated subject of a new modernity, was often travelling abroad, leaving his family behind. While his autobiographical writings did not convey information on his wife and children, his letters are rich testimony to his emotions and closeness with them. The intimacy expressed in this letter by Rabindranath was significantly different from what he himself experienced with his father Debendranath. Certainly, there is nothing in any of the narratives by Debendranath's children suggesting that their father, when away from his family, sent his spirit home to visit.

Another letter written in 1890 captured how Rabindranath and his sister-in-law Jnadanandini Devi (wife of Satyendranath Tagore, whom we encountered earlier), when living in Bombay, carefully picked out clothes for his wife and daughters before his departure to England. Rabindranath selected a bright red sari and a "border" for his elder daughter Bela (aka Madhurilata) while his sister-in-law selected "a blue and a white one." Rabindranath mused, "I hope Rani (aka Renuka) likes it—the fusspot that she is. Does she ever ask for me? Who knows how grown Khoka [his son, Rathindranath] will be when I see him on my return ... I am sure he will not recognize me. I may turn into such a sahib that none of you may recognize me."[36]

We find in these expressions not the philosopher-poet but an anxious father deeply in love with his children and wife,[37] a picture missing in his own childhood experience. Rabindranath was an affectionate and playful father who mused over his joy and sorrow with his children and with his nephew and nieces (See Figure 5.3). His niece Indira Devi in reminiscences of her childhood in England recalled when Rabi-Kaka (Uncle Rabi) visited them, he amused Indira and her brother Surendranath by singing a Hindi song faster and faster until they could only see his trembling lips.[38] A letter written to Rabindranath by his youngest daughter

---

[36] Tagore, *Chitthi Patra*, 13–15.
[37] For parallels in Victorian England, see Tosh, *Man's Place*, 83.
[38] Indira Devi Chaudhurani, "Jivan-Kawtha," in *Smriti-Samput*, vol.1(Santiniketan: Visvabharati, 1997 [1953]), 7.

Figure 5.3 Rabindranath Tagore with family. Left to right: youngest daughter Mira Devi, eldest son Rathindranath Tagore, Rabindranath Tagore, wife of Rathindranath, Pratima Devi, eldest daughter of R. Tagore Madhurilata Devi (1909)

Mira Devi (1894–1969), when she was a little girl, was filled with stories of her dolls and toys. The letter testifies to an intimate father-daughter bonding.[39] Rabindranath's son Rathindranath provides us with a more detailed picture by conveying "glimpses of some aspects" of his illustrious "father's personality" that were "not dealt with by his biographers."[40] Rabindranath was remembered as a down-to-earth father whose august personality did not stand in the way with his children. Rabindranath's friendly approach also was recalled through his attempts to introduce his children to the many worlds of practical learning such as allowing them to handle a precious heirloom clock from his grandfather, Prince Dwarkanath, and teaching them how to wind it. He also nurtured affectionately the literary and artistic talents of his nephews and nieces. Rathindranath noted:

[39] Mira Devi, *Smritikatha* (Calcutta: Visvabharati, 1975), 7–8.
[40] Tagore, *On the Edges of Time*, preface (not paginated).

Father never treated any of his children harshly, nor did he, on the other hand, lavish sentimental affection upon them. I do not remember any occasion when Father subjected any of us to physical punishment. Temperamentally it was impossible for him to use violence. During all the years of my boyhood and youth, only thrice have I seen him get really angry with me.[41]

Rabindranath, to an extent, represented a departure from the fathers we encountered in the last chapter. His attitude towards and behaviour with children were quite controlled as opposed to the angry fathers we witnessed earlier in this book. His playfulness with children and closeness with his wife remind us of the virtues of Victorian men as John Tosh described, but unlike Tosh's fathers, "distance" or "tyranny" never underlined his relationship with children. Neither temperamental nor effusive, Rabindranath was nevertheless a strict disciplinarian. One area of commonality between him and his own father was that Rabindranath subjected his son Rathindranath (See Figure 5.4) to rigorous training and hardship.[42] It is best to capture the authoritarian aspect of his parenting style in the words of his son Rathindranath, who described how his father decided to send him to a hiking trip to "the shrine of Kedarnath in the Western Himalayas" with a group of monks:

> Father thought that this sort of hiking trip would be a good preliminary training for the life of hardship he intended me to take up, as a pupil of Brahmacharya Asrama at Santiniketan. I wonder how many parents even today would let a boy of such immature age risk a journey on foot trekking through the Himalayas...[43]

Rabindranath might have pushed his son to develop physical stamina, but towards his young daughters, he seems to have been far more tender.[44] He describes his involvement in a reminiscence-filled letter:

---

[41] Tagore, *On the Edges of Time*, 149.
[42] Mira Devi, *Smritikatha*, 19.
[43] Rathindranath Tagore, *On the Edges of Time*, 38.
[44] We may recall in this instance that most daughters in the last chapter also recalled fond memories of their affectionate fathers despite the latter's ambivalent attitude towards girls' marriage and education.

Figure 5.4 Rathindranath Tagore

Yesterday, my mind went back to Bela's childhood time and again. I raised her with such loving care. I remember how she would play with the pillows in bed and jump on to the little toys that came her way... I remembered how I used to bathe her in our Park Street house, and when we were in Darjeeling how I used to wake her up and feed her with warm milk in the nights. Those early days of having her so close keep haunting me.[45]

The haunting likely was produced by the circumstances under which he wrote this letter: he sent it to his wife in 1901, just after leaving a fourteen-year-old Bela aka Madhurilata, his eldest daughter, at the home of her

---

[45] Tagore, *Chitthi Patra*, 67–69.

new husband (I discuss the child marriages of the Tagore daughters later in the chapter.).

Rabindranath was also solicitous towards his daughter Renuka aka Rani, although she, too, had been married off in 1901. His son might have trekked through the Himalayas without his father, but in 1903, Tagore himself took Renuka, who contracted tuberculosis, to the Himalayas: "at one stage in the mountains the poet had to carry his ailing daughter in his arms... [H]e had not only to tend and look after his daughter but keep her entertained and cheerful, for she was moody and high-strung."[46] Renuka was married, but it was her father, and not her husband or in-laws, who took her to the mountains.[47]

In his care for his children, Rabindranath may have been an atypical example and an outlier; but it is more likely that he represented the "new father" through his thoughts and actions. He was an active caregiver, bathing and feeding his children; and like any loving parent, grieved over the loss of child, whether by death or early marriage.[48] Rabindranath marked a shift in generations and paternal behaviour, with concomitant changes in the emotional experience of filial relations. As a loving father, Rabindranath symbolized a role model displaying complex emotions of love, affection, and trust distinctly different from his father Debendranath. However, similar to his father Debendranath, Rabindranath's autobiographical writings omit extensive discussions of his wife and children. But his correspondence fills in the gap—it describes the intimate experiences comprising fatherhood that accord with the views espoused by the *bhadralok* authors of scientific journals and children's literature described in earlier chapters. In this changed conjugal relationship the wife/mother or servants were not solely responsible for the bodily care of children, thus blurring the gendered division of labour among couples and

---

[46] The trip was, sadly, ineffective; Renuka died months later, at the age of thirteen. Krishna Kripalani, *Rabindranath Tagore: A Biography* (New York: Grove Press, 1962), 216, cited in Christine Kupfer, "Renuka Devi," Scottish Centre of Tagore Studies website, http://www.scots-tagore.org/renuka-devi (accessed on January 7, 2019).

[47] In this journey while tending his sick daughter Renuka, Tagore wrote several poems for children which, along with others written earlier, were published as *Shishu* (*The Child*, 1903). *Shishu* later was translated by the author as *The Crescent Moon* (London and New York: The Macmillan Publishers, 1913).

[48] Of Rabindranath's five children, only his eldest son Rathindranath and youngest daughter Mira Devi survived him. Two died while still children, Renuka (d. 1903) and Shamindranath (d. 1907). Eldest daughter Madhurilata, aka Bela, also died of tuberculosis at age thirty-two in 1918.

classes and opening a space for a "new father" who personally cared for his children.[49] His attitude, behaviour, and practices closely adhered to the model prescribed in the Brahmo household compendium, *The Duties of Women* (1890) that scripted the duties of husband, wife, and children in a paradigmatic nuclear family in late colonial India.[50] Rabindranath's ideas and actions reconciled the instructions of the normative texts with his everyday practices of a father and husband.

As Tosh explained in the context of Victorian fathers, Tagore's grieving or loving tenderness for his wife and children did not compromise his manliness.[51] As an iconic cultural figure, he received tremendous awe and respect from his children, but he eschewed the distance so characteristic of his own relationship with his father. Generational conflict or economic dependence and support did not surface in his children's recollections. For Tagore, in addition to economic sustenance and protection, parental responsibilities included providing emotional support based on "guidance, tenderness and pity," a view that resonated with Unitarian principles.[52] It is worth noting that following his wife's death in 1902, Rabindranath single-handedly took care of his five children, and often their spouses as well, through their joys and sorrow, life and death.

The parental intimacy that Rabindranath practised in his own life was also manifest in his commitment to the causes of children and educational reforms that he envisioned and implemented as a public intellectual. It likewise emerged from his pen, both in his representations of fathers and their children and through his pioneering work in the world of children's literature.[53] His children, in other words, were not simply biological; he was the father to children in his school and through his writings, in India and the world. This was the role of father as educator. For his followers, he was a mentor—they called him *Gurudev* (Teacher-God).

---

[49] For non-kin caregivers of children see Swapna Banerjee, "Blurring Boundaries, Distant Companions: Non-kin Female Caregivers for Children in Colonial India," *Paedagogica Historica* 46, no. 6 (December 2010): 777–790.

[50] Judith E. Walsh, *Domesticity in Colonial India: What Women Learned When Men Gave Them Advice* (New Delhi: Oxford University Press, 2004).

[51] Tosh, *Man's Place*, 100.

[52] Broughton and Rogers, *Gender and Fatherhood in the Nineteenth Century*, 18.

[53] Gautam Chando Roy, "The Pathshala and the School: Experiences of Growing up in Nineteenth and Twentieth Century Bengal," in *Mind, Body, and Society: Life and Mentality in Colonial Bengal*, ed. Rajat Kanta Ray (Delhi: Oxford University Press, 1995), 195–231; Tanika Sarkar, "The Child and the World," 268–298.

It is worth emphasizing that he took on this role for a diverse body of students. He empathized with fathers of poor background and lower social status through his short stories, poems, and novels. With his privileged socio-economic status, he did not have to struggle himself to meet the needs of his family, but he powerfully brought home the precarity of poor fathers as providers.

The poem "Puja-r Shaaj" ("Puja Attire") in Rabindranath's collection of children's poetry *Shishu* captured the sentiment of poor parents while also sending children a message to honour their parents. On the joyous celebration of the annual Durga Puja, which for the Bengalis involves buying new clothes, the father of two brothers, Madhu and Bidhu, was only able to procure some frugal attire for his sons. Madhu, seeing those simple clothes, flew into a rage and managed to receive a set of expensive satin dress from their landlord neighbour. Brother Bidhu, on the contrary, was happy wearing the clothes given by his father and earned the happiness and blessings of his parents: "The affection of the poor father and the cheap printed outfit illuminated the body of the poor boy," the mother exclaimed at the end of the poem.[54] More poignant was the short-story "Dena Paona" ("Profit and Loss") that portrayed the pathos of a penury-stricken father's inability to provide the dowry demanded by the in-laws of his only daughter Nirupama. By the time the poor father managed to pay the dowry, the daughter Nirupama, yielding to the humiliation and torture at the hands of her in-laws, committed suicide.[55] His other poems and stories such as "Karma" (Work) and "Khokababur Protyaborton" (Little Master's Return), among others, also captured the heart-wrenching pathos of poor fathers.[56] Tagore, no doubt, resorted to this imaginative literature to offer a critique of unjust social practices and awaken sensibilities that recognized inequities and injustice. Yet it is significant, given the argument of my book, that these and other stories and novels by Rabindranath Tagore (e.g. *Gora* and *Noukadubi*) harboured numerous characters of loving and domineering fathers—fathers that, in many respects, acted out his (Tagore's) own concern and care. The

---

[54] Rabindranath Tagore, "Puja-r Shaaj," in *Shishu* (Kolkata: Viswabharati, 1901), 145–148.
[55] Rabindranath Tagore, "Dena Paona," in *Galpaguchha*, trans. William Radice, "Profit and Loss," *Selected Short Stories* (Kolkata: Penguin, 1991), 48–54.
[56] Swapna M. Banerjee, *Men, Women, and Domestics: Articulating Middle-Class Identity in Colonial Bengal* (Delhi: Oxford University Press, 2004), 146–149.

fictional fathers that came from Rabindranath's pen were imaginary fathers—but that imaginary was based on the lived experience of his relationship with his children. Those children included his own, of course, but as I describe in the following pages, also the children on his estate and in his school, along with a large body of imagined children who were the audience for an important part of his oeuvre.

Tagore's Intervention in Pedagogy: The Family, the Nation, and the World

As an adult, Tagore's first formal intervention in educational movements corresponded with his life as a family man. An aristocratic man in his thirties, a husband, and a father, he pushed educational reforms that were not far removed from his family. His zeal for reforms was part of a larger social experiment in India in which other leaders, including his predecessors, played an active part. His grandfather Dwarkanath Tagore donated money for education and institution building;[57] his father Debendranath was an important votary for education as well. His family had a close connection with reformers and educationists such as Iswarchandra Vidyasagar, Keshub Chandra Sen, and Dayanand Saraswati. In his later life, Tagore developed his own link with leaders dedicated to education. He joined the National Education Movement in the early 1890s under the leadership of Sir Gooroo Dass Banerjee, the first Indian Vice-Chancellor of the University of Calcutta, to actively champion vernacular education.[58]

The family continued to be Tagore's major arena of play and support in every project he undertook. He launched his initial educational experiments in his family estates in eastern Bengal. As early as the 1890s, hoping to alleviate the hunger and poverty of his tenants, he tried, without much success, to educate villagers in collective farming. Identifying the divisive nature of colonial educational policies, and influenced by his childhood

---

[57] Pradip Bose, *Samayiki*.
[58] H.B. Mukherjee, *Education for Fullness* (New York: Routledge, 2013 [1962]). O'Connell, *Tagore: The Poet as Educator*. Seth, "Vernacular Modernity." Kumkum Bhattacharya, *Rabindranath Tagore: Adventure of Ideas and Innovative Practices in Education* (London: Springer Publications, 2014).

experiences in the Normal School, he stated in no uncertain terms that "if we place education in the hands of the Government, they will attempt through that education to fulfill their own interests and not ours. They will so arrange that a farmer may remain a farmer in his village; they will not bother to make him a true citizen (*odhivasi*) of India."[59] Since those early days the ideals of self-realization and self-determination were at the heart of his educational principles. In his later lectures he urged, "nothing is more absurd than to seek freedom through the diametrically opposite path of dependence... We have to find out that source in the mind of the villagers. And the very first preparation for it is to create in them faith in their own power and their power of co-operation."[60]

His speech, "Shikshar Herpher" ("Our Education and Its Incongruities," 1892), delivered in the Rajshahi district in eastern Bengal (now Bangladesh), contained his most scathing critique of colonial education. Reflecting on his boyhood experience when he felt the disconnect with rote English learning, he argued that the failure of the Bengalis to communicate their ideas and opinions effectively like *adults* (*sabalok*) could be explained by the lack of connection they felt with Western-style education imparted in schools and colleges. Echoing the sentiment of the time he blamed the enfeeblement of the Bengalis on the colonial system, a point that Tanika Sarkar emphasized in a different context.[61] He stressed that being forced to master English, the children neither learned nor played: they did not have the leisure to enter the "true-land" (*satyarajya*) of nature; the doors to the imaginary lands of literature were sealed. The only way to strike a balance between thought and expression, between education and life, was by promoting vernacular language and literature, not English.[62] When requested to write the Constitution for the National College founded by the nationalist leader Aurobindo Ghose (1872–1950), he authored the essay "Shiksha Samasya" ("Problem with

---

[59] Rabindranath Tagore, "Purbo-Prashnér Anubritti (1905 [1312 B.S.])," in *Rabindra-Rachanabali* (Kolkata: Visva-Bharati Granthan Bibhag, 1995 ed.), 720. Also cited in Mukherjee, *Education for Fullness*, 30.

[60] *Visva-Bharati Patrika*, Agrahayan (1942 [1349 B.S.]), 314. Cited in Mukherjee, *Education for Fullness*, 125.

[61] Tanika Sarkar, *Hindu Wife, Hindu Nation*.

[62] Rabindranath Tagore, "Shikshar Herpher (1892)," in *Shiksha* (Kolkata: Visvabharati Granthan Bibhag, 1990), 8–10.

Education") that addressed the key issues of colonial education. For Tagore, the problem lay in the unfathomable distance between Western-style education mechanically disseminated in schools and the experiences of common people in India.[63]

Tagore's positioning as a public paternal figure was further evident in his response to the critique of his pedagogic vision. Following Tagore's article "Shikshar Herpher," he was attacked by contemporary educationists for his denunciation of university education. To that Tagore retorted sharply that the main intention of that piece was to point out the lack of opportunity for Bengali children to read and think in their mother tongue and that this stunted their intellectual growth and maturity. He further emphasized that education could only spread to the masses by instruction in the mother tongue. He stated in no uncertain terms that he was not opposed to the learning of the English language and the cultivation of English studies.[64] But, English as a language should be supplemented by study of the mother tongue, and the vehicle for the spread of western education should be the vernacular language. Accordingly, he promoted the teaching and cultivation of science in vernacular languages. Pointing out the elitist nature of scientific education in India, he asserted that scientific studies could take root in the country only when they were spread among the masses in the mother tongue.[65]

In his role as a pedagogical father, Tagore pushed hard promoting the Bengali language; at the same time, he also nurtured a deeply felt conviction that Indian learning ought to come in contact with western learning. He believed "our powers will awaken only through vital contact with the real world ... European learning is a living and dynamic thing, which is growing and changing and is seeking for expression in man's day-to-day problems of life."[66] Tagore was open to ideas of European educationists and thinkers like Pestalozzi and Rousseau and had ties to the Unitarian movement. But his pedagogy differed from that of the missionaries and the early reformers. In his proposal for the

---

[63] Rabindranath Tagore, "Shiksha Samasya (Problem with Education)," in *Shiksha* (Kolkata: Visva-Bharati Granthan Bibhag, 1990 [1906]), 38–55.
[64] See Michael Collins, *Empire, Nationalism and the Postcolonial World: Rabindranath Tagore's Writings on History, Politics, Society* (New York/London: Routledge, 2012).
[65] Mukherjee, *Education for Fullness*, 19–20.
[66] Mukherjee, *Education for Fullness*, 110.

National College as well as in his own school (Brahmacharya Asrama) in Santiniketan, he rejected the popular "gallery model" championed by the Scottish educator David Stow and adopted by early Bengali educators like Bhudev Mukhopadhyay.[67] To promote his idea of freedom for children he advocated a spatio-structural transformation of the classroom. He moved the classroom to the heart of nature and he stripped it of any furniture. For him, students and teachers sitting on floors and preferably holding classes in natural surroundings would be the most effective way of lowering the cost of education.[68] By the time he was engaging with these questions, the vernacularization of education was already underway under the initiatives of nationalist-reformers and missionaries. They all shared a Western model and their demand was infused with strong religious overtones.[69] But Rabindranath's curriculum, creative and secular, offered an alternative, drawing on the best of both India and the West.[70]

Tagore and Children: The Father as Educator

Tagore's experimentation with children's education started around the same time he embarked on training peasants in eastern Bengal. Confronted with a school system that belied his vision, it was in eastern Bengal that Tagore started home-schooling his three children—Bela (thirteen), Rathindranath (eleven), and Renuka (nine)—a practice that he had encountered in his own childhood but for different reasons and with a very different pedagogy. As his son Rathindranath (See Figure 5.4) noted, fully aware of the ill-effects of the stereotypical teaching practiced in colonial schools,

---

[67] For more on Bhudev Mukherjee's pedagogy, see Parna Sengupta, *Pedagogy for Religion: Missionary Education and the Fashioning of Hindus and Muslims in Bengal* (Berkeley: University of California Press, 2011), 84.
[68] Rabindranath Tagore, "Shiksha Samasya," in *Shiksha*, 38–55.
[69] Sengupta, *Pedagogy for Religion*; Manu Goswami, *Producing India* (Chicago: University of Chicago Press, 2004).
[70] In his later life after visiting Russia Tagore was deeply inspired by the communist model that spread education to all. See Rabindranath Tagore, *Russia-r Chithi* (*Letters from Russia*) (Kolkata: Visvabharati, 1930).

Father was anxious that his own children should be spared such unhealthy and stifling influences, so he engaged teachers who lived with us. But the teachers had to be taught first. Father began to devise his own methods and to train the teachers to learn and follow them. Very often he would take the classes himself.[71]

In the domain of his family Tagore acted as a sovereign and asserted his authority. The children were taught English by a British tutor who lived with them; they also learned mathematics and Sanskrit; Bengali was taught by Rabindranath himself. He would make his daughter, Bela, and son, Rathindranath, meticulously go over every piece for his recent collection *Katha-o-Kahini*. At the end of the lesson, the children could "recite whole books of poems and descriptive pieces of prose from well-known writers."[72] But they never learned grammar. In English, Rabindranath would assign passages from his favourite book, Amiel's *Journal*; in Sanskrit, the children would read from the *Upanishads* contained in *Brahmo Dharma*, written by his father Debendranath. He insisted that the children read the two Indian epics, *The Ramayana* and *The Mahabharata*, and being unhappy with the existing printed editions, he entrusted his wife to translate from Sanskrit an abridged version of *The Ramayana*, a task that Mrinalini arduously undertook but left unfinished due to her untimely death.[73] The responsibility of translating *The Mahabharata* fell on his nephew, Surendranath Tagore, his elder brother Satyendranath Tagore's son and Indira Devi's brother. As part of a multigenerational extended family, Tagore always displayed paternal behaviour towards his nephews and nieces and often worked as a team, inspiring and guiding them in different directions.[74]

In emphasizing the training of the teachers and in insisting on familiarity with the epics, Tagore had actualized the dreams of the early educators. Bhudev Mukhopadhyay (1827–1894), a conservative social critic from colonial Bengal who served as a headmaster and worked for the Department of Public Instruction, regretted that in India, there was

---

[71] Rathindranath Tagore, *On the Edges*, 20.
[72] Rathindranath Tagore, *On the Edges*, 21.
[73] Rathindranath Tagore, *On the Edges*, 21–22.
[74] See Abandindranath Tagore and Rani Chanda, *Gharoa* (Kolkata: Visvabharati Granthanbibhag, 1941).

"very little effort to encourage mutual affection and understanding between fathers and sons." In his teacher training manual Bhudev urged school teachers to take on the role of an understanding and affectionate father: the behaviour between the teacher and the students "should be the same as between fathers and sons."[75] Tagore succeeded in translating that vision into practice—first, by training the teachers; second, by positioning himself as a father-cum-educator and becoming a role model for the teachers.[76] As one commentator noted: Tagore "succeeded in establishing a cordial atmosphere of mutual understandability and warmth of sympathy as a teacher-father-Gurudev of the *Ashrama*."[77]

As his commitment to social justice deepened, Tagore increasingly saw his family members "less as individuals than as part of the greater cause to which he felt his life was dedicated."[78] As a father-cum-educator, Tagore extended his pedagogical experiments far beyond his immediate family. His major educational reforms were launched in the thick of political controversies and nationalist upheavals. On December 22, 1901, with permission and assistance from Debendranath, he inaugurated his school in Santiniketan, a small town, west of Kolkata in the Birbhum district of West Bengal, with less than ten students, including his son.

Departing from a Western model, Tagore invoked the ancient Indian ideal of *brahmacharya* (a life-stage prescribed for high-caste males) where male disciples studied in the secluded areas of the guru's house, restraining themselves through strict rules and hardship. All clothed in long yellow robes, the students rose at four in the morning, bathed, meditated, prayed, and chanted Vedic hymns. Tagore's son Rathindranath recounted:

> The life led by both pupils and teachers was not only simple but almost austere. The ideal of Brahmacharya was the keynote of everything. The

[75] Sengupta, *Pedagogy for Religion*, 81.
[76] For Tagore's rigorous training of teachers for his school at Santiniketan, see "'Ashram-er Rup o Bikash' (The Form and Growth of the Ashram, 1941)," in *Rabindra-Rachanabali*, vol. 14 (Kolkata: Visva-Bharati, 1989), 226. "Ashramer Rup O Bikash" includes three essays. The first of these was published as "Ashramer Shiksha" (The Education of the Ashram) in 1936.
[77] Mohit Chakrabarti, *The Gandhian Dimension of Education* (Delhi: Daya Publishing House, 1990), 94. Tagore's school is often referred to as the *ashrama*.
[78] Rabindranath Tagore, *Selected Letters of Rabindranath Tagore*, in eds. Krishna Dutta and Andrew Robinson, *Rabindranath Tagore: The Myriad-Minded Man* (Cambridge: Cambridge University Press, 1997), 45.

yellow uniform, which covered up the poverty of clothes; a pair of blankets, which served as our only bedding; the vegetarian meals comparable to jail diets in their dull monotony—these were the standards laid down. Nobody wore shoes or even sandals and such luxuries as toothpaste or hair oil were taboo.[79]

It might be worth mentioning that notwithstanding the frugality that the ashram boys underwent, Tagore, like the medical practitioners in the past chapter, was equally mindful of students' diet. But his position was different from his predecessors—while the latter quoted the meal plan of English boarding schools, Tagore argued for the distinct and specific situation of Indian students. Away from Santiniketan, Tagore wrote the following letter in 1914 to his close friend C.F. Andrews, who was in charge of running the school:

> I was surprised to read in the "Modern Review" that our Bolpur boys are going without their share of sugar and ghee in order to open a relief fund. Do you think this is right? In the first place, it is an imitation of your English schoolboys and not their original idea. In the second place, so long the boys live in our institution, they are not free to give up any portion of their diet which is absolutely necessary for their health. For any English boy, who takes meat and an amount of fat with it, giving up sugar is not injurious. But for our boys in Santiniketan, who can get milk only in small quantities, and whose vegetable meals contain very little fat ingredients, it is mischievous.[80]

This school suffered from an acute shortage of funds since it did not collect any fees from students at first and provided them with food, lodging, and often clothing as well. The school was funded by a trust set up by Debendranath; the money gained from selling his wife's jewellery; and his own meagre resources. Tagore hoped to realize his ideal of democracy and self-reliance by reaching out to the wider public and transgressing class-caste and religious boundaries. Through his conception of

---

[79] Rathindranath Tagore, *On the Edges*, 44–45.
[80] Rabindranath Tagore, "Letter written to C.F. Andrews," *Visva-Bharati Patrika* (Agrahayan, 1349 B.S.), 308.

the *ashrama* (hermitage), an ancient Indian institution, Tagore "sought to imagine a space where his ideas of self-reliance and democracy could be translated into praxis."[81] In his new school, modelled after the ancient Indian system of *tapovan* (forest schools), Tagore attempted to establish "real *swaraj*" in his *ashrama*, where students were tied in a bond of fraternity underscored by a devotion to the *guru* and the new order.

In its initial phase, the constitution of the school upheld two objectives: "to establish the 'sacred relationship' between teacher and disciple in which the communication of traditional wisdom becomes possible"; and "to make the students of Brahma Vidyalay especially devoted to their country. Just as there is a special manifestation of deity in one's father and mother, so too for us there is special presence of deity in our own country, the place where our forefathers were born and taught."[82] Tagore approximated the environment of an *ashrama* by imparting spiritual training to all his students: he insisted on their understanding and chanting the Gayatri mantra, an ancient hymn that he, like other high-caste Hindu boys, learned as a child.[83] According to Tagore, the mantra made the connection between individual consciousness and external reality, linking the inner self with its deepest aspects and transcending boundaries of race, class, nationality, and religion. Displaying the influence of the Father as the god-head Absolute, he reminded children that "God is our father, and like a father always gives us lessons of wisdom. The teachers are only the vehicles, but the real knowledge comes from our universal father."[84] Tagore's strong enunciations testified to his own authoritarianism and control, a streak akin to his father's, but he expressed himself in a different idiom for an imaginary public. His invocation of God as "Father" displayed the Christian (Unitarian) influence that his father publicly denied yet enigmatically upheld in the faith he propounded. While Father for

---

[81] Sukalyan Chandra, "Towards Swaraj: The Ideals of Democracy and Self-Reliance at Rabindranath Tagore's Ashram," in *Phalanx: A Quarterly Review of Continuing Debate*, August 2014 (http://www.phalanx.in/pages/article_i0010_Rabindranath_Tagore.html) (accessed on February 19, 2015).

[82] O'Connell, *Tagore: The Poet as Educator*, 65–67.

[83] At eleven, Tagore's father made him go through the caste-specific practice of *upanayan*, a rite of passage for Brahmin boys that introduced them to the Gayatri mantra. Traditionally, this rite would mark the start of their period of study in an *ashrama* as a *brahmacharin*.

[84] O'Connell, *Tagore: The Poet as Educator*.

Tagore might not have been an intentionally sexist symbol, it represented an all-pervading masculinity as a sovereign source of power.

Teaching Sons and Daughters

In his massive educational schemes, how did Rabindranath, the father and educator, imagine children as the future generation? And to what extent, in his pedagogy, his literary works, and in his relations to his own children, did Tagore differentiate between girls and boys? Tagore's poems, short stories, and plays imagined children, both boys and girls, in various subject positions. While he captured the pathos of a father and the sorrows, joy, and excitement of children in various scenarios, his "ideal" image of a brave boy was embodied in "Birpurush" ("The Hero"), a poem that vividly narrates the fantasies of a young male child rescuing his mother from the hands of fierce dacoits.

Bravery was a constant theme with Rabindranath that he defined and invoked in various contexts, especially when writing and speaking for and about boys. On the foundation day of his school in December 1901, he gave his blessings to the first batch of schoolboys: "Gentle children, long time ago our country *Bharatvarsha* was great in many ways. Its people were brave; they are our ancestors." He described the ancestors as "fearless," as not being afraid of anything but *dharma*. "They were so happy and enlightened within themselves that they did not accept the unjust rule of any king, they were not afraid of death." Likewise, he exhorted his students: "If our effort succeeds, you will become *brave*, you will not be afraid of anything, you will not become restless when in pain, you will not be greedy toward wealth, you will not hate death, will always be in search for truth, will keep untruth away from your mind, speech, and work" (emphasis mine).[85] Although he founded his institution on the ideals of the simplicity of the ancient *rishis* (saints) and *tapovans*, he also pointed out that "[I]t is not entirely true that a simple mode of life within

---

[85] Rabindranath Tagore, first essay from *Initiation: Santiniketan Brahmacharyashram* (republished in *Santiniketan*, West Bengal: Visvabharati Publications, 1951). Cited in Devi Prasad, *Rabindranath Tagore: Philosophy of Education and Painting* (Delhi: National Book Trust, 2001), 59–61.

a narrow compass is the highest ideal ... Rather, that activity has to be respected which ultimately retains its vitality in spite of all the errors that it may commit in the course of its onward progress along a rough and wide path."[86]

In one of his addresses he remarked about the students of his institutions in its early years: They were "not quite gems of the first water," and "[t]hey were mostly the despair of their guardians. They were uncontrollable, turbulent, dare-devil young fellows, who were the terror of their teachers and came frequently into conflict with those among them with conventional ideas about education and discipline ... "[87] However, they never failed to respond to him. It was perhaps with these students in mind that he composed his famous song: *Amra Chonchol, amra odbhut, amra notun joubon-er-i doot* ("We are restless; we are odd; we are harbingers of a new youth").

Rabindranath's bias towards a male child and a student was also explicit in the ideal of his institution. According to Rathindranath Tagore, Rabindranath's son, the "ideal of Brahmacharya was the keynote of everything," in his school. *Brahmacharya*, of course, is implicitly a gendered and caste-based institution.[88] *Brahmacharya*, the first of the four stages of life set out as ideals in Hindu legal codes, was not open to all: just to boys belonging to the upper three social classes. Women, Shudras, and Dalits were not eligible. Thus, by evoking *brahmacharya* and study in an *ashrama* as the model for his pedagogical experiments, Tagore, despite opening the doors of Santiniketan to all social classes, valorized a Brahminic male institution.

At this point, if we juxtapose Rabindranath's personal life as a biological father with his public career as a pedagogical father, the contradiction was even more flagrant. The year 1901 was when he founded Santiniketan and

---

[86] Rabindranath Tagore, *Prabashi* (Phalgun 1934 [1341 B.S.]); reprinted in *Visva-Bharati* (1951 [1358 B.S.]): 137. Cited in Mukherjee, *Education for Fullness*, 120.

[87] Mukherjee, *Education for Fullness*, 124.

[88] *Brahmacharya*, which entails celibacy, was a key theme in educational movements with strong nationalist overtones across India in late nineteenth century. Gurukul Kangri, an educational wing of the Arya Samaj in Punjab, actively championed *brahmacharya* for its students who they envisioned as the citizen and the harbinger of a new nation. Tagore's vision of *brahmacharya* advocated frugality and restraint but no separate emphasis on celibacy could be discerned. For Gurukul Kangri see Harald Fischer-Tiné, "From Brahmacharya to Conscious Race-Culture: Victorian Discourses of 'Science' and Hindu Traditions in Early Indian Nationalism," in Crispin Bates, ed., *Beyond Representation*, 241–269.

gave his speech extolling bravery; it was also the year he published his novella *Nashtanirh* (*The Broken Nest*) capturing the agony of child marriage and a lonely wife; it was also the year in which Rabindranath arranged for the marriages of his two daughters.[89] Bela was fourteen; Renuka was ten or eleven. In striking contrast, Tagore's nieces, Indira Devi (1873–1960; m. 1899) and Sarala Devi Chaudhurani (1872–1945; m. 1905) were married in their twenties and thirties respectively.[90] As discussed in previous chapters, throughout the nineteenth century, the age of marriage for girls was heavily debated among the social reformers and colonial administration. The Age of Consent Act (1891) made consummation of marriage with brides below twelve a punishable offence. Even earlier, the Brahmo community split into three factions over the Marriage Act of 1872 that aimed to formalize Brahmo marriages by designating the specific age of marriage, fourteen for girls and eighteen for boys.[91] Rabindranath's elder brother Satyendranath, brother-in-law Janakinath Ghoshal, and his father Debendranath publicly championed higher age of marriage for girls. Somehow, Rabindranath was strapped in the custom of child-marriage while nurturing and disseminating feminist and antipatriarchal sentiments through his writings even before the girls were married.

On arranging child marriages for his daughters Rabindranath justified himself on the grounds that given the uniqueness of the Tagores in social and cultural matters, early marriage would facilitate their integration with their in-laws more easily. In the same letter to his wife quoted earlier, Tagore says: "We must forget our own joy and sorrow where our children are concerned ... We must make room for them so that they can mould their lives in their own way."[92] It is possible that Rabindranath's dependence on his father Debendranath for financial support led to these early marriages, rather than concern for the girls' well-being. Furthermore,

---

[89] On Rabindranath's conflicted position on gender see Geraldine Forbes, "Dependent on Patriarchy: Rabindranath's Widows and Widows' Lived Lives in Late Nineteenth Century Bengal," in Blanka Knotková-Čapková, *Tagore on Discriminations: Representing the Unrepresented* (Prague: Metropolitan University Prague Press, 2015), 29–41.

[90] Indira Devi was the daughter of Satyendranath Tagore we discussed in Chapter 4; Sarala Devi Chaudhurani was the daughter of his sister Swarnakumari.

[91] Rochona Majumdar, *Marriage and Modernity* (Durham: Duke University Press, 2009), 167–205.

[92] Tagore, *Chitthi Patra*, 67–69.

scholars surmise that Rabindranath had a strong disdain for the family atmosphere in Jorasanko and perhaps wanted to devote himself full-time to the newly evolved ideas of his school.

Whatever the reason, the inescapable fact is that while Rabindranath was seeking to free boys from the constraint of colonial pedagogy and encouraging them to become brave and independent citizens, he forced his girls to marry. Notably, following the death of his eldest daughter Bela (1918), Rabindranath published in the same year the collection of poems *Palataka*, which were deeply resonant of his feminist perspective and critical of the existing patriarchy, of which he considered himself a part.[93] Rabindranath was gripped by similar inconsistencies and ambivalence that beset the reformers we examined in Chapter 2. In his later life, he expressed guilty feelings on the marriage of his three daughters.[94]

Rabindranath followed the reformist trend when it came to the marriage of his son Rathindranath. He was twenty-one when Rabindranath arranged for him to marry seventeen-year-old Pratima Devi, a child-widow, in 1910. Later, Rabindranath trained and educated her to be part of his educational schemes. Again, he exerted his paternal authority, like that of his father, in arranging his son's marriage; but his choice of a widow for his son was consonant with legislation, the Widow Remarriage Act (1856), passed in the previous century. His closeness with Pratima Devi defied the conservatism that his father displayed towards his daughters-in-law. He signalled a change from the domineering father like Debendranath to a more self-confident, engaging father in his own right.

There are some grey areas between Rabindranath's private and public life. Though in his personal life he yielded to the practices (and perhaps the persuasion) of his own father, as did the leaders we studied in the earlier chapters, he did, in 1908–1909, take the unprecedented step of admitting six girls to his school. By 1920, the school became both co-residential as well as coeducational. Despite contradictions in his personal life, Rabindranath was a public advocate for education for women, like

---

[93] Rabindranath Tagore, *Palataka (Fugitive)*(Kolkata: Visvabharati, 1918). See *In Memorium: Smaran and Palataka by Rabindranath Tagore*. Translated by Sanjukta Dasgupta. (Delhi: Sahitya Academy, 2020).

[94] For possible explanation of Rabindranath's compromised position regarding early marriage of his daughters, see Krishna Dutt and Andrew Robinson, *Rabindranath Tagore: The Myriad-Minded Man*, pp. 130-132.

his elder brother and father. In response to a letter written to him by a woman, he wrote an essay, "Streeshiksha" ("Education of Women"), exclusively devoted to women's education.[95] In tune with the philosophy of his curriculum, he declared that knowledge for the sake of knowing should be equally accessible to both men and women. He rejected the prevailing idea that in sharing the common curriculum with men, women would lose their femininity. He urged, "even if women read Kant and Hegel, they would still love children and would not disregard men."[96] But he did maintain a distinction between men's and women's education. Dividing knowledge into two categories, pure and utilitarian, he advocated that women should acquire pure knowledge along with men to develop into matured individuals. But women should gain utilitarian knowledge to become "true women." Echoing the opinions of the intelligentsia of the time, he urged:

> It is the nature of woman to be a wife and a mother; not to be a maid... Love dominates in the nature of women. A mother rears her child because she has so much affection, not because it is her responsibility; she serves her husband out of love and not because it is her duty.[97]

Extolling women's disposition for love and sacrifice, he also offered a critique of masculinity. He continued: love entailed sacrifice and it also brought pride. It was out of true love that women whole-heartedly accepted the social ideals of dogged self-sacrifice. Some selfish men took advantage of this sacrifice and used it against women. "Where men have fallen from the true ideals of manliness (*pourush*), there women are tortured by and deprived of their high ideals ... One needs to bear in mind that in a society slavery of men is no less than that of women."[98]

In his later addresses to students, he laid out in detail the three components of his educational ideals for both boys and girls: physical education, intellectual education, and character training. Physical education, for him, consisted of exercises and games; training and use of limbs; personal

---

[95] Rabindranath Tagore, "Streeshiksha," in *Shiksha* (Kolkata: Visva-Bharati Granthan Bibhag, 1997 [1907]), 137–141.
[96] Rabindranath Tagore, "Streeshiksha," 139.
[97] Rabindranath Tagore, "Streeshiksha," 140.
[98] Rabindranath Tagore, "Streeshiksha," 141.

hygiene and sense training. Intellectual education constituted the development of the spirit of questioning, thinking, and observation; joyful interests in varied aspects of nature; and exact and thorough knowledge of the human world, especially of one's country and its rural life. With character training, Rabindranath echoed themes discussed in previous chapters: he emphasized cleanliness, orderliness, and observation of rules and regulations. In particular, he stressed, "the cultivation of good manners, specially towards the menials; the cultivation of proper regard and love for peoples of other countries."[99]

It is to this last directive, the cultivation of "proper regard and love for peoples of other countries," that I turn in the following section as I trace the development of a universalist pedagogy in Tagore's writings and activism. Through this, Tagore moved from being a father not just for his own children, not just for his own school, and not even just for the children of India. Tagore's innovative pedagogy might have begun at home and been tested in the classrooms of his family estate, but then this father-cum-educator presented himself as a father to the world at large.

Pedagogy Unbound: Beyond Nation and on to the World

Rabindranath Tagore, over the course of his life, expanded his role as a father-teacher ever outward, from family to nation to the world, becoming a moral and educational leader over an ever-larger body of imaginary children-pupils. The pedagogy he formulated was as innovative as his new role. As an artist and a poet, Tagore emphasized joy in creative work. He contended that "[If] there is no joy in the heart, life lacks sufficient power to protect itself." Joy comes from an aesthetic culture, and aesthetic culture, he astutely pointed out, was condemned in prevalent India as an "effeminate luxury." He argued that those who criticize "do not know that manly heroism is closely related to beauty; when there is want of joy in life, there is also want of heroism. A hard, dried-up log of wood has no strength; strength resides in a mighty tree that has burst

---

[99] "Address to Students, 1935." The English version of this address appeared in *Visva-Bharati Patrika*, April 1935. Also cited in Mukherjee, *Education for Fullness*, 121–122.

into flowers and foliage through sheer joy of vitality."[100] Tagore tied together bravery, joy, and masculinity—and thereby created a new image of fatherhood, one that he then offered to the world.

His natural impatience with formalism led him to formulate a new prose-form and invent new institutional structures that privileged nature over artificial boundaries and constructions. He produced his collection of poetry for children, Shishu, while taking care of his ailing daughter Renuka (aka Rani) during the last days of her life. His joyous approach to learning resonated with the progressive spirits of the literary movements of the late nineteenth century that emphasized reading for pleasure.[101] It is this new spirit and vitality that Tagore attempted to infuse in his new universal pedagogy, a pedagogy that for all its global reach, nonetheless commenced in his family estate and thrived with the active support of his family members.

Tagore's vast repertoire of children's literature, consisting of poems, plays, short stories, primers, and essays, let loose his imaginings of an idealized childhood. But his imaginings were also rooted in a colonial reality and frustration that he experienced as a child; his emphasis on self-help and focus on building citizens were also likely motivated by the colonial situation. Tagore's special relationship with the child commenced from "his own lived experiences" and it was his "poetic words" that acted as the primary site of the relationship between the adult and the child.[102]

A major turn in Tagore's personal conviction and public action came when the anti-partition Swadeshi movement (1905–1908) against Lord Curzon's plan to divide Bengal gave way to Hindu-Muslim antagonism, self-aggrandizement, and violence. Abandoning his nationalist agenda, he resigned from the National Council of Education and disassociated himself from the movement to which he had given active leadership. Tagore developed a stringent critique of parochial patriotism and shifted his focus to ideas of universalism and rural reconstruction.[103] Following a visit to the United States, he advocated a spirit of democracy among his

---

[100] Visva-Bharati Patrika, 1942 (1349 B.S.), 315.
[101] Sarkar, "The Child and the World."
[102] Sarkar, "The Child and the World," 268–298.
[103] Bipasha Raha, Living a Dream: Rabindranath Tagore and Rural Resuscitation (New Delhi: Manohar, 2014).

students urging that "boys should be left as much as possible to themselves, and manage their own affairs without any interference from outside." This view meshed well with Tagore's insistence on education for the common people.[104]

Tagore won the Nobel Prize in Literature in 1913, and its money was spent on the improvement of his school. As the war broke out in 1914, he became more convinced of his message of universalism and proclaimed in a lecture in the United States in 1916 that "the highest education is that which does not merely give us information but makes our life in harmony with all existence.[105] His reaction against parochial nationalism was expressed in his condemnation of Western education. He claimed that his countrymen would gain their India by "fighting against the education which teaches them that a country is greater than the ideals of humanity."[106] For him, "the highest education is that which does not merely give us information but makes our life in harmony with all existence." He believed that "the object of education is the freedom of mind...—though freedom has its risk and responsibility as life itself has." In his *ashrama* the "guiding spirit" of children was "personal love" and life was "fully awake" in its activities:

> [w]here boys' minds are not being perpetually drilled into believing that the ideal of the self-idolatry of the nation is the truest ideal for them to accept; where they are bidden to realize man's world as God's Kingdom, to whose citizenship they have to aspire; where the young and the old, the teacher and the student, sit at the same table to partake of their daily food and the food of their eternal life.[107]

Tagore's convictions, stressing children's connection with nature and describing them as citizens of "God's kingdom" clearly marked his shift from nationalism to universalism. Tagore, as a father–teacher, evolved

---

[104] Rabindranath Tagore, "Bhashabichhed," *Rabindra-Rachanabali* 6: 739–742. On Tagore's vision of educating the masses, see also Mukherjee, *Education for Fullness*.
[105] Rabindranath Tagore, "My School," lecture delivered in America in 1916; published in *Personality* (London: Macmillan, 1933).
[106] Partha Chatterjee, "Tagore's Non-nation," in *Lineages of Political Society* (New York: Columbia University Press, 2011), 99.
[107] Rabindranath Tagore, "My School."

Figure 5.5 Rabindranath Tagore reading to others (1925)

through the ages of his life, transcending nationalistic limits and extending his moral and pedagogic leadership over a larger body of pupils (See Figure 5.5).

His commitment to a universal pedagogical ideal (and thus his implicit claim of universal fatherhood) and his concern for the future generation led him to establish in 1918 his university, Visva-Bharati, as "the Center of Indian culture" with the motto "where the world meets in one nest," where individuals of different backgrounds connected through humanity and not through nationality. As a global learning centre based on a multi-racial network, Visva-Bharati emphasized a nonsectarian and aesthetic curriculum that drew on both Eastern and Western materials to teach fine arts, music, Indian folk culture, and literature.[108] Central to Tagore's institution-building was the Jorasanko extended-family model, as O'Connell pointed out, where creative artists from all over the world were invited and they were sought to bring out unique aspects of their

---

[108] Nussbaum, "Tagore, Gandhi, Nehru."

cultures that would harmonize and afford maximum development of the human personality.[109] Visva-Bharati was not the only institutional setting for Tagore's universalist pedagogy. His paternalistic concern for the common people, evident in his early efforts to educate the peasantry, reached its culmination in the establishment of Sriniketan in 1922 with the help of Leonard Elmhirst, the British agro-economist, and twelve of his former students. Based on international cooperation since its inception, Sriniketan's objective was rural reconstruction to make the villagers "self-reliant and self-respectful, acquainted with the cultural traditions of their country and competent to make use of modern resources for improvement of their physical, intellectual and economic conditions."[110] Organizing boys and girls in ways that were modelled on the Boy Scouts, Girl Guides, and the 4-H movement of America, village children were trained in practical skills and were made to overcome caste prejudices through group participation.[111] This last major educational experiment belies the criticism that Tagore's aesthetic moralism did not provide a viable model for mass education and that he was elitist in his approach.[112]

For Sriniketan, as well, the family provided the pillar of support. Rabindranath delegated the main responsibility of Sriniketan to his son, Rathindranath (See Figure 5.4), who was sent abroad to study agriculture.[113] Upon his return from the West, Rathindranath served on his family estates training poor farmers in the art of scientific farming. For the next four decades, he worked for Visva-Bharati and became its first

---

[109] O'Connell, *Tagore: The Poet as Educator*, 97–99.
[110] O'Connell, *Tagore: The Poet as Educator*, 195.
[111] Sriniketan's ideology and program had a striking resemblance with that of Gandhi's ideals of self-supporting education. When the ideas of Sriniketan were taking shape, Gandhi was launching his first non-cooperation movement, to which Tagore was vehemently opposed. Tagore always kept his school at Santiniketan above politics. Yet, a decade later when Gandhi was envisioning his Basic Education Plan in 1932, he sought Tagore's permission to seek help from the headmaster at Sriniketan. When Gandhi visited Santiniketan in 1940, the last time before Tagore's death, the latter entrusted the future responsibility of Visva-Bharati to him. On the eve of Gandhi's departure, Tagore pressed a letter in Gandhi's hand making "a fervent appeal" to accept his institution under his protection and to give it "an assurance of permanence" if he considered it to be "a national asset." "Visva-Bharati is like a vessel which is carrying the cargo of my life's best treasure, and I hope it may claim special care from my countrymen for its preservation." In his response, Gandhi promised "Gurudev" (mentor), "all the assistance" he was "capable of rendering" and after the poet passed away in 1941, he actively raised funds for his institutions. O'Connell, *Tagore: The Poet as Educator*, 221.
[112] Partha Chatterjee, "Tagore's Non-nation."
[113] He studied at the University of Illinois in the United States and Göttingen University, Germany.

vice-chancellor when it became a central university; his wife, Pratima Devi, also was involved. Through the ages of life Tagore relied on the strength and support of his family, abided by family rules and customs, but also offered resistance to the limitations imposed by them.

Committed to nineteenth-century values of liberal individualism, the entanglements of Tagore's familial side with his pioneering educational experiments reveal in him an insurgent consciousness that challenged both colonial oppression and native injustices. Rabindranath's masculinity rested on being the son of his father (and father figures like his older brothers[114]) and then a father himself.[115] The sense of freedom he inculcated among the future generation was restrained by his authority as the paterfamilias in the geographical locale of the *ashrama*. While in his imaginings, the child, mostly male, was "Indian but not orthodox, modern but not [a] mimic," and its "rebelliousness was contained within a formalized context and limited authority,"[116] understanding Rabindranath only within the post-Enlightenment analytic is too limiting. By focusing on the nexus between his personal life and his public pedagogical experiments, I have endeavoured to foreground his familial context from which he drew sustenance and the experiential reality of becoming and assuming the role of a father.

Conclusion

The Tagore family's long involvement in education over four generations reached a pinnacle with Rabindranath's experiments. In that sense, the pedagogical enterprise was a family project. Neither he nor his family entirely superseded prevailing caste, class, and gender norms, but the family as a whole, and Rabindranath's meditations and activism on social ills,

---

[114] Rabindranath was the youngest son, and his elder brothers were an important influence on him as well as being important figures in their own right. For instance, his brother Satyendranath (1842–1923) was the first Indian to join the civil service in British India; it was with Satyendranath that in 1878, the teenage Rabindranath travelled to London, a trip that had a profound influence on the youth. His brother Hemendranath (1844–1884), the third son of Debendranath, actively championed Bengali or vernacular for promotion of children's education. It was through Hemendranath that Rabindranath learned the urgency of disseminating education in one's mother tongue.

[115] Sen, "Remembering Robi," 58–74.

[116] Sen, "Remembering Robi," 60.

gender norms, and education, gestured towards a radicality that set the Tagores apart as trend-setters and culture-builders in colonial India. The novelty lay in Rabindranath's new pedagogic model, one that aimed to ignore differences of age, gender, sex, caste, class, or religion. As a father-cum-educator he transcended the home (*ghar*) and reached out to the world (*bahir*). While his experiments—localized and limited but within a global framework—failed in the long run, his critique of the Raj and its educational institutions still remains salient for understanding colonial modernity.

Tagore's enactment of masculinity and fatherhood can be tracked along interconnected trajectories: as a rebellious thinker, Tagore rejected the authoritarianism of British institutions. He blamed colonial education for the emasculation of Indians. Unlike the majority of his contemporaries, including his own niece Sarala Devi Chaudhurani, he did not participate in a movement for body-building and wrestling that would strengthen the "weak" body of the Indians. Manliness for him was rooted in an aesthetic culture and encompassed fatherhood, traits of which he chiefly inherited from his predecessors: fatherhood that commanded compliance but also nurtured freedom. Through the ages of his life, his model of *Pitridev* (father-god) evolved into his own archetype as *Gurudev* (teacher-god), the father-cum-teacher that the early native educators emphasized. His "empire" of fatherhood extended beyond his immediate familial, religious, and ultimately even national domain. He encouraged the independent spirit of his students as world citizens but did not subscribe to the Enlightenment notion of private individuals entrenched in property rights and predicated on a separation with the father.[117] The mutual deference (*bhakti*) that sustained the relationship between him and his disciples did not undermine the autonomy of either but fostered a culture of creativity unfettered by the "technologies of power."[118] The politics of everyday life shaped by many competing forces reconstituted his fatherhood in its nurturing, care-giving roles both within home and outside, thus giving a new meaning to masculinity that was not just an expression of physical might but also an "education in emotional literacy."[119]

---

[117] Chakrabarty, "Family, Fraternity, Salaried Labor."
[118] Chatterjee, "Tagore's Non-nation," 126.
[119] Trev Lynn Broughton and Helen Rogers, eds., *Gender and Fatherhood in the Nineteenth Century* (London: Palgrave Macmillan, 2007), 22.

Samir Dayal has argued that the "fulcrum" of Tagore's universal humanism was "an erotic economy of love" that could be best identified in the notion of *sahridayata* or empathy, as Dipesh Chakrabarty argued. Dayal writes: "Tagore's preferred version of patriotism was couched in the rhetoric of love, rather than the received modality of aggressive nationalist self-affirmation."[120] If "Tagore's counternarrative was calculated to destabilize the hegemony of a hypermasculinist discourse of nationalism,"[121] I suggest that Tagore's counternarrative could be traced to his pedagogical experiments in which his family played a central role. His "love" for humanity (including children) was not confined to the microcosm of the home but became a blueprint for his public action. By taking care of a larger community of children as dependents, by protecting them through training and education, by giving them a home in his *ashrama* outside of home, by nurturing deeply spiritual, yet secular, democratic principles, Tagore displayed his larger concern as a modern father endowed with altered sensibilities.

As an imperial subject of international stature, Tagore felt a bigger onus of freeing children's minds and preparing them with skills and knowledge as autonomous, independent subjects of the modern world. Beset with ambivalence and contradictions, his sensibility was also conditioned by his contextual reality as a son and father. In each phase of his life, family played an important role through its enabling dynamics and restrictive presence. By focusing on the private and the quotidian aspects that are subsumed under his more popular image of a benign, universalist poet, this chapter has attempted to establish the link between the history of a notable family and more widespread notions of gender, masculinity, and fatherhood. Tagore's involvement in educational movements and his embeddedness in family offered us the opportunity to explore the role of fathers as mentors-educators and interrogate notions of masculinity that were not connected to gender-specific sex-roles as biological parents. While one aspect of Tagore's masculinity was anchored in everyday acts of reformed fatherhood, the other aspect of masculinity de-linked itself from maleness and acquired its meaning through the enunciation of education programmes that challenged colonial forms of domination.

---

[120] Samir Dayal, *Resisting Modernity* (Manchester: Cambridge Scholars Publishing, 2007), 78.
[121] Samir Dayal, *Resisting Modernity*, 79.

6
Beyond Bengal—Gandhi and Nehru: Fathers at Home and Fathers of the Nation

This last chapter opens up a broader comparative picture of India by bringing into view two iconic figures, Mohandas Karamchand Gandhi (1869–1948) and Jawaharlal Nehru (1889–1964), who publicly held father-like positions in modern India.[1] Like all our interlocutors, big and small, they too were products of colonial culture and governance; western educated and entrenched in colonial politics, they were global in their stature and were architects of a postcolonial nation. In historical scholarship, their larger-than-life political profiles occlude their engagement with children. Before Gandhi became *Bapuji* (Father) of the nation and Jawaharlal Nehru became *Chacha* (Uncle), they both mobilized their own children to embark on projects of educating the future generation who would be free citizens and not colonial subjects. Their life-works bring into sharper relief our concerns with imaginary fathers and children beyond Bengal. They both harnessed the potentiality of children trained in an alternate pedagogy that emphasized self-determination, self-help, and self-reliance that would constitute their manhood (*pourush*) as liberated citizens of a new world. These duo's lives as sons, fathers, and educators are crucial for sensing the all-India resonances in practices of fathers and children that we saw in the localized experiences of Bengal. A focus on two leaders who enjoyed national and international preeminence also allows us to track continuities and changes over time, from the tentative self-assertion of the early literary activists

---

[1] For an astute assessment of Gandhi, Nehru, and other Indian leaders as advocates of peace and human rights see Manu Bhagavan, *India and the Quest for One World: The Peacemakers* (New York: Palgrave Macmillan, 2013).

in primers, children's periodicals, normative and scientific texts to confident crystallization of full-fledged ideology and programmes for the new generation. By connecting Gandhi's and Nehru's familial experiences with their public experimentation in education, I attempt to demonstrate the ways their experiential reality translated into their public practices as pacifists, statesmen, and nation-builders. This will hammer home my argument that in the face of colonial subjection, fatherhood was a domain of deliberation for educated Indian men. The fathers, through a creative appropriation and assimilation of an indigenous and colonial culture, the latter disseminating post-Enlightenment thoughts, entertained a vision that was transnational and global. The pedagogical experiments of the leaders, driven initially by a familial concern to educate their children, reflected their changing notions of masculinity. What made each of the father-leaders a "man" was contingent on their relationship with their own biological as well as the imaginary body of children. Their emphasis on freedom of mind and spiritual training, in addition to physical strength, for the younger generation displaced the colonial critique of Indian effeminacy. While the scholarship on and primary sources by Gandhi and Nehru are vast and complex, I restrict my focus on specific aspects of their familial life and pedagogy by drawing chiefly on their rich autobiographical accounts and writings related to their "education of desire." By adopting a biographical approach my hope is to flag the wider significance of the entangled story of family and nation, of the home and the world that this book seeks to unravel.

Mohandas Karamchand Gandhi, the *Bapuji* (1869–1948)

Born into a powerful family of Gujarati trading caste (Banya), Gandhi, the Bapuji (an endearing term for father that was and is widely used to refer to Gandhi), came from a family that held important political positions (See Figures 6.1).[2] His father, Karamchand Gandhi (See Figure 6.2),

[2] Gandhi was addressed as Bapu/Bapuji among his close and distant associates alike. For example, members of the Nehru family, including Nehru himself, addressed him as Bapuji; distant and common people too addressed him as Bapu. See Begum Qudsia Zaidi, *Our Bapu* (with a foreword by Nehru), (Ahmedabad: Navajivan Publishing House, 1952).

236 FATHERS IN A MOTHERLAND

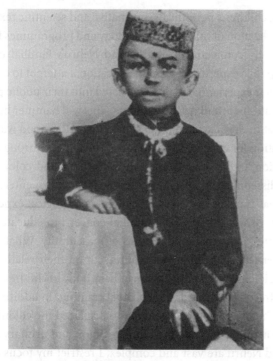

Figure 6.1 Mohandas K. Gandhi (Age 7)

was the chief administrator and member of the court of Porbandar and so was his grandfather in the tiny neighbouring state of Junagadh. Gandhi started his *Autobiography* tracing his paternal heritage, but he also left a detailed account of his mother, wife, and children, which was not a common practice by the standard of his time. He described his father as "a lover of his clan, truthful, brave and generous, but short-tempered." Gandhi in his characteristic frankness, which was fairly uncommon in Indian sons' remembrances of fathers, noted that his father "might have been even given to carnal pleasures. For he married for the fourth time when he was over forty."[3] He had no ambition to "accumulate riches" and bequeathed little property for his successors. Neither was he highly educated; but his "rich experience of practical affairs stood him in good

---

[3] M.K. Gandhi, *Autobiography: The Story of My Experiments With Truth* (Washington, D.C.: Public Affairs Press, 1948), 1. As a contrast, we may recall from Chapter 4 that Bipin Chandra Pal did not make any subjective judgemnet about his father who married at age sixty-four as a reaction to Bipin's conversion to Brahmoism.

Figure 6.2 Karamchand Gandhi, Mohandas Gandhi's Father

stead" in his profession and in his life.[4] Gandhi's mother, Putlibai (See Figure 6.3), "well-informed about matters of state" and possessing strong common sense, left an indelible impression on her son through her saintliness and religiosity.[5] Gandhi by his own confession was a mediocre student but always truthful and respectful towards his teachers: "I had learnt to carry out the orders of elders, not to scan their actions."[6] Although not particularly drawn to reading, a book that seized Gandhi's attention as a child was *Shravana Pitribhakti Nataka* (*A Drama on Shravana's Devotion to his Father*), a play about the mythical character Shravana's devotion to his parents. His love for Shravana was further fuelled by an enactment of the story by itinerant "showmen" (performers) and a picture of Shravana carrying, by means of slings fitted on his shoulders, his blind parents on a

---

[4] Gandhi, *Autobiography*, 2.
[5] Gandhi, *Autobiography*, 2–3.
[6] Gandhi, *Autobiography*, 4.

238 FATHERS IN A MOTHERLAND

Figure 6.3 Putlibai, Mohandas Gandhi's Mother

pilgrimage. At that young age, Gandhi told himself: "Here is an example for you to copy."[7]

This re-telling of his childhood experience through the lens of filial piety was a clear testimony to supreme respect that parents enjoyed in Indian children's lives. Devotion to parents, which Iswarchandra Vidyasagar emphasized through his primers and Bengali autobiographers such as Bipin Chandra Pal and Rabindranath Tagore vouched through their commemorative writings, was also a major theme in Gandhi's *Autobiography*. But no other writer we discussed had engaged in such a candid, perhaps transgressive conversation as Gandhi did about early marriage and the conflict it posed between filial obligation and carnal pleasure (See Figure 6.4). Gandhi confessed in his *Autobiography* of a critical moment when his desire for physical closeness with his wife stood in the way of fulfilling his duty as a son. He was married to Kasturba Makanji (See Figure 6.5)

---

[7] Gandhi, *Autobiography*, 5.

Figure 6.4 Mohandas Gandhi as a teenager (1876)

Figure 6.5 Mohandas Gandhi and his wife Kasturba (1902)

when they were both thirteen years old, an experience that later turned him into a staunch opponent of the "cruel custom" of child marriage. Recalling his marriage ceremony, he wrote: "I was devoted to my parents. But no less was I devoted to the passions that flesh is heir to. I had yet to learn that all happiness and pleasure should be sacrificed in devoted service to my parents."[8] It may be worth noting that in his chapter "Child Marriage" he devoted a significant amount of time to his father who arranged the marriage for him. When he was sixteen and still a student, his father was sick and bed-ridden, and Gandhi was his principal attendant. One night he left his dying father to spend time with his wife. His father died in the span of his short absence, leaving Gandhi emotionally devastated. He remained deeply ashamed of his behaviour for the rest of his life, because "carnal lust got the better of what I regarded as my duty to study, and of what was even a greater duty, my devotion to my parents..."[9]

Between 1888 and 1900 Gandhi fathered four sons with his wife (Harilal, Manilal, Ramdas, and Devadas); he then took the vow of celibacy at age thirty-seven. In 1888, leaving his wife and their newborn son with his family in India, he left for England to study law. It was in England that Gandhi came of age—he lived the life of an English gentleman; joined the vegetarian movement; read widely from European, American, and Asian authors; came in contact with theosophists; and studied Christianity, the Bhagavad-Gita, and Edwin Arnold's *Light of Asia*. Upon completion of his degree and return to India in 1891, he was determined to reform children's education at home. He liked the company of children and enjoyed playing and fooling around with them. Inspired by the British system, he wanted to train his own son, almost four, and his nephew in physical education to make them hardy.[10]

Gandhi's political activism started in Natal, South Africa, where he went to launch his career as a lawyer in 1893 and witnessed first-hand the brutal racial discrimination Indians were subjected to (See Figure 6.6). It was in opposition to such practices that he developed his unique method of non-violent resistance (*Satyagraha* or Quest for Truth). Along with inspirations from Indic traditions and especially the new Hindu monk, Swami Vivekananda, whom he never met, three seminal books magically transformed his life: Thoreau's "masterly treatise," *On the Duty of Civil Disobedience* (1847); Tolstoy's *The Kingdom of God Is Within You* (1893), the fountainhead of his non-violence and love; and Ruskin's *Unto This Lust* (1862)—the ideas of which became the source of his non-violent

---

[8] Gandhi, *Autobiography*, 7.
[9] Gandhi, *Autobiography*, 25.
[10] Gandhi, *Autobiography*, 79.

Figure 6.6 Mohandas Gandhi in South Africa (1909)

passive resistance and self-reliance that he inculcated among his children and the future generation. The development of Gandhi's worldview and methods were therefore truly global and transnational.

In South Africa, he launched a number of experiments with child-rearing, diet, nature-cure, and in his personal and professional life.[11] As a modern responsible husband and father, a trend we witnessed in Tagore, Gandhi went further to read an advice manual for mothers—Dr Tribhuvandas's *Ma-ne Shikhaman* (*Advice to Mothers*) before two of his sons were born in South Africa, and his medical knowledge came in handy during the birth of his youngest son when he had to assist with the delivery.[12] He also displayed all the qualities of an authoritarian patriarch, commanding obedience from his sons and wife, any exception to which

---

[11] For a succinct account of Gandhi's life, see Bhikhu Parekh, *Gandhi: A Brief Insight* (New York: Sterling, 2010).
[12] Gandhi, *Autobiography*, 178.

Figure 6.7 Mohandas Gandhi's wife Kasturba and her Sons (1902)

often led to acrimony and break-up with his offspring (See Figure 6.7).[13] Gandhi had a conflicted relationship with his eldest son, Harilal, who disliked his father's experimentation with education and non-violent resistance. Harilal broke away from Gandhi in South Africa and trained as a lawyer in India. He took to drinking, converted to Islam, and passed away in 1948.[14]

But even prior to subjecting his sons to his experiments, Gandhi was quick to realize the potential of children as crucial mobilizers. He harnessed their labour and cooperation from the very onset of his revolutionary career. Contra Tagore's "imagined community" of children endowed with a new spirit of freedom, Gandhi counted on children's actual participation and support to attain his nationalist goals. In 1896 on

---

[13] David Hardiman, *Gandhi in His Time and Ours* (Delhi: Permanent Black, 2003), 94–102.
[14] For details, see Rajmohan Gandhi, *Mohandas: A True Story of a Man, His People and an Empire* (Delhi: Penguin/Viking, 2006).

his first trip back home to bring his wife and sons to Natal, he had to take the train from Calcutta to reach Bombay before he could reach his hometown in Gujarat. As the train stopped at Allahabad, a major North Indian town, Gandhi decided to quickly explore the city, eventually missing the train and being stuck there for another day. Taking advantage of this situation he managed to see the editor of a leading English newspaper, *The Pioneer*, and got permission to publish a pamphlet describing the condition of Indians in South Africa. Faced with the daunting task of circulating ten thousand copies of those pamphlets, he gathered all the children in his locality and "asked them to volunteer two or three hours' labour of a morning, when they had no school" to post those booklets. Gandhi wrote: "This they willingly agreed to do. I promised to bless them and give them, as a reward, used postage stamps which I had collected. They got through the work in no time. That was my first experiment of having little children as volunteers."[15] This singular event in the late years of the nineteenth century presaged Gandhi's assumption of guardianship and his first effort to mobilize children for a political cause.

Educating Children: The Father as Teacher

Gandhi's experiments with education, like Tagore's, started with his own family, beginning when he landed in Durban in 1897 with his two sons, age nine and five, and his nephew, then ten.[16] Indian students in South Africa could only attend special schools set up by the missionaries where the medium of instruction was English, and they received a smattering of Tamil or Gujarati. Gandhi, as a special privilege, had the option of sending them to European schools, where no other Indian students were accepted. Dissatisfied with the choices, he temporarily hired a teacher for regular instruction at home supplemented by his own irregular coaching whenever possible. Barring his eldest son, who went back to Ahmedabad for high school, three of Gandhi's sons never had any public education and only attended a school that was staffed by *Satyagrahi* parents and

---

[15] Gandhi, *Autobiography*, 148–149.
[16] For debates between Tagore and Gandhi see Sabyasachi Bhattacharya, compiled and edited with an Introduction. *The Mahatma and the Poet: Letters and Debates Between Gandhi and Tagore, 1915–1941* (Delhi: National Book Trust, 1997).

whose lessons were improvised by him: a school that taught them "the simplicity and spirit of service" over "literary education."[17] Gandhi admitted in his *Autobiography* that although his system of educating his sons was inadequate, resulting in the boys lacking any formal training, he could not convince himself to send his sons to a school run by the British. These unilateral decisions by Gandhi for his sons in the late years of 1890s led to disagreements with his sons and wife, but it was his decision that prevailed all the time. His confident recounting of his decisions in his *Autobiography* about thirty years later bears testimony to his sternness and authoritarianism as a biological father. He affirmed that the "ultimate result" of his educational experiments lay in the "womb of the future." His objective was to bring to attention that "a student of the history of civilization may have some measure of the difference between disciplined home education and school education, and also the effect produced on children through changes introduced by parents in their lives." As one of his early experiments with truth, he made a choice between liberty and learning and gave his children "an object-lesson in liberty and self-respect" at the cost of a less-than-complete education that he called "literary training."

These initial experiments with pedagogy in the late 1890s and early 1900s prepared him to call Indian youths for the non-cooperation movement in 1920 to boycott their schools and colleges—the "citadels of slavery." He advised them: "it was far better to remain unlettered and break stones for the sake of liberty than to go in for a literary education in the chains of slaves."[18] He prioritized a moral/political education over book learning. Commencing with pedagogical decisions in his familial environment, Gandhi came to posit himself as the father who determined that British education took second place to Indian liberty. Although sceptical of missionary education, Gandhi carried forward the idea of "teacher as father" as it was professed by evangelists and Indian educators—but he inverted the roles. Contradicting the Anglican headmaster's, Reverend Gmelin's, assumption that the "modern" male teacher should serve as a model for "modern" father,[19] Gandhi foregrounded the role of the father as model for the teacher, as he voluntarily acquired the responsibility of

---

[17] Gandhi, *Autobiography*, 175.
[18] Gandhi, *Autobiography*, 176.
[19] Parna Sengupta, *Pedagogy for Religion*, 87.

fatherhood over his students and later of the nation. He firmly believed that being at home and having constant contact with their parents would provide his sons the best possible education, inculcating in them a spirit of service and simplicity. Gandhi was more concerned about their moral and spiritual development than he was with their academic prowess in traditional school subjects.

Central to Gandhi's personal-political philosophy was his deployment of the idea of family. His very idea of *swaraj* as self-rule that involved not only political self-government but also a personal and spiritual self-governance blurred the boundaries between his private interests and the public good. During his stay in South Africa his exhortation, "We are one family," addressing the larger society was key to his mobilization of the diasporic South Asian community. His mission of imparting education thus went beyond his own biological children to the world at large when he launched his experiment of communal living, first in his school at Phoenix (1904) and then in the Tolstoy Farm (1910). As the Farm started growing, it was imperative to make provisions for education of its boys and girls. Students came from different caste, class, regional, socioeconomic, and religious backgrounds—Hindu, Muslim, Parsi, and Christian. Gandhi lacked confidence in outside teachers and believed that only parents could impart the best education. Considering the inhabitants of Tolstoy Farm a family in which he occupied "the place of the father," he took upon himself "the responsibility for the training of the young."[20]

Gandhi assumed the role of the "father" long before he was construed as the "father of the nation," the *Bapuji*. At the same time, he also recognized the limitation of assuming the role of the "paterfamilias" in the farm—of a group of unfamiliar children of varying ages and backgrounds with whom he had limited personal contact. But convinced that moral training could be given to all alike, irrespective of age, sex, religion, or background, he decided to live among the children of the Tolstoy Farm for twenty-four hours a day as their *father* to lay the foundation of their character-building, which he believed was fundamental for good education. Gandhi thus materialized through his pedagogical practices what

---

[20] Gandhi, *Autobiography*, 298.

Figure 6.8 Mohandas Gandhi and his wife Kasturba with Tagore (1940)

the missionaries and early educators yearned to achieve—the abstract equation of the teacher and the father. His manhood rested on being the father in charge of protecting and taking care of his children and dependents and also providing them with a sense of belonging in the spatiotemporal setting of his schools as a "farm" and later as "ashram" (hermitage).[21] Gandhi, like Tagore, represented the engaged, sympathetic male pedagogue who listened, played with, and most importantly guided his students beyond the classroom (See Figure 6.8).[22]

As a "father-teacher" Gandhi also deliberated on the role of teachers. He saw himself as "an eternal object-lesson to the boys and girls" living with him.[23] At the core of Gandhi's teaching was spiritual training

---

[21] Later he would also assume the role of a caring mother for his followers. There is a substantial body of literature on Gandhi's femininity and masculinity but this complex topic is beyond the parameters of the present study. In short, Gandhi vehemently denounced the hyper-masculine culture of the West and rejected Western ideas of scientific rationalism. I have restricted my discussion on Gandhi's emphasis on masculinity to his critique of colonial education. Readers interested in this question should see, for a start, Ashis Nandy, *The Intimate Enemy* (Delhi: Oxford University Press, 1983); Joseph Alter, *Gandhi's Body: Sex, Diet, and the Politics of Nationalism* (Philadelphia: University of Pennsylvania Press, 2000); *Moral Materialism: Sex and Masculinity in Modern India* (London: Penguin, 2011); Joseph Lelyveld, *Great Soul: Mahatma Gandhi and His Struggle With India* (New York: Knopf, 2011).

[22] For elaboration on the ideas of object-lesson see Parna Sengupta, *Pedagogy for Religion*, 81–101.

[23] Gandhi, *Autobiography*, 303.

comparable to Tagore's, training that he enforced on his family as well. According to Gandhi, familiarity with one's own religion and scriptures was part of intellectual training, but the development of the spirit involved the building of character and work towards a knowledge of God and self-realization. Initially, he started to impart this spiritual training by making children "memorize and recite hymns" and by "read[ing] to them from books on moral training," such as the manuals I described in Chapters 2 and 3. But he soon realized that training of the spirit could not be achieved through books; rather,

> [t]he training of the spirit was possible only through the exercise of the spirit. And the exercise of the spirit entirely depended on the life and character of the teacher. The teacher has always to be mindful of his p's and q's, whether he was in the midst of his boys or not.[24]

The students also became his teachers. He vouched that the increasing discipline and restraint that he imposed on himself at Tolstoy Farm was mostly due to his students. Contrary to the disciplinary regimes of teachers and fathers using corporal punishment, Gandhi left no room for the physical chastisement of students in his Farm. Gandhi regretted that on one occasion, irritated by the repeated unruly behaviour of a student, he struck the latter with a ruler. The incident involving violence on his part left him with so much regret that it taught him a better method of correcting students. He was always opposed to corporal punishment. He recalled only one incident in which he physically punished one of his sons.[25]

That Gandhi assumed the fatherhood of the larger community, the would-be nation, was evident when he refused to make any distinction between his own children and other pupils attending his school. The student population at Tolstoy Farm was mixed, and Hermann Kallenbach, Gandhi's close friend and associate who donated the land for Tolstoy Farm, once warned Gandhi about the possible ill-effects on his sons of the company of a mixed student body. Gandhi responded that he could not afford to differentiate between his sons and the "loafers" for, he was

---

[24] Gandhi, *Autobiography*, 302.
[25] Gandhi, *Autobiography*, 303.

in charge of all of them. He urged that his sons, instead of enjoying an advantageous position that would arouse in them a feeling of superiority, should associate with the rest of the boys and teach themselves self-discipline so that they could discriminate between good and evil.[26] Gandhi always privileged the greater public good over individual self-interest.

Equally important for Gandhi was vocational training—Gandhi himself learned shoe-making from Kallenbach and shared his knowledge with the students; Kallenbach taught carpentry, and all the students knew how to cook. On Tolstoy Farm, it was the rule that "the youngsters should not be asked to do what the teachers did not do, and therefore, when they were asked to do any work, there was always a teacher cooperating and actually working with them."[27] This principle along with vocational training, we may recall, strongly echoed Tagore's ideals at Santiniketan and Sriniketan. But unlike Tagore's emphasis on new methods of literary training, Gandhi's literary training was rudimentary—imparted in Tamil, Hindi, Gujarati, Urdu, and English taught by Gandhi himself. For Gandhi, the labour of the mind and that of the body had equal significance. In that regard, Gandhi described himself as a scientist working in the laboratories of his own making, experimenting on himself and his close associates. He was confident in his experimentation and unflinching in his role as a father-cum-teacher.

Educating the Nation: *Nai Talim*

Gandhi's education philosophy was evident in *Hind Swaraj* (1908) where he claimed elementary or higher education did not "make of us men." Gandhi's pedagogical principles emanated from his overall critique of Western civilization and the colonial government's professed system of education. Like Tagore's identification of English education as the root cause of Indian men's inability to attain adulthood, Gandhi too proclaimed repeatedly:

---

[26] Gandhi, *Autobiography*, 304–305.
[27] Gandhi, *Autobiography*, 299.

[t]he Government schools have *unmanned* us, rendered us helpless and Godless... They have made us what we were intended to become—clerks and interpreters... The *youth* of a nation are its hope. I hold that, as soon as we discovered that the system of government was wholly, or mainly evil, it became sinful for us to associate our children with it.[28] (emphasis mine)

Gandhi maintained his position on education through the 1920s when he addressed Tagore's public critique of his non-cooperation movement. Tagore had urged Gandhi that students should not give up Government schools unless they had alternate schools to attend. Emphasizing the independent importance of character-building, Gandhi assured Tagore that non-cooperation was not "intended to build a Chinese wall between India and the West" but was intended "to pave the way to real, honourable, and voluntary cooperation based on mutual respect and trust."[29]

Gandhi's educational experiments culminated into a full-fledged blueprint of "Basic Education" (*nai talim*) when the Indian National Congress adopted his ideas as the Wardha Scheme in 1937.[30] The Wardha Scheme emerged out of Gandhi's frustration in the wake of the Indian National Congress's decision to cooperate with the British in its implementation of the provisions of the 1935 Government of India Act. The Act, passed by the British Government with limited input from Indians, had provided for a limited form of self-government in the provinces under which elected ministers, chosen by provincial legislatures, were endowed with the responsibility of all matters related to provincial administration. Gaining the majority in the countrywide election, as Congress stepped into power in the elected provinces, education became a major area of reform and revitalization. Committed to the policy of prohibition, as Congress leaders grappled with the financial crisis of propagating education without dependence on funding from the excise duty on liquor, Gandhi, in July 1937, launched his radical idea in his newspaper *Harijan* that "education should be self-supporting":

---

[28] Ronald Duncan, ed., *Gandhi: Selected Writings* (New York: Dover Publications, 2005), 112.
[29] Duncan, *Gandhi, Selected Writings*, 112.
[30] The scheme's name is due to it being based on Gandhi's inaugural speech at the All-India National Education Conference in Wardha, Maharashtra, on October 22, 1937.

By education I mean an all-round drawing out of the best in child and man—body, mind and spirit. Literacy is not the end of education nor even the beginning. It is only one of the means by which man and woman can be educated. Literacy in itself is no education. I would therefore begin the child's education by teaching it a useful handicraft and enabling it to produce from the moment it begins its training. Thus every school can be made self-supporting, the condition being that the State takes over the manufactures of these schools. I hold that the highest development of the mind and the soul is possible under such a system of education. Only every handicraft has to be taught not merely mechanically as is done today, but scientifically, i.e. the child should know the why and wherefore of every process... This method does not exclude a knowledge of history and geography. But I find that this is best taught by transmitting such general information by word of mouth. One imparts ten times as much in this manner as by reading and writing. The signs of the alphabet may be taught later.[31]

With an emphasis on the use of mother tongue and an equal stress on the labour of the mind and the body, the radicality of Gandhi's self-sustaining, secular education proposal lay not only in its introduction of productive handicrafts as an integral part of the school curriculum but to make the learning of the craft the crux of the entire teaching programme. As Krishna Kumar argued, "it restructured the sociology of school knowledge in India, where productive handicrafts had been associated with the lowest groups in the hierarchy of castes."[32] By favouring the child belonging to the lowest echelons of society, Gandhi's social philosophy and Basic Education turned the existing education policy upside down. Gandhi's vision of basic education combined the physical and the spiritual faculties inherent in a child. He claimed "true education of the intellect" was "only" possible "through a proper exercise of and training of the bodily organs, e.g. hands, feet, eyes, ears, nose, etc." In other words, "brain should be educated through the hand."[33] Basic Education also envisaged

---

[31] *Harijan*, July 31, 1937.
[32] Krishna Kumar, "Mohandas Karamchand Gandhi (1869–1948)," in *Prospects, the Quarterly Review of Education* (Paris, UNESCO: International Bureau of Education) 23, no. 3/4 (1993): 507–557.
[33] Mohit Chakrabarti, *The Gandhian Dimensions of Education* (Delhi: Daya Publishing House, 1990), 68–69.

a cooperative model that treated the child as a member of a cooperative group. The objective of education should be to reintegrate the individual and develop him/her as a member of a living society. Basic Education would inculcate in the child a spirit of co-operation and a sense of responsibility from the very beginning. The goal of Gandhi's Basic Education was to make education accessible to all.[34] Gandhi revolutionized the idea of education although the appeal of his ideas was narrow. At the same time, he also represented a long tradition of Indian men, such as those described in Chapters 2 through 4, who used the educational policy as a means of making themselves fathers. While, on the one hand, Gandhi's educational experiments were unique and perhaps as unique as Tagore's, on the other they served to place him in the same position—as the virtual father to a broad community of future citizens. The details of the pedagogy varied, but nonetheless, Gandhi-as-educator and moral exemplar was implicitly using educational recommendations as a way of asserting his identity as a father

Despite their failings with their biological children and differing attitudes towards nationalism, it is important to note that Tagore's and Gandhi's fatherly anxieties travelled from their homes to the world, envisioning a new culture of childhood in India that championed simultaneous training of the mind and the body by defying the prevailing colonial system. Tagore's educational mission, based on universalism and aesthetic moralism, had limited practicability.[35] Gandhi's educational proposal for the new nation, a plan that intersected with and diverged from Tagore's, offered a practical solution, yet it was incommensurable for the nation and its citizens, just as Tagore's was. Neither of them rejected the study of English, but their insistence on vernacular education (like other nationalists of the period) was a move away from the dominant middle-class culture that projected knowledge of English as a sign of virile masculinity.[36] Shefali Chandra has demonstrated the

---

[34] Humayun Kabir, "Theory and Practice of Basic Education," *Education in New India* (London: George Allen and Unwin Ltd., 1959), 22–23.

[35] Partha Chatterjee, "Tagore's Non-Nation," in *Lineages of Political Society* (New York: Columbia University Press, 2011), 94–128.

[36] For the connection between knowledge of English and Indian masculinity see Shefali Chandra, "Mimicry, Masculinity and the Mystique of Indian English: Western India, 1870–1900," *Journal of Asian Studies* 68, no. 1 (February 2009): 199–225 and "Gendering English: Gender, Sexuality and the Language of Desire in Modern India, 1850–1940," *Gender & History* 19, no. 2 (August 2007): 284–304.

Figure 6.9 Mohandas Gandhi with Jawaharlal Nehru (1946)

multiple ways Indian English was "materially and symbolically" associated with the management of "cultural mimicry, masculinity, and heterosexual affect." By deploying the cultural authority of English into "sexually differentiated spaces," Indians (from western India, for Chandra's research) self-consciously bolstered their "native" and masculine authority.[37] Tagore and Gandhi's denunciation of English and Western-style learning, therefore, was a significant departure from the dominant ethos, but their moves certainly symbolized their hegemonic aspirations. By empowering the younger generation with a secular, democratic, and self-supporting education, the fathers empowered themselves. In the decades to follow, it would be Jawaharlal Nehru who would implement national educational policies (See Figures 6.9). But he acted differently from both Gandhi and Tagore. It is thus imperative that we examine Nehru as a father and a founder of a new nation who set Indian democracy on its way.

---

[37] Chandra, "Mimicry, Masculinity," 200.

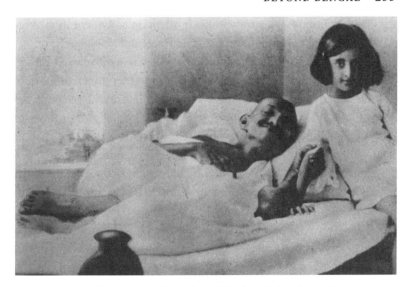

Figure 6.10 Mohandas Gandhi with child Indira Nehru (1924)

Jawaharlal Nehru: The *Chacha* (1889–1964)

If Gandhi was *Bapu*, Jawaharlal Nehru was *Chacha* (uncle), as he was affectionately called, and his birthday, November 14, is celebrated as the "Children's Day" in India. Nehru was not an educator and he did not launch pedagogical experiments; neither did he adopt a paternalistic position as a mentor (Gurudev) or a father (Bapuji) as Tagore and Gandhi did. But, as is well known, Nehru was deeply engaged in raising his daughter Indira, later to become the prime minister of India, and had a unique way of training her young mind. His vast collection of letters to Indira (written between 1917 and 1964), retelling the history of the world, indicated his zeal for a broad-based education for the future generation. Written mostly from prison cells, the privacy of the letters was already compromised by his very location in a strictly surveilled colonial prison system. Not only were his writings subject to scrutiny by the colonial government, the fact that they were written in English and were circulated internationally, ensured a transcendence of his ideas from the home to the world. His collection of 196 letters to daughter Indira written during his periods of incarceration between 1930 and 1933 were published as the *Glimpses of World History* in 1934, and in the decades to come, with new reprints, it continued to earn worldwide attention as evident in rave reviews published in several international journals and newspapers.

Nehru's life was distinct from any of the leaders we discussed earlier. His autobiography, *Toward Freedom*, was also written in jail and began with his experience of confinement and reflections on the relations between Englishmen and Indians, of "official and nonofficial, of those in authority and those who have to obey." He waited until the third chapter of his autobiography to share his heritage and family history.[38] Even more interestingly, in contrast with his contemporaries' memoirs, which generally began one or more generations back, he began the book with a description of himself, "an only son of prosperous parents" likely to be spoiled, "especially so in India," given that he was born more than a decade before his two younger sisters. He grew up as a lonely child with no companions of his age. He even missed the opportunity of making friends in school for, instead of attending primary and kindergarten institutions, he was educated by governesses and private tutors at home (See Figures 6.11 and 6.12).[39]

Nehru was born into an affluent household in Allahabad, UP, tracing ancestry to the Kashmiri Pandit community who came and settled in and around Delhi, serving first the Mughals and then the British Raj. His father, Motilal Nehru (1861–1931), was a posthumous child raised under the "sheltering care" of his elder brother, who worked for the British judiciary.[40] Nehru provided a candid account of a young Motilal that we missed in the Bengali writers we examined before. He described Motilal as a far from a model student who was more interested in games and adventures than in study.[41] Although Motilal never graduated from college, once he chose to study law for his career, he came out first in the High Court vakils' examination and won a gold medal. Despite his law practice he was drawn towards sports and other amusements, especially wrestling, in which he won many matches. A self-made man with an exuberant spirit and confidence, Motilal established himself as a successful

---

[38] For an interesting reading on autobiography and decolonization, see Philip Holden, *Autobiography and Decolonization: Modernity, Masculinity, and the Nation-State* (Madison: University of Wisconsin Press, 2008).

[39] Jawaharlal Nehru, *Toward Freedom: The Autobiography of Jawaharlal Nehru* (New York: The John Day Company, 1941 [1936]), 16.

[40] Nehru, *Toward Freedom*, 17.

[41] Nehru, *Toward Freedom*, 18.

Figure 6.11 Child Jawaharlal Nehru with father Motilal and mother Swaruprani

lawyer, and as his practice flourished he embraced a lavish Westernized lifestyle while taking care of a large Hindu joint family. Having lost his first wife in childbirth, Motilal fathered with his second wife, Swaruprani Thussu (1868–1938), three children—the eldest, Jawaharlal, followed by two daughters, Vijaya Lakshmi Pandit, a diplomat, politician, and the first female president of the United Nations General Assembly; and Krishna Hutheesing, a noted writer who authored several books on her brother. Jawaharlal Nehru had a "sheltered and uneventful" childhood surrounded by luxury, love, and affection from both parents (See Figure 6.12).[42] Unlike Tagore or Gandhi, he enjoyed a close relationship with his father despite sharp political differences in later life. Nehru noted in his *Autobiography*:

---

[42] S. Gopal, *Jawaharlal Nehru: A Biography* (Delhi: Oxford University Press, 2004), 4; Nehru, *Toward Freedom*, 20.

Figure 6.12 The Nehru Family (Seated, L to R): Swaruprani Thussu, Motilal Nehru, and Jawaharlal's wife Kamala. (Standing, L to R): Jawaharlal Nehru, Vijaya Lakshmi Pandit, Krishna Hutheesing, Indira Nehru, and Ranjit Pandit (1927)

> I admired father tremendously. He seemed to me the embodiment of strength and courage and cleverness, ... I treasured the hope that when I grew up I would be rather like him. But as much as I admired him and loved him I feared him also. I have seen him lose his temper at servants and others; he seemed to me terrible then, and I shivered with fright, mixed sometimes with resentment, at the treatment of a servant.[43]

As strongly as he was attracted to his father, Jawaharlal was equally afraid of him. One of his earliest recollections was of his father's temper on an occasion when he was a victim. When he was five or six, he found two fountain pens on his father's table, and unable to resist himself, he took one of them. When his father looked for the pen he did not confess; at the end, when he was caught, his father beat him so severely that he was

---

[43] Nehru, *Toward Freedom*, 21–22.

blind with pain and mortified by his disgrace. He ran to his mother and for several days creams and ointments were applied to his "aching and quivering little body."[44] Jawaharlal felt closer to his mother and had no fear of her because he knew she would always forgive him; he would confide in her when he would not even dream of doing so to his father.[45] This incident of brutal physical punishment resonated with the experiences of Vidyasagar, Sivnath Sastri, and Premankur Atarthi we documented in chapter 4. It testifies to the prevalence of corporal punishment received by children from all classes, ethnicities, and cultures in India. Reform-minded parents like Tagore, Gandhi, and Nehru stayed away from such practices.

As mentioned earlier, Nehru was home-schooled by British teachers such as the Irish-French Theosophist, F.T. Brooks, who introduced him to the world of English literature, poetry, and science as well as Theosophy, the Upanishads, and the *Bhagavad Gita*. His father, Motilal Nehru, unhappy with Brook's teaching, sent Jawaharlal to Harrow, a British public school, in 1905, and Jawaharlal subsequently attended Trinity College at Cambridge, followed by a law degree from the Inner Temple, London. Although Nehru empathized with the radical nationalists at home and exulted over Japan's victory over Russia in 1905, as a student he showed "no real signs of fire or distinction; neither did he stand out among his generation."[46] His father had already decided for him in 1910 that he would not sit for the Indian Civil Service Examination, anticipating the British bias against Indian students and also because of the fear of his only son being posted in a remote Indian village.[47]

In fact, Motilal's overbearing presence in Jawaharlal's life stymied his confidence as a youth and made him somewhat passive in decision-making. He fulfilled everything that his father wanted from him but with no real enthusiasm. Nehru came back to India not so much with a stellar academic achievement but with a "nurtured mind and imagination." As S. Gopal, Nehru's biographer, argued, "he brought back with him attachments to Britain, and the values he considered British, which were never

---

[44] Nehru, *Toward Freedom*, 21.
[45] Nehru, *Toward Freedom*, 21–22.
[46] Gopal, *Jawaharlal Nehru*, 8.
[47] Gopal, *Jawaharlal Nehru*, 8.

Figure 6.13 Jawaharlal Nehru and wife Kamala (before 1936)

to leave him. They molded his outlook, sustained him in his struggles and influenced his policies in the days of his power."[48]

On his return to India, Nehru embarked on his professional and social life in the footsteps of his father and carried on moderate nationalist activities. He married in 1916 his betrothed, Kamala Kaul, a middle-class Kashmiri Brahmin girl of seventeen from Delhi (See Figure 6.13). Political activism and incarceration interrupted Nehru's conjugal and family life. He enjoyed a deep emotional and physical connection with Kamala, and their relationship intensified as she developed a deeper commitment to nationalist politics and often faced imprisonment. Their only child, Indira, was born in November 1917 (See Figure 6.14).

Increasingly annoyed by the reactionary policies of the colonial government against the nationalist movement, Nehru was radicalized by the massacre at Amritsar in April 1919 and the final call for him came from Gandhi to join the civil disobedience movement. As he later remarked, it was the acceptance of the mentorship of Gandhi, civil disobedience,

---

[48] Gopal, *Jawaharlal Nehru*, 10.

Figure 6.14 Jawaharlal Nehru with wife Kamala and daughter Indira (1918)

and being jailed that made the man of him.[49] The lengthy periods in jail, covering a period worth ten years of his life, matured him as a writer and augmented his political vision.

Nehru: The Father of Indira

Despite the physical distance caused by frequent imprisonment, Nehru developed an intense emotional bonding with Indira as a child. His

[49] Gopal, *Jawaharlal Nehru*, 13–17.

affection was poured out in the letters that he wrote, mostly from prison, narrating the history of humankind and the world. As a dutiful father, Nehru first wrote his series of thirty letters to his daughter when she was attending a boarding school in Mussoorie, India. As Indira Gandhi (née Nehru) wrote in the preface to the third edition of the book, *Letters from a Father to a Daughter*: "The letters ... deal with the beginnings of the earth and of man's awareness of himself. They were not merely letters to be read and put away... They taught one to treat nature as a book."[50] In the only letters that were written from home, Nehru made his purpose clear: he was going to write to Indira "from time to time short accounts of the story of our earth, and the many countries, great and small into which it is divided." As a story-teller, Nehru cast a wide net: "If we want to know something about the story of this world of ours we must think of all the countries and all the peoples that have inhabited it, and not merely of one little country where we may have been born."[51] From the very outset Nehru's position as a global citizen was evident: his vision was not restricted by national or geographical boundaries.

It was in these letters that one can trace Nehru's pedagogical principles. Nehru's passion for rewriting world history was heightened by his lingering years in prison, allowing him for introspection and giving him the respite from political action. The bunch of letters (196) he wrote to Indira from Naini jail in the early 1930s, later to be published as *Glimpses of World History* (1934–35), on the one hand, unpacked his deeply felt emotions as a father forcibly separated from his daughter by an authoritarian state; on the other, they were poised to overcome the physical distance through bringing the larger world closer to his child.[52] The letters did not even reach Indira until two years later, but despite this delay, they established Indira as an iconic daughter and Nehru, as the emblem of an ideal father in charge of feeding young minds. With restricted access to sources and based on memory and personal notes, each letter in *Glimpses* was devoted to a specific theme. Nehru claimed that the letters were "personal and there were many intimate touches in them" which were meant for Indira alone. But the fact that he prefaced these letters saying, "I do

---

[50] Jawaharlal Nehru, *Letters From a Father to a Daughter* (Delhi: Penguin Books, 1973; orig. published by Allahabad Law Journal Press, 1929), Preface to the third edition.

[51] Nehru, *Letters From a Father*, 1–2.

[52] Jawaharlal Nehru, *Glimpses of World History* (Delhi: Oxford University Press, 1998, 13th impression; orig. published as 2 volumes, Kitabistan, Allahabad, 1934–35).

Figure 6.15 Jawaharlal Nehru and Rabindranath Tagore

not know when or where these letters will be published, or whether they will be published at all ..." was a testament to his commitment to a wider audience.[53] The content of his letters, however imperfect but challenging the Eurocentric view of the world, changed Nehru's own outlook on history and their dissemination to a larger public made him an imaginary "father." For his daughter he positioned himself as a teacher—not only through his specific instructions alerting her about the significance of dates in history, about making her aware of the importance of the year 1917, the year of her birth, when a leader like Lenin, "with heart full of love and sympathy for the poor and the suffering" started "the great Revolution" changing "the face of Russia and Siberia"; but also awakening in her the awareness that she was witness to the great movement of India's freedom struggle under Bapuji's (Gandhi's) leadership! His message to her was to be brave and fearless.[54]

His letters revealed an insurgent consciousness that we also witnessed in Tagore and Gandhi (See Figure 6.15). The call for fearlessness harked

---

[53] Nehru, "Preface to Original Edition," *Glimpses* (1998), vii–viii.
[54] Nehru, *Glimpses of World History*, 1–3.

back to Tagore's addresses to his students in Santiniketan. Nehru himself described his work as an "unfortunate mixture of elementary writing for the young and a discussion at times of the ideas of grown-ups." Devoid of other instruments of protest, writing as a *father* and formulating an alternate history of the world, acted as an enabler for Nehru. Letter-writing was both an act of defiance and an assertion of his autonomous fatherhood and subjecthood, as well. Nehru's attempt was not just to educate his daughter but also a reading public by offering a new historiography that dislodged Euro-centric views of history.[55]

A deep thinker influenced by the spirit of science and rationalism, Nehru was also committed to the ideologies of the twentieth century. *Glimpses* was not deeply analytical; but it demonstrated, as S. Gopal argued, his lifelong commitment to half-liberal and half-Marxist ideologies of history that gave his book a unity. Nehru conceived the history of humankind as one connected whole, hence the only way he could represent history was through a history of the world. Global forces, such as class conflict and social struggle, shaped the history of the past centuries and were more important for him than individual actors or leaders. If Tagore had fought against the narrow Western conception of nationalism and statecraft and Gandhi held machinery and the modern civilization as the true enemy, for Nehru, it was the system of imperialism that called for condemnation. Nehru, like Tagore, was cautious about nationalism as "an unreliable friend and an unsafe historian." He devoted time to explaining the shortcomings of his people as much as those of the British, but he firmly believed that imperialism and nationalism could not go together.[56] Interestingly, in the preface to the original edition of *Glimpses*, Nehru, not knowing when or where his letters would be published, urged the readers to "begin at the end," referring to his last letter, which he concluded with a poem by Tagore that captured the essence of the poet's educational philosophy:

Where the mind is without fear and the head is held high;
Where knowledge is free;

---

[55] Nehru, "Preface to Original Edition" in *Glimpses* (1998).
[56] Nehru, Letter 14, December 1932, in *Glimpses*, cited in Gopal, 92–93; 138.

Where the world has not broken up into fragments by narrow domestic walls;
Where words come out from the depth of truth.[57]

No wonder Nehru sent Indira to study at Tagore's school in Santiniketan. Both as a young girl and an adult, Indira was Nehru's closest emotional companion, more so since her mother died in 1936. The closeness between the father and the daughter are also evident in the letters Indira wrote to her father as "a child (1922–29);" as a girl growing up (1930–36); as she came into her own (1937–39); and as a companion and politician in the making.[58] Indira's letters as intimate and insightful as they are form a subject of a separate investigation. The kind of intimacy Nehru fostered with his daughter was noticeable between an equally caring father Tagore with his surviving daughter Mira Devi. But Tagore's exchanges were not as extensive as between Nehru and Indira (See Figures 6.16 and 6.17).

As undeliverable letters written in the prison brought Indira's image closer to Nehru, in real life, too, the latter tested his ideas with child Indira. The singularly important event that established Nehru as the future leader of India was his election as the president for the Lahore session of the Indian National Congress in 1929, succeeding his father Motilal. Jawaharlal had long resisted his father's moderate politics and was particularly incensed by his demand, supported by Gandhi, for India's dominion status in 1928. When his turn came he boldly proclaimed in his presidential address: "independence for us means complete freedom from British dominion and British imperialism." While Nehru was fervently working on his speech, Indira was by his side, and when a secretary handed him the typed copy of the final draft, which included a demand for complete independence for India, he immediately gave it to her and made her read it out slowly and clearly. After Indira read the whole text, Nehru said to her, "Well, now that you have read it, you are committed to it." When Gandhi moved the resolution in the Congress the next day,

---

[57] Nehru, *Glimpses*, 953. He drew more heavily from Tagore in *The Discovery of India* (New York: Anchor Books, 1960 [1946]).
[58] Sonia Gandhi, ed., *Freedom's Daughter: Letters Between Indira Gandhi and Jawaharlal Nehru 1922–1939* (London: Hodder & Stoughton, 1989); *Two Alone, Two Together: Letters Between Indira Gandhi and Jawaharlal Nehru, 1922–1964* (Delhi: Penguin Books, 2005).

Figure 6.16 Playful Jawaharlal Nehru with daughter Indira and grandsons Rajiv and Rahul Gandhi (1940s)

thirteen-year-old Indira realized that she had been the first person to take the pledge. While Nehru's forcing her to read the independence statement might be seen as simply another example of an authoritarian father imposing his will upon his child, it also signalled Nehru's induction of his own child—and, with the child volunteers he encouraged Indira to lead, the children of the nation—in the anti-colonial offensive.

Nehru did not just see children as future citizens; he saw them as current political actors who could join the independence movement. To the father as guru, we must therefore add the figure of father as political

Figure 6.17 Jawaharlal Nehru and Indira at Disneyland (1961)

mentor. Thus Indira Nehru, with her father's encouragement and her mother's organizational assistance, took on the leadership of child activists. The Vanar Sena ("monkey brigade," named after the monkey army that supported Rama in his war against Ravana) was significant because it ascribed agency to the child volunteers and brought to fruition Gandhi's efforts to deploy children for political mobilization.[59] With the help of Biswambhar Nath Pande, the then-secretary of the Allahabad Congress Committee, twelve-year-old Indira recruited about a thousand students from schools in Allahabad. As the leader of the Vanar Sena, Indira donned the male Congress volunteer uniform of *khadi* and a Congress cap. Interestingly, this very act of leadership and dressing up also immediately transformed Indira from a thin, sickly girl to "Indu-Boy," as her

---

[59] Katherine Frank, *Indira: The Life of Indira Nehru Gandhi* (Boston, NY: Houghton Mifflin, 2002), 62–63.

biographer describes her, laden with all masculine attributes. She urged children to collect rations for the *satyagraha* camps, distribute *satygraha* bulletins, and to collect one *paisa* per day from each household for the Vanar Sena fund.[60] In addition to distributing leaflets and banned literature, the young members of the monkey brigade were soon entrusted with gathering intelligence from the police camps and conveying them to the Congress leaders. These incidents from the life of Indira, the daughter of Nehru, bring alive a process that we have traced from the nineteenth century—of harnessing biological and imaginary children to the service of the nation.

Nehru and the Children of the Nation

Nehru not only attempted to train his daughter but was equally committed to educating the children of the nation he conceived. Strikingly, he did not make any distinction between a girl's and a boy's education, eschewing a dichotomy that was so rampant among the early reformers. Akin to Tagore in many respects, he condemned parochial nationalism and endorsed internationalism more as a necessity than choice. To him, isolation from other cultures meant backwardness and decay. He wrote, "we march to the One World of tomorrow where national cultures will be intermingled with the international culture of the human race."[61] He agreed with Gandhi on principles of basic education. He echoed Gandhi's dictum that learning "to work with our own hands does not involve any indignity."[62] He admitted that "[I]t is well recognized now that a child's education should be intimately associated with some craft or manual activity. The mind is stimulated thereby, and there is a coordination between the activities of the mind and the hands." But at the same time, he maintained his difference with Gandhi when he championed the worthiness of simple scientific experiments and know-how that would foster self-confidence and cooperative spirit among the younger generation and reduce their frustration arising out of the "miasma of the past."[63] As far

---

[60] Frank, *Indira*, 63.
[61] Nehru, *Discovery of India*, 417.
[62] R.P. Singh, *Nehru on Education* (Delhi: Sterling Publishers, 1966), 67.
[63] Nehru, *Discovery of India*, 330.

as curriculum is concerned, he was biased towards the "literary aspects of education" and admired the classics. But he was also convinced that "some elementary scientific training in physics and chemistry and especially biology, as also in the applications of science, is essential for all boys and girls. Only thus can they understand and fit into the modern world and develop, to some extent at least, the scientific temper."[64] On the whole, Nehru too championed, like Tagore and Gandhi, the supremacy of mind and spirit in life and the harmony with nature.[65]

Nehru's fatherhood, like that of so many of the men described in this book, made him not just a breadwinner, but a teacher for biological and metaphorical children; but it also made him their political guide as well (See Figure 6.18). Nehru's scheme of education was deeply embedded in his political philosophy as a modern statesman. His central critique of the British empire rested on its economic exploitation of India, and the only way this could be redressed was through the establishment of an independent, autonomous state that would ensure social justice for all. Social justice could be attained only through new institutional apparatus that embodied the spirit of progress and modernity, which for Nehru meant primacy of the economic sphere.[66] True to the spirit of the twentieth century, the "highest ideals of the age" for Nehru were "humanism and the scientific spirit" that India (and China) ought to learn from the modern West. But the West also needed to learn "some of the deeper lessons of life, which have absorbed the minds of thinkers in all ages and all continents." Criticizing the West for not fully developing the real temper of science, Nehru drew from the Indian past:

> ... the essential basis of Indian thought for ages past, though not its later manifestations, fits in with the scientific temper and approach, as well as with internationalism. It is based on a fearless search for truth, on the solidarity of man, even on the divinity of everything living, and on the

---

[64] Nehru, *Discovery of India*, 330.
[65] For parallels between Tagore and Gandhi see Tapan Raychaudhuri, *Perceptions, Emotions, Sensibilities: Essays on India's Colonial and Postcolonial Experiences* (Delhi: Oxford University Press, 2000).
[66] For detailed elaboration of this thesis see Partha Chatterjee, "The Moment of Arrival: Nehru and the Passive Revolution," in *Nationalist Thought and the Colonial World* (Delhi: Oxford University Press, 1986), 133.

Figure 6.18 Jawaharlal Nehru at the Doon School (1959)

free and co-operative development of the individual and the species, ever to greater freedom and higher stages of human growth.[67]

Here the vision of Nehru closely coincided with that of Tagore's and even of Gandhi's; but his commitment to a modern, independent nation-state whose progress relied on a sound economy backed up by science and technology determined the future course of his action that would ultimately sideline the education of the masses. Thus, while Tagore, Gandhi, and Nehru all served as fathers to the larger community and the nation through their commitment to the education of future generations, they differed in the pedagogy and curricula they promoted.

From his early days of Congress leadership, Nehru advocated free compulsory primary education, first in the "Draft Programme" of the India League in 1928, then in the Karachi Resolution on Fundamental Rights in 1931; the policy was finally adopted in the Constitution of independent

---

[67] Nehru, *Discovery of India*, cited in Chatterjee, *Nationalist Thought*, 138–139.

India and was advocated through his Five-Year Plans, but its reach remained restricted.[68] After assuming the position of the head of state, in his address to the Ministry of Education in 1948, he urged that with the great changes that were unleashed in the country, "the entire basis of education must be revolutionized."[69] To the Indian National Congress in January 1955, he stated: "Nothing saddens me so much as the sight of children who are denied even food and clothing. If our children today are denied education, what is our India of tomorrow going to be?" He emphatically added: "It is the duty of the state to provide good education for every child in the country. And I would add that it is the duty of the state to provide free education to every child in the country."[70] In the same speech, he was equally enthusiastic of women's education, proclaiming that woman's economic dependence on man had led to her degradation in Indian society. In a free country and socialist democracy, every member of the society had to bear equal responsibility; every individual should be "a producer as well as a good citizen." He further asserted, "If you educate the women probably men will also be affected thereby, and in any case children will be affected... it is necessary for women to be educated, if not for themselves, at any rate for their children."[71] With his vision riveted on the future, Nehru's India, in the end, was an industrialized India, and he believed that Indian schools would provide with the personnel to man the industries. He urged, "Now, in India, we are bound to be industrialized, we are to be industrialized, we must be industrialized, for greater wealth and production.[72] Fatherhood for Nehru thus required training children not in handicrafts, but in industry.

As a founding father and the prime minister (1947–64), Nehru was undoubtedly instrumental in the educational policies of newly liberated India. Inspired by the Soviet model, he endorsed scientific and technical learning leading to the establishments of the All India Institute of Medical

---

[68] Michael Brecher, *Nehru: A Political Biography* (Delhi: Oxford University Press, 2005), 130, 176.
[69] Naik, *Educational Planning in India* (Bombay: Allied Publishers, 1965), 13.
[70] J. Nehru, *Hindustan Ki Samasyayen* (Delhi: Sasta Sahitya Mandal), 87. Cited in Singh, *Nehru on Education*, 36.
[71] J. Nehru, *Hindustan Ki Samasyayen* (Delhi: Sasta Sahitya Mandal), 87. Cited in Singh, *Nehru on Education*, 36.
[72] *Nehru's Speeches,* Vol. 1 (New Delhi: Publication Division), 370. Cited in Singh, *Nehru on Education*, 45.

Sciences, the Indian Institutes of Technology, the Indian Institutes of Management, and the National Institutes of Technology—giving India a body of highly skilled professionals and an infrastructure for excellence in science, technology, and industry. He gave India foundations of a strong secular democracy that would maintain equal respect for all religions, a foreign policy of non-alignment and internationalism, and an economic policy of socialist welfare far removed from communism.[73] Still, his rationalistic policies, his lack of connection with religion that he admitted repeatedly in his writing and correspondence, and his immersion in the Western culture and values alienated him from the masses. He was, in this sense, a distant father. Basic education that he championed along with Gandhi, after all, was not implemented and enforced nationwide.

In her comparative assessment of Tagore, Gandhi, and Nehru, Martha Nussbaum argued that Nehru's limited imagination of humanity, his neglect of critical thinking, arts, history, and music that constituted Tagore's "Public poetry" led to his "failure to create a system of public education that would provide robust underpinnings for a democratic political culture."[74] Nussbaum's analysis has its values, but it calls for a more nuanced reading: Nehru was driven by the spirit of his age and the exigency of the political situation as a national leader. He made a deliberate decision to privilege economics over social causes, reason, and science over emotions and public poetry. It is in his commitment to the ideologies of the twentieth century—the belief that science and technology enshrined in the policies of a sovereign nation-state would lead to progress and modernity—overshadowed his commitment to mass education. As he averred in his autobiography, "If there is one thing that history shows it is this: that economic interests shape the political views of groups and classes. Neither reason nor moral considerations override those interests."[75] In his educational scheme for the advancement of a new nation, he chose to favour those on the top of the socio-economic ladder over the ones who crowded the bottom rungs.

---

[73] Shashi Tharoor, *Nehru: A Biography* (New York: Arcade Publishing, 2011).
[74] Martha C. Nussbaum, "Tagore, Gandhi, Nehru," in *The Clash Within* (Cambridge, MA: Harvard University Press, 2007), 80–121, here 119.
[75] Nehru, *Toward Freedom*, 568, cited in Chatterjee, *Nationalist* Thought, 140.

Nehru's contribution as an educator was limited compared to Tagore's and Gandhi's. But his vision for children as free citizens of the modern world was embodied in his writings which attempted to free their minds by providing them with an alternate sense of history and a scientific temper. If his demanding political career and frequent incarceration had hindered his proximity to his own child during her growing years, he wielded considerable influence over her and subsequently over the children of the nation through his writings and institutions, encapsulating his vision of a new India. Not only are his writings still widely read in Indian schools and colleges, no other Indian leader arguably enjoys as much popularity with children as he does (due to the celebration of his birthday as the Children's Day). His hegemonic aspirations as the leader of a new nation were further carried forward by his daughter, who remained by his side through thick and thin and carried the political legacy of the family as the first woman prime minister of India (1968–77; 1980–84). In Nehru's case, everyday practices of fatherhood thus acquired an extra-national dimension through family lineage and succession.

Committed to the public good, Gandhi and Nehru, like other leaders discussed in the book, embodied deep concerns of paternal responsibilities that went beyond providing economic support in the form of food, clothing, and shelter. They were neither trying to make ends meet nor relying on their children's support for the sustenance of their family. As imperial subjects of international stature, they felt a bigger onus of freeing their children's minds and preparing them with skills and knowledge as autonomous, independent citizens of the modern world. Breaking conventions and freeing themselves from dogma, doctrine, and prejudice, Tagore, Gandhi, and Nehru defined and defied prevailing norms of education to train their own children but also to prepare the children of the nation. Their mediation in pedagogical practices betrayed the confluence of their global selves and their local concerns.

Conclusion

This chapter has attempted to demonstrate the symbiotic and an interlocking connection between a rising nationalist offensive and a performative self-fashioning of elite leaders as fathers at home (and in prison) and fathers of the nation. By self-consciously positioning themselves as "fathers as teachers," these men actualized the dream of earlier educators and traversed the domain of the private and the public, moving from guiding their biological children to aspiring to shape future citizens. By self-consciously positioning themselves as "fathers as political mentors," by mobilizing the younger population to engage in the freedom struggle and, in Nehru's case, also viewing private letters as being of public interest, they added another nuance to the manifold identity of the Indian father. If the first generation of Congress leaders had conceived of India as "a bounded and organically constituted national space and economy," as Manu Goswami argued,[76] my research tends to fill out that re-constituted space with an active body of citizenry that the "fathers" envisioned through their revised schemes of education.

An exploration into the familiar and familial biographies of Gandhi and Nehru shines a light on their intimate experiences as fathers and public leaders. Family experiences shaped and mediated their public concerns, particularly in their handling of issues related to education. In everyday practices, they were hands-on fathers—to educate their children they developed a model that was also geared to the larger public. They both firmly believed in the expansion of basic education: Nehru, like Tagore, believed in ideas of progress based on the scientific knowledge that ensured better living conditions. Equating freedom with progress, Tagore emphasized individual self-realization through establishing an organic connection with nature via creative imaginations, arts, and literature. Although Gandhi described his experiments in scientific terms he differed from both Tagore and Nehru in his disapproval of Western science and reason and his critique of modern civilization based on technological advancement. But all three shared the mantle of father to children from across the nation and the world.

Gandhi and Nehru, like Tagore, appropriated and positioned India in distinct ways. But they all emphasized a syncretic Indian civilization and secular (or mostly secular, in the case of Tagore and Gandhi) education, and despite Tagore and Nehru's rejection of Gandhi's stand against science, technology, and reason, they relied on Gandhi at crucial moments

---

[76] Manu Goswami, *Producing India: From Colonial Economy to National Space* (Chicago: University of Chicago Press, 2004), 12.

for fulfilling their mission. Although Gandhi's template for education remained imaginary and utopian, his ideas were most effective in mobilizing children as self-reliant, active agents through his self-supporting programme. Notwithstanding their differences, the three leaders sustained each other.

Parna Sengupta has argued that modern educational techniques and institutions in the colonies actually opened up new ways of articulating Hindu and Muslim identities along religious lines. This and the preceding chapter's study of the three leaders reveals a different direction—to move towards more inclusive and tolerant education by breaking away from the mould of mission schools and madrasas. In achieving this goal each leader's vision and endeavour remained limited and incomplete. I further contend that the breeding ground of Tagore, Gandhi, and Nehru's pedagogy was their own home and started with their biological children before their ideals were shared with the world. Family resources and children provided the fathers with social and human capital. Their everyday performance of fatherhood within the domestic domain straddled with their enunciative efforts envisaging a new model of education outside of the home.

Conceptualization of a new educational curriculum for children gave these leaders both the epistemic and the public space to proclaim their autonomy and sovereignty as both fathers at home and as fathers of the nation. In the life and activities of these individuals we see a culmination of a discourse started in the long nineteenth century—children in their writings were no longer hapless victims and embodiments of aberrations, indicating deficiencies in nineteenth-century Indian culture;[77] rather, they appeared as free citizens of an independent nation trained in a new curriculum modelled by their fathers and not by alien masters. These children were endowed with a promise of hope. The educational programmes—well in tune with the larger movement for a "vernacular modernity"[78] and their relative emphasis on self-help, vocational exercise, spiritual discipline, and higher level of scientific and educational training—were aimed at overcoming a cognitive enslavement. Audacious

---

[77] Ishita Pande, *Medicine, Race, and Empire in British Bengal* (New York: Routledge, 2009).
[78] Sanjay Seth, "Vernacular Modernity," in *Subject Lessons: The Western Education of Colonial India* (Durham: Duke University Press, 2007).

yet restraining, they prepared and welcomed a new body of citizenry able to govern themselves.

These leaders also signalled a change from the iconicity of domineering, sanctimonious paterfamilias like Debendranath Tagore and Motilal Nehru, to more self-confident, engaging fathers as subjects in their own right. Identifying imperialism as the principal enemy, the drafting of alternate educational strategies suggested an overturning of the colonial system and a refusal to be treated like "children" by the colonial state.[79] Their individual imaginings of alternate education, contradicting one another and inconsistent and incomplete by themselves, was contingent on their own positionality in family life and public responsibility. With the archetypal home representing the gendered organization of social relations, elite fathers, as heteronormative subjects, asserted their authority over their family members, especially wives and children, and did not visualize any major reconfiguration of gender roles or household structure. But as "imperial social formations"[80]—the power of "men at home" vied with the power of the colonial state in which children and their education became the principal enabler to establish their sovereign authority as male heads of household and of the larger population. For each of them, like most other nationalists of the time, it was the British education system that was the root cause of India's misery and degradation, deluding its people of its rich heritage and emasculating them in the process. Therefore, by rethinking and redesigning a new roadmap, these leaders threatened the foundation of colonial domination on the one hand, and mobilized its own younger generation, on the other. Fatherhood, both literally and figuratively, with its supporting, nurturing, protective, and didactic responsibilities, empowered Indian men with supreme authority to mobilize children as ubiquitous subalterns, as vehicles of their desires and dreams for a nation in the making.

---

[79] See Ashis Nandy, *Intimate Enemy*.
[80] Mrinalini Sinha, *Colonial Masculinity: The 'Manly Englishman' and the 'Effeminate Bengali' in the Late Nineteenth Century* (Manchester: Manchester University Press, 1995).

Conclusion

The book historicizes two forgotten actors, fathers and children, in the realm of colonial Indian history. Examining different literary genres, it documents the many ways the Indian intelligentsia assumed moral guardianship as "fathers," both biological and imaginary, by harnessing the power of children through alternate pedagogical practices and ideology. The chapters concentrate on the local to understand the ramifications and contestations of global trends in the life-works of Indian men assuming paternalistic positions. These reformers shifted the registers of colonial masculinity by advocating an alternate education that emphasized filial piety and freedom of mind. Departing from colonial policies and institutions, the book focuses on the private-public worlds of the literati inhabiting multiple subject positions as fathers (and sons) by imagining a gendered citizenry and by being, in turn, imagined by their own adult children. The book establishes the connection between the home and the world through a deeply contextualized history of fathers and children.

Legitimizing patriarchal visions and their tentativeness, the harnessing of the power of youth and children through various literary modes demonstrate the complexity and the diverse experiences that went into the making of fatherhood in colonial India. I have historicized fathers and children in the realm of troubled encounters with the colonial state and have attempted to recuperate the subject-position of Bengali educated males as "fathers," both biological and putative, who assumed a moral guardianship of an incipient nation and rested their hopes and despairs on the future generation. My work shifts focus from colonial policies on education, children, and citizenship to reform-minded men who envisioned an alternate pedagogy, mostly in vernacular languages, outside the state domain and beyond the individual home. The book endeavours to shed light on an important aspect of manhood that has remained hidden in the current historical literature. Through an exploration of experiences of fathers and children in the colonial era, I have attempted to tease out the inseparable connection between the home and the world while pointing towards the ways in which fathers' socio-economic positions and the gender of their real and imagined offspring shape the experiences and practices of their fathering.

Current historiography recognizes the significance and plasticity of children as important political subjects who were appropriated and mobilized by the colonial state and the indigenous reformers and nationalists. In British colonial projects, the attempt to educate its Indian subjects underscored the political significance of the child. Undergoing many changes through the nineteenth century, educating children became a major source of anxiety and contention for the colonial government. This project has shown that fathers were equally significant and equally plastic. Educated native men worked first hand in glove with, and then against, the colonial government and were active participants on matters related to children's education. My research underscores the literary and political activism of these educated Indian males and their initiative to disseminate, independent of the colonial government, an alternate education that emphasized devotion to parents and elderly members, filial piety, health, hygiene, art, and self-sufficiency. The new epistemic space, thanks to the vernacular print culture, allowed these men to assert their sovereignty and subjecthood as "fathers" of an imagined community of children who would be the future citizens of the country. Ironically, in the domain of the family, these men were unable to transcend the reigning social customs and family demands. The anomalous behaviour as father, husband, and son that ran contrary to the public image of the leaders attested to the unrestricted patriarchal authority of the head of the household, be it the fathers of the leaders or the leaders themselves. The influential patriarchy professed its desired education to free the minds of its pedagogical subjects on the one hand, but also demanded their obedience to paternal authority, on the other. It was in that tension, in the contradictory pulls between the local and the global, that one could locate their subjectivity.

I examined different genres of literature to identify the many ways these fathers imagined the shifting and gendered category of the child as future citizen-subject, if male, and a good wife and mother, if female. The genre-based analysis allowed me to track how fathers were "imagined" in auto/biographical literature where adult authors reflect on their childhood interaction with fathers. While there is no absolute way to determine "what really happened" or what went through the minds of these writers, my study emphasized the imaginary constitution of the father and the child that approximated reality. Following Charles Taylor, I invoked the term "social imaginary" to explain how ordinary people imagined their familial lives and ethnic community through pedagogical literature, normative texts, scientific journals, letters, and personal narratives. The imaginaries envisaged prevalent norms and practices in filial relationships among the literate segment of the Bengali population and conveyed a sense of shared understanding and legitimacy. My research demonstrates that parallel to motherhood and mother-craft, fatherhood, too, became an important domain of reflection for Bengali men. As the examples of Gandhi and Nehru suggest, fatherhood was of equal significance in other regions of India. Furthermore, I argue that it was inextricably connected to their masculine identity. The authorial voice of male writers in different kinds of sources—political essays, normative texts, health and medical journals, women's magazines, biographies, autobiographies, letters, stories, and poems—attest not only to their polyvocality, doubts, and conflicts but also an articulation of male identity as moral guardians of a new society, signalling hegemonic possibilities.

The writings and experiences of Bengali males that are presented here are testimonies of their dividual selves—their individual identities and interests were tied to family, community, the nation, and sometimes the larger public. The fathers as moral guardians asserted a subject position trying to break out of the mold into which they were cast by the colonial government. They also asserted their individual preferences and choices going against the will of their fathers and guardians. From their position as subjugated subjects in the public realm, they made interventions in various literary genres in vernacular languages that interrupted the dominant narrative by imagining an implicit community of children and proposing for them an education of their desire: the young generation, a fleeting and gendered category, would be trained in Western sciences, reason, and new sensibilities but they would not challenge family and patriarchal hierarchies or undermine cultural expectations. The Indian fathers, even when sovereign and independent, abided by the authority of their own fathers and forefathers, and they tempered their sense of justice with devotion and obedience to authority, family lineage, and often religion. Nonetheless, in the assertion of their individual identity and subjecthood, in their endorsement of restricted freedom of male children, in the gendered education of girls as ideal mothers and wives, the stamp of European and Victorian influence was evident. Modern humanism constructed by the fathers to shape the mind and body of children were patriarchal and "non-liberal" if judged by paradigms of the contemporary West. In understanding these fathers, who envisioned a new body of citizenry and paved the foundation of education for posterity, we thus need to recognize the historical difference in contexts where reason and conscience coexisted with patriarchal values and allegiance to familial authority.[1]

The book highlights the enabling dynamics of children that allowed educated men not only to assert their patriarchal authorities but also forge their identities through an articulation of a different modernity based on new pedagogical and cultural practices. Focusing on new educational models offered by later leaders like Tagore, Gandhi, and Nehru, this study makes a vital point that these men had completely dismissed the earlier colonial critique of Indian men by shifting the register of masculinity. In designing a new curriculum of education that transcended religious and caste-class boundaries, the trio did not just react to the colonial regime but had actually responded to the exigencies of their personal life. Anxious to provide the best education for their children, each leader was compelled to conceptualize a new model of pedagogy. Yet, as apparent from their records and legacy, in implementing their scheme for education and making it a possibility for future generations, the fathers did not succeed. Their biggest shortcoming lay in accommodating differences based on caste, class, gender, religion, and ethnicity. Neither the fathers nor the colonial state succeeded in nurturing the idea of independent or

---

[1] Dipesh Chakrabarty, *Provincializing Europe* (Princeton: Princeton University Press, 2000).

universal children, a point that other scholars raised in the context of the postcolonial Indian state, as well.[2]

This book is not a comprehensive account of all fathers and children (or even all Bengali fathers and children) in the past two centuries; neither is it a story of "perfect" or "successful" fathers—as borne out by the conflictual intergenerational relationships. Rather, it selectively engages with seminal representatives who were major interlocutors from the intermediary position of the educated middle-class community (*shikshito bhadralok sampraday*) with its hegemonic aspirations to give leadership to the future nation. By taking on the question of fathers and children, it unravels the entanglements of the private-public worlds of the intelligentsia, an aspect of social history that has not received adequate attention. I have infused the public career of prominent male figures of the nineteenth and the early twentieth century with their private lives, thus delineating not only their contradictions, ambivalence, and ambiguities but also capturing their power or the lack thereof within the home and outside. Recognizing the implication of personal lives in the larger sociocultural currents of a colonial political economy, I have treated household and family life not in isolation but as an integral part of colonial and nationalist history.

At the heart of my argument resides the question of spatiality as a continuum that extends from the so-called private to the public, from the domestic realm of the family to the domain of public culture that included education and social reforms. In the continuing swathe of the home and the world, I have projected the agency of male actors as fathers at home and as fathers of the nation and beyond (as it was the case with Tagore). By focusing on groups of men from elite and not-so-elite backgrounds, I reclaimed the agentiality of these men and their many layers of masculinity that were embedded in a complex network of hierarchy and power. By emphasizing the ordinariness and everyday practices in family life with their inextricable connection with an embattled nation engaged in a struggle with the colonial state, I demonstrated that fathers were a crucial presence in the colonial-era motherland.

[2] Nita Kumar, *Lessons from School: The Theories of Education in Benares* (Delhi: Sage Publications, 1999); *The Politics of Gender, Community, and Modernity: Essays on Education in India* (Delhi: Oxford University Press, 2011); Sarada Balagoplan, *Inhabiting Childhood: Children, Labor, and Schooling in Postcolonial India* (New York: Palgrave Macmillan, 2014).

Selected Bibliography

Primary Sources in Bengali and Sanskrit

"Adarsha Janani [Ideal Mother]," *Bamabodhini Patrika* (n.d.).
"Ahaar-er Poriman [Diet Portions]," *Swasthya* (Jaishtha, 1307 B.S. [1900]).
Atorthi, Premankur. *Mahasthabir Jatak*, vol. 3. Kolkata: De's Publishing, 1964.
Atorthi, Premankur. "Satyabadi" [One Who Always Says Truth], *Mouchak* 15, no. 5 (Jyaistha, 1331 B.S. [1924]), 66–72.
Bandyopadhyay, Bhabanicharan. *Kalikata Kamalalaya*. Kolkata: Nabapatra Prakashan, 1987 [1825].
Basu, Bani, ed. *Bangla Shishusahitya: Granthapanji*. Kolkata: Bangiya Granthagar Parishad, 1965.
Basu, Buddhadeb. "Bangla Shishu-sahitya," in *Prabandha Sankalan*. Kolkata: De's Publishing, 1952.
Basu, Pradipa, ed. *Samayiki: Purono Samayikpatre-r Probondhoa Sankalan*, vol. 1, *Bijnan o Samaj, 1850–1901*. Kolkata: Ananda Publishers, 1998.
Chattopadhyay, Aruna, ed. *Sakha, Sakha o Sathi*. Kolkata, 2002.
Datta, Akshay. *Charupath*. Kolkata, 1852.
Devi, Indira. *Smriti-Samput*, vol. 1. Santiniketan: Visvabharati, 1997 [1953].
Devi, Kanan. *Sabare Ami Nomi*. 1st ed. Kolkata: M.C. Sarkar and Sons, 1974.
Devi, Maitreyi. *Na Hanyate*. Kolkata: Manisha Granthalaya, 1974.
Devi, Mira. *Smritikatha*. Calcutta: Visvabharati, 1975.
Devi, Santa. *Purvasmriti*. Kolkata: Thema, 2006.
Devi, Santa. *Bharat Muktisadhak Ramananda o Ordho Satabdir Bangla*. Kolkata: De's Publishers, 2005 [originally published by Prabasi Press, 1950].
Devi, Saudamini. *Pitrismriti o Anyanya Rachana*. Ed. Sutapa Bhattacharya. Kolkata: De's Publishers, 2010.
Devi, Swarnakumari. "Shekélé Kawtha," in *Shekélé Kawtha: Shatak Shuchona-i Meyeder Smritikawtha*, eds. Abhijit Sen and Abhijit Bhattacharya. Kolkata: Noya Udyog, 1997.
Ghosh, Jagadishchandra, ed. *Chanakya-Sloka*. 11th ed. Kolkata: Presidency Library, 2009.
"Jatiya Daihik Punurujjiban [Regeneration of National Health]," in *Chikitsha Sammilani* (Baishakh, 1292 B.S. [April, 1885]), reprinted in Bose, *Health and Society in Bengal*, 135–141.
Kaviraj, Pyarimohan Sengupta. "Hastamaithun-e Balak o Naba Jubakgan," in *Chikitsha Sammilani* (1229 B.S. [1887]), reprinted in Basu, *Samayiki*, 227–229.
Majumdar, Leela. *Pakdandi*. Kolkata: Ananda Publishers, 1986.
Mitra, Khagendranath. *Shatabdir Shishu-sahitya*. Calcutta, 1958.

Pal, Bipin Chandra. "Surendra-Babu-r Karabash," *Sakha* (6th issue), in Khagendranath Mitra, *Shatabdir Shishu-sahitya*, 21.

"Pathshal-r Chhele-der Ahaar [School Boys' Diet]," *Swasthya* (Karttick, 1307 B.S. [1900]), reprinted in Basu, *Samayiki*, 158–161.

"Pathyaboshthar Khadya [Diet for Students]," *Swsasthya* (Agrahayan, 1307 B.S. [1900]), reprinted in Basu, *Samayiki*, 161–162.

Ray, Bharati, Collected and Edited. *Nari o Poribar: Bamabodhini Patrika (1270–1329 Bangabda)*. Kolkata: Pustak Bipani, 1999.

Sastri, Sibnath. *Grihadharma*. Calcutta, 1963.

Sastri, Sibnath. *Ramtanu Lahiri o Tatkalin Bangla Samaj*. Calcutta, 1957 [1907].

Sastri, Sibnath. *Dharmajivan*, vol. 3. Calcutta, 1933.

Sastri, Sibnath. *Atmacharit*. Calcutta, 1918.

Sen, Promodacharan. "Bhim-er Kapal. *Sakha* year #1" (January 1883–October 1883), in Aruna Chattopadhyay, *Sakha, Sakha o Sathi*, 19–44.

"Shaishab o Koumar Obostha-y Sharirik Bidhan o Kriya-r Bisheshattva," in *Vishak-Darpan, A Monthly Magazine of Medicine in Bengali*, ed. Maulavi Ahiruddin Ahmed and Debendranath Ray, vol. 6 (July 1896–June 1897): 230–241.

Sinha, Kaliprasanna. *Hutom Penchar Naksha*. Calcutta, 1862.

Sukthankar, Vishnu S., ed. *The Mahabharata*, vol. 1. Poona: Bhandarkar Oriental Research Institute, 1933.

Tagore (Thakura), Abanindranath and Chanda Rani. *Gharoa*. Kolkata: Visvabharati Granthanbibhag, 1941.

Tagore (Thakura), Debendranath. *Brahma Dharma*. Kolkata: Brahmo Samaj, 1848.

Tagore (Thakura), Rabindranath. "Bhashabichhed," in *Rabindra-Rachanabali*, vol. 6. Kolkata: Visvabharati, 1997 [1898], 739–742.

Tagore (Thakura), Rabindranath. "Vidyasagarcharit," in *Rabindra-Rachanabali*, vol. 2. Kolkata: Visvabharati, 1997 [1895].

Tagore (Thakura), Rabindranath. "Dena Paona," in *Galpaguchha* [Profit and Loss, 1891], translated by William Radice, *Selected Short Stories*, 48–54. Kolkata: Penguin, 1991.

Tagore (Thakura), Rabindranath. *Rabindra-Rachanabali* [Collected Works]. 16 vols. Kolkata:, 1991 (new release).

Tagore (Thakura), Rabindranath. "Shikshar Herpher," *Shiksha*. Kolkata: Visvabharati Granthan Bibhag, 1990 [1892].

Tagore (Thakura), Rabindranath. "Shiksha Samasya [Problem with Education," *Shiksha*. Kolkata: Visva-Bharati, 1990 [1906]): 38–55.

Tagore (Thakura), Rabindranath. "Ashramer Shiksha," in *Rabindra-Rachanabali*, vol. 14. Kolkata: Visva-Bharati, 1989 [1936].

Tagore (Thakura), Rabindranath. "Ashram-er Rup o Bikash," in *Rabindra-Rachanabali*, vol. 14. Kolkata: Visva-Bharati, 1989 [1941].

Tagore (Thakura), Rabindranath. *Chitthi Patra*, vol. 1. Kolkata: Visvabharati, 1966.

Tagore (Thakura), Rabindranath. *Chithi Patra*. Calcutta: Visva-Bharati Granthan Bibhag, 1942 [1901].

Tagore (Thakura), Rabindranath. *Russiar-r Chithi*. Kolkata: Visvabharati Granthagar, 1930.

Tagore (Thakura), Rabindranath. "Puja-r Shaaj," in *Shishu*, 145–148. Kolkata: Visvabharti, 1901

Vidyasagar, Iswarchandra. "Balyabibaher Dosh" [Evils of Child Marriage, 1850], in *Vidyasagar Rachanabali*, vol. 1, ed. T. Datta. Kolkata: Tuli Kalam, 2001.
Vidyasagar, Iswarchandra. *Varnaparichay*, part 1 and 2 in *Vidyasagar Rachanabali*, vol. 1, ed. T. Datta, 1259–1260. Calcutta, 2001.
Vidyasagar, Iswarchandra. *Vidyasagar Rachanabali*, ed. Tirthapati Datta, vol. 2. Kolkata: Tuli-kalam, 2001 [1262 B.S.].
Vidyasagar, Iswarchandra. "Vidyasagar Charit," in *Vidyasagar Rachanabali*, vol. 1. Kolkata: Tuli-Kalam, 1997.
Vidyasagar, Iswarchandra. "Bohubibaha Rohit Hoya Uchit Kina Etodbishoyok Prostab" [Proposal on Whether It Is Justified to Ban Polygamy, 1828], in *Vidyasagar Rachanabali*, vol. 2, ed. Tirthapati Datta, 840–916. Calcutta: Tuli Kalam, 1994.

Journals and Magazines

Abodhbandhu (1866).
Balak (1885).
Balakbandhu (1878).
BibhidharthaSangraha (1851–61).
Chikitsha Sammilani (1884–94).
Digdarshan (1818).
Gnanodoy.
Mouchak (1920).
Mukul (1875–90).
Onubeekshan (1875).
Pashwabali (1822).
Sakha o Sathi (1883–84).
Sandesh (1913–34).
Shishu-Bandhav (1889).
Swasthya (1897–1902).
Tattvabodhini Patrika (1843–1932).

Primary Sources in English

Adam, William. *Adam's Reports on Vernacular Education in Bengal and Behar with a Brief View of Its Past and Present Condition*. Calcutta: Home Secretariat Press, 1868.
Bhattacharya, Sabyasachi, comp., ed., and introduction. *The Mahatma and the Poet: Letters and Debates between Gandhi and Tagore, 1915–1941*. Delhi: National Book Trust, 1997.
Bose, Rajendralal. *A Scheme for the Rendering of European Scientific Texts in India*.
Chanda, Monika. *Days with Dinko and Other Memories*. Ed. Malavika Karlekar. New Delhi: Archana Press, 2018.
Das Gupta, Uma, ed. *Rabindranath Tagore: My Life in My Words*. New Delhi: Viking, 2006.
Devee [Devi], Sunity. *The Autobiography of an Indian Princess*. London: J. Murray, 1921.

SELECTED BIBLIOGRAPHY

Devi, Maitreyi. *It Does Not Die: A Romance*. Chicago: University of Chicago Press, 1994.

Doniger, Wendy, with Brian K. Smith, trans. *The Laws of Manu*. Delhi: Penguin Books, 1991.

Duncan, Ronald, ed. *Gandhi: Selected Writings*. New York: Dover Publications, 2005.

Dutt, Manmatha Nath, ed. and publisher. *A Prose English Translation of the Mahaharata* (translated literally from the original Sanskrit text). Calcutta: H.C. Dass, Elysium Press, 1895. https://books.google.com/books?id=Wy0MAAAAIA AJandpg=PA449#v=onepageandqandf=false (accessed June 18, 2016).

Dutta, Krishna and Andrew Robinson, eds. *Selected Letters of Rabindranath Tagore*. Cambridge: Cambridge University Press, 1997

Dutta, Krishna and Andrew Robinson. *Rabindranath Tagore: The Myriad-Minded Man*. London: Bloomsbury, 1995.

Gandhi, M.K. *Autobiography: The Story of My Experiments with Truth*. Washington D.C.: Public Affairs Press, 1948

Gandhi, M.K. *Harijan*. July 31, 1937.

Gandhi, Sonia, ed. *Two Alone, Two Together: Letters Between Indira Gandhi and Jawaharlal Nehru, 1922-1964*. Delhi: Penguin Books, 2005.

Gandhi, Sonia, ed. *Freedom's Daughter: Letters between Indira Gandhi and Jawaharlal Nehru, 1922-1939*. London: Hodder and Stoughton, 1989.

Locke, John. *Thoughts Concerning Human Education*. 1692.

Long, James. *Descriptive Catalogue of Bengali Works*. 1855.

Macaulay, Thomas Babington. "Minute of Education," in Kumar, *Science and the Raj*, 49.

Mahmood, Syed. *History of English Education in India, 1781-1893*. Aligarh: M.A.O. College, 1895.

Mazumdar, Sudha. *Memoirs of an Indian Woman*. Ed. with an Introduction by Geraldine Forbes. New York: M.E. Sharpe, 1989.

Nehru, Jawaharlal. *Glimpses of World History* (originally published in 2 volumes). 13th impression. Delhi: Oxford University Press, 1998 [Kitabistan, Allahabad, 1934-1935].

Nehru, Jawaharlal. *Nehru's Speeches*, vol. 1. New Delhi: Publication Division, 1983.

Nehru, Jawaharlal. *Letters from a Father to a Daughter*. Delhi: Penguin Books, 1973 [originally published by Allahabad Law Journal Press, 1929].

Nehru, Jawaharlal. *Discovery of India*. New York: Anchor Books, 1960 [1946].

Nehru, Jawaharlal. *Toward Freedom: The Autobiography of Jawaharlal Nehru*. New York: The John Day Company, 1941 [1936].

Pal, Bipin Chandra. *Memories of My Life and Times*. New Delhi: UBS Publishers' Distributors, 2004 [1932].

Rousseau, Jean-Jacques. *Emile, or On Education*. 1762.

Sastri, Sivnath. *Atmacharit*. Kolkata: Signet Press, 1952.

Sastri, Sivnath. *Ramtanu Lahiri, Brahman and Reformer; a History of the Renaissance in Bengal*. Ed. and trans. Sir Roper Lethbridge. 1907.

Sen, Haimabati. *"Because I am a woman": A Child Widow's Memoirs from India*. Trans. Tapan Raychaudhuri, ed. Geraldine Forbes and Tapan Raychaudhuri. New Delhi: Chronicle Books, 2011.

Tagore, Debendranath. *The Auto-Biography of Maharshi Devendranath Tagore*. Trans. Satyendranath Tagore and Indira Devi. Calcutta: S.C. Sarkar and Sons, 1994 [1914].

Tagore, Rabindranath. "My Childhood," in *Oxford Tagore Translations: Selected Writings for Children*, ed. Sukanta Chaudhury, 205–209. Delhi: Oxford University Press, 2010.

Tagore, Rabindranath. *Boyhood Days*. Trans. Radha Chakrabarty. London: Hesperus Worldwide, 2007 [1940].

Tagore, Rabindranath. *My Reminiscences*. Gutenberg E-Book, 2007 [1917] http://www.gutenberg.org/files/22217/22217-h/22217-h.htm#Page_30 (accessed on 20 March 2016).

Tagore, Rabindranath. "Talks in China," in *Rabindranath Tagore: My Life in My Words*, ed. Uma Das Gupta New Delhi: Viking, 2006 [1925].

Tagore, Rabindranath. "My Ideals with Regard to the Sreebhavana [1934]," in *The English Writings of Rabindranath Tagore*, vol. 3, ed. Sisir Kumar Das. New Delhi: Sahitya Akademi, 1996.

Tagore, Rabindranath. Letters from Russia, translated from Bengali by Sasadhar Sinha. Calcutta, 1960 [1930–1931].

Tagore, Rabindranath. "My School," Lecture delivered in America in 1916; published in *Personality*. London: Macmillan, 1933.

Tagore, Rabindranath. "An Eastern University," in *Creative Unity*. London: Macmillan, 1922.

Tagore, Rabindranath. *Gitanjali* (English Translation). London: Macmillan, 1912.

Tagore, Rathindranath. *On the Edges of Time*. Calcutta: Visva-Bharati, 1958.

Secondary Sources

Adhikary, Sayantani. "The Bratachari Movement and the Invention of a 'Folk-Tradition,'" *South Asia: A Journal of South Asian Studies* 38, no. 4 (2015): 656–670.

Ananthalakshmy, S. and M. Bajaj. "Childhood in Weavers Community in Varanasi," in *Socialization of the Indian Child*, ed. D. Sinha. New Delhi: Concept, 1981.

Agamben, Giorgio. *Remnants of Auschwitz*, translated by Daniel Heller-Roazen. New York: Zone Books, 1999.

Agarwal, Bina. *Gender and Legal Rights in Landed Property in India*. Delhi: Kali for Women, 1999.

Agarwal, Bina. *A Field of One's Own: Gender and Land Rights in South Asia*. Cambridge: Cambridge University Press, 1994.

Agnes, Flavia. "Women, Marriage and Subordination of Rights," in *Subaltern Studies XI Community, Gender, and Violence*, eds. Partha Chatterjee and Pradeep Jaganathan. Delhi: Permanent Black, 2000.

Agnes, Flavia. *Law and Gender Inequality: The Politics of Women's Rights in India*. Delhi: Oxford University Press, 1999.

Agnes, Flavia. "Economic Rights of Women under Muslim Personal Law," *Economic and Political Weekly* 31, no. 2832 (October 1996).

Alter, Joseph. *Moral Materialism: Sex and Masculinity in Modern India*. Delhi: Penguin Books, 2011.

SELECTED BIBLIOGRAPHY

Alter, Joseph. "Celibacy, Sexuality, and the Transformation of Gender into Nationalism in North India," *Journal of Asian Studies* 53 (1994): 45–63.

Alexander, Kristine. "Can the Girl Guide Speak? The Perils and Pleasures of Looking for Children's Voices in Archival Research," *Jeunesse Young People, Texts, Cultures* 4, no. 1 (2012).

Alexander, Kristine and Stephanie Olsen. "Emotions and Global Politics of Childhood," in *Childhood, Youth and Emotions in Modern History: National, Colonial, and Global Perspectives*, ed. Stephanie Olsen. London: Palgrave Macmillan, 2015.

Alexander, Emma. "The 'Special Classes' of Labour: Women and Children Doubly Marginalized," in *Labour Matters:Towards Global Histories*, eds. Micahel van der Linden and Prabhu Mahapatra. New Delhi, 2009.

Alexander, Emma. "Child-Labor in the Bombay Presidency, 1850–1920," Ph.D. dissertation, University of Cambridge, UK, 2002.

Allender, Tim. *Learning Femininity in Colonial India*. Manchester: University of Manchester Press, 2016.

Allender, Tim. *Ruling Through Education: The Politics of Schooling in Colonial Punjab*. Elgin, IL: The New Dawn Press, 2006.

Amin, Sonia Nishat. *The World of Muslim Women in Colonial Bengal, 1876–1939*. Leiden: Brill, 1996.

Anagol, Padma. *The Emergence of Feminism in India, 1850–1920*. London: Ashgate Publishing, 2015.

Anderson, Benedict. *Imagined Communities*. London: Verso, 1991.

Appadurai, Arjun. *Modernity at Large*. Minneapolis: University of Minnesota Press, 1998.

Ariès, Phillippe. *Centuries of Childhood: A Social History of Family Life*. New York: Vintage, 1965 [1960].

Armstrong, Nancy. *Desire and Domestic Fiction: A Political History of the Novel*. London: Oxford University Press, 1987.

Arnold, David. *Science, Technology and the Raj, The New Cambridge History of India*, vol. 3, part 5. Cambridge: Cambridge University Press, 2000.

Arnold, David. *Colonizing the Body: State, Medicine, and Epidemic Disease in Nineteenth-Century India*. Berkeley: University of California Press, 1993.

Arnold, David and Stuart Blackburn. *Telling Lives in India: Biography, Autobiography and Life History*. Bloomington: Indiana University Press, 2004.

Arunima, G. *There Comes Papa: Colonialism and the Transformation of Matriliny in Kerala, Malabar, c. 1850–1940*. Hyderabad: Orient Longman, 2003.

Ashar, Meera. " ... And What Can We Learn from That: Learning and Instruction in Gujarati Folk Stories," *South Asia History and Culture* (forthcoming).

Bagchi, Barnita. "Cheery Children, Growing Girls, and Developing Young Adults: On Reading, Growing, and Hopscotching Across Categories," Working Papers id:1993, eSocialSciences (https://ideas.repec.org/p/ess/wpaper/id1993.html (accessed on December 3, 2019) .

Bagchi, Jasodhara. ."Socializing the Girl Child in Colonial Bengal," *Economic and Political Weekly*, 28, no. 41 (October 9, 1993): 2214–2219.

Bagchi, Jasodhara, Jaba Guha, and Piyali Sengupta. *Loved and Unloved: The Girl Child in the Family*. Kolkata: Stree, 1997.

Bajpai, Asha. *Child Rights in India: Law, Policy, and Practice*. Delhi: Oxford University Press, 2006. 2nd ed.
Balagopalan, Sarada. "Childhood, Culture, History: Redeploying 'Multiple Childhood,'" in *Reimagining Childhood Studies*, eds. Spyros Spyrou, Rachel Rosen, and Daniel Thomas Cook, 23–40. London: Bloomsbury, 2019.
Balagopalan, Sarada. *Inhabiting "Childhood": Children, Labour and Schooling in Postcolonial India*. New York: Palgrave Macmillan, 2014.
Balagopalan, Sarada. "An Ideal School and the Schooled Ideal: Educational Experiences at the Margins," in *Educational Regimes in Contemporary India*, eds. P. Jeffrey, et al. New Delhi: Sage Publications, 2005.
Ballantyne, Tony and Antoinette Burton, eds. *Bodies in Contact: Rethinking Colonial Encounters in World History*. Durham, NC: Duke University Press, 2005.
Bandyopadhyay, Aparna. *Desire and Defiance: A Study of Bengali Women in Love, 1850–1930*. Hyderabad: Orient Blackswan, 2016.
Bandyopadhyay, Aparna. "Towards a History of Women in Love in Colonial Bengal," Paper presented at the International Conference on *Shifting Contours, Widening Concerns: Women's History, Historiography and the Politics of Historical Representation*, held at Research Centre for Women's Studies, SNDT Women's University, Mumbai, 11–13 February 2015.
Bandyopadhyay, Sekhar. "Texts of Liminality: Reading Identity in Dalit Autobiographies from Bengal," in *Memory, Identity and the Colonial Encounter in India: Essays in Honor of Peter Robb*, ed. Ezra Rashkow, Sanjukta Ghosh, and Upal Chakrabarti. London and New York: Routledge, 2018.
Bandyopadhyay, Sekhar. "Popular Religion and Social Mobility in Colonial Bengal: The Matua Sect and the Namasudras," in *Readings on Dalit Identity*, ed. S. Basu, 306–334. New Delhi: Orient Black Swan, 2016.
Bandyopadhyay, Sekhar. "Rabindranath Tagore, Indian Nation and Its Outcasts," *Harvard Asia Quarterly*, 15, no. 1 (Spring 2013): 28–33.
Bandyopadhyay, Sekhar. *Caste, Protest, and Identity in Colonial India: the Namasudras of Bengal, 1872–1047*. 2nd enl. ed. Delhi: Oxford University Press, 2011.
Bandyopadhyay, Sekhar. *Caste, Culture and Hegemony: Social Dominance in Colonial Bengal*. Delhi: Sage Publications, 2004.
Bandyopadhyay, Sekhar. *From Plassey to Partition: A History of Modern India*. Hyderabad: Orient BlackSwan, 2004.
Bandyopadhyay, Sibaji. *Abar Shishu-Sikkha*. Kolkata, 2010.
Bandyopadhyay, Sibaji. *Bangla Shishu Sahityer Chhoto Meyera*. Kolkata, 2008.
Bandyopadhyay, Sibaji. *Gopal-Rakhal Dwandwa Samas*. Calcutta: Papyrus, 1991.
Bandyopadhyay, Sibaji. "Shiksha o Adhunikata-r Pawth," in *Gopal-Rakhal Dwandwa Samas*, 78–191. Calcutta: Papyrus, 1991.
Banerjee, Prathama. "Chanakya/Kautilya: History, Philosophy, Theater and the Twentieth-Century Political," *History of the Present* 2, no. 1 (Spring 2012): 24–51.
Banerjee, Sikata. *Make Me a Man: Masculinity, Hinduism, and Nationalism in India*. Albany: State University of New York Press, 2005.
Banerjee, Sumanta. "Marginalization of Women's Popular Culture in Nineteenth-Century Bengal," in *Recasting Women: Essays in Colonial History*, eds. Kumkum Sangari and Sudesh Vaid. New Delhi: Kali for Women, 2006 [1989].
Banerjee, Sumanta. *The Parlour and the Street*. Calcutta: Seagull, 1989.

Banerjee, Swapna. "Children's Literature in Nineteenth-Century India: Some Reflections and Thought," in *Stories for Children, Histories of Childhood / Histoires d'enfant, histoires d'enfance*, vol. 2, *GRAAT Journal* 36, eds. Rosie Findlay and Sébastien Salbayre, 337–351. Tours: Presses universitaires François-Rabelais, 2017; now in open access at http://books.openedition.org/pufr/4974?lang=en.

Banerjee, Swapna. "Through the Ages of Life: Rabindranath Tagore—the Son, Father, and Educator (1861–1941)." Also in French, "À travers les âges de la vie : Rabindranath Tagore – fils, père et éducateur (1861–1941)," *Enfances Familles Générations* 27 (2017) (Open Edition) https://journals.openedition.org/efg/1508.

Banerjee, Swapna. "Emergent Youth Culture in Nineteenth-Century India: A View from Colonial Bengal," in *Lost Histories of Youth Culture*, ed. Christine Feldman, 239–255. New York: Peter Lang, 2015.

Banerjee, Swapna. "Everyday Emotional Practices of Fathers and Children in Late Colonial Bengal, India," in *Childhood, Youth and Emotions in Modern History*, eds. Stephanie Olsen, et al., 221–241. London: Palgrave Macmillan, 2015.

Banerjee, Swapna. "Baby Halder's *A Life Less Ordinary*—A Transition from India's Colonial Past?," in *Colonization and Domestic Service*, eds. Victoria Haskins and Claire Lowrie, 239–255. New York: Routledge, 2014.

Banerjee, Swapna. "Debates on Domesticity and Position of Women in Late Colonial India," *History Compass Journal* [Blackwell Publishing, Oxford, UK] 8, no. 6 (2010): 455–473.

Banerjee, Swapna. *Men, Women, and Domestics: Articulating Middle-Class Identity in Colonial Bengal*. Delhi: Oxford University Press, 2004.

Banerjee-Dube, Ishita. *A History of Modern India*. New York: Cambridge University Press, 2014.

Bannerji, Himani. *Inventing Subjects: Studies in Hegemony, Patriarchy and Colonialism*. London: Anthem Press, 2001.

Basak, N.L. "Origin and the Role of the Calcutta School Book Society in Promoting the Cause of Education in India," *Bengal Past and Present* 78 (January–June 1959).

Basu, Srimati. *Trouble with Marriage*. Berkeley: University of California Press, 2015.

Basu, Srimati. *She Comes to Take Her Rights: Indian Women, Property, and Propriety*. Albany: State University of New York Press, 1999.

Basu, Subho, and Banerjee, Sikata. "The Quest for Manhood: Masculine Hinduism and Nation in Bengal," *Comparative Studies of South Asia, Africa and Middle East* 26, no. 3 (2006): 476–490.

Berger, Rachel. *Ayurveda Made Modern: Political Histories of Indigenous Medicine in North India, 1900–1955*. London: Palgrave Macmillan, 2013.

Berger, Stefan and Bill Niven, eds. *Writing the History of Memory*. London: Bloomsbury Press, 2014.

Bhaba, Homi K. *Location of Culture*. New York: Routledge, 1994.

Bhadra, Gautam. "Bangali-r Boi Pora," in *Nyara Bat talai Jaye Kabar?* Kolkata: Chhatim Books, 2011.

Bhadra, Gautam. "The Mentality of Subalternity: Kantanama or Rajdharma," in *Subaltern Studies Reader, 1986–1995*, ed. Ranajit Guha, 63–99. Minneapolis: University of Minnesota Press, 1997.

Bhagavan, Manu. *India and the Quest for One World: The Peacemakers*. New York: Palgrave Macmillan, 2013.

Bhattacharji, Sukumari. "Economic Rights of Ancient Indian Women," in *Women and Society in Ancient India*, 42–61. Calcutta: Basumati Corporation Ltd., 1994.

Bhattacharya, Kumkum. *Rabindranath Tagore: Adventure of Ideas and Innovative Practices in Education*. London: Springer Publications, 2014.

Bhattacharya, Rimli. *My Story and My Life as An Actress*. New Delhi: Kali for Women, 1998.

Bhattacharya, Sabyasachi and Mukhopadhyay, Ashoke, eds. *The Common Pursuit: Convocation Addresses at Visva-Bharati, Santiniketan, 1952–1993*. Kolkata: Visva-Bharati, 1995.

Bhattacharya, Tithi. *The Sentinels of Culture: Class, Education, and the Colonial Intellectuals of Bengal* (1848–85). New Delhi: Oxford University Press, 2005.

Bilgrami, Akeel. *Secularism, Identity, and Enchantment*. Cambridge, MA: Harvard University Press, 2014.

Blackburn, Stuart and Vasudha Dalmia. *India's Literary History: Essays on the Nineteenth Century*. New Delhi: Permanent Black, 2004.

Bloch, Emily K. "Making Sense of Nonsense: A Contextual Study of the Art of Sukumar Ray," Ph.D. dissertation, University of Chicago, 2013.

Bloch, Emily K. "Questions of Identity in the Nonsense Literature of Sukumar Ray," in *Identities: Local and Global*, eds. Kailash C. Baral and Prafulla C. Kar. Delhi: Pencraft International, 2003.

Boddice, Rob. "The Affective Turn: Historicizing the Emotions," in *Psychology and History: Interdisciplinary Explorations*, eds. Cristian Tileagă and Jovan Byford, 147–165. Cambridge: Cambridge University Press, 2014.

Borthwick, Meredith. *Changing Roles of Women in Bengal (1849–1905)*. Princeton, NJ: Princeton University Press, 1984.

Borthwick, Meredith. *Keshub Chunder Sen: A Search for Cultural Synthesis*. Kolkata: Minerva Publishers, 1977.

Botre, Srikant and Douglas Haynes. "Sexual Knowledge, Sexual Anxieties: Middle-class Males in Western India and the Correspondence in Samaj Swasthya, 1927–53," *Modern Asian Studies* 51, no. 4 (2017): 1–44.

Bose, Pradip. *Health and Society in Bengal: A Selection from Late 19th-Century Bengali Periodicals*. New Delhi: SAGE, 2006.

Bose, Pradip. "Sons of the Nation: Child Rearing in the New Family," in *Texts of Power*, ed. Partha Chatterjee, 118–144. Minneapolis: University of Minnesota Press, 1995.

Bose, Sugata. *The Nation as Mother and Other Visions of Nationhood*. New Delhi: Penguin Random House Publishing, 2017.

Bose, Sugata and Ayesha Jalal. *Modern South Asia: History, Culture, Political Economy*. 3rd ed. London/New York: Routledge, 2011.

Bose, Sugata and Ayesha Jalal, eds. *Nationalism, Democracy, and Development: State and Politics in India*. Delhi: Oxford University Press, 1997.

Bowen, Zazie and Hinchy, Jessica. "Introduction: Children and Knowledge in India," *South Asian History and Culture* 6, no. 3 (July 2015): 317–319.

Brecher, Michael. *Nehru: A Political Biography*. Delhi: Oxford University Press, 2005.

Broughton, Trev Lynn, and Helen Rogers. *Gender and Fatherhood in the Nineteenth Century*. London: Palgrave Macmillan, 2007.

Buettner, Elizabeth. "Fatherhood Real, Imagined, Denied: British Men in Imperial India," in *Gender and Fatherhood in the Nineteenth Century*, eds. Trev Lynn Broughton and Helen Rogers, 178–189. London: Palgrave Macmillan, 2007.

Buettner, Elizabeth. *Empire Families: Britons and Late Imperial India*. Oxford: Oxford University Press, 2004.

Burton, Antoinette. *Dwelling in the Archive: Women Writing House, Home, and History in Late Colonial India*. New York: Oxford University Press, 2003.

Calhoun, Craig. "Nation and Imagination: How Benedict Anderson Revolutionized Political Theory," *ABC Religion and Ethics* (9 May 2017), http://www.abc.net.au/religion/articles/2017/05/09/4665722.htm (accessed on 5 May 2018).

Canning, Kathleen. "The Body as Method? Reflections on the Place of the Body in Gender History," *Gender and History* 11 (1999): 499–513.

Castañeda, Claudia. *Figurations: Child, Bodies, Worlds*. Durham, NC: Duke University Press, 2002.

Chakrabarti, Mohit. *The Gandhian Dimension of Education*. Delhi: Daya Publishing House, 1990.

Chakrabarty, Dipesh. *Habitations of Modernity: Essays in the Wake of Subaltern Studies*. Chicago: University of Chicago Press, 2002.

Chakrabarty, Dipesh. *Provincializing Europe: Postcolonial Thought and Historical Difference*. Princeton, NJ: Princeton University Press, 2000.

Chakraborty, Aishika. "Gender, Caste and Marriage: Kulinism in Nineteenth-Century Bengal," in *Intimate Others: Marriage and Sexualities in India*, eds. Samita Sen, Ranjita Biswas, and Nandita Dhawan, 35–65. Kolkata: Stree, 2011.

Chakraborty, Aishika. "Contract, Consent, Ceremony: The Brahmo Marriage Reform (1868–1920)," *Journal of History* [Department of History, Jadavpur University, Kolkata] 26 (2008–2009).

Chakraborty, Chandrima. *Masculinity, Asceticism, Hinduism: Past and Present Imaginings of India*. Delhi: Permanent Black, 2011.

Chakraborty, Sambuddha. *Andare Antare: Unish Shatake Bangali Bhadramahila*. Calcutta: Stree, 1995.

Chakramakkil, Anto Thomas. "The Polemics of Real and Imagined Childhood(s) in India," *International Research in Children's Literature* 10, no. 1 (2017): 74–88.

Chakravarti, Uma. "Conceptualizing Brahmanical Patriarchy in Early India: Gender, Caste, Class, and State," *Economic and Political Weekly* 28, no. 14 (April 3, 1993): 579–585.

Chando Roy, Gautam. "Science for Children in a Colonial Context: Bengali Juvenile Magazines, 1883–1923," *British Journal of History of Science*, Themes 3 (2018): 43–72.

Chando Roy, Gautam. "Childhood Conditions: Moral Education in Early 20th Century Bengal," *History* [Journal of the Department of History, Burdwan University] 7, no. 1 (2005).

Chando Roy, Gautam. "Swadeshikal, Swadeshbodh O Bangla Shishusahitya," in *Shatabarser Aaloy Bangabhanga*, ed. Debabrata Ghose (2005).

Chando Roy, Gautam. "Themes of 'National' Identity in Bengali Children's Literature, c.1880–c.1920: A Note," *Journal of History* [Mahisadal Raj College], 1 (2005).

Chando Roy, Gautam. "The Pathshala and the School: Experiences of Growing Up in 19th and 20th Century Bengal," in *Mind, Body and Society*, ed. Rajat Kanta Ray. Calcutta, 1995.

Chandra, Nandini. *The Classic Popular: Amar Chitra Katha, 1907–1967*. New Delhi: Yoda Press, 2008.

Chandra, Shefali. "Mimicry, Masculinity, and the Mystique of Indian English: Western India, 1870–1900," *Journal of Asian Studies* 68, no. 1 (February 2009): 199–225.

Chandra, Shefali. "Gendering English: Gender, Sexuality and the Language of Desire in Modern India 1850–1940," *Gender and History* 19, no. 2 (August 2007): 284–304.

Chandra, Sukalyan. "Towards Swaraj: The Ideals of Democracy and Self-Reliance at Rabindranath Tagore's Ashram," *Phalanx: A Quarterly Review of Continuing Debate* (August 2014) http://www.phalanx.in/pages/article_i0010_Rabindranath_Tagore.html (accessed on February 19, 2015).

Chatterjee, Amitava. "An Introduction" to "Body, Men, and Sports: Construction of Masculinity in Bengal," *Cultural Cartographies of Media: Exploring Media Spaces and Digital Cultures* (DigiMagazine) http://mltspaces.blogspot.com/2014/12/evolution-of-colonial-bengali-identity.html (accessed on September 5, 2016).

Chatterjee, Indrani. *Forgotten Friends Monks, Marriages, and Memories of Northeast India*. New Delhi: Oxford University Press, 2013.

Chatterjee, Indrani. "When 'Sexualities' Floated Free of Histories in South Asia," *Journal of Asian Studies* 71, no. 4 (November 2012): 945–962.

Chatterjee, Indrani, ed. *Unfamiliar Relations*. New Delhi: Permanent Black, 2004.

Chatterjee, Kalyan. *Media and Nation-Building in Twentieth-Century India: Life and Times of Ramananda Chatterjee*. London/New York: Routledge, 2020.

Chatterjee, Nandini. "English Law, Brahmo Marriage, and the Problem of Religious Difference: Civil Marriage Laws in Britain and India," *Comparative Studies in Society and History* 52, no. 3 (2010): 524–552.

Chatterjee, Partha. "Tagore's Non-Nation," in *Lineages of Political Society*, 94–128. New York: Columbia University Press, 2011.

Chatterjee, Partha. *The Politics of the Governed: Popular Politics in Most of the World*. New York: Columbia University Press, 2004.

Chatterjee, Partha. *The Nation and Its Fragments*. Princeton, NJ: Princeton University Press, 1993.

Chatterjee, Partha. *Nationalist Thought and the Colonial World*. New Delhi: Oxford University Press, 1986.

Chaudhuri, Nupur. "Nationalism and Feminism in the Writings of Santa Devi and Sita Devi," in *Interventions: Feminist Dialogues on Third World Women's Literature and Films*, eds. Bishnupriya Ghosh and Brinda Bose. New York: Routledge, 1996.

Chopra, Radhika. "Invisible Men: Masculinity, Sexuality and Male domestic Labour," *Men and Masculinities* 9, no. 2 (2006): 152–167.

Chopra, Radhika. "Muted Masculinities: Introduction to the Special Issue on Contemporary Indian Ethnographies," *Men and Masculinities* 9, no. 2 (2006): 127–130.

Chopra, Radhika, ed. *Reframing Masculinities: Narrating the Supportive Practices of Men*. Hyderabad: Orient Longman, 2006.

Chopra, Radhika. "From Violence to Supportive Practice: Family, Gender and Masculinities," *Economic and Political Weekly* 38, no. 17 (April 26–May 2, 2003): 1650–1657.

Chopra, Radhika, Osella, Caroline, and Osella, Filippo. eds. *South Asian Masculinities: Context of Change, Sites of Continuity*. New Delhi: Women Unlimited, 2004.

Chowdhury, Indira. *The Fragile Hero and Virile History*. New Delhi: Oxford University Press, 2001.

Cohn, Bernard. "Recruitments of Elites in India under British Rule," in *Essays in Comparative Social Stratification*, eds. Leonard Plotnicov and Arthur Tuden. Pittsburgh: University of Pittsburgh Press, 1970.

Collins, Michael. *Empire, Nationalism and the Postcolonial World: Rabindranath Tagore's Writings on History, Politics, and Society*. New York: Routledge, 2012.

Connell, R.W. *Masculinities*. Oxford: Polity Press, 1995.

Courtright, Paul B. "Fathers and Sons," in *Vishnu on Freud's Desk: A Reader in Psychoanalysis and Hinduism*, eds. T.G. Vaidyanathan and Jeffrey J. Kripal, 137–146. New Delhi: Oxford University Press, 1999.

Curley, David. *Poetry and History: Bengal Mangal Kabya and Social Change in Precolonial Bengal*. New Delhi: Chronicle Books, 2008.

Dayal, Samir. *Resisting Modernity: Counternarratives of Nation and Masculinity in Pre-Independence India*. Newcastle: Cambridge Scholars Publishing, 2007.

DeMause, Lloyd. ed. *The History of Childhood*. Baltimore: Johns Hopkins Press, 1974.

Desai, Priti, Neela D'Souza, and Sonal Shukla. *Indelible Imprints: Daughters Write on Fathers*. Calcutta: Stree, 1999.

Doniger, Wendy. *The Hindus: An Alternate History*. New York: Penguin Books, 2000.

Dutta, Manomohini. *Inheritance, Property, and Women in the Dāyabhāga*, Ph.D. Dissertation, University of Texas, Austin, 2016.

Ellis, Catriona. "Education for All: Reassessing the Historiography of Education in Colonial India," in *History Compass* 6 (December 2008).

Eustace, Nicole, Eugenia Lean, et al. "AHR Conversation: The Historical Study of Emotions," *American Historical Review* 117, no. 5 (2012): 1487–1531.

Finucci, Valeria. *The Manly Masquerade: Masculinity, Paternity and Castration in the Italian Renaissance*. Durham, NC: Duke University Press, 2003.

Fischer-Tiné, Harald. "From Brahmacharya to Conscious Race-Culture: Victorian Discourses of 'Science' and Hindu Traditions in Early Indian Nationalism," in *Beyond Representation: Colonial and Postcolonial Constructions of Indian Identity*, ed. Crispin Bates, 241–269. New Delhi: Oxford University Press, 2006.

Flora, Giuseppe. "On Fairy Tales, Intellectuals and Nationalism in Bengal (1880–1920)," *Alla Revista Degli Studi Orientali* LXXV, no. 1 (2002): 7–84.

Forbes, Geraldine H. "Dependent on Patriarchy: Rabindranath's Widows and Widows' Lived Lives in Late Nineteenth Century Bengal," in *Tagore on Discriminations: Representing the Unrepresented*, ed. Blanka Knotková-Čapková, 29–41. Prague: Metropolitan University Prague Press, 2015.

Forbes, Geraldine H. *Women in Modern India*. Cambridge, UK: Cambridge University Press, 1996.

Forbes, Geraldine H. "Women and Modernity: The Issue of Child Marriage in India" *Women's Studies International Quarterly* 2, no. 4 (1979): 407–419.

Foucault, Michel. *Discipline and Punish: The Birth of the Prison*. New York: Pantheon, 1978.

SELECTED BIBLIOGRAPHY 293

Frank, Katherine. *Indira: The Life of Indira Nehru Gandhi*. Boston: Houghton Mifflin, 2002.

Gandhi, Rajmohan. *Mohandas: A True Story of a Man, His People and an Empire*. Delhi: Penguin/Viking, 2006.

Ghosh, Anindita. *Power in Print*. New Delhi: Oxford University Press, 2006.

Ghosh, Anindita. "Literary Bengali and Low-Life Print Culture in Colonial Calcutta: Revisiting the 'Bengal Renaissance,'" *Economic and Political Weekly* 37, no. 42 (October 2002).

Ghosh, Durba. *Gentlemanly Terrorists: Political Violence and the Colonial State in India, 1919–1947*. Cambridge, UK: Cambridge University Press, 2017.

Ghosh, Durba. "Revolutionary Women and Nationalist Heroes in Bengal, 1930 to the 1980s," *Gender and History* 25, no. 2 (2013): 355–375.

Ghosh, Jayatri. "Satyavati: The Matriarch of the Mahabharata," in *Faces of the Feminine in Ancient, Medieval, and Modern India*, ed. Mandakranta Bose. New Delhi: Oxford University Press, 2000.

Gopal, Sarvepalli. *Jawaharlal Nehru: A Biography Volume 1, 1889–1947*. New Delhi: Oxford University Press, 2015.

Goswami, Manu. *Producing India: From Colonial Economy to National Space*. Chicago: University of Chicago Press, 2004.

Goswami, Supriya. *Colonial India in Children's Literature*. New York: Routledge, 2012.

Goonesekere, S. *Children, Law and Justice: A South Asian Perspective*. New Delhi: Thousand Oaks; London: Sage Publications, 1997.

Grinshpon, Yohanan. "Under-reading Multiple Vocality: The Case of the Good Boy and the Angry Father," in *Crisis and Knowledge: The Upanishadic Experience and Storytelling*. New Delhi: Oxford University Press, 2003.

Guha, Ranajit. "Discipline and Mobilize: Hegemony and Elite Control in Nationalist Campaigns," in *Dominance Without Hegemony*, 100–151. Cambridge, MA: Harvard University Press, 1997.

Guha, Sumit. "Did the British Empire Depend on Separating Parents and Children," *Not Even Past* (blog) (January 24, 2020). https://notevenpast.org/did-the-british-empire-depend-on-separating-parents-and-children/.

Guha, Sumit. *History and Collective Memory in South Asia (1200–2000)*. Seattle: University of Washington Press, 2019.

Guha, Sumit. "The Family Feud," in *Unfamiliar Relations*, ed. Indrani Chatterjee. New Delhi: Permanent Black, 2004.

Gupta, Charu. "Anxious Hindu Masculinities in Colonial North India: Shuddhi and Sangathan Movements," *CrossCurrents* 61, no. 4 (November 2011).

Gupta, Charu. "Feminine, Criminal, or Manly? Imaging Dalit Masculinity in Colonial North India," *Indian Economic Social History Review* 47, no. 3 (July/September 2010): 309–342.

Gupta, Charu. "Sanskrit Pandits Recall Their Youth: Two Autobiographies from Nineteenth-Century Bengal," *Journal of the American Oriental Society* 121, no. 4 (October–December 2001): 580–592.

Habib, Irfan and Dhruv Raina, eds. *Social History of Science in Colonial India*. New Delhi: Oxford University Press, 2007.

Hardiman, David. *Gandhi in His Time and Ours*. New Delhi: Permanent Black, 2003.

Harrison, Mark. *Climates and Constitution: Health, Race, Environment and British Imperialism in India 1600–1850*. New Delhi: Oxford University Press, 1999.

294 SELECTED BIBLIOGRAPHY

Harrison, Mark and Pati Biswamoy, eds. *The Social History of Health and Medicine in Colonial India*. London: Routledge, 2011.

Hasan, Mushirul. *Modernity and Nationalism*. New Delhi: Oxford University Press, 2009.

Hatcher, Brian. "Father, Son and Holy Text: Rabindranath Tagore and the Upanisads," *Journal of Hindu Studies* 4, no. 2 (2011): 119–143.

Haynes, Douglas E. "Selling Masculinity: Advertisements of Sex Tonics and the Making of Modern Conjugality in Western India, 1900–1945," *South Asian Journal of South Asian Studies* 35, no. 4 (2012): 1–45.

Haynes, Douglas E. *Rhetoric and Ritual in Colonial India: The Shaping of a Public Culture in Surat City, 1852–1928*. Berkeley: University of California Press, 1991.

Herder, Hans. "The Modern Babu and the Metropolis: Reassessing Early Bengali Narrative Prose (1821–1862)," in *India's Literary History: Essays on the Nineteenth Century*, eds. Stuart Blackburn and Vasudha Dalmia, 358–401. New Delhi: Permanent Black, 2004.

Husain, Md Hamid and High Sarwar, Firoj. "A Comparative Study of Zamindari, Raiyatwari And Mahalwari Land Revenue Settlements: The Colonial Mechanism of Surplus Extraction in 19th-century British India," *Journal of Humanities and Social Sciences* 2, no. 4 (September–October 2012): 16–26.

Ilaiah, Kancha. *Why I Am Not a Hindu*. Kolkata: Samya, 1996.

Indramitra. *Vidyasager Chhlebela*. Kolkata: Ananda Publishers, 2002.

Indramitra. *Karunasagar Vidyasagar*. Rev. 2nd ed. Kolkata: Ananda Publishers, 1992.

Ingalls, Daniel H.H. "The Cānakya Collections and Nārāyana's Hitopadeśa," *Journal of the American Oriental Society* 86, no. 1 (January–March 1966): 1–19.

Isin, Engin F. *Citizenship After Orientalism: An Unfinished Project*. Houndmills, Basingstoke, Hampshire, UK: Palgrave Macmillan, 2014.

Jackson, Peter. "The Cultural Politics of Masculinity: Towards a Social Geography," *Transactions of the Institute of British Geographers* 16, no. 2 (1991): 199–213.

Joshi, Sanjay, ed. *The Middle Class in Colonial India*. New Delhi: Oxford University Press, 2010.

Joshi, Sanjay. *The Fractured Middle Class*. New Delhi: Oxford University Press, 2001.

Kakar, Sudhir, ed. *Identity and Adulthood*. New Delhi: Oxford University Press, 1998.

Kakar, Sudhir. "Setting the Stage: The Traditional Hindu View and the Psychology of Erik H. Erikson," in *Identity and Adulthood*, ed. Sudhir Kakar, 3–12. New Delhi: Oxford University Press, 1998 [1979].

Kakar, Sudhir. *The Inner World: A Psychoanalytic Study of Childhood and Society in India*. 2nd ed. New Delhi: Oxford University Press, 1982.

Kamani, Ginu. "A Terrible Hurt: The Untold Story Behind the Publishing of Maitreyi Devi." https://www.press.uchicago.edu/Misc/Chicago/143651.html (accessed on February 11, 2020).

Karlekar, Malavika. *Voices from Within: Early Personal Narratives of Bengali Women*. New Delhi: Oxford University Press, 1993.

Kasturi, Malavika. "Asceticising' Monastic Families: Ascetic Genealogies, Property Feuds and Anglo-Hindu Law in Late Colonial India," *Modern Asian Studies* 43, no. 5 (September 2009): 1039–1083.

Kaviraj, Sudipta. *The Invention of Private Life: Literature and Ideas*. New York: Columbia University Press, 2015.

Kaviraj, Sudipta. *The Imaginary Institution of India: Politics and Ideas*. New Delhi: Permanent Black, 2010.
Kaviraj, Sudipta. "Tagore and Transformations in the Ideals of Love," in *Love in South Asia: A Cultural History*, ed. Francesca Orsini, 161–182. Cambridge: Cambridge University Press, 2006.
Khilnani, Sunil. *The Idea of India*. New York: Farrar Straus Giroux, 1997.
King, Laura. *Family Men: Fatherhood and Masculinity in Britain, 1914–1960*. Oxford: Oxford University Press, 2015.
King, Margaret L. *Mothers and Sons: A History*. Lewiston, NY: Edwin Mellen Press, 2014.
King, Margaret L. *The Death of the Child Valerio Marcello*. Chicago: University of Chicago Press, 1994.
Kling, Blair B. *Partner in Empire: Dwarkanath Tagore and the Age of Enterprise in Eastern India*. Berkeley: University of California Press, 1976.
Knotková-Čapková, Blanka. *Tagore on Discriminations: Representing the Unrepresented*. Prague: Metropolitan University Prague Press, 2015.
Kopf, David. *The Brahmo Samaj and the Shaping of the Indian Mind*. Princeton, NJ: Princeton University Press, 1979.
Kopf, David. *British Orientalism and the Bengal Renaissance: The Dynamics of Indian Modernization, 1773–1835*. Berkeley: University of California Press, 1969.
Kripalani, Krishna. *Rabindranath Tagore: A Biography*. New York: Grove Press, 1962.
Kumar, Deepak. *Science and the Raj*. New Delhi: Oxford University Press, 2006.
Kumar, Krishna. *The Political Agenda of Education: A Study of Colonialist and Nationalist Ideas*. New Delhi: Sage Publications, 2004.
Kumar, Krishna. "Mohandas Karamchand Gandhi (1869–1948)," in *Prospects*, the *Quarterly Review of Education* (Paris, UNESCO: International Bureau of Education) 23, no. 3/4 (1993): 507–517.
Kumar, Nita. *The Politics of Gender, Community, and Modernity: Essays on Education in India*. New Delhi: Oxford University Press, 2011.
Kumar, Nita. *Lessons from School: The Theories of Education in Benares*. New Delhi: Sage Publications, 1999.
Lal, Ruby. *Coming of Age*. Cambridge: Cambridge University Press, 2013.
Lal, Ruby. "Recasting the Women's Question: The Girl-Child/Woman in the Colonial Encounter," *Interventions* 10, no. 3 (2008): 321–339.
Laqueur, Thomas W. "The Facts of Fatherhood," in *Conflicts in Feminism*, eds. Marianne Hirsch and Evelyn Fox Keller, 205–221. New York: Routledge, 1990.
LaRossa, Ralph. *The Modernization of Fatherhood: A Social and Political History*. Chicago: University of Chicago Press, 1997.
Lejeune, Philippe. *On Autobiography*, ed. P.J. Eakin and trans. Katherine Leary. Minneapolis: University of Minnesota Press, 1989.
Lelyveld, David. "*Naicari* Nature: Sir Sayyid Ahmad Khan and the Reconciliation of Science, Technology and Religion," in *The Cambridge Companion to Sir Sayyid Ahmad Khan*, eds. Yasmin Saikia and Raisur Rahman. Cambridge: Cambridge University Press, 2018.
Lelyveld, David. "Young Man Sayyid: Dreams and Biographical Texts," in *Muslim Voices: Community and the Self in South Asia*, eds. David Gilmartin, Sadria Freitag, and Usha Sanyal. New Delhi: Yoda Press, 2013.

Lelyveld, David. *Aligarh's First Generation: Muslim Solidarity in British India*. New Delhi: Oxford University Press, 2003.
Lockridge, Kenneth A. *On the Sources of Patriarchal Rage: The Commonplace Books of William Byrd and Thomas Jefferson and the Gendering of Power in the Eighteenth Century*. New York: New York University Press, 1992.
Madan, T.N. *Non-Renunciation: Themes and Interpretations of Hindu Culture*. New Delhi: Oxford University Press, 2004.
Majumdar, Rochona. *Marriage and Modernity*. Durham, NC: Duke University Press, 2009.
Manderson, Lenore and Pranee Liamputtong, eds. *Coming of Age in South and Southeast Asia: Youth, Courtship and Sexuality*. Richmond, UK: Curzon: 2002.
Mazlish, Bruce. *James and John Mill: Father and Son in the Nineteenth Century*. New York: Basic Books, 1975.
McDaniel, June. "Emotion in Bengali Religious Thought: Substance and Metaphor," in *Emotions in Asian Thought: A Dialogue in Comparative Philosophy*, ed. Joel Marks and Roger T. Ames, 39–63. Albany: State University of New York Press, 1995.
McKeon, Michael. *The Secret History of Domesticity: The Public, Private, and the Division of Knowledge*. Baltimore: Johns Hopkins Press, 2005.
Menon, Dilip. *Blindness of Insight: Essays on Caste in Modern India*. New Delhi: Navayana Publishers, 2006.
Metcalf, Thomas. *Aftermath of Revolt: India 1857–1970*. Princeton, NJ: Princeton University Press, 2015 [1964].
Minault, Gail. *Secluded Scholars: Women's Education and Muslim Social Reform in Colonial India*. New Delhi: Oxford University Press, 1999.
Mintz, Steven. "Mothers and Fathers in America: Looking Backward, Looking Forward," *Digital History* (2003). http://www.digitalhistory.uh.edu/historyonline/mothersfathers.cfm.
Mintz, Steven and Susan Kellogg. *Domestic Revolution: A Social History of American Family Life*. New York: The Free Press, 1988.
Mitra, Durba. "Indian Sex Life: Sexuality and the Colonial Origins of Modern Social Thought." (Princeton: Princeton University Press, 2020).
Mitra, Samarpita. "Periodical Readership in Early Twentieth Century Bengal: Ramananda Chattopadhyay's Prabasi," *Modern Historical Studies* 47, no. 1 (2013): 204–249.
Mitra, Subal Chandra. *Isvar Chandra Vidyasagar: A Story of His Life and Works*. Kolkata: New Bengal Press, 1907.
Mukharji, Projit Bihari. *Doctoring Traditions: Ayurveda, Small Technologies, and Braided Sciences*. Chicago: University of Chicago Press, 2016.
Mukharji, Projit Bihari. *Nationalizing the Body: The Medical Market, Print, and Daktari Medicine*. London: Anthem Press, 2009.
Mukherjee, H.B. *Education for Fullness*. Reprint. New York: Routledge, 2013.
Mukherjee, S.N. *Calcutta: Myths and History*. Calcutta: Subarnarekha, 1977.
Naik, J.P. and Nurullah, Syed. *A Student's History of Education in India (1800–1973)*. 6th revised ed. Delhi: Macmillan and Co. Ltd., 1974 [1945].
Nandy, Ashis. "Reconstructing Childhood: A Critique of the Ideology of Adulthood," in *Traditions, Tyranny and Utopia: Essays in the Politics of Awareness*. New Delhi: Oxford University Press, 1992.

Nandy, Ashis. *Intimate Enemy: Loss and Recovery of the Self under Colonialism*. New Delhi: Oxford University Press, 1983.

Narayan, Rochisha. "Widows, Family, Community, and the Formation of Anglo-Hindu Law in Eighteenth-Century India," *Modern Asian Studies* 50, no. 3 (2016): 866–897.

Narayanan, Vasudha. "Renunciation and Law in India," *Religion and Law in Independent India* (1993): 279–291.

Nayeem, Asha Islam. "How to Educate the Girl Child? Financing Female Education in Colonial Bengal," in *Readings in Bengal History: Identity Formation and Colonial Legacy*, eds. Asha Islam Nayeem and Aksadul Alam, 179–202. Dhaka: Bangladesh History Association, 2017.

Nayeem, Asha Islam and Avril A. Powell. "Redesigning the Zenana: Domestic Education in Eastern Bengal in the Early Twentieth Century," in *Rhetoric and Reality: Gender and the Colonial Experience in South Asia*, eds. Avril A. Powell and Siobbhan Lambert-Hurley, 50–81. New Delhi: Oxford University Press, 2006.

Nelson, Claudia. *Invisible Men: Fatherhood in Victorian Periodicals, 1850–1910*. Athens: University of Georgia Press, 1995.

Newbigin, Eleanor. *The Hindu Family and the Emergence of Modern India: Law, Citizenship, and Community*. Cambridge: Cambridge University Press, 2013.

Newbigin, Eleanor. "Personal Law and Citizenship in India's Transition to Independence," *Modern Asian Studies* 45, no. 1 (2011): 7–32.

Nieuwenhuys, Olga. "Keep Asking: Why Childhood? Why Children? Why Global?," *Childhood* 17, no. 3 (2010): 291–296.

Nieuwenhuys, Olga. "Is There an Indian Childhood?," *Childhood* 16, no. 2 (2009): 147–153.

Nieuwenhuys, Olga. "Global Childhood and the Politics of Contempt," *Alternatives: Global, Local, Political* 23, no. 3 (July–September 1998): 267–289.

Nijhwan, Shobhna. *Women and Girls in the Hindi Public Sphere: Periodical Literature in Colonial North India*. New Delhi: Oxford University Press, 2012.

Nijhwan, Shobhna. "Hindi Children's Journals and Nationalist Discourse (1910–1930)," *Economic and Political Weekly* 39, no. 33 (2004): 3723–3729.

Nurullah, Syed and ,J.P. Naik. *A History of Education in India*. Bombay: Macmillan and Co. Ltd., 1951.

Nussbaum, Martha C. "Tagore, Gandhi, Nehru," in *The Clash Within: Democracy, Religious Violence, and India's Future*, 80–121. Cambridge, MA: Harvard University Press, 2007.

O'Connell, Kathleen M. *Rabindranath Tagore: The Poet as Educator*. Kolkata: Visva-Bharati, 2002.

O'Hanlon, Rosalind. "Issues of Masculinity in North Indian History: The Bangash Nawabs of Farrukhabad," *Indian Journal of Gender Studies* 4, no. 1 (1997): 1–19.

Olivelle, Patrick, ed. *Gṛhastha: The Householder in Ancient Indian Religious Culture*. New York: Oxford University Press, 2019.

Olsen, Stephanie. *Juvenile Nation: Youth, Emotion, and the Making of Modern British Citizen, 1880–1914*. London: Bloomsbury, 2014.

Olsen, Stephanie et al., eds. *Childhood, Youth and Emotions in Modern History*. London: Palgrave Macmillan, 2015.

Pande, Ishita. "'Listen to the Child': Law, Sex, and the Child Wife in Indian Historiography," *History Compass* 11, no. 9 (September 2013).

Pande, Ishita. "Sorting Boys and Men: Unlawful Intercourse, Boy-Protection, and the Child Marriage Restraint Act in Colonial India," *Journal of the History of Childhood and Youth* 6, no. 2 (January 2013): 332–358.

Pande, Ishita. "Coming of Age: Law, Sex, and Childhood in Late Colonial India," *Gender and History* 24, no. 1 (April 2012).

Pande, Ishita. *Medicine, Race, and Liberalism in British Bengal: Symptoms of Empire*. London/New York: Routledge, 2010.

Pawde, K. "The Story of My 'Sanskrit,'" in *Subject to Change: Teaching Literature in the Nineties*, ed. Susie Tharu. Hyderabad, India: Orient Longman, 1998.

Pernau, Margrit. *Ashraf into Middle Class: Muslims in Nineteenth-Century Delhi*. Oxford: Oxford University Press, 2013.

Pernau, Margrit. "Male Anger and Female Malice: Emotions in Indo-Muslim Advice Literature," *History Compass* 10, no. 2 (2012): 119–128.

Perrot, Michelle, ed. *A History of Private Life: From the Fires of Revolution to the Great War*. Trans. Arthur Goldhammer. Cambridge, MA: The Belknap Press of the Harvard University Press, 1990.

Prakash, Gyan. *Another Reason: Science and Its Imagination in Modern India*. Princeton, NJ: Princeton University Press, 1999.

Raha, Bipasha. *Living a Dream: Rabindranath Tagore and Rural Resuscitation*. New Delhi: Manohar, 2014.

Raman, Vasanthi. "The Diverse Life-Worlds of Indian Childhood," in *Family and Gender: Changing Values in Germany and India*, eds. Margrit Pernau, Imtiaz Ahmad, and Helmut Reifeld, 84–111. New Delhi: Sage Publications, 2003.

Raman, Vasanthi. "Politics of Childhood: Perspectives from the South," *Economic and Political Weekly* 35, no. 46 (November 11–17, 2000): 4055–4064.

Ramaswamy, Sumathi. *The Goddess and the Nation: Mapping Mother India*. Durham, NC: Duke University Press, 2010.

Ramaswamy, Sumathi. *The Lost History of Lemuria: Fabulous Geographies, Catastrophic Histories*. Berkeley: University of California Press, 2004.

Ramusack, Barbara. *Women in Asia: Restoring Women to History*. Bloomington: Indiana University Press, 1999.

Rao, Velcheru Narayan, David Shulman, and Sanjay Subrahmanyam. *Textures of Time: Writing History in South India, 1600–1800*. New Delhi: Permanent Black, 2001.

Ray, Bharati, ed. *From the Seams of History: Essays on Indian Women*. New Delhi: Oxford University Press, 1995.

Ray, Rajat Kanta. *Exploring Emotional History: Gender, Mentality and Literature in the Indian Awakening*. New Delhi: Oxford University Press, 2003.

Ray, Utsa. *Culinary Culture in Colonial India: A Cosmopolitan Platter and the Middle Class*. Cambridge, UK: Cambridge University Press, 2015.

Ray, Utsa. "Consumption and the Making of the Middle Class in South Asia," *History Compass* 12, no. 1 (January 2014): 11–19.

Ray, Utsa. "The Body and Its Purity: Dietary Politics in Colonial Bengal," *Indian Economic and Social History Review* 50, no. 4 (October–December 2013): 395–421.

Raychaudhuri, Tapan. "Gandhi and Tagore: Where the Twain Meet," in *Perceptions, Emotions, Sensibilities: Essays on India's Colonial and Postcolonial Experiences*, 141–154. New Delhi: Oxford University Press, 1999.

Raychaudhuri, Tapan. "Love in a Colonial Climate: Marriage, Sex and Romance in Nineteenth-Century Bengal," in *Perceptions, Emotions, Sensibilities: Essays on India's Colonial and Postcolonial Experiences*. New Delhi: Oxford University Press, 1999.

Raychaudhuri, Tapan. *Europe Reconsidered: Perceptions of Europe in Nineteenth Century Bengal*. New Delhi: Oxford University Press, 1989.

Reddy, William M. *The Making of Romantic Love: Longing and Sexuality in Europe, South Asia, and Japan, 900–1200 CE*. Chicago: University of Chicago Press, 2012.

Reddy, William M. *The Navigation of Feeling: A Framework for the History of Emotions*. New York: Cambridge University Press, 2001.

Riggan, Jennifer. *The Struggling State: Nationalism, Mass Militarization, and the Education of Eritrea*. Philadelphia: Temple University Press, 2016.

Robb, Peter. *Empire, Identity, and the India: Liberalism, Modernity, and the Nation*. New Delhi: Oxford University Press, 2006.

Rocher, Ludo. *Jimutavahana's Dayabhaga: The Hindu Law of Inheritance in Bengal*. New York: Oxford University Press, 2002.

Rohner, Ronald Preston and Majushri Chaki-Sircar. *Women and Children in a Bengali Village*. Hanover, NH: Published for University of Connecticut by University Press of New England, 1988.

Roopnarine, J. and P. Suppal. "Kakar's Psychoanalytic Interpretation of Childhood: The Need to Emphasize the Father and Multiple Caregivers in the Socialization Equation," in *Childhood, Family and Socio-cultural Change in India: Reinterpreting the Inner World*, ed. D. Sharma, 115–137. New Delhi: Oxford University Press, 2003.

Roper, Michael. "Slipping Out of View: Subjectivity and Emotion in Gender History," *History Workshop Journal* 59, no. 1 (2005): 57–72.

Rosaldo, Michelle Z. and Louise Lamphere, eds. *Woman, Culture, and Society*. Stanford, CA: Stanford University Press, 1974.

Rosenwein, Barbara H. *Emotional Communities in the Early Middle Ages*. Ithaca, NY: Cornell University Press, 2006.

Rosenwein, Barbara H. "Worrying about Emotions in History," *American Historical Review* 107, no. 3 (2002): 821–845.

Rosselli, John. "The Self Image of Effetness: Physical Education and Nationalism in Nineteenth-Century Bengal," *Past and Present* 86 (1980): 121–148.

Roy, Kumkum. *The Emergence of Monarchy in North India: Eighth to Fourth Centuries B.C.* New Delhi: Oxford University Press, 1994.

Roy, Manisha. *Bengali Women*. Chicago: University of Chicago Press, 1992 [1972].

Roy, Parama. "Meat-Eating, Masculinity, and Renunciation in India: A Gandhian Grammar of Diet," *Gender and History* 14, no. 1 (April 2002): 62–91.

Sanders, Valerie. "'What do you want to know about next?' Charles Kingsley's Model of Educational Fatherhood," in *Gender and Fatherhood in the Nineteenth Century*, eds. Trev Lynn Broughton and Helen Rogers. London: Palgrave Macmillan, 2007.

Sarkar, Oishik and Dutta, Debolina. "Beyond Compassion: Children of Sex Workers in Kolkata's Sonagachi," *Childhood* 18, no. 3 (2011): 333–349.

Sarkar, Sumit. "Vidyasagar and Brahmanical Society," in *Writing Social History*, 246–247. New Delhi: Oxford University Press, 2009.

Sarkar, Sumit and Tanika Sarkar, eds. *Women and Social Reform in Modern India: A Reader*. Bloomington: Indiana University Press, 2008.

SELECTED BIBLIOGRAPHY

Sarkar, Tanika. *Words to Win: Making of a Modern Autobiography.* Reprint ed. New Delhi: Zubaan Books, 2014.

Sarkar, Tanika. *Rebels, Wives, Saints: Designing Selves and Nations in Colonial Times.* Calcutta: Seagull Books, 2009.

Sarkar, Tanika. *Hindu Wife, Hindu Nation.* New Delhi: Permanent Black, 2001.

Savary, Luzia. "Vernacular Eugenics? *Santati-Śāstra* in Popular Hindi Advisory Literature (1900–1940)," *South Asia: Journal of South Asian Studies* 37, no. 3 (2014): 381–397.

Scheer, Monique. "Are Emotions a Kind of Practice (And Is that What Makes them Have a History)? A Bourdicuian Approach to Understanding Emotion," *History and Theory* 51, no. 2 (2012): 193–220.

Scheper-Hughes, Nancy and Carolyn Sargent. *Small Wars: The Cultural Politics of Childhood.* Berkeley: University of California Press, 1998.

Sen, Amartya. "Tagore and His India," in *The Argumentative Indian*, 89–120. New York: Picador, 2003.

Sen, Asok. *Iswar Chandra Vidyasagar and His Elusive Milestones.* Kolkata: Riddhi, 1977.

Sen, Krishna. "Lessons in Self-Fashioning: 'Bamabodhini Patrika' and the Education of Women in Bengal," in *The Victorian Periodicals Review* 37, no. 2 (Summer 2004): 176–191.

Sen, Nivedita. *Family, School, and Nation: The Child and the Literary Constructions in 20th-Century Bengal.* New Delhi: Routledge, 2015.

Sen, Samita. "Crossing Communities: Religious Conversion, Rights in Marriage, and Personal Law," in *Negotiating Spaces: Legal Domains, Gender Constructs, and Community Concerns*, eds. Flavia Agnes and Shoba Venkatesh. New Delhi: Oxford University Press, 2012.

Sen, Samita. "Offences Against Marriage: Negotiating Customs in Colonial Bengal," in *A Question of Silence: The Sexual Economies of Modern India*, ed. Mary E. John and Janaki Nair, 77–110. New Delhi: Kali for Women, 1998.

Sen, Samita. "Motherhood and Mothercraft: Gender and Nationalism in Bengal," *Gender and History* 5, no. 2 (1993): 231–243.

Sen, Satadru. "Remembering Robi," in *Traces of Empire: India, America, and Postcolonial Cultures: Essays and Criticism*, 58–74. Chennai: Primus Books, 2014.

Sen, Satadru. *Colonial Childhoods: The Juvenile Periphery of India, 1850–1945.* London: Anthem, 2005.

Sen, Satadru. "A Juvenile Periphery: The Cartographies of Literary Childhood in Colonial Bengal," *Journal of Colonialism and Colonial History* 5, no. 1 (2004).

Sen, Simonti. *Travels to Europe: Self and Other in Bengali Travel Narratives.* Hyderabad: Orient Blackswan, 2005.

Sengoopta, Chandok. *The Rays Before Satyajit: Creativity and Modernity in Colonial India.* New Delhi: Oxford University Press, 2016.

Sengupta, Indra and Daud Ali, eds. *Knowledge Production, Pedagogy and Institutions in Colonial India.* New York: Palgrave, 2011.

Sengupta, Parna. *Pedagogy for Religion.* Berkeley: University of California Press, 2011.

Seth, Sanjay. *Subject Lessons: The Western Education of Colonial India.* Durham/London: Duke University Press, 2007.

Singh, R. P. *Nehru on Education.* New Delhi: Sterling Publishers, 1966.

Sinha, Mrinalini. "Nations in an Imperial Crucible," in *Gender and Empire*, ed. Philipa Levine. Oxford University Press, 2011.
Sinha, Mrinalini. *Specters of Mother India*. Durham, NC: Duke University Press, 2006.
Sinha, Mrinalini. "Giving Masculinity a History," *Gender and History* 11, no. 3 (1999): 445–460.
Sinha, Mrinalini. *Colonial Masculinity: The "Manly Englishman" and the "Effeminate Bengali" in the Late Nineteenth Century*. Manchester, UK: University of Manchester Press, 1995.
Smith, Sidonie and Julia Watson. *Reading Autobiography: A Guide for Interpreting Life Narratives*. 2nd ed. Minneapolis: University of Minnesota Press, 1989.
Sreenivas, Mytheli. *Wives, Widows, and Concubines: The Conjugal Family Ideal in Colonial India*. Bloomington: Indiana University Press, 2008.
Stearns, Carol and Peter Stearns. *Anger: The Struggle for Emotional Control in America's Society*. Chicago: University of Chicago Press, 1986.
Stearns, Peter. "Obedience and Emotion: A Challenge in the Emotional History of Childhood," *Journal of Social History* 47, no. 3 (Spring 2014): 593–611.
Stearns, Peter. *Be a Man: Males in Modern Society*. New York: Holmes and Meier, 1990.
Stearns, Peter and Carol Stearns. "Emotionology: Clarifying the History of Emotions and Emotional Standards," *American Historical Review* 90, no. 4 (1985): 813–836.
Steedman, Carolyn. *Strange Dislocations: Childhood and the Idea of Human Interiority*. Cambridge, MA: Harvard University Press, 1998.
Stevens, John A. *Keshab: Bengal's Forgotten Prophet*. London: Hurst Publishers, 2017.
Stevens, John A. "Marriage, Duty, and Civilization: Keshab Chandra Sen and the Cuch Behar Controversy in Metropolitan and Colonial Context," *South Asian History and Culture* 7, no. 4 (2016): 401–415.
Stoler, Ann Laura. *Race and the Education of Desire: Foucault's History of Sexuality and the Colonial Order of Things*. Durham, NC: Duke University Press, 1995.
Sträth, Bo and Wagner, Peter. *European Modernity: A Global Approach*. London: Bloomsbury, 2018.
Subramanian, Narendra. *Nation and Family: Personal Law, Cultural Pluralism, and Gendered Citizenship in India*. Stanford, CA: Stanford University Press, 2014.
Taylor, Charles. *Modern Social Imaginaries*. Durham, NC: Duke University Press, 2007.
Tharoor, Shashi. *Nehru: A Biography*. New York: Arcade Publishing, 2011.
Thorat, S.K. "Passage to Adulthood," in *Identity and Adulthood*, ed. Sudhir Kakar. New Delhi: Oxford University Press, 1979.
Topdar, Sudipa. "The Corporeal Empire: Physical Education and Politicising Children's Bodies in Late Colonial Bengal," *Gender and History* 29, no. 1 (April 2017): 176–197.
Topdar, Sudipa. "Duties of a 'Good Citizen': Colonial Secondary Textbook Policies in Late Nineteenth-Century India," *South Asian History and Culture* 6, no. 3 (2015): 417–439.
Tosh, John. *A Man's Place: Masculinity and the Middle-Class Home in Victorian England*. New Haven/London: Yale University Press, 2007 [1999].
Tosh, John. "Father and Child," in *A Man's Place*. New Haven/London: Yale University Press, 2007 [1999].

Tosh, John. *Manliness and Masculinities in Nineteenth-Century Britain.* New York: Pearson, 2005.
Vallgårda, Karen. *Imperial Childhoods and Christian Mission: Education and Emotion in South India and Denmark.* London: Palgrave Macmillan, 2015.
Vallgårda, Karen, Kristine Alexander, and Stephanie Olsen, eds. *Childhood, Youth and Emotions in Modern History: National, Colonial, and Global Perspectives.* London: Palgrave Macmillan, 2015.
van der Veer, Peter. *Imperial Encounters: Religion and Modernity in India and Britain.* Princeton, NJ: Princeton University Press, 2001.
Vatuk, Sylvia. "'Family' as a Contested Concept in Early-Nineteenth-Century Madras," in *Unfamiliar Relations,* ed. Indrani Chatterjee. New Delhi: Permanent Black, 2004.
Viswanathan, Gauri. *Masks of Conquest: Literary Studies and British Rule in India.* 25th year ed. New York: Columbia University Press, 2014.
Wadley, Susan. "Women and the Hindu Tradition," *Signs* 3, no. 1, Women and National Development: The Complexities of Change (Autumn, 1977): 113–125.
Walsh, Judith. *Domesticity in Colonial India: What Women Learned When Men Gave Them Advice.* Lanham, MD: Rowman and Littlefield, 2004.
Watt, Carey Anthony. *Serving the Nation: Cultures of Service, Association, and Citizenship.* New Delhi: Oxford University Press, 2005.
Weiner, Myron. *The Child and the State in India.* 4th imprint. New Delhi: Oxford University Press, 1994 [1991].
White, Daniel. *From Little London to Little Bengal.* Baltimore: Johns Hopkins University Press, 2013.
Wink, Andre. *Land and Sovereignty in India.* Cambridge: Cambridge University Press, 2007.
Zaidi, Qudsia (Begum). *Our Bapu* (with a foreward by Nehru). Ahmedabad: Navajivan Publishing House, 1952
Zastoupil, Lynn. "Defining Christians, Making Britons: Rammohun Roy and the Unitarians," *Victorian Studies* 44, no. 2 (2002): 215–243.
Zehfuss, Maja. *Wounds of Memory: The Politics of War in Germany.* Cambridge: Cambridge University Press, 2007.

Index

For the benefit of digital users, indexed terms that span two pages (e.g., 52–53) may, on occasion, appear on only one of those pages.

Figures are indicated by *f* following the page number

Abodhbandhu, 71
Act III of 1872 (Marriage Act of 1872), 75–76, 119n.65, 151n.38, 222–23
Adam, William, 39–40, 201 2
adoption, 9–10, 13, 15–16
Aesop, 61, 66
agency
   children's, 27–29, 74–75, 82–83, 94, 100–1, 189–90
   defined, 53n.6
   father's, 53n.6, 92–94
   in pedagogy, 61
agentiality, 52–55, 68–69, 71, 92–94, 279
   defined, 53n.6
age of consent, 70–71, 118–19, 120
Age of Consent Act, 59–60, 121n.70, 222–23
agriculture, 57, 105–6, 230–31
allopathy, 112–15
alphabet, 63, 250
Anagol, Padma
Anderson, Benedict, 37–38, 58n.14, 99, 129–31
Andhra Pradesh, 25–26
Andrews, C. F., 219
Anglicists, 63
Anglo-Hindu laws, 10n.30, 13–15, 32–33
Anjali, 84n.97
Antahpur, 121–22
anti-colonialism, 79–80
Ariès, Phillippe, 27n.99
Armstrong, Nancy, 93n.120
Arnold, Edwin, 240
Arya Samaj, 222n.88

Ashalata Singha, 177n.103
ashrama, 217–18, 219–21, 222, 228, 231, 233
Asiatic Society, 56–57, 107
Atorthi, Premankur, 183–84, 188–89
authority, 33, 57–58, 70–71
   accepted by (adult) children, 63, 64–65, 157–58, 180
   contingent, 157–58
   in India vs. Europe, 157–58
   literati claim, 44, 45–46, 131–32
   masculine, 16–17, 66–67, 157–58
   naturalization of, 34–35
   paternal, 10–11, 15–16, 30, 34–35, 64–65, 66–67, 68–69, 90–91, 131–32, 157–58, 191–92, 224, 276–77
   patriarchal, 7–8, 10–11, 13–15, 82, 103, 276–77, 278–79
   in public sphere, 47, 66–67
   restricted (or not), 13–15, 66–67
   subordination and, 47, 52–55
   unquestioned, 135–36, 137, 183
   Western doctors' or scientists', 122–23
autobiographies, 25–26, 43
   fathers' places in, 138–39
   as genre, 138–40, 141–42, 191
   men's vs. women's, 164–65, 191
   tropes in, 141–42
Ayurveda, 23–24, 102n.22, 112–15, 127, 128–29

babus, 5–6, 17–18, 44, 57–58
Badheka, Girjashankar (Gijubhai), 49n.167
Balagopalan, Sarada, 27–28, 47–48

Balak, 73–74n.71
Balakbandhu, 72–76
Ballal Sen, King, 18
Bamabodhini Patrika, 121–22
Bandyopadhyay, Aparna, 187n.124, 188n.130
Bandyopadhyay, Sekhar, 4n.9, 18n.65, 40n.147, 196n.6
Bandyopadhyay, Thakurdas, 54f
Banerjee, Gooroo Dass, 213
Banerjee, Prathama, 1n.1
Banerjee, Surendranath, 79–80
Baptists, 28–29, 57, 103–5
basic education (*nai talim*), 49–50, 249–51, 266–67, 269–70, 272
Basu, Dwijendranath, 82n.92
Basu, Pradipa (Pradip Kumar Bose), 101n.18
Bela. *See* Devi, Madhurilata
Bengal, 39–40, 227–28
Bengali, 61, 91–92
Bethune School, 147–50
Bhadra, Gautam, 16n.56
bhadralok, 28–29, 59n.19, 126–27n.87, 144–46, 163
bhadralok authors, 130–31, 210–11
bhadralok children, 142–44
bhadralok fathers, 18–20, 52–55, 89–90, 92, 142–44, 174–77
  contradictions of, 89–90
  gender biases of, 164–66, 185
  hegemonic aspirations of, 92
bhadralok men, 163–64
bhadramahila, 163–64
Bharati, 73–74n.71
Bharat Mata, 67
Bhattacharya, Nabakrishna, 82n.92, 83n.94
Bhisma, 11, 12–13
Bibidhartha-Sangraha, 96, 103–5, 107, 118–19
  readers of, 111, 111n.51
Binodini Dasi, 163–64
biographies, 79
biopolitics, 108, 177–78
Birajmohini, 87–88
boarding schools, 124–25, 127, 219

bodies, 101–2
  feeble, 5–6, 107, 111–12, 128, 232
  Muslim women's, 128–29
  punished (*see* physical punishment)
  as sites of control, 177–78
  worry about, 128
body building, 30, 232
Bombay, 112–15
Bombay presidency, 17–18, 39–40
Booth, Marylyn, 164–65
Bose, Jagadish Chandra, 82–83
Bose, Pradip Kumar (Pradipa Basu), 101n.18
boys
  agency of, 74–75
  brave, 221–23
  diet of, 124–26, 127, 219
  education of, 141, 225–26
  as future citizens, 44, 100–1, 109–10, 115–16, 125–26, 191–92, 197–98, 222–23
  as gender-neutral term, 72–74
  good, 51, 64–65
  marriage age for, 75–76, 110–11, 115–16, 118–20, 222–23
  middle-class, 79
  poetry by, 75–76, 83–84
Boy Scouts, 98, 229–30
Boy's Own Annual and *Paper*, 83–84
brahmacharya, 128–219, 222, 222n.88
Brahmacharya Ashrama, 208, 215–16.
  See also Santiniketan
Brahmanical norms, 63, 68–69
Brahmins, 18, 23–24
Brahmo Dharma Grantha, 198–99, 217
Brahmos, 3–4, 28–29, 70–71, 72, 158–59
  dissention among, 76–77, 158–59, 222–23
  marriage age for, 75–76, 151n.38, 222–23
  sons disowned after becoming, 78–80, 88, 88n.108, 180, 185
  women, 210–11
Brahmo Samaj, 146
breadwinning, 3, 100–1
British Crown, 41–42, 76–77, 83–84
Broughton, Trev Lynn, 95

INDEX

Buddhists, 13
Burton, Antoinette, 33

Calcutta, 3–4, 57, 112–15, 126–27n.87
Calcutta Journal of Natural History, 107
Calcutta Medical College, 42
Calcutta School Book Society, 4, 47, 59–60, 70–71, 71n.66, 74–75
   intelligentsia's role in, 61
Canning, Kathleen, 99
Carpenter, Mary, 72–74
caste, 4, 18, 23–24, 49–50, 70–71, 103–5, 229–30, 231–32
   elided (or not), 123, 128–30
   rejection of, 75–76
celibacy, 128
Chakrabarti, Satishchandra, 96n.3
Chakrabarty, Biharilal, 71, 203–4
Chakrabarty, Dipesh, 35n.135, 47, 64–65, 91, 139–40, 233
Chakrabarty, Punyalata, 74n.72
Chakraborty, Aishika, 18n.66, 76n.77
Chanakya, 1n.1, 2n.4, 8–9, 134–35
Chanda, Monica, 171–72, 186–87
Chandra, Shefali, 251–52
Chando Roy, Gautam, xiv, 74n.21, n17.59, n61.70, 53n.211
character building or training, 35–36, 44, 51–52, 96–98, 103n.26
   of daughters vs. sons, 165–66
   magazines stress, 69, 71, 78–79, 91–92
   M. K. Gandhi on, 245–47, 249
   physical punishment and, 177–78
   Rabindranath Tagore on, 225–26
   Satischandra Chakravarti on, 96n.3, 138n.15
Charaka, 124–25, 128–29
Charitabali, 79
Charter Act of 1813, 39–40, 56–57, 105n.30
Chatterjee, Indrani, 10–11, 13, 38–39
Chatterjee, Partha, 36–37, 38n.144, 58n.14, 90–91, 99n.11, 129–31
Chattopadhyay, Bankim Chandra, 78–79, 92–94, 203–4
Chattopadhyay, Ramananda, 82–83, 164n.76, 172–74

Chattopadhyay, Saratchandra, 177n.103
Chaudhurani, Indira Devi, 152, 153, 162–63, 206–7, 222–23
Chaudhurani, Sarala Devi, 151n.38, 159–60, 222–23, 232
Chaudhuri, Pramatha, 162–63
chhelebela (boyhood), 72–74
Chikitsha Sammilani, 47–48, 112–15, 118–20, 122–23, 124–25
Child Marriage Restraint Act, 110–11
child, category of, 21–22, 47–48, 59–60, 110–11
childhood, 4–5
   as battleground, 28–29, 132–33
   in classical texts, 23–24
   differing views of, 21–22, 24–28
   "new idea" of, 134–35
   as trope, ix–x
child marriage, 18, 47–48, 59–60, 67–68, 70–71, 115–16
   age restrictions on, 110–11, 115–16, 118–19
   Bibidhartha-Samgraha article on, 103–5
   defended, 118–20, 222–23
   eugenicist arguments about, 103–5, 122–23
   impact of, 118–19, 122–23
   M. K. Gandhi on, 238–40
   national health and, 120
   Suniti Devi's, 76–77
children
   absent, x, 128–29
   as agents, 4–5, 69, 94, 99, 100–1, 272–73
   as audience or readers, 68–69, 70–71, 74–75, 81–83, 94
   caste and, 25–26
   as category, 99, 110–11, 115–16
   as citizens or future citizens (*see* citizens: children as)
   conditional love for, 51–52
   diet of, 124–25
   disowned, 78–80, 88, 88n.108, 177–78, 180, 185, 188–89
   as enablers or enabling agents, 20–21, 68–69, 100–1, 133, 274, 278–79
   female, 47–48

children (cont.)
  as gendered category, 47–48, 99, 110–11, 130–31, 138, 277
  as homogenous category, 128–30
  imagined, 4, 20–21, 37–38, 58–59, 129–30, 133
  imperilled, 29, 59–60
  male, 47–48, 66–67
  middle-class, 4–5, 58–59
  mobilized, 49–50, 52–55, 70–71, 234–35, 242–43, 263–66
  modernity and, 27–28, 99
  Muslim, 128–29, 245
  physical well-being of, 96–97
  scholarship on, 21–24, 27–28
  as social imaginaries (*see* social imaginaries)
  story-telling, 188–89
  as subalterns, 130, 274
  as subjects, 70–71, 98, 276–77
  as subjects of reform, 47–48, 96, 108
  in tribal communities, 26
  as victims (or not), 47–48, 99, 100–1, 103–5, 273
children's literature, 59–60, 70–71, 73–74n.71, 74–75, 79, 82, 90–91
children's magazines or periodicals, 43, 69–71, 72–74, 79, 92–94
  contents of, 57, 71, 73–74n.71, 81
  nationalism and, 91–92
  paternalism of, 81
Christianity, 81
Christians, 28–29, 72–74. *See also* Baptists; Unitarians
citizens
  as bio-moral concept, 98–99
  children as (future), 4–5, 6–7, 29, 44, 49–50, 58–60, 97–98, 99, 108, 115–16, 128–29, 132–33, 191–92, 234–35, 264–66, 273
  terms *nagarik* or *odhibasi* for, 98–99
citizenship, 56n.9, 99
civil service, 4, 151, 169, 231n.114
classrooms, 215–16
clubs or associations (*sabha*, *samiti*), 100–1, 107n.38, 109–10
Colebrook, H. T., 13–15

Collins, Michael, 197n.9
colonial education system, 3–4, 38–43, 194–95, 201–3
  critiques of, 6–7, 19, 197–98, 199, 213–15, 231–32, 248–49, 274
  Indian vs. non-Indian views of, 40–41, 202–3
  resistance to, 43, 78–79
colonial state, 20n.71, 21–22, 35–37, 38n.144, 45, 52–55, 89–90, 132
  adulthood defined by, 115–16
  children's significance for, 276–77
  criticisms by, 29, 90–91, 100, 103–5, 108, 130
  interference or interventions of, 41–42, 75n.76, 92–94, 111–12
  liberal-utilitarian principles of, 22–23
  literati or reformers in, 45–46
  literati or reformers challenge, 41–42, 105–6, 126, 274, 276–77
  literati or reformers work with, 40–41, 47, 49n.167, 56–57, 103–5, 202–3, 276–77
  paternalistic, 16–17, 21–22, 56–57, 58–59, 77–78, 82, 110–11, 274
  view of Bengalis of, 5–6, 18–19, 20–21, 36–37, 57–58, 107
  view of subjects or citizens of, 38n.144, 98–99
companionate marriage, 67–68
conversions, 78–80, 88, 158–59
Cooch Behar, 76–77, 165–66
corporal punishment. *See* physical punishment
Courtright, Paul, 33–34
crisis idiom, 47–48, 100–1, 103–5, 128–29

Dalhousie, Lord, 15–16, 62
Dalits, 18n.65, 25–26, 28–29
Darwin, Charles, 112
Dasgupta, Surendranath, 187–88
Dasi, 172–74
daughters, 9, 11–12, 26–27, 121–22, 185
  imaginary, 140–41

narratives by, 137, 141–42, 163–77, 191
Dayabhaga, 13–15
Dayal, Samir, 233
Deb, Radhakanta, 61
Debi, Hemlata, 82n.92
degeneration trope, 100–1, 112–15, 122–23, 124–25, 127–28, 132–33
Department of Public Instruction, 62
Devi, Ashapurna, 177n.103
Devi, Bhagabati, 53f
Devi, Dinamayi, 55f, 67–68
Devi, Hemlata, 88, 89f
Devi, Jaganmohini, 72–74, 74f
Devi, Jnadanandini, 73–74n.71, 148f, 152–53, 152n.45, 162–63, 206
Devi, Kanan, 163–64
Devi, Madhurilata (Bela), 204–6, 209, 216, 222–23
Devi, Maitreyi, 187–89
Devi, Mira, 206–7, 210n.48, 263–64
Devi, Mrinalini (Bhabatarini), 156–57, 204
Devi, Pratima, 224, 230–31
Devi, Rassundari, 163–64
Devi, Renuka (Rani), 210, 210n.48, 216, 222–23, 227
Devi, Santa, 164n.76, 172–74
Devi, Saudamini, 147–50
Devi, Sita, 164n.76, 172–74, 177n.103
Devi, Suniti (Sunity Devee), 72–74, 75–78, 165–66, 191
Devi, Swarnakumari, 147–51, 152–53, 159–60, 223n.90
dharma, 2, 221–22
dharmashastras, 9–10, 12–13, 222
diaries, 138–39
diet, 96–97, 169–71
  Gandhi's experiments with, 241–42
  in Santiniketan, 218–19
  scientific periodicals on, 96–97, 115–16, 122–23, 124–26, 127, 128, 129–30
Digdarshan, 57
divorce, 9–10
domestic workers. *See* servants
Dooti Bilash, 17–18

dowry, 120, 120n.66
Dutt, Michael Madhusudan, 203–4
Dutta, Akshay Kumar, 40–41, 109–10, 202–3
Dutta, Ramesh Chandra, 82–83

East India Company, 13–15, 39–40, 41–42, 57
education
  colonial (*see* colonial education system)
  modern, 141, 185
  objectives of, 250–51
  Western, ix–x, 215–16, 225–26, 251–52
educational curriculum, 20–22, 43–44, 62, 70–71, 105–6
  colonial government control of, 70–71
  Gandhi's, 250–51
  Vidyasagar's, 63
effeminacy, 5–6, 18–19, 20–21, 36–37, 40–41, 44, 57–58
elementary schools. *See* primary schools
Eliade, Mircea, 187–88
Elmhirst, Leonard, 229–30
emotions, 48–49, 131–32, 142–44, 156, 188–89, 191–93
England, 19–20, 30, 45–46, 98, 112, 128, 191–92
  masculinity or manliness in, 103, 211
  "patterns" of fathers in, 136–37
  Tagores in, 153, 203–4, 206, 231n.114
English, 5–6, 40–41, 61, 105–6, 111, 151, 162–63, 217
  as language of instruction (or not), 41, 202, 214–15, 251–52
  as language of power, 92–94
environmentalism, 112
ethics, 63, 71
eugenics, 102n.22, 103–5, 112, 128, 182–83
everyday practices, 35–36, 46, 94–95, 141, 210–11, 279
  public discourses vs., 47, 68–69
exercise, 124–25, 169–71, 225–26

INDEX

father–child relationship
   father–daughter relationship, 165–66, 165n.81, 172–77
   father–son relationship, 8–9, 134–35, 142, 157–58, 174–77, 182–84
fatherhood
   breadwinning aspect of, 3, 6–7, 100–1, 137, 267
   as category, 13, 50
   "enunciative" and "performative" aspects of, 19, 48–49, 90–91
   Indian views of, 38–39, 58–59, 100–1, 182–83
   masculinity or manhood and, 32–33, 94–95, 137–38, 161, 191–92, 231, 234–35, 277
   naturalization of, 7–8, 135–36
   norms of, 3, 141
   patriarchy and, 7–8, 48–49
   scholarship on, 33–35
   self-fashioning and, 3, 130–31, 271–72
fathers
   absent-present, x
   British, 136–37, 140–41
   as category, 32–33, 36–37, 50
   Chanakya on, 1
   in cinema or fiction, 177n.103
   in classical texts, 2, 8–10, 11–12
   contradictions in lives of, ix–x, 47, 77–78, 89–90, 276–77
   daughters vs. sons for, 3, 9, 137–38, 191
   as disciplinarians, 48–49, 136–37, 144, 155–56, 162–63, 177–78, 183–84, 189–90, 208
   distant (or not), 34–35, 136–37, 141, 144–46, 154–55, 158–59, 191–92, 208
   health of, 120
   as hegemonic and subaltern subjects, 47, 55–56
   ideal or idealized, 137, 181, 191
   imagined or imaginary, 139–42, 144–46, 160–61, 190
   leadership role of, 19
   metaphorical, 3–4, 11
   middle-class, 4, 18, 19–20, 47, 55–56, 90–91, 165–66, 185
   "modern," 48–49, 58–59, 81–82, 91, 158–59
   as moral guardians, 4–5, 18–19, 44–45, 55–56, 69, 92, 94, 100–1, 137, 198, 275–76, 277–78
   of nation, 49–50, 234–35
   playful, 136–37, 186–87
   as political mentors, 264–66, 267, 271–72
   in popular literature, 11–12
   power of, 2
   protective, 100–1, 136–37
   as teachers or gurus, 13, 17–22, 211–12, 217–18, 226–27, 228–29, 232, 245–47, 260–61, 271–72
   upper-caste, 4
   veneration of, 137, 144, 157–58, 164–65, 183, 189–90, 204
filial piety, 9, 11, 35–36, 44, 51–52, 65–66, 96–97, 137, 238–40
   in different genres, 139–40, 144, 164–65, 180
Forbes, Geraldine, 42–43n.158, 74n.73, 121n.70, 223n.89
Fort William College, 56–57, 61n.26
Foucault, Michel, 93n.120, 177–78

Gandhi, Indira, 49–50, 263–66
Gandhi, Karamchand, 235–38
Gandhi, Kasturba Makanji, 238–40
Gandhi, Mohandas K., 49–50, 189–90, 230n.111
   authority or authoritarianism of, 241–42
   as *Bapu-ji*, 49, 234–35, 245–46
   children mobilized by, 242–44
   in England, 240
   family conflicts of, 241–42, 243–44
   as father, 96, 240, 241–42, 243–44, 245–46
   Hind Swaraj by, 248
   influences on, 240–41
   on liberty vs. education, 243–44
   marriage of, 238–40

as mother, 246n.21
parents of, 235–40
pedagogy of, 234–35, 244–46, 248, 250–51, 272, 273, 278–79
at Phoenix or Tolstoy Farm, 245–48
in South Africa, 240–42, 243–44, 245
Ganesha, 33–34
garhasthya, 12–13
Garos, 26–27
gender-binaries, 30–31, 38–39
geography, 57, 63, 71, 73–74n.71
Ghosal, Janakinath, 150–51, 151n.38
Ghose, Aurobindo, 214–15
Ghosh, Anindita, 59
Ghosh, Jogendranath, 71
Ghosh, Prasannakumar, 166
girls, 26, 120
　absent or elided, 67, 69, 72–74, 101n.17, 121n.70, 121–22, 125–26
　agency of, 119, 132–33
　as audience or readers, 85
　births celebrated, 166, 168–69, 174–77
　as future mothers, 4–5, 44, 67, 100–1, 115–16, 117–18, 119, 120–21, 125–26, 132–33, 191–92, 277–78
　as future wives, 44, 125–26, 191–92, 277–78
　marriage age for, 75–76, 110–11, 115–16, 118–19, 120, 150–51, 151n.38, 152–53, 222–23
　men claim to speak for, 119
　Muslim, 117n.59
　parents worried by, 120
　schools or education for, 147–50, 165–66, 169, 171–72, 174–77, 201–2, 224–26, 266–67
　scientific literature on, 120–21
　as subjects of reform, 78–79
　as victims, 100–1, 103–5
Gleanings in Science, 107
Gnanodoy, 71
Goonesekere, S., 26–27
Gopal, S., 257–58, 262
Gopal/Rakhal stories, 63, 64–65, 201–2
Goswami, Manu, 271–72
governmentality, 42, 45

technologies of, 45
Governors-General of India, 39–40
Grant, Charles, 39–40
Guha, Ranajit, 20n.71
Guha, Sumit, 16–17
Gupta, Durgadas, 112–15
Gupta, Jnanendra Nath, 171–72
Gurukul Kangri, 112, 128, 222n.88
gurus, 13, 34–35, 220–21

Hanafi School, 26–27
Haq, Mojammel, 84n.97
Hatcher, Brian, 61–62, 139–40, 161
Haynes, Douglas, 17n.62, 128n.92
health, ix–x, 96–98, 100–1, 103–5
　scholarship on, 101–2
hegemony, 19–20
heteronormativity, 6–7, 10–11, 38–39, 274
Hindu legal systems, 13–15, 18. *See also* Anglo-Hindu laws
Hinduism, 2n.3, 3–4, 5–6, 9–10, 12–13, 28–29
　"invented" past of, 57–58, 135–36, 140–41, 183
　masculinity and, 32–33, 35–37
　reformist, 72–74, 112, 177n.103
historicity, 53n.6
history education, 63, 71, 73–74n.71
home schooling, 201–2, 216–17, 254, 257
homes, 19–20, 33, 36–37, 44–45, 64–65, 66–67, 103
homoeopathy, 112–15
householders, 12–13, 36–37, 182–83
housewives, 4–5, 121–22
Hunter Commission, 41–42
Hunter, Sir William, 41–42
hygiene, ix–x, 100–1, 112–15, 123n.78, 225–26

identity
　national, 4–5
　social or religious, 59, 273
Ilaiah, Kancha, 25–26
Ilbert Bill, 57–58
illegitimacy, 26–27

imagination, 46, 52–55, 63, 81–82, 91, 99, 130–31, 188–89, 191, 197–98, 224, 257–58
imperial legislations, 21–22
Indian National Congress, 79–80, 151n.38, 249, 263–64, 268–69
Indira Gandhi. *See* Gandhi, Indira
individualism, 35–36, 231, 232
infancy (*shaishab*), 115–16, 117–19
Ingalls, Daniel H. H., 1n.1
inheritance, 9–10, 12, 13–15, 26–27
  disputes of biological vs. spiritual heirs over, 12
intelligentsia, ix–x, 4, 21–22
  critiques by, 6–7, 19–20
Islamic law, 26–27

Jimutavahana, 13–15
Jones, Sir William, 9–10n.28, 107
juvenile magazines, 78–79

Kakar, Sudhir, 23–24, 45–46, 139n.17
Kallenbach, Hermann, 247–48
Karim, Abdul, 84n.97
Karlekar, Malavika, 171–72
karta (husband and father), 36–37
Kasturi, Malavika, 10n.30
Kathamala, 66
Katha-o-Kahini, 217
Kaviraj, Sudipta, 86–87, 91–92, 139–40, 181
Kaviraji, 128–29
Kellogg, Susan, 19n.68
Kerala, 15n.48
King, Laura, 7n.18
King, Margaret, 31n.113
kings, 15–17
koumar obostha, 115–16. *See also* youths
kulins, 18
Kumar, Krishna, 69, 250–51
Kumar, Nita, 47–48
Kusum, 84n.97

labour policies, 21–22
Laqueur, Thomas, 30
Laws of Manu. *See Manusmriti*
legal codes, Hindu, 9, 222

legal systems, 13–15
lekhapora (education), 51–52
literary societies, 96
Locke, John, 91, 97–98, 157–58
Long, James, 108–9
love marriages, 10–11, 187–88

Macaulay, Thomas Babington, 5–6, 41, 105–6
Madan, T. N., 12–13
madrasas, 61, 273
Mahabharata, 1n.1, 2, 11, 217
Mahar, 25–26
Mahila, 121–22
Majumdar, Leela, 185–87, 188–89
Majumdar, Rochona, 76n.77, 91n.114, 120n.66, 121n.70
Manavadharmashastra. *See Manusmriti*
Mangal Kabyas, 11–12
manhood
  reformers' practices of, 1
  Victorian, 19–20
manliness, 3, 35–36, 103, 137, 211, 225, 232
  colonial critique of, ix–x
  Hindu, 35–36
Manusmriti (*Laws of Manu*; *Manavadharmashastra*), 2n.3, 9–10, 13, 23–24
Marathas, 5–6
Marathi, 126
Marriage Act of 1872 (Act III of 1872), 75–76, 119n.65, 151n.38, 222–23
marriage laws, 9–10
Marshman, John Clark, 57
masculinity, 3, 132, 137, 191–92, 198–99, 225
  changes in registers of, 18–19
  compromised, 94–95
  factors constituting, 6–7, 20–21, 44, 92–94
  historiography of, x, 5–6
  paternalistic, 94–95
  reformers' conception of, ix–x, 20–21
  scholarship on, 30, 199n.12
  subaltern, 32–33
  in Victorian England, 30, 45–46

INDEX

mass education, 63, 215, 229–30, 268, 270
masturbation, 118–19, 122–23, 126–28, 129–30
medical practitioners, 4, 47, 96–98, 100, 108, 112–15, 122–23, 128
medicine, 108, 109
   journals or publications on, 108–9, 111–15, 128n.92
   "local" or traditional, 111–15, 128–29
   Western, 101–2, 111–15, 127, 128–29
Meghalaya, 26
memoirs, 138–39
memories, 137, 142, 144–46, 190, 191
men
   home as archive for, 33
   "modern," 86–87, 91
Menon, Dilip, 4n.9
middle class, 4, 18, 61–62, 102n.22, 128n.92, 138–39, 251–52
   anxiety or tension of, 36–37, 50
   as audience or readers, 129–30
   British, 19–20, 93n.120
   British view of Bengali, 5–6, 18–19
   daughters vs. sons of, 165–66
   educated, 88, 192–93, 200, 279
   gender-binaries and heteronormativity of, 38–39
   middleness of, 55–56, 90–91
   paradoxical nature of, 5–6, 47, 55–56
   paternity for, 185
   pedagogical experiments by, 40–41, 202–3
   self-identity or self-fashioning of, 126, 130–31
   See also children: middle-class; fathers: middle-class
middleness, 55–56, 90–91
Mill, James, 22–23
Mills, John Stuart, 152–53
Mintz, Steven, 19n.68
missionaries, 28–29, 36–37, 56–57, 105n.30, 158n.66
   magazines or periodicals of, 70–71, 83–84
   schools set up by, 39–40, 41–42, 168–69, 243–44
   vernacular publications by, 57, 103–5

missionary education, 59n.19
Mitakshara, 13–15
Mitra, Jogendranath, 115–16
Mitra, Krishnadhan, 71
Mitra, Rajendralal, 47, 96, 103–5, 107, 111
Mitra, Tarinicharan, 61
Modern Review, The, 172–74
monastic lineages, 10–11, 13
Montessori education, 49n.167
moral education or training, 43–44, 47, 83–84, 144, 183–84, 245–46. *See also* character building or training
morality, 63, 68–69
morality tales, 63
mother-craft, 6–7
motherhood, 6–7, 121–22
   male authors define, 7–8
motherland, 37–38, 67, 81, 100–1, 127, 132
mothers, 34–35
   as audience or readers, 111
   in autobiographies or memoirs, 178–79, 181–82, 183–84, 190
   in classical texts, 2, 11–12
   distant, 138–39
   education needed for, 117–18, 121–22
   ideal or idealized (*adarsha janani*), 121–22, 135–36
   in Vidyasagar's works, 67
Mukharji, Projit, 97n.4, 127n.91, 130n.96
Mukherjee, Iswar, 160
Mukherjee, Raja Dakhinaranjan, 109n.47
Mukhopadhyay, Bhudev, 40–41, 62, 78–79, 202–3, 215–16, 217–18
Mukhopadhyay, Snehalata, 120n.66
Mukhopadhyay, Trailokyanath, 82n.92
Mukul, 82–84
Muslims, 3–4, 13, 26–27, 58–59, 227–28, 273
   British laws for, 13–15
   works for children by, 84n.97

Naba-babu Bilash, 17–18
Naba-Bibi Bilash, 17–18
Nandy, Ashis, 24–25

Narayan, Prince Nripendra, 76–77
Narayanan, Vasudha, 12
National College, 214–16
National Council of Education, 227–28
National Education Movement, 213
nationalism, 50, 85, 233, 251–52
  fundamentalist Hindu, 32–33
  gender and, 36–37, 67
  Nehru's views of, 262, 266–67
  Rabindranath Tagore's view of, 199, 227–29, 233, 262, 266–67
nationalist organizations or movement, 95, 128, 144–46, 199–200, 242–43, 258–59, 271–72
nationalists, 40–41, 119n.65, 122–23, 258, 276–77
  brahmacharya in educational plans of, 168n.89
  children's magazines on plight of, 79–80, 91–92
  colleges or schools founded by, 214–15
  educational programmes of, 215–16, 251–52, 274
  homes and families of, 131–32, 279
  scientific discourse of, 47–48, 132–33
Neetibodh, 66
Neetikatha, 61
Nehru, Jawaharlal, 4–5, 49–50, 189–90
  autobiography of, 254
  background and childhood of, 254–55
  as *Chacha*, 49, 234–35, 253–54
  educational policies of, 266–70
  as father of Indira, 49–50, 96, 253–54, 259–66
  as father of the nation, 49–50, 271
  Glimpses of World History by, 49–50, 253–54, 260–62
  influences on, 49–50
  as nationalist, 257
  pedagogy of, 234–35, 253–54, 260–62, 268–62, 278–79
Nehru, Kamala Kaul, 258
Nehru, Motilal, 254–57, 263–64
Nelson, Claudia, 19–20
Newbigin, Eleanor, 15n.51

"new child," 20–21, 58–59, 70–71
"new father," xiv–xv, 58–59, 141–42, 190, 192–93, 204, 210–11
"new woman," 20–21, 34–35, 36–37, 58–59, 67, 94, 121–22, 135–36, 192–93
Nieuwenhuys, Olga, 27–28
non-cooperation movement, 230n.111, 244–45, 249
nongovernmental organizations, 27–28
non-violent resistance, 240–42
Normal School, 165–66, 202, 203–4, 213–14
novels, 139–40, 177n.103, 188
nuclear families or households, 15–16, 162, 210–11
Nussbaum, Martha, 195–96, 270
nutrition, 112–15, 124–26

O'Hanlon, Rosalind, 30
obedience, 11n.33, 35–36, 44, 63, 77–78, 87–88, 141, 179, 191
Oedipus, 33–34
Olsen, Stephanie, xiv, 103n.26, 132n.100
Onubeekshan, 47–48, 127
Orientalists, 61, 63

Pal, Bipin Chandra, 91–92, 188–89
  autobiography by, 134–35, 138–39, 169–71, 181–83
  disowned, 181
  Sakha articles by, 79–81, 82n.92
Pande, Biswambhar Nath, 264–66
Pande, Ishita, 101n.17, 121n.70, 127n.88
Parashurama, 11n.33
parents, 2
  as audience or readers, 78–79, 101–2, 108, 111–12, 124–26, 144
  devotion to, 235–40, 276–77
  duties of, 26–27
  as educators, 243–44
  as gods, 1, 66–67
  obedience to (or not), 35–36, 51, 64–65, 66, 77–78, 177–78, 180, 188–89
  as role models, 66–67
  worries of, 120
Paricharika, 121–22
Paswabali, 61n.25

paternity, 26–27, 30
patriarchal culture, 2, 119, 125–26
patriarchs, 11, 19, 82
patriarchy, 5–6, 7–8, 12, 19–20, 89–90, 91, 163–64
   role of fathers or fatherhood in, 34–35, 192–93
patriotism, 71–72, 79–80, 96–97, 227–28
Pawde, K., 25–26
pedagogical innovations (alternate pedagogy), ix–x, 6–7, 48–49, 59–60, 94, 226–27, 234–35, 274, 275–76, 278–79
pedagogy, x, 97n.5
Perrot, Michelle, 30
Persian, 41, 61
personal narratives, 48–49
physical debility, 112–15, 123n.78, 124–25, 131–33
physical education, 108, 225–26, 240
physical health, 122–23, 124–25
physical punishment, 63–64, 141, 177–79, 183–85, 186–87, 188–90, 208, 247, 256–57
   in autobiographical vs. other works, 141–42, 144–46, 177–78, 190
   by teachers, 183–85
physical strength, 6–7, 20–21, 30, 44, 197–98, 232, 234–35
pita (father), 4–5, 8–9, 12
pitri-bhakti (father-veneration), 91, 144, 204
pitritantra (patriarchy), 12, 35–36
pitritwo (fatherhood, paternity), 4–5, 12, 35–36, 137, 185, 195–96, 198–99
poetry, 75–76, 83–84, 139–40
polygamy, 18, 59–60, 88, 122–23
postcolonial state, 22–23, 25–26, 27–28
pourush (manhood), 44, 195–96, 200, 225, 234–35
power, 5–6, 7–8
Prabasi, 172–74
Prakriti, 84n.97
primary schools, 39–40, 201–2, 268–69
primers, 38–39, 40–41, 59–60, 198–99, 202–3
   Vidyasagar's, 51–52, 63, 65, 71, 144

print culture or media, 59, 64–65, 103, 108–9, 128–29, 131–33
private sphere, 20–21, 30, 36–37, 90–91
property rights, 13–16, 88n.108, 91, 177–78, 232
   Banaras vs. Bengal schools on, 13–15
   disputes over, 10n.30, 12
   fatherhood and, 10–11, 12
   Manu on, 9
   masculinization of, 15–16
prose, 59–60, 61, 74–75, 111
Prosonnomoyee, 87–88
prostitution, 126, 126–27n.87
proverbs, 2, 9
psychoanalysts, 23–24, 33–34
public/private dichotomy, 20–21, 90–91
public schools, 39–40, 257
Punjab, 39–40, 112, 128
Puranas, 8–9
purushotwo (masculinity, manliness), 12, 35–36, 192–93, 195–96, 198–99
Putli Bai, 235–38

racism, 36–37, 105–6
Raha, Bipasha, 227n.103
Rajputs, 5–6
Rakhal. See Gopal/Rakhal stories
Raman, Vasanthi, 24n.83, 26n.94
Ramanujan, A. K., 33–34
Ramaswamy, Sumathi, 38n.143, 67n.51, 101n.16, 142n.25
Ramayana, 11, 13, 217
Ray, Bharati, 6n.16, 118n.63
Ray, Bhubanmohan, 82
Ray, Dasarathi, 61–62
Ray, Rajat Kanta, 142–44, 143n.29, 192
Ray, Satyajit, 83–84
Ray, Sukumar, 83–84, 91–92
Raychaudhuri, Tapan, 143n.29
Raychaudhuri, Upendrakishore, 82n.92
Rebellion of 1857–1858, 5–6, 41–42
reflexivity, 53n.6
reformists or reformist organizations, 18n.65, 94, 103–5, 109, 112, 146, 165–66
regeneration trope, 29, 99, 100–2, 103–5, 107, 122–23, 132–33

restraint, 44, 137, 193, 222n.88, 247
Rogers, Helen, 95
Roper, Michael, 142–44
Rose, Sonya O., 99
Rosenwein, Barbara, 142–44, 143n.28
Rosselli, John, 107
Rousseau, Jean-Jacques, 97n.5
Roy, Gautam Chando, xiv, 21n.74, 59n.17, 70n.61
Roy, Rammohun, 28–29, 39–40, 57, 88n.108, 146, 147–50
rural reconstruction, 227–28, 229–30
Ruskin, John, 240–41

sabhas. See clubs or associations
Sadharan Brahmo Samaj, 76–77, 86–87
Sakha, 69, 78–82, 89
Sakha o Sathi, 82
samiti. See clubs or associations
Sandesh, 83–84, 91–92
Sanskrit, 1n.1, 2, 25–26, 61, 66n.48, 74–75, 155, 160–61, 203–4, 217
Sanskrit College, 86–87
santati-sastra, 102n.22
Santiniketan, 208, 215–16, 218–21, 222, 224–25, 263
Sanyal, Pulinchandra, 118–19
Saraswati, Dayanand, 213
Sarkar, Jogindranath, 82, 82n.92, 83n.94
Sarkar, Pyari, 201
Sarkar, Tanika, 5–6, 36–37, 119n.65, 121n.70, 214–15
Sastri, Sivnath, 47, 72, 82n.92, 95
  Brahmos or Sadharan Brahmo Samaj and, 76–77, 86–87, 88, 180, 188–89
  colonial officials and, 85, 85–86n.99
  daughters of, 86–87, 88
  on education of women, 86–87
  marriages of, 87–88, 157–58
  as *Mukul* editor, 82–85, 89
  punished by father, 178–81
  as reformer, 86–87, 95
Sathi (Companion), 82, 89
sati, 61, 103–5
satires, 126
Scheduled Castes, 25–26
Scheduled Tribes, 25–26

schools, 20–21, 39–40, 249
  British or English, 124–25, 127, 257
  funding for, 249–50
  girls', 86–87
  statistics about, 42
science, 63, 73–74n.71, 105–11, 266–70, 272
  applied sciences, 105–6
  life sciences, 57
  natural sciences, 107, 109–10
scientific journals, ix–x, 43, 47–48, 100–1, 130, 139–40, 144
  male vs. female children in, 47–48
  proliferation of vernacular, 108–9, 111–12
"second patriarchy," 36–37
self-help, 49–50
Sen, Haimabati, 166–68
Sen, Keshub Chandra, 46, 47, 61n.26, 72–78, 86–87, 95, 158–59, 213
  daughter of (*see* Devi, Suniti)
  on education of women, 86–87
  popularity of, 72–74
  as reformer, 74–76, 77–78, 95, 165–66
Sen, Promodacharan, 78–79, 82
Sen, Ram Comul, 61, 74–75
Sen, Samita, 7n.19, 75n.76
Sen, Satadru, 20–21
Sengupta, Parna, 59n.19, 273
Serampore, 57
servants, 19, 23–24, 154–55, 178, 210–11, 256
sexuality, 100–1, 111, 117n.60, 122–23, 126–28
shaishab (infancy), 4–5, 115–16
Shaivas, 13
Shekele Kawtha, 147–50
shikshito bhadralok sampradaya, 4–5, 186–87, 279
shikshito sampradaya (educated community), 4–5
shishu sahitya (children's literature), 59–60
Shiva, 33–34
Shravana, 235–38
Shudha Mazumdar, 168–71
Sikhs, 5–6
Sinha, Kaliprasanna, 126–27n.87

Sinha, Mrinalini, 5–6, 30, 33, 132n.101, 199n.12
social imaginaries, 37–38, 100, 130–31
   children as, 37–38, 47–48, 99–100, 129–31, 277
social reformers, ix–x, 3–4, 52–55, 147–50
   interventions by, 58–59
Society for the Acquisition of General Knowledge, 109
spatiality, 279
Spencer, Herbert, 112
sportsmanship, 103, 186–87
Sriniketan, 229–30
state, the. *See* colonial state; postcolonial state
Stoler, Ann Laura, 93n.120
Stow, David, 215–16
Sträth, Bo, 53n.6
subalterns, 19, 35–36
   children as, ix–x
   middle-class fathers as, 47, 55–56
   reformers as, 57
subjectivity, 90–91, 92–95, 129–30, 142–44, 179
Sufis, 13
sugrihini, 121–22, 135–36
Sushruta, 124–25, 128–29
swadesh, 71
Swadeshi movement, 227–28
swaraj, 219–20, 245
Swasthya, 47–48, 96, 112–15, 117–18, 119, 124–26

Tagore, Abanindranath, 160
Tagore, Debendranath, 144–63, 199–200, 206, 210–11, 218
   Auto-biography of, 147, 152, 160–61
   background and education of, 146
   as Brahmo leader, 146, 152, 158–59, 160–61
   education stressed by, 147–50, 151, 153, 154–55, 160–61, 213
   marriages arranged by, 150–51, 157–58, 204
   as patriarch, 147, 156–57, 160–61
   as reformer, 147
   venerated, 147, 152, 156, 159–60, 163, 204
Tagore, Dwarkanath, 42, 126–27n.87, 146–47, 199–200, 206–7, 213
Tagore, Girindranath, 146–47
Tagore, Hemendranath, 231n.114
Tagore, Jyotirindranath, 150*f*
Tagore, Nagendranath, 146–47
Tagore, Rabindranath, 35–36, 49–50, 73–74n.71, 82–83, 147, 153, 172–74, 188
   Amra Chonchol by, 222
   authority or authoritarianism of, 208, 217, 220–21, 224
   as *Bibidhartha-Sangraha* reader, 111n.51
   bravery emphasized by, 221–22, 226–27
   childhood of, 71n.67, 153–56, 158–59, 197, 198, 200–4
   children imagined by, 221, 226–27, 231
   children of, 139n.18, 204–8, 210n.48, 211–12
   colonial education system and, 200–4, 213–15, 231–32
   on education of women, 224–26
   as educator, 194–95, 197–98, 200, 211–12, 213–14, 216–18, 222, 231–32, 272
   empathy of, 212–13, 233
   as estate manager, 155–57
   as father, 96, 198, 206–12, 232
   Gandhi and, 230n.111, 243n.16, 248, 249
   girls admitted to school of, 224–25
   Gora by, 177n.103, 212–13
   as Gurudev, 49, 162–63, 211–12, 232
   imagined fathers of, 212–13
   influences on, 196, 203–4, 215–16, 216n.70, 220–21
   manliness for, 232
   marriage of, 204–6
   marriages arranged by, 222–24
   Noukadubi by, 177n.103, 212–13
   pedagogy of, 195–96, 197–98, 200, 215–16, 226–27, 231–32, 233, 262, 278–79

Tagore, Rabindranath (*cont.*)
  as reformer, 213
  religious views of, 220–21
  Reminiscences by, 153
  universalism of, 227–29, 233, 251–52
  vernacular languages stressed by, 214–15
Tagore, Rathindranath, 155–56, 204–5, 206–8, 210n.48, 218, 222, 230–31
  Himalayan trip of, 208
  home-schooled, 216–17
  marriage of, 224
  on Santiniketan, 218–19, 222
Tagore, Satyendranath, 147, 151–53, 161–63, 217, 231n.114
Tagore, Shamindranath, 210n.48
Tagore, Surendranath, 162, 206–7, 217
Tantrics, 13
Tattvabodhini Patrika, 109–10, 110n.49, 150–51
Tattvabodhini Sabha, 109–10
Taylor, Charles, 37–38, 47–48, 100, 129–31, 277
teachers, 78–79, 166, 202, 218–19, 220–21
  authority of, 64–65
  corporal punishment by, 183–85, 247
  fathers as, 1, 243–48
  spiritual, 13, 246–47
  training of, 41–42, 217–18
textbooks, 38–41, 47
  British-produced, 98
  missionaries and, 57
  vernacular-language, 61
Thakur, Harichand, 28–29
Theosophists, 240, 257
Thorat, S. K., 25–26
Thoreau, Henry David, 240–41
Tolstoy, Leo, 240–41
Topdar, Sudipa, 101–2
Tosh, John, 30, 45–46, 103, 138, 208, 210–11
Trall, R., 122–23, 123n.78
translations, 47, 61, 108–9, 111–12
tribal communities, 25–26
Tribedi, Ramendrasundar, 59–60, 82n.92, 82–83

Unani, 128–29
Unitarians, 39–40, 158–59, 211, 215–16, 220–21
universities, 62, 194, 229–30
Upanishads, 8–9, 160–61, 217, 257
Utilitarians, 36–37, 41

Vaishnavas, 13
Vanar Sena, 264–66
Varnaparichay, 51–52, 63, 64–65, 201–2
Vedanta, 28–29
Vedas, 160–61, 218, 220–21
vernacular education, 34–35, 56–57, 197–98, 213, 251–52
  Rabindranath Tagore advocates, 215–16, 231n.114
  Vidyasagar advocates, 62–63
vernacular languages, 62, 101–2, 200, 214–15, 250–51
  scientific or medical terms in, 111–12, 215–16
vernacular literature, 21–22, 44, 57–58, 91–92, 214–15, 277–78
  youths in, 126
vernacular periodicals, 101–2, 103–5
Victoria, Queen, 83–84, 85
Victorian ideology, 19–20, 45–46
Vidyaratna, Narayan Chandra, 56f, 67–68
Vidyasagar, Iswarchandra, 18, 47, 78–79, 95, 103–5, 144, 213
  ear-biting-orphan story by, 65–66
  father of, 63–64, 178
  as father of Bengal, 61–62
  female children elided by, 67
  Gopal/Rakhal stories by, 63, 64–65, 201–2
  parental devotion of, 63–64, 66–67, 238–40
  pedagogy of, 62–63, 64–67, 68–69, 178, 202–3
  personal life of, 67–68, 92
  as *purush singha* (lion man), 35–36
  students of, 86–87
  virtual fatherhood of, 65
Vijnanesvara, 13–15
Vishak Darpan, 115–16

Visva-Bharati, 229–31
Vivekananda, Swami, 240–41
vocational training, 248, 250, 266–67

Wagner, Peter, 53n.6
Walsh, Judith, 139n.17
Wardha Scheme, 249
warrior monks, 30
widow remarriage, 18, 61–62, 67–68, 103–5
Widow Remarriage Act, 67–68, 224
widows, 13–16, 67–68
    burning of, 61, 103–5
    diet of, 117–18
    marriage of, 224
    Vidyasagar and, 67–68
Wilberforce, William, 39–40
wives, 7–8, 34–35, 135–36
"woman question," 34–35, 36–37, 58–59
women
    articles about, 71n.68, 117–18
    articles by, 121–22
    as audience or readers, 117–18
    autobiographies by, 141–42, 163–65, 191
    Brahmo, 210–11
    in classical texts, 9
    education for, 42, 67–68, 103–5, 147–50, 152–53, 224–25, 268–69
    home as archive for, 33
    Keshub Chandra Sen and, 72–74
    modern, 152n.45, 153
    traditional, 58n.15
    Vidyasagar and, 61–62, 67–68
    Westernized, 58n.15
women's magazines or periodicals, 85, 121–22
Wood's Despatch, 41–42, 59n.19, 62, 105–6
working classes, 43–44, 58n.15, 78–79
wrestling, 232

Young Bengal, 109
youths, 82–83, 89, 96
    as elided category, 110–11, 126
    as gendered category, 110–11
    imagined, 129–30
    as implicit category, 99
    male, 100–1, 109–10, 122–25
    sexual behavior of, 126–27
Yudhisthira, 2